Moving with the Ball

Moving with the Ball

The Migration of Professional Footballers

Pierre Lanfranchi and Matthew Taylor

BERG

Oxford • New York

First published in 2001 by
Berg
Editorial offices:
150 Cowley Road, Oxford, OX4 1JJ, UK
838 Broadway, Third Floor, New York, NY 10003-4812, USA

Berg is an imprint of Oxford International Publishers Ltd.

Library of Congress Cataloging-in-Publication Data
A catalogue record for this book is available from the Library of Congress.

British Library Cataloguing-in-Publication Data
A catalogue record for this book is available from the British Library.

ISBN 1 85973 302 6 (Cloth)
1 85973 307 7 (Paper)

Typeset by JS Typesetting, Wellingborough, Northants
Printed in the United Kingdom by Biddles Ltd, Guildford and King's Lynn

Contents

Acknowledgements

The idea for this book was born when our separate projects on the history of professional players in France and the development of the English Football League converged in the little known story of the British footballers who travelled to France during the 1930s. Long discussions followed on the possibility of an integrated study of football and migration. We hope that the book we have produced will interest students of migration, history and social sciences as well as appealing to anybody with an interest in the development and character of international sport.

We have had a great deal of help in the course of researching and writing this book. Within De Montfort University, present and former colleagues and post-graduate students have always been ready to discuss chapters and propose new ideas. We are particularly grateful to Daryl Adair, Franco Bianchini, Nick Carter, Fabio Chisari, Tony Collins, Mike Cronin, Richard Holt, David Hudson, Allanna McAspurn, Jason McDonald, Tony Mason, Panikos Panayi, David Ryan, Mark Sandle, Jonathan Thomas, Wray Vamplew, Francesco Varrasi and Jean Williams. Dick, Mike, Tony C., Wray and the members of the International Centre for Sports History and Culture provided useful comments on many of the book's ideas when we presented them formally in lectures and seminars and in informal discussions. Tony M. and Panikos read and commented on early versions of chapters, as did Eduardo Archetti, Chuck Korr and Bert Moorhouse (three members of the old Florence connection). We also owe a debt of gratitude to John Bale, Marco Brunelli, Christian Bromberger, Neil Carter, Vittorio Dini, Christiane Eisenberg, Jean-Michel Faure, Jeff Hill, Martin Johnes, Paolo Piani, Stefano Pivato, Alfred Wahl, John Williams and the late Gianni Isola and Ian Taylor, all of whom contributed to our understanding of the subject.

The book could not have been completed without the support and assistance of many people outside our daily university lives. Andy Lyons provided useful guides (and long discussions) on Yugoslav football, Jim Creasy and Paul Taylor give us access to their impressive data on British players abroad. Stan Skinner and Brian Spurrell provided us with invaluable material, including letters and photographs, on the 'West Kent' group in southern France. In addition, we are grateful to the many members of the Association of Football Statisticians who answered our plea for information in their newsletter. Matteo Marani was generous enough to let us use the cover photograph while Gordon Taylor of the Professional Footballers' Association and David Barber of the Football Association allowed us to consult their archives. We would also like to thank Kathryn Earle and the team at Berg who have been patient and encouraging throughout.

Academics are often on the move. It is surely fitting that one of us migrated during the writing of this book. As we preferred to work together rather than via fax and e-mail, this meant a number of journeys between Italy and England. We would like to think that rather than suffering from the *Saudade* and the differences of language, food and lifestyle, the book has benefited from much of it being written 'away from home', in the contrasting cultural environment and physical landscape of Tuscany and Leicester.

Introduction

In a French novel published in 1932, the author related the atmosphere of the dressing-room of Lyons Football Club at the turn of the century. It was, he wrote, 'A mixed society in which the German-speaking Swiss was together with the Italian, the Englishman with the Egyptian, and the man from Lyons with the one from Marseilles'.[1] The situation was not fundamentally different in reality. The tradition of cosmopolitan teams is deeply rooted in world football history. From the very start of the game, men have moved across national borders, and from city to city, to play football. Foreign players have been imported in large numbers to the major nations of Western Europe and the Americas. Such has been the case in France since the 1930s and Italy from the fascist period, while skilled workers emigrated en masse from Europe to North America in the 1920s and again in the 1970s and 1980s to staff the new professional leagues. In Argentina, Brazil and Yugoslavia, footballers have been able to sell their talent abroad and by so doing have contributed to making football one of their nation's staple export products for over seventy years.

Football was the people's game before becoming the world game. It was born in Britain, where the professional game emerged in a specific class context. For the best part of a century British football was dominated by working-class lads from the urban centres of the north and midlands of Britain. The social, cultural, economic, ethnic and geographical backgrounds of the profession's early practitioners were extremely narrow. Footballers seem to have come from the same background as those who watched the game; they could literally be next-door neighbours.[2] They did move, of course, but generally not very far. David Jack's journey of over 200 miles in 1928, when Arsenal paid Bolton Wanderers £10,000

1. Joseph Jolinon, *Le joueur de balle*, Paris: Ferenczi, 1932, p. 83.

2. See Tony Mason, *Association Football and English Society, 1863–1915*, Brighton: Harvester, 1980; Nicholas Fishwick, *English Football and Society, 1910–1950*, Manchester: Manchester University Press, 1989; Richard Holt, 'Football and Regional Identity in the North of England: The Legend of Jackie Milburn', in S. Gehrmann (ed.), *Football and Regional Identity in Europe*, Münster: Lit Verlag, 1997, pp. 49–66. For a modification of this view as it relates to the geographical origins of professionals from the 1950s and beyond, see John Bale, 'From Ashington to Abingdon?: Some Regional Changes in Post-War British Professional Soccer', in A. Tomlinson (ed.), *Explorations in Football Culture*, Eastbourne: LSA Publications, 1983, pp. 73–93. Alain Ehrenberg, *Le culte de la performance*, Paris: Calmann-Lévy, 1991, for the idea of sporting heroes as 'next door neighbours'.

for his registration, was longer than most. Twenty years later Stanley Matthews, the most famous footballer of his day, was the subject of an eighty-mile transfer from Stoke-on-Trent to Blackpool. He returned to Stoke in 1961 but these were to be the only moves in his 33-year career. In Britain, of course, players could cross national boundaries without moving to another state. There was nothing stopping Irish, Welsh or Scottish footballers, for instance, from working for English clubs. So intranational migration has been commonplace. Indeed, many of the first professionals in the 1880s were Scottish players who travelled south to sign contracts with prominent clubs in the north and the midlands of England. International migration, on the other hand, took some time to develop. Handfuls of professionals left the home of football to try their luck as players and coaches in Europe before the Second World War and others travelled to Italy, France and North America after 1945. But foreigners were rarely let in. Indeed, the recruitment of foreign talent in the birthplace of the game is a relatively recent phenomenon. Ten years ago, Chelsea fielded hardly any non-British players: today there are only one or two regulars with British passports. Even the most insular of islanders have gradually come in line with the rest of the world.

From its beginnings, football was a universal game. As well as being simple to learn and play, it did not require the use of a specific national language, a recognized diploma or acquired qualification, and its rules became standardized across the globe. Moreover, for many of its overseas promoters, football was a product of transnational connections and the ideology of free trade. In continental Europe, particularly, it was linked to ideas of modernization and technical progress. When Bari Football Club was founded in 1908, Swiss, German, Austrian, French, Spanish, British (and Italian) tradesmen played in the same team, embodying a belief in an ideal world promoting international trade and cutting across economic frontiers.[3] And Bari was hardly exceptional. Many of the first football teams in continental Europe reflected this modern, urban and transnational society.

Yet football also became a site for the expression of national sentiment. In many countries the use of British terms in football started to be prohibited in the years immediately preceeding the First World War. Football became *Fußball* in Germany, *Calcio* in Italy, *Labdarugas* in Hungary and *Nogomet* in Croatia.[4] If the nineteenth century is considered as the era of 'nation-building', the first half of the twentieth century saw the advent of nationalistic values and the consolidation of the nation state. As Eric Hobsbawm has noted, the emergence of national football teams before 1914, and of national leagues in the 1920s and early 1930s, contributed to the

3. Gianni Antonucci, *Bari 90, 1908–1998*, Bari: Corcelli, 1998, pp. 14–18.

4. Fabio Marri, 'Metodo, sistema e derivati nel linguaggio calcistico', *Lingua nostra*, 44, 2–3, 1983, pp. 70–83; Wolfgang Schweickard, *'Die Cronaca calcistica': Zur Sprache des Fußballberichterstattung in italienischen Sportzeitungen*, Tübingen: Niemeyer, 1987, p. 62.

broader recognition of national distinctions.[5] As such, international sporting contests became a means of expressing a recognized hierarchy of nations while the organization and administration of the game came to reflect national boundaries.[6] But this emerging football nationalization did not prevent the movement of players from one country to another, even if national governments and football associations retained jurisdiction over the inward flow of labour. National peculiarities abound. While the English Football League remained staunchly protectionist in the interwar period, the newly formed French league allowed its clubs to field up to five foreign players in every match. The Italian league, meanwhile, banned non-nationals but exploited the possibilities offered by the dual citizenship of players from South America. In the United States and Canada, no restrictions were made on the grounds of nationality and citizenship. The question of whether to accept foreign footballers was never independent of broader political debates. When he came to power in 1933, Hitler outlawed the planned professional league and the German federation banned the involvement of foreign players and managers at every level. There was therefore always a tension between the universalistic and the nationalistic elements of football, which came to be expressed in the fierce debates over the access of clubs to foreign players.

The migration of footballers has been fundamentally bound up with general migratory patterns. From the mid-nineteenth century large population movements significantly altered the composition of world societies. Different regions and countries have been involved in different ways, some as senders and some as recipients. The United States received around thirty-three million immigrants from Europe between 1820 and 1924. By the 1880s, most of these came from Ireland, Italy, and other parts of Southern and Eastern Europe, areas in which industrialization was generally limited.[7] The colonization of Africa, Eastern Asia and South America by European powers provoked dense movements of population from the metropolis to the colony and, later, a reverse migration from colonial periphery to imperial centre. The main routes of professional footballers have barely differed from those of mass migration, although the directional flow has not always been the same. The Scots and Irish, for example, have sought work in England, North America and Australia in football as in other occupations. If South America was a destination for Italian and Spanish emigrants before the First World War, the goal

---

5. Eric Hobsbawm, *Nations and Nationalism Since 1780: Programme, Myth, Reality*, Cambridge: Cambridge University Press, 1990.

6. As the inventors of the game, the British were once again allowed to stand apart, keeping four national associations and thus a distinction between nation and state.

7. Roger Davids, *Coming to America: A History of Immigration and Ethnicity in American Life*, Princeton: Harper Perennial, 1990, pp. 23–4; A.W. Carlson, 'One Century of Foreign Immigration to the United States: 1880–1979', *International Migration*, 23, 3, September 1985, pp. 309–33.

of Brazilian, Argentinian and Uruguayan footballers was to seek fortune in the land of their parents. And from the 1920s, as the Algerian emigrant workforce began to opt almost exclusively for a French destination, the nation's footballers, in the same way, have practised their profession almost singularly in France. In the post-war period, international migration has expanded to include more regions and has intensified in volume. Professional football, as a universal economic activity, reflects many of the features of this so-called 'age of migration'.[8]

It is important to locate the position of football professionals within migratory groups more generally. While most migratory movements have both political and economic causes, the former are of little significance in this case. The international football market has rarely been inflated by political refugees although there are, of course, exceptions. There is no doubt that the Spanish Civil War and the Budapest uprising of 1956 precipitated the dispersal of the best Spanish and Hungarian players of the day. The Basque and Catalan players did not turn back from their tour of Mexico in the summer of 1937 and many found contracts with various South American clubs, others preferring France. Ferenc Puskas and his Honved team, playing a European Cup match in Bilbao, refused to return to Hungary after the arrival of the Soviet troops. Puskas signed a contract with Real Madrid; Sandor Kocsis and Zoltan Czibor chose Barcelona.[9] A further example involved the Jewish Hakoah Vienna club, which lost all its players in the aftermath of the *Anschluß*.[10] Finally, a small number of political dissidents from Eastern Europe have, over the years, left their countries illegally and signed contracts in the West. This trickle might have turned into a flood were it not for international football regulations which prevented these refugees from playing for a year after their arrival. Notwithstanding these instances, the motives of football migrants have mainly been economic.

We can identify three main situations, involving both push and pull factors, which favour the economic migration of professional footballers. First, economic crises and national financial weakness have been a catalyst for the departure of players. Good results at international level, and established domestic professional leagues, have not been enough to prevent players leaving. In the 1920s and 1930s,

8. For broad overviews of the history of world migration see Stephen Castles and Mark J. Miller, *The Age of Migration: International Population Movements in the Modern World,* London: Macmillan, 1993; Lydia Potts, *The World Labour Market: A History of Migration,* London: Zed, 1990.

9. Carlos Fernandez Santander, *El fútbol durante la guerra civil y el franquismo,* Madrid: San Martin, 1990, pp. 151–59; Ferenc Puskas, 'A Few Precious Years', in R. Melcon and S. Smith (eds), *The Real Madrid Book of Football,* London: Consul, 1961, pp. 52–61.

10. John Bunzl, *Happauf Hakoah: Jüdischer Sport in Österreich. Von den Anfängen bis in die Gegenwart,* Vienna: Junius, 1987, pp. 127–8; Matthias Marschik, *Vom Nutzen der Unterhaltung. Der Wiener Fußball in der NS-Zeit: Zwischen Vereinnahmung und Resistenz,* Vienna: Turia und Kant, 1998, pp. 115–29.

the collapse of the Austrian and Hungarian economies proved to be the incentive for a large-scale emigration of players and managers to Southern Europe. Clubs such as Rapid Vienna toured Europe every year, regularly selling players as they travelled and finishing their tours without part of the original squad.[11] In the last twenty years, the inflation rates of the indebted South American states have persuaded footballers at all professional levels to look for more lucrative contracts in Europe or Japan. In addition, the weakness of post-colonial economies has left African teams unable to compete with European clubs in keeping their promising youngsters. Secondly, in certain countries football's amateur or semi-professional status has prevented the game from becoming a lucrative activity. Before the 1980s, the Scandinavian leagues were amateur and still are largely conducted on a semi-professional basis. All players seeking to earn a living through their footballing skills have had to go abroad. The Dutch authorities took the step of recognizing professionalism in 1954 specifically to prevent the departure of the nation's best players. Thirdly, for the elite of the profession, the wealthy European leagues (Italy, Spain and, in the past three or four years, England) have been able to offer unrivalled contracts. In football, as in computer science, the concentration of highly specialized human resources is increasing: Serie A, the Premier Liga and the Premiership have become the football equivalents of Silicon Valley.

Historians have also highlighted the importance of enabling factors in explaining migration. In the early part of the century developments in transport, such as the steamship, undoubtedly facilitated the movement of South Americans to European leagues and Europeans to the professional competition established in the United States in the 1920s. Air transport has had an even greater impact since 1945. More important, perhaps, were those bodies or individuals which either encouraged emigration from the donor country or attempted to attract players to the receiving society. The football players' union in England encouraged its members to seek contracts abroad during the inter-war depression and to organize loan periods with North American Soccer League (NASL) clubs in the 1970s, although no funds were allocated to subsidize journeys. Agents have been particularly important figures in the movement of football labour. They have taken many guises over the years: representatives of clubs eager to attract foreign talent; journalists or former players who act as middlemen in negotiations; and increasingly in recent years, independent agents from outside the football world who represent a string of clients and are often transnational in their dealings. As well as being crucial in the historical development of the international transfer market, agents are widely regarded as a key factor in the acceleration of football migration in the 1990s.

11. Fonje Lang, *Das ist Rapid. Der Weg der Grünweissen Meistermannschaft*, Vienna: Josef Faber, 1952, p. 10; Joachim Wendt, 'Grundzüge der Geschichte des Deutschen Fußball-Bundes und die bürgerlichen deutschen Fußballsports im Zeitraum von 1918 bis 1933', Unpublished PhD Thesis, Halle Wittenberg, 1975, p. 160.

Distinctions have to be made between particular kinds of 'foreign' footballer. For this work, we have decided to limit our consideration of the migration of professional footballers to those who effectively moved *with* the ball; those who migrated with the intention of earning a living playing football. We are less concerned, therefore, with those who arrive in the host country in their youth.[12] Three main categories of football migrants emerge: the 'itinerants', the 'mercenaries' and the 'settlers'. The notion of the 'itinerant', who travelled, often over long distances, to sell his labour skills for short periods, has a long tradition in agriculture, industry and forms of commercial entertainment. It may well apply to those footballers who spend their summer on short, match-by-match contracts in the United States, Australia or South Africa. But more often it can be related to players spending one or two years in a foreign league before returning to their previous countries, and often to their previous employers. The football 'mercenaries' change country as soon as they get a better offer. Many Yugoslav and Scandinavian players sign contracts in three or four different national leagues during the course of their careers. After leaving his Danish club Naestved, Jesper Olsen, for instance, made a name for himself in the 1980s and early 1990s at Ajax, then at Manchester United, before spells with Bordeaux and Caen in France; Vladimir Durkovic left Red Star Belgrade in 1966 to play for Borussia Moenchengladbach, moving then to Saint-Etienne, before being stabbed by a policeman in a pub in Sion in 1972, where he had hoped to finish his career. The third category is the 'settler'. Because football is a profession practised by young men, many find a home and a wife, along with a stable job, in their host country. Of the five foreign players under contract with Montpellier in 1934, four married French women, took French citizenship and put down roots in France. More than thirty years after the end of his career, Alfredo Di Stefano is still living in the farm he bought outside Madrid. And many players have continued to be employed in the host country as managers or coaches. Players such as these are symbolic of the potential of football to act as a means of integration for immigrants.

Not all cases fit neatly into this typology. For some players, a move abroad represents the swansong of a successful career at home. The NASL was often viewed, somewhat disparagingly, as a retirement home for European and South American stars. Others, especially the British and Northern Europeans, have followed the familiar routes of tourists and well-off retirees. Terry McDermott, for instance, was given a two-year contract in sunny Cyprus at the end of a fifteen-year career with Bury, Liverpool and Newcastle United. Brian Talbot preferred

---

12. Recent work has taken a different perspective, which in our opinion does not take into account the specific nature of football as a direct cause of migration. Marc Barreaud, *Dictionnaire des footballeurs étrangers du championnat professionnel français (1932–1997)*, Paris: L'Harmattan, 1998.

the charm of another Mediterranean island, Malta, as a setting for his last professional games.

Much of the discussion concerning the migration of football talent to date has seen it in terms of globalization. This is the perspective adopted by the editors of an important contribution to the subject. In their introduction, they chose to view sports labour migration as an aspect of a broader globalization process. Emphasizing the importance of 'the global dimension' and 'the global system', the authors suggested a variety of possible cross-disciplinary frameworks for studying sports labour migration, from modernization and imperialism to dependency theory and Wallerstein's world system theory.[13] Another study has tried to adapt Wallerstein's theory to a study of football migrants in Britain. In an attempt to establish a model for football labour migration, the author suggests that the flow of football labour has been from the external area of Oceania, Asia and North America, to the periphery of Africa, the semi-periphery of South and Central America, and ultimately to Europe (and implicitly England) at the core. The European core acts, in this account, 'as a magnet for labour migrants on a global scale'.[14] Neither approach, however, takes much account of history. Globalization itself can be a nebulous concept which explains very little if used without care. According to one recent account, it 'is in danger of becoming . . . the cliché of our times'.[15] Too often it is introduced uncritically, as if it were an established fact rather than a contested concept. For globalization to have any real meaning in this context it must involve a process of economic and cultural interconnectedness which is historically unprecedented.[16] It is not sufficient to say that the increasing movement of professional footballers reflects broader processes of globalization or to assume that earlier examples were mere precursors of the recent migration 'explosion'. If, as we will argue, the migration of footballers has taken place on an *international* scale from the beginning of the twentieth century, what exactly are the factors which have transformed this into a *global* phenomenon in recent years? Any convincing answer to this question must be sensitive to historical change.

13. John Bale and Joseph Maguire (eds), *The Global Sports Arena: Athletic Talent Migration in an Interdependent World*, London: Frank Cass, 1994, pp. 1–21. Also Joseph Maguire and David Stead, 'Border Crossings: Soccer Labour Migration and the European Union', *International Review for the Sociology of Sport*, 33, 1, 1998, pp. 59–73; Joseph Maguire, *Global Sport: Identities, Societies, Civilizations*, London: Polity Press, 1999, chapter 5.

14. Jonathan Magee, 'Historical Concepts of Football and Labour Migration in England', unpublished paper presented at the 18th Conference of the British Society of Sports History, Eastbourne, April 1999, p. 4.

15. David Held, Anthony McGrew, David Goldblatt and Jonathan Perraton, *Global Transformations: Politics, Economics and Culture*, Cambridge: Polity Press, 1999, p. 1.

16. The most powerful critique of the economic dimension of the concept is in Paul Hirst and Grahame Thompson, *Globalization in Question*, 2nd edn, Cambridge: Polity Press, 1999.

This is not to say that we are outright sceptics of globalization. The movement of footballers in the 1990s, in particular, is clearly very different from that in earlier periods. The increasing volume of players exported from Eastern Europe to the West can be related to what has been labelled the 'new' migration in Europe, initiated by the end of the cold war, the collapse of Communist regimes and the opening of national borders.[17] More significantly, the Bosman ruling of 1995 is said to have radically changed the circumstances of professional footballers. Its consequences are evident every weekend throughout Europe, when increasing numbers of non-nationals line up alongside nationals. A number of authors have seen this as evidence of the globalization of the football market and the concomitant dissolution of national boundaries.[18] There is little doubt that the football scene at the end of the twentieth century, in Britain as elsewhere, is no longer confined to the nation. Television coverage has allowed viewers across Europe access to the matches of the major championships of other nations, while the new organization of the European Champions League has also helped to increase the amount of non-domestic football shown on national television.[19] This has facilitated the development of a vibrant international transfer market and means that managers, as well as spectators, are more likely to have seen their new foreign signings on the screen before they witness them in the flesh. National associations have seen their importance diminishing drastically in football's 'new' economic order. As one commentator recently noted: 'Since Bosman, players are only dealing with their direct employers: the clubs. The associations are becoming marginal'.[20] More than this, it can be argued that the transfer market in Europe has become tiered according to wealth and status, with a distinct transnational elite market emerging for the continent's richest 'Super Clubs'. Thus when a young international player such as Nicolas Anelka decides to leave his employer, as he did during the summer

17. Khalid Koser and Helma Lutz (eds), *The New Migration in Europe: Social Constructions and Social Realities*, London: Macmillan, 1998; Council of Europe, *People on the Move: New Migration Flows in Europe*, Strasbourg: Council of Europe, 1992; Vic Duke, 'The Flood from the East?: Perestroika and the Migration of Sports Talent from Eastern Europe' in Bale and Maguire (eds), *Global Sports Arena*, London: Frank Cass, pp. 153–67.

18. John Williams, *Is It All Over?: Can English Football Survive the Premier League*, London: South Side Press, 1999; Vic Duke and Liz Crolley, *Football, Nationality and the State*, London: Longman, 1996. For the notion of globalization pre-Bosman, see John Williams and Stephen Wagg (eds), *British Football and Social Change: Getting into Europe* Leicester: Leicester University Press, 1992.

19. British viewers are currently offered by terrestial television weekly features of the Italian, Dutch, Argentinian and North American leagues. Sky offers live Spanish matches while Eurosport has weekly programmes including French, Belgian and Portuguese football. In France, Canal Plus offers a Sunday night programme with extended highlights of some of the major European matches.

20. Denis Musso, 'Conséquences de l'arrêt Bosman: Réflexions sur la situation juridique du sportif', in H. Hélal and P. Mignon (eds), *Football: jeu et société*, Paris: INSEP, 1999, pp. 245–55.

of 1999, his choice of new club is restricted to those members of the continental football aristocracy who can afford his wages. While he could plausibly have moved to either Marseilles, Lazio or Real Madrid, he would never have gone to Lens, Venezia or Celta Vigo.

The changing composition of international teams is a good indicator of the increasing impact of labour migration in recent decades. Until about the mid-1980s, a move abroad could signal the end of a player's international career. The successful World Cup nations, such as the Brazilian sides of 1958, 1962 and 1970, were built exclusively around home-based players. Even the members of the winning Argentinian and Italian squads of 1978 and 1982 played their football mostly in domestic leagues. Yet possibly influenced by the success of the French European Championship winning side of 1984, with Juventus' inspirational Michel Platini at its core, national coaches were increasingly more prepared to accept, and perhaps even encourage, their best players moving to another country to gain experience. Argentina's 1986 team was dominated by three European-based stars – Maradona at Naples, Burruchaga at Nantes and Valdano at Real Madrid. Half of the German team at Italia 90 worked outside Germany, with its heart of Matthaeus, Klinsmann and Brehme playing at Inter. Brazil's 1994 Cup winners, in stark contrast to earlier squads, included a number of exiles. And most recently, there were just three players in France's victorious 1998 side employed by French clubs. The improved performance of African nations in international competition can also be related to more of the continent's footballers playing abroad, mainly in Europe but also in the Middle East and South Africa. Thus Africa's two representatives in the 1982 World Cup, Algeria and Cameroon, both had almost half their side playing in the French league and, more recently, Morocco, Nigeria and even South Africa have based their World Cup squads around players at European clubs.

The victory of the French national team in the 1998 World Cup has had a far-reaching impact over questions of race, citizenship and national identity. The 'Black-Blanc-Beur' (Black-White-Arabs) integration model advanced on the football pitch was transformed into a broader political message which represented the defeat of xenophobes, such as Jean-Marie Le Pen and his Front National in France. The World Cup winners epitomized the culture of 'the Melting Pot'. The adulation for a team composed of players from different ethnic backgrounds, and born in four different continents – America, Africa, Oceania and Europe – but all of whom were French *before* playing professional football, has developed interest in football as an integratory force for minorities. Unfortunately, however, in the popular discourse two questions with no necessary connection have been combined: the increasing migration of footballers and the integration of second-generation minorities. As in England, the migration of *footballers* has had no impact on the increasing multi-ethnic composition of the national side. In the English case, football has become in the last twenty years, alongside popular music, one of the main routes of achievement for ethnic minorities, although Asians, in football at least, are notably absent from these developments.[21] Increasingly the integration of minorities in professional football has been seized upon by politicians as a positive expression of their multi-ethnic achievement.

National definitions of citizenship and rules of naturalization are complicated by the interpretations of national and international football federations. Moreover, different countries have defined 'national' and 'non-national' footballers in a variety of ways. In certain respects, the broader rules of citizenship have been irrelevant to national football bodies, who have attempted to create sporting laws which exist outside the proper legal system.[22] In football today, the notions of dual or multi-nationality do not exist: one can be either Dutch or Surinamese, French or Moroccan but not both. For talented players who are dual nationals this involves deciding at some point which international side to play for. The difference in approach to issues of nationality can be highlighted by a few examples. Portuguese football teams, at domestic and international level, have been based on a mixture of national origins. The rise of the national team in the 1960s was constructed around the participation of players from the colonies, such as Eusebio and Mario Coluna from Mozambique. Brazilians in general have found it particularly easy to 'become' Portuguese, an attitude which has largely determined the multi-national constituency of the domestic league. In 1984, for instance, there were some 340 footballers born outside Portugal playing in the three divisions of the national league. The Italian and German federations, in contrast, have been less concerned to incorporate minority groups. In Italy, in the years from 1966 until about 1990, citizenship was not sufficient to allow an Italian to play as an Italian professional in the League. A player also had to have begun his career at home. Thus there has been little opportunity for those brought up abroad, such as Enzo Scifo in Belgium, to be selected for the *Azzurri*. In German football, meanwhile, the most significant ethnic groups, particularly the Turks, have barely featured at professional level because they are still considered to be foreigners.

Since the Second World War in particular, almost all domestic competitions have applied restrictions on foreign players. Two distinct conceptions of citizenship have emerged. In the countries where the legal system favoured the principle of *jus soli* (law of the soil), the naturalization of foreign footballers has led leagues to be perceived as melting pots of nationalities. In the countries applying *jus*

---

21. On this see Jez Bains and Sanjiev Johal, *Corner Flags and Corner Shops: The Asian Football Experience*, London: Victor Gollancz, 1998.

22. For the legal interactions between nationality law and football, Hans Ulrich Jessurun d'Oliveira, 'Calcio e nazionalità: le Olimpiadi, la Coppa del Mondo', in P. Lanfranchi (ed.), *Il calcio e il suo pubblico*, Naples: ESI, 1992, pp. 353–67.

sanguinis, or the law of the blood (Germany but also Italy, the Low Countries and Scandinavia), the opposite tendency emerged.[23] Because football federations, like governments, have defined citizenship in many different ways, the category of 'foreigner' has varied from country to country. What is more, some football federations have adopted policies which run counter to the nation's broader legal definitions.[24] In Belgium, a 'sporting citizenship' was introduced in the 1960s. A professional footballer acquired a 'Belgian football citizenship' after four years' residence which allowed him to play in the league as a 'national', but as a legal foreigner he could not play for the national team. Around 1980, Anderlecht had as many as nine non-Belgians in its team but only three were defined as 'foreigners'. The six others, including Rensenbrink, Haan and Brylle, enjoyed this strange privilege as semi-nationals. In Switzerland, a special status has for some time been attached to the 'border residents': foreign players previously living within thirty kilometres of the Swiss border. So players from Mullhouse, Weil am Rhein, Como or Bregenz could all play in Switzerland as nationals. We should not forget that overseeing the changing national and international framework of football labour migration has been FIFA, the world governing body. As well as its role in the organization of international competition, FIFA has been central in regulating the registration and contractual rights to football players across national and continental borders. The international transfer market which developed from the early part of the twentieth century under the auspices of FIFA ensured that, unlike most migrant workers, a professional football player could not move from one part of the world to another without the agreement of both his former and prospective employers.

This book considers the migration of football talent in an international and historical context. It is an attempt to explain the changes, but also outline the continuities, in patterns of migration over time and to look at the movement of footballers to and from particular regions and nations. Although the book provides a significant amount of quantification, we are not concerned only with patterns, flows and numbers. It is all too often forgotten that migration involves more than groups being propelled to and fro by structural forces. Migrants are individuals and members of families and social networks. Most actually make a decision to move. Where they go may be affected by a range of economic, cultural and traditional considerations – specific as well as general – and the impact of this migration is felt in both the place of origin and the destination. We are interested

---

23. Stephen Castles and Alastair Davidson, *Citizenship and Migration: Globalization and the Politics of Belonging*, Basingstoke: Macmillan, 2000. For a detailed exploration of conceptions of citizenship in France and Germany see Rogers Brubaker, *Citizenship and Nationhood in France and Germany*, London: Harvard University Press, 1992.

24. Andreas Malatos, *Il calcio professionista in Europa. Profili di diritto comparato*, Padua: CEDAM, 1989, pp. 114–20.

in football migrants as individuals as well as groups. Their experiences, perceptions and stories play a central role in our work and are crucial, we think, to understanding the phenomenon of migration. Moreover, we are as concerned with what happens when footballers step off the boat or the plane as in why they are there in the first place. As in any other profession, living and working abroad offers opportunities but also presents problems. Players have to adapt to a new cultural environment, often a different way of working and a new way of life. This can also mean learning a new language. Some find adjustment impossible while others become assimilated or integrated, to varying degrees, into the host society. Yet while it may be possible to distinguish between different types of experience – based on the motivations, national origin and number of immigrants and the attitude of receiving societies – it is nonetheless important to remember that the experiences of migrants and the stories they tell are personal and unique.[25]

The present study is not intended as a definitive history of football migration. The scope of the phenomenon is so vast that it would be unrealistic to attempt an analysis of this kind. We have focused instead on what we regard as some of the most significant and interesting aspects of the movement of footballers. Chronologically, the study traces football migration from its beginnings in late nineteenth-century Britain and the foundation of the first clubs in continental Europe right through to the post-Bosman period of the late 1990s. In doing so, we have chosen a number of case studies which focus on particular nations or regions and which, though specific, illuminate more general themes. South American, particularly Argentinian and Brazilian, and Yugoslavian footballers are considered as prime examples of football migrants. North America and Africa are treated respectively as key continents of immigration and emigration. Britain, meanwhile, is worthy of consideration because of its formative role in the creation and diffusion of the professional game but also because of its apparent isolationism and reticence towards both the in- and out-migration of footballers. In the course of these chapters, and other thematic ones, key countries such as Italy, Spain, Germany and France will be considered, as will regions such as Scandinavia, the Low Countries and Eastern Europe.

Naturally there are omissions. The development of football in recent years in south-east Asia has led to further extensions of the international labour market. Indonesia, Malaysia, Singapore, Hong Kong, South Korea and even China have all started to admit foreign players and have reciprocated by sending their best talent abroad. Japan is a particularly interesting case in view of the government's long-standing opposition to foreign labour. Non-nationals had played as amateurs

---

25. On typologies of migrant experience in the host society, see Charles Price, 'The Study of Assimilation', in J.A. Jackson (ed.) *Migration*, Cambridge: Cambridge University Press, 1969, pp. 181–237.

in Japanese football for some years but it was the acceptance of full-time professionals, and the creation of the J-League in 1993, which encouraged the influx of migrant footballers, mainly Brazilian Japanese alongside the big names such as Zico, Pierre Littbarski and Gary Lineker. Japanese emigrants have been few and far between, although some, like Okudera at Cologne in the late 1970s and more recently Nakata at Perugia and now Roma, have been extremely successful.[26] Similarly, little attention has been paid to the countries of Australasia, although we recognize their significance as exporters and importers of football talent and their key role in the complex international migratory flows of the late 1990s. This more 'global' interchange of football talent – if that is what it is – is only at its formative stage. It remains to be seen whether football's status as the world game will be reflected in an increasing diversification of the routes and equalization of the volume of player movement. Only then could we begin to talk about a truly global market for football talent.

26. On football in Asia and Oceania more generally see Bill Murray, 'Cultural Revolution: Football in the Societies of Asia and the Pacific', in S. Wagg (ed.) *Giving the Game Away*, London: Leicester University Press, pp. 138–62. On Japanese football, John Horne and David Jary, 'Japan and the World Cup: Asia's first World Cup Final hosts?' in J. Sugden and A. Tomlinson (eds), *Hosts and Champions: Soccer Cultures, National Identities and the USA World Cup*, Aldershot: Arena, 1994, pp. 161–82; Harua Nogowa and Hiroko Maeda, 'The Japanese Dream: Soccer Culture towards the New Millennium', in G. Armstrong and R. Giulianotti (eds), *Football Cultures and Identities*, London: Macmillan, 1999, pp. 223–33.

–1–

Migrants and the Foundation of European Football

The modern sport known as association football was codified in the middle of the nineteenth century in England. The game soon became in its English version a male preserve and an expression of working-class culture. Yet in its formative phase in continental Europe, football acquired values which were more representative of the Victorian *middle* class. At first, the spirit of the game involved a liberal *Weltanschauung* – with the ideas of universal and open competition, fair play, the acceptance of rules and the authority of the referee paramount. It also represented a complete rupture with older forms of game which cultivated distinction and were based on local ceremonies and parochial customs.[1] As Christiane Eisenberg notes: 'Along with tourism, fashion, jazz, photography and cinema, it [football] represented modernity, a phenomenon which challenged the self-evidence of eternal customs.'[2] With its simple and universally recognized rules, football rapidly became the sport which unified the promoters of progress.

The adoption of football outside Britain marked a fundamental breach with ancient forms of ball game. Hundreds of different types of game had existed all over Europe before the mid-nineteenth century and shared some of the rules and many of the characteristics of association football. But they varied from place to place and their players remained, in essence, confined to particular areas. Standardization has often been regarded as the major innovation of modern sport. Yet we would argue that the introduction of egalitarian values and the mobility of playing talent were also crucial distinctions which initially separated modern football from traditional games. The spread of the game on the continent in the final decades of the nineteenth century was not simply an expression of British imperialism. Football was in fact closely linked with a range of technical innova-

1. On the difference between pre-modern sports and football see Roger Chartier and Georges Vigarello, 'Les trajectoires du sport', *Le Débat*, 19, February 1982, pp. 35–58; Guy Laurens, 'Qu'est-ce qu'un champion? La compétition sportive en Languedoc au début du siècle', *Annales ESC*, 45, September 1990, pp. 1047–69; Horst Bredekamp, *Calcio Fiorentino. Il Rinascimento dei giochi*, Genoa: Il Melangolo, 1995.

2. Christiane Eisenberg, 'Sportgeschichte: Eine Dimension der modernen Kulturgeschichte', *Geschichte und Gesellschaft*, 23, 1997, pp. 295–310.

tions – from electrification to the development of railway networks – all of which required a massive migration of skilled and highly qualified workers. Playing football was one of the many ways of expressing the passage from an archaic to an industrial world.

Ball Games before Football

The migration of participants in ball games is a modern phenomenon. In an Italian book published in 1949, the authors tried to write the history of football from antiquity to the year 2000 and chose as their front cover an image of Piazza della Signoria in Florence during a match of Florentine *calcio*. Through this, they tried to demonstrate a direct link between modern football and the Florentine game.[3] This genealogical tendency is also present in Jusserand's *Les sports et jeux d'exercice dans l'ancienne France* (Sports and games in ancient France), published at the beginning of the twentieth century. The author considered the French game of *soule* as the 'source and major origin of the present football'.[4] *Hornusse* in Switzerland, *Lapta* in Russia, the *Kalagut* played by the Eskimos and the various forms of folk football have all been identified as predecessors of the association game.[5] In Britain, Norbert Elias and Eric Dunning have insisted on the importance of 'folk football' and Dennis Brailsford identified 'communal football' as the direct antecedent of the modern game.[6] These possible links indicate the continuity of interest in ball games at different periods and in different areas. However, the continuity between the participants (or players) in these games is less clear. In *calcio*, a code written in the sixteenth century defines the players as eligible 'only if they are gentlemen, honoured soldiers, nobles and princes'.[7] The *calcio* represented the ideal definition of the city; it helped to reinforce the Florentine social order. To be able to compete, participants needed to fulfil three criteria associated with their birth: temporal (the age group), social (being a member of the gentry) and spatial (being born in one of the parishes of the city). Crucially,

---

3. L.C. Romanato and R. Marmiroli, *Il gioco del calcio dalle origini al 2000*, Modena: Dini, 1949.

4. Jean-Jules Jusserand, *Les sports et jeux d'exercice dans l'ancienne France*, Paris: Plon, 1901, p. 266.

5. Henning Eichberg, 'Einheit oder Vielfalt am Ball? Zur Kulturgeschichte des Spiels am Beispiel der Nuit und der Altisländer', in O. Gruppe, H. Gabler and U. Göhner (eds), *Spiel–Spiele–Spielen*, Schorndorf: K. Hoffmann, 1983, pp. 131–53.

6. Norbert Elias and Eric Dunning, *Quest for Excitement: Sport and Leisure in the Civilizing Process*, Oxford: Blackwell, 1986; Dennis Brailsford, *Sport, Time and Society: The British at Play*, London: Routledge, 1991, pp. 3–10.

7. Giovanni de Bardi, *Discorso sopra il giuoco del calcio fiorentino*, Florence, 1580, p. 10.

players were not permitted to choose their teams. The distinction between most teams was immutable and these distinctions continued after the contest.

Most descriptions of the composition of pre-modern football teams are similar. The distinction between opponents seems to have been only partially dependent on sporting ability. The playing groups were not composed of young men in search of leisure but reproduced an image of the communities from which they came. The world they portrayed was static.[8] As the local patrons differed from parish to parish, so the nature of the game varied from village to village.[9] Parish, occupation or marital status could divide the protagonists of the contests. Playing games was, as Jean Delumeau writes, one of the reassuring rituals of the pre-industrial Western world.[10] The contest pointed out the nature of social differences, and each of the participants was aware of these distinctions. The remark of Clifford Geertz on the cockfights in Bali, that 'Bringing a cock to an important fight was, for an adult male, a compulsory duty of citizenship', may well apply to the organization of pre-modern ball games in the Western world.[11] In this form of 'deep play', foreigners and outsiders may have watched but they could not possibly have taken part. Participation was not the result of individual choice but the affirmation of a tangible and permanent anchorage in a group.

A *calcio* player, then, was bound to the team of his native parish for his entire sporting career.[12] John Huizinga observed the stable image of social orders when he noted that pre-modern playing communities tended to stay together longer, to consider themselves as unique.[13] For this reason, *calcio* was presented as 'an old and specific game of the city of Florence'.[14] Its appeal came from the fact that it

---

8. André Rauch, 'Des jeux aux sports: Pour une histoire des différences', *Cahiers d'histoire*, 34, 1, 1989, pp. 156–63; Pedro Cordoba, 'Exercices et jeux physiques, repères pour une analyse', in A. Redondo (ed.) *Le corps dans la société espagnole des XVIe et XVIIe siècles*, Paris: Editions de la Sorbonne, 1990, pp. 267–76.

9. Jean-Michel Sallmann, 'Il santo patrono cittadino nel 1600 nel regno di Napoli e in Sicilia', in *Per una storia sociale e religiosa del mezzogiorno d'Italia*, vol. 2, Naples: Guida, 1982, pp. 191–210.

10. Jean Delumeau, *Rassurer et protéger. Le sentiment de sécurité dans l'occident d'autrefois*, Paris: Fayard, 1989, pp. 156–63.

11. Clifford Geertz, 'Deep Play: Notes on the Balinese Cockfight', in *The Interpretation of Cultures*, New York: Basic Books, 1973, pp. 412–53. The quotation is from page 424.

12. By contrast, in Siena's *Palio* the jockeys were mercenaries and their geographic origins were irrelevant. Yet even in this case, the true actors of the event were the horses and the *contradaioli* (the parish inhabitants), see Pier Giorgio Solinas, 'Le sort, le hasard, la lutte: le Palio de Sienne', *Ethnologie française*, 2–3, 1997, pp. 170–7.

13. John Huizinga, *Homo Ludens: A study of the play-element in culture*, Boston: Beacon Press, 1955.

14. Definition of the Florentine *calcio* from the Crusca Dictionnary, quoted in S. Capelli, 'Il calcio fiorentino', in *Azzurri: 1990, Storia della nazionale italiana di calcio e del calcio a Firenze*,

was inextricably linked to the city and its inhabitants – it was *the* Florentine game and thus by definition could not be exported. By contrast, the rules of modern football may have been translated into various languages in the 1880s, but they remained the same independently of where the game was being played. In many respects, the attraction of the modern association game derived from its universality. It was not bound by place and therefore could be 'transferred', 'diffused' or 'spread'. Its participants could also migrate.

The rigidity of group divisions was also evident in the Eton Wall Game. The wall was the protagonist of the game: it was the object, the boundary and the arena. The opposing sides were defined by their spatial relationship to it. The oppidans, the village people or outside boarders, were positioned on the external side and the collegers on the internal. At the end of the match everyone returned to his side and the wall remained in place. The players could not possibly have moved from one side to the other because to do so would have altered their social status.[15] *Soule* matches in Normandy opposed two teams of single (the young) and married (the old) men in the same rural community. For the young Freemen Marblers of Corfe Castle, participation in an annual ball game against married opponents was, in part at least, conceived as a display of physical prowess and vigour which could help to attract a girl.[16] Similarly in the Tlatchi played by the Aztecs, 'it is unthinkable to be able to modify your own destiny, to have the illusion to one day change your status'.[17] This is one of the features which distinguishes pre-modern forms of football from the modern association game. In these pre-modern games, we are facing a limited world. The challengers had to know each other off the field; often they were neighbours, and their opposition on the field was never accidental. Any conception of leagues or championships was absent: competition was still based on a direct challenge from one group to another.[18] This was a binary world: you were in either one group or another, you were either a loser or a winner, but never a runner-up. When the contest finished, you had to wait another year to challenge again, with the same people in the same teams.

Rome: Meridiana, 1990, pp. 147–9. In the nearby city of Prato, the *calcio* players used a different ball and different rules 'because the place is smaller than the one used by the young Florentines'. C. Gausti, 'Il giuoco del calcio a Prato', *Archivio storico pratese*, 1919, pp. 59–70.

15. R.E. Macnaghton, 'The Eton Wall-Game', *Badminton Magazine of Sports and Pastimes*, Vol. 6, London: Longmans, 1898, pp. 171–83; J. Chandos, *Boys Together: English Public Schools, 1800–1864*, Oxford: Oxford University Press, 1984.

16. Richard Holt, *Sport and the British*, Oxford: Clarendon, 1989, p. 15; Sire de Gouberville, *Journal*, Caen: Beaurepaire, 1892; Michel Manson, 'La choule (soule) en Normandie au XVIe siècle d'après le Sire de Gouberville', in L. Burgener (ed), *Sport und Kultur. Sport et civilisations*, Bern: Lang, 1982, pp. 97–106.

17. C. Duverger, *L'esprit du jeu chez les aztèques*, Paris: Mouton, 1978, p. 172.

There were no associations or extended fixture lists, and recruitment was based on local membership. Sporting ability was secondary.

Englishness and Modernity

The Britain that invented modern football was also the Britain of the industrial and urban revolution. Above all, Britain represented modernity. The distinctions which emerged here – between work and leisure time, skilled and unskilled workers, urban and rural communities – became the key boundaries which defined modernity. So it was not football's Englishness[19] alone which fascinated various sections of the continental urban middle class, but its obvious association with elements of modernity. The early success of football in continental Europe was directly connected with the mobility of economic elites in the second half of the nineteenth century. British citizens were certainly involved in these initial stages but intra-European migration played a major role often neglected in the British literature. In one of the first historical texts about the development of sport on the continent, Eugen Weber identified the pioneering role of Switzerland in the early spread of football.[20] The Ecole de la Chatelaîne in Geneva had a football team from 1869, probably the first registered team on the continent.[21] Other private schools such as the Villa Ouchy, the Clauselet School and Villa Longchamp in Lausanne quickly followed. Mountaineering, football and athletics had all been included in the curriculums of these schools by 1890.[22] They recruited a large number of their students from Britain, and built football grounds on their premises.[23] Private schools of this kind were in charge of the education of the future international economic elite, dominated largely by British capitalists. The fresh air, the proximity to the

18. Laurens, 'Qu'est-ce qu'un champion?', focuses rightly on the intermediate period of the beginnings of modern sports in Southern France, showing the importance of archaic values such as the direct challenge. In football, cup competitions maintained the idea of the challenge match.

19. The term 'Englishness' is used to refer to Britishness in almost every European text.

20. Eugen Weber, 'Gymnastics and Sport in Fin de siècle France', *American Historical Review*, 76, 1, 1971, pp. 70–98.

21. Disagreeing with this idea, Allen Guttmann writes: 'The palm for priority seems to have been awarded wrongly. Soccer was played in Belgium as early as 1863, the year of the foundation of England's Football Association'. Allen Guttmann, *Games and Empires: Modern Sports and Cultural Imperialism*, New York: Columbia University Press, 1994, p. 44. We would argue that rather than being an isolated case, the Swiss development shows a whole strategy by a large group of private schools. The team of La Chatelaine, for instance, continued to field a team for decades.

22. Pierre Lanfranchi, 'Football et modernité: La Suisse et la pénétration du football sur le continent', *Traverse, revue d'histoire*, 5, 1998, 3, pp. 76–88.

23. Fritz Klippstein (ed.), *Festschrift zum 30 Jährigen Bestand des Schweiz. Fussball- und Athletik-Verband*, St Gall: Tschudy, 1925, pp. 25–6.

Alps and the exclusive recruitment these institutions offered were a large part of their attraction. In Switzerland, more than anywhere else, English sports were associated with a new system of education which aimed to diffuse the ideals of the industrial revolution, along with the knowledge of foreign languages and new technologies. The choice of football as *the* sport of modernity in Switzerland, and later throughout the continent, had an English explanation. In England, the other major team sports of rugby and cricket were associated respectively with the traditional universities and the Empire. Football, also popular in the elite public schools and universities, had spread to become the dominant sport in the engineering schools and technical institutions which provided a more practical education.[24] The international migration of wealthy students to Switzerland, the rapid increase in the number of Swiss polytechnics, and the 'discovery' of the Alps from the end of the eighteenth century, contributed to the scattering of football throughout continental Europe.[25]

Irrespective of their nationality, the modern 'sportsmen' spoke English.[26] The use of English words was a sign of the modern and a rejection of the traditional local culture. The White Rovers club in Paris was open to players of any nationality but at its AGM in 1892 decided that 'Football being essentially an English game, all players must use the English language exclusively when playing together'.[27] In Genoa, Naples, Antwerp, Milan and Vienna, clubs adopted the *English* translation of the local town in their name. The *Grasshoppers* of Zurich, *Old Boys* of Basle, *Young Boys* of Bern, *Young Fellows* of Zurich – and the two Dutch clubs with the most curious of names of all, *Go Ahead Eagles* in Deventer and *Be Quick* in Groningen – all played for the most part without English players but were nonetheless keen to express the anglophilia of their members. A degree of anglophilia was also evident in the choice of clothes, the growth of gentlemen's clubs, the names attached to new games (whist, steeple-chase, lawn-tennis) and the development of tourism. Together with other forms of leisure activity, playing football contributed to the reproduction of an English way of life. A Basque commentator writing at the beginning of the twentieth century could identify the type of person who was likely to play the game: '[football] is a modern and open-

24. Robert Angus Buchanan, 'Institutional Proliferation in the British Engineering Profession, 1847–1914', *Economic History Review*, 38, 1985, pp. 42–60.

25. Philippe Joutard, *L'invention du Mont Blanc*, Paris: Gallimard, 1986, especially chapters 3–4.

26. From this point of view, Germany certainly constitutes an exception. Football rules were translated very early and clubs names were mainly German. See Christiane Eisenberg, 'Deutschland' in C. Eisenberg (ed.), *Fußball, Soccer, Calcio. Ein englischer Sport auf seinem Weg um die Welt*, Munich: DTV, 1997, pp. 94–129.

27. Alfred Wahl, *Les archives du football*, Paris: Gallimard, 1989, p. 34.

minded tendency directed at upper and middle class people with "advanced" and cultivated ideas'.[28]

By contrast, in this period of nation-state building, national gymnastic organizations all over Europe (representing a much larger group of participants) refused to adopt foreign names. They opted instead for patriotic titles such as the *Patriote* or *Jeanne d'Arc* (Joan of Arc) in France, *Borussia* (Prussia in Latin) *Germania* or *Teutonia* in Germany,[29] and Latin terms such as *Juventus* (Youth) and *Pro Patria* (For the Fatherland) in Italy. In Switzerland, as in many other countries, state schools associated with the nationalist movements chose gymnastics while the cosmopolitan private schools and polytechnics encouraged English sports in general, and football in particular, to epitomize their faith in progress and the industrial revolution.[30] Similarly, playing football meant challenging the classical form of education which ignored the body. Football proposed new concepts of lifestyle expressed in the ideas of 'fair play' and the 'self-made man' – terms not translated when used in other European languages. Links were drawn between the 'winning' economy and the 'winning' pastimes. The French educationalist Edmond Demolins, a disciple of Le Play, wrote in 1897: 'The English do not seek strength through too much physical education – they prefer sport. It is evident that this type of game helps them to acquire serenity and self-confidence. These are the conditions of triumph.'[31] A similar approach was expressed by the progressive Italian Catholic priest and theoretician Giovanni Semeria: 'The Englishman loves sport, he loves difficulty. He does not run from adventure: he looks for it.'[32]

This distinction between football and gymnastics is essential for understanding the issues of citizenship and xenophobia. Whereas football clubs rarely discriminated on the basis of citizenship, a nationality clause was inserted in the regulations of almost every gymnastics club.[33] The case of Italy highlights the importance of

28. John Walton, 'Football and Basque Identity: Real Sociedad of San Sebastián, 1909–1932', *Memoria y Civilización*, 2, 1999, pp. 261–89.

29. Christiane Eisenberg, *'English Sports' und deutsche Bürger. Eine Gesellschaftsgeschichte 1800–1939*, Paderborn: Schöningh, 1999, p. 185.

30. Fritz Prith, *Sport in der Schweiz*, Olten: Walter, 1979, pp. 29–75; Marco Marcacci, 'La ginnastica contro gli sport', *Traverse*, 5, 3, 1998, pp. 69–73.

31. Edmond Demolins, *A quoi tient la supériorité des Anglo-Saxons?*, Paris: Firmin-Didot, 1897, pp. 103–4.

32. Giovanni Semeria, *L'Alpinismo*, Genoa, 1909, quoted in Stefano Pivato, 'Foot-ball e neotomismo', *Belfagor*, 16, 5, 1990, pp. 579–86.

33. Pierre Chambat, 'Les fêtes de la discipline: gymnastique et politique en France (1879–1914)', in P. Arnaud and J. Camy (eds), *La naissance du Mouvement Sportif Associatif en France*, Lyon: Presses Universitaires de Lyon, 1986, pp. 85–96; Marcel Spivak, 'Un concept mythologique de la Troisième République: Le renforcement du capital humain de la France', *International Journal of the History of Sport*, 4, 2, 1987, pp. 155–75.

this contrast. Footballers were criticized by the gymnastics organization because 'they dress, eat, drink, and abuse in English'.[34] Their Anglomania was ridiculed: 'People only play football to look like Englishmen and to be able to use an exotic vocabulary. For some time, this was considered fashionable and a sign of good taste. Fortunately, everybody recognises now the grotesqueness of this attitude.'[35] Consequently, football competitions arranged by the Italian Gymnastics Organization were open only to Italian citizens. Having established a majority inside the Italian football federation from 1908, the gymnastics clubs decided, as a first step, to ban foreigners from the national championship. Genoa, Torino, Milan and Inter then withdrew in protest from the national league they had previously monopolized. A typical Italian compromise was reached the following year. The so-called 'English' teams and their foreign players agreed to take part in the competitions again while, as compensation, the Italian federation changed its name from *Federazione Italiana di Foot-Ball* to *Federazione Italiana Giuoco Calcio* in order to emphasize the Italian character of the game and acknowledge its assumed link with the Florentine game.[36]

Where discrimination existed within the early European football clubs, it was more likely to apply to social distinction than citizenship. The First Vienna Football Club, formed in 1894 under the patronage of the banker Rothschild, explicitly excluded 'manual workers, journeymen and other unskilled workers' in its internal regulations.[37] Moreover, continental footballers were keen to elicit the help of aristocrats. Many of the continent's 'sportsmen' considered themselves to be members of an international aristocracy. In 1907, Paul Adam observed in his book *La morale des sports* that:

> Over the last fifty years, a general type of elite has emerged. They share a number of common ideas about philosophy, science, arts and morality. They reign and prosper in spa towns, winter resorts and where international conferences take place. This elite is composed of doctors, bankers, professors, rentiers, authors, diplomats, dandies, artists, princes and dilettantes of various kinds. They agree on about one hundred essential values. They consider themselves the brothers of the same intellectual family and have faith in universality and rationalism . . . Already the yachtsmen and the horse owners are among them. They like car racing and through sport they may unite and soon dominate the world.[38]

34. *Il ginnasta*, 15 October 1903.

35. T. Morgagni and V. Brusca, *Annuario sportivo 1907–1908*, Milan: Corriere della sera ed., 1907.

36. 'Regolamento organico della FIGC', *Letteratura sportiva*, 22 August 1909.

37. Michael John, 'Österreich' in Eisenberg (ed.), *Fußball, soccer, calcio*, p. 65.

38. Paul Adam, *La morale des sports*, Paris: Librairie mondiale, 1907, pp. 189–91.

This aristocratic model may initially seem rather surprising to those who have always regarded football as 'the people's game'. The first football team in Italy, the International Football Club of Turin, was established by Edoardo Bosio, a former employee of the Thomas Adams factory in Nottingham, who was able to recruit the Marquis of Ventimiglia and the Duke of Abruzzi, nephew of the king.[39] Influenced by the social elitism of the Jockey Club, these aristocrats saw sport as an ideal meeting place.[40] Baron Edouard de Lavelaye was the chairman of the Belgian FA from 1895 to 1924; his successor Comte d'Outremont was another aristocrat.[41] Yet the spirit associated with sport and the playing of games were two entirely different things. The personal investment of aristocrats and lower social groups in football contrasted greatly. If members of high society considered playing football as just one of a range of leisure activities, for white-collar workers it became a major preoccupation.[42] This kind of cross-class alliance was casual and necessitated by the limited number of potential players. In short, the aristocrat regarded playing football as a new adventure; the white-collar worker saw in it a way of distancing himself from the working class.

The First Cosmopolitan Footballers

Switzerland, the 'little England' of the continent, could be defined as a point of connection between Britain and Southern Europe in the diffusion of football and the introduction of 'foreigners' to the game.[43] In the first ten years of the twentieth century, Swiss players were present throughout Europe and three figures are particularly emblematic of the first cosmopolitan footballers educated in Switzerland: Hans Gamper, Henry Monnier and Vittorio Pozzo.

39. Luciano Serra, *Storia del calcio 1863–1963*, Bologna: Palmaverde, 1964, p. 28; Antonio Ghirelli, *Storia del calcio in Italia*, 3rd edn, Turin: Einaudi, 1990, p. 19; Antonio Papa and Guido Panico, *Storia sociale del calcio in Italia*, Bologna: Il mulino, 1993, p. 46.

40. Edoardo Grendi, 'Lo sport, un'innovazione vittoriana?', *Quaderni storici*, 17, 2, 1983, pp. 679–94; Monique de Saint-Martin, 'La noblesse et les sports "nobles"', *Actes de la recherche en sciences sociales*, 80, 1989, pp. 22–32; Joseph-Antoine Roy, *Histoire du Jockey-Club de Paris*, Paris: Rivière, 1958.

41. Victor Boin, *Het gulden Jubilaeumboek van het KBVB*, Brussels: Leclercq & De Haas, 1945, p. 151.

42. On leisure and the Italian aristocracy, see Anthony L. Cardoza, *Aristocrats in Bourgeois Italy: The Piedmontese Nobility, 1861–1930*, Cambridge: Cambridge University Press, 1997, pp. 187–225.

43. Peter Dudzik, *Innovation und Investition*, Zurich: Chronos, 1987; Rudolf Jaun, *Management und Arbeiterschaft. Verwissenschaftlichung, Amerikanisierung und Rationalisierung der Arbeitsverhältnisse in der Schweiz, 1883–1959*, Zurich: Chronos, 1986.

Hans Gamper was born in 1877 in Winterthur, an industrial town in the Zurich Canton, and studied in Basle and at Zurich Polytechnic Institute. In 1897, he was one of the founders of the Football Club Zurich. The following year he moved to Geneva and played football with the Servette Football Club, at the same time taking part in athletics and cycling competitions and even winning the Swiss 200 metres championship.[44] In 1898, Gamper crossed the border to live in Lyons, where he was employed by the Crédit Lyonnais and played with the Football Club de Lyon, but more often in rugby than football or athletics. Finally, in 1899, he arrived in Barcelona, where his uncle owned a major business, to represent the interests of various Swiss and French companies. At the end of that year, he established the Football Club Barcelona. According to Gamper's biography, the blue and red colours of FC Barcelona were based on the flag of the Swiss canton of Basle.[45] In this first Barcelona team, players came from as far afield as Switzerland, Britain, Germany and Austria.

The first words of Henry Monnier's biography portray his sporting life as a ritual: 'In 1898, aged eighteen, he entered the sporting sanctuary. The initiation took place in Switzerland, in Geneva'.[46] The son of a Protestant banker, he had been sent to a banking institution in the city of Calvin to develop his knowledge of international trade.[47] The following year, Monnier's apprenticeship as a banker brought him to Liverpool, where he studied at Liverpool polytechnic and continued to play football.[48] Back home in France in 1901, working in the family bank, one of his first moves was to create a football club: the Sporting Club de Nîmes. He donated a ball which he had acquired in England and taught local youths the official rules of the game (in English) which he had brought home with him. Every aspect of Monnier's life reflected his Anglophilia. His Christian name was the English *Henry,* rather than the French *Henri*, and he named his son Willy.[49] During the First World War, he even worked as an English translator on the Somme.

44. 'Hans Gamper', *La Suisse sportive*, 25 June 1898.

45. Nicolau Casaus, *Gamper*, Barcelona: Labor, 1984; Antoni Closa and Jordi Blanco, *Diccionari del Barça*, Barcelona: Enciclopèdia catalana, 1999, pp. 157–8; Jacques Ducret, *Le livre d'or du football suisse*, Lausanne: L'âge d'homme, 1994, p. 13.

46. *Nîmes Sport*, 11, 7 January 1922.

47. This combination of international trade and sporting education on the Geneva lake was far from exceptional. Jean-Louis Jullien and Jules Falgueirettes the founders of Olympique de Sète, another successful southern French club, learnt football in their colleges in Geneva and Franz Calì, the captain of the first Italian national team, had been educated in Lausanne. Yves Dupont, *La Mecque du football ou les mémoires d'un dauphin*, Nîmes: Bène, 1973.

48. *Nîmes Sport*, 11, 7 January 1922; Handwritten and unpublished memoirs of Henry Monnier, *Le Sporting Club de Nîmes* (66 pages) written in 1954, photocopy in possession of the authors, p. 1.

49. The Belgian referee of the first World Cup Final in 1930, *John* Langenus is another good example of this Anglomania expressed by the choice of an English name. See John Langenus, *En*

Born in Turin in 1886, Vittorio Pozzo spent two years in Winterthur and Zurich where in 1908 he was awarded a degree in commercial techniques and languages and played with the Grasshoppers second team. After two more years abroad, in Germany and in Manchester, he came back to his native town to become a member of Torino Football Club.[50] His international football experience gave him an unchallenged expertise. He was only twenty-six years old when he became responsible for the national team at the Olympic Games in Stockholm in 1912. His playing career had not been exceptional but his involvement in football would continue for half a century.[51] He became one of Italy's first sports journalists, writing for *La Stampa*, as well as a referee and later the manager of the Italian national team which won the World Cups of 1934 and 1938.[52]

Football pioneers generally came from wealthy families and were particularly influenced by the British traditions associated with the industrial revolution. They would often go to England or Switzerland (or both) to complete their education, arriving home with a football. Yves du Manoir, a member of the Breton aristocracy, studied in public schools in Lausanne and Jersey, then at the Lycée Saint-Louis in Paris and concluded his pilgrimage at the highly prestigious Ecole Polytechnique in the same city. In the 1920s, he became one of the most famous rugby players in France. His impact was such that the Olympic Stadium in Paris was named after him when he died in an air crash in 1928.[53] Raymond Dubly, the son of a textile broker from Roubaix, spent a year at Uckfield College in Sussex improving his English and his football skills. He later became a famous French international and a wealthy businessman.[54]

These migrants did not consider themselves as champion sportsmen but as missionaries of free-market enterprise and opponents of the protectionist and xenophobic visions of nationalism. Sport was not a career but it became a central part of their lives. Religion also played an important role. Monnier enlisted the first members of his Sporting Club de Nîmes from the local branch of the Calvinist

---

sifflant par le monde: souvenirs et impressions de voyage d'un arbitre de football, Gent: Snoeck-Ducajou, 1943.

50. Biography of Pozzo in *Il calcio, cronache illustrate della vità sportiva italiana*, 1 March 1924.

51. See his autobiography, Vittorio Pozzo, *Campioni del Mondo. Quarant'anni di storia del calcio italiano*, Rome: CEN, 1960.

52. Brian Glanville, *Soccer Round the Globe*, London: The Sportmans Book Club, 1961, p. 59; Brian Glanville, *Football Memories*, London: Virgin, 1999, pp. 102–5.

53. Pierre Lafond and Jean-Pierre Bodis, *Encyclopédie du rugby français*, Paris: Dehédin, 1989, p. 693.

54. Alfred Wahl and Pierre Lanfranchi, *Les footballeurs professionnels des années trente à nos jours*, Paris: Hachette, 1995, p. 15.

Church Youth Club.[55] In Sète, two of the more active sporting promoters were eminent Swiss protestant bankers.[56] In Marseilles, the Stade Helvétique was closely connected with the local reform church.[57] And in Barcelona, Gamper based the recruitment of FC Barcelona on local Protestant organizations. As late as 1912, a match between FC Barcelona and Bishop Auckland Wanderers was refereed by a Swiss Protestant priest.[58] In Catholic southern Europe, the Protestant sportsmen reproduced through football an 'alternative culture' which was able to attract Protestants from different national origins.[59] Given the elitist character of football in its continental dimension, the young Protestants and the business and commercial classes were very often one and the same and provided one of the most fertile environments for the diffusion of the game. As Allen Guttmann (referring to the work of Bero Rigauer) has shown, sports have historically developed more rapidly and successfully in a Protestant milieu, as a kind of transposition to physical activity of Max Weber's theory of secular asceticism.[60]

The British, the 'Swiss' and Economic Progress

British citizens were of course far from absent in the foundation and the initial development of football on the continent.[61] The case of Genoa Cricket and Football

55. Monnier, *Le Sporting Club de Nîmes*, pp. 1–3. Also, Jean-Daniel Roques, 'Nouveaux aperçus sur l'Eglise protestante de Nîmes dans la seconde moitié du XIXe siècle', *Bulletin de la société de l'histoire du protestantisme français*, 120, 1974, pp. 48–96.

56. Jean Gaussent, 'L'Eglise protestante de Sète 1851–1905', *Bulletin de la Société de l'histoire du protestantisme français*, 135, 1987, pp. 25–40.

57. Renée Lopez,'Les Suisses à Marseille: une immigration de longue durée', *Revue européenne des migrations internationales*, 3, 1–2, 1987, pp. 149–72.

58. Joan Garcia Castell, *Història del futbol català*, Barcelona: Aymà, 1968, p. 107.

59. For the concept of alternative culture and the German Social Democrats during the same period, Vernon Lidtke, *The Alternative Culture: Socialist Labor in Imperial Germany*, Oxford: Oxford University Press, 1984.

60. Allen Guttmann, *From Ritual to Record: The Nature of Modern Sports*, New York: Columbia University Press, 1978, pp. 57–89. Aside from football, Protestant youth organizations such as the YMCA were vital in the introduction of new sports such as basketball in the 1890s, and in the diffusion of women's team sports (especially volleyball) between the wars. See Gérard Cholvy, 'Les organisations de jeunesse d'inspiration chrétienne ou juive', in G. Cholvy (ed.), *Mouvements de jeunesse*, Paris: Le Cerf, 1986, p. 21; Remy Fabre, 'Les Unions chrétiennes de jeunes gens de la rue de Trévise', in G. Cholvy (ed.), *Le patronage, Ghetto ou vivier?*, Paris: Nouvelle Cité, 1988, pp. 145–63.

61. The English literature on this subject is vast. From James Walvin who entitled one chapter of his book 'Britain's most durable export', references to the British influence have been numerous, sometimes perhaps overestimating their impact. James Walvin, *The People's Game: A History of British Football*, London: Allen Lane, 1975, pp. 92–112; Lincoln Allison, 'Association Football and the Urban Ethos', *Stanford Journal of International Studies*, 13, 1978, pp. 203–28; John Bale, 'The Adoption of Football in Europe: An Historical-Geographic Perspective', *Canadian Journal of Sport History*, 2, 11, 1980, pp. 56–66.

Club is symptomatic of the complex link existing between the British and the locals, as well as of the importance of 'other' nationals in the development of football. The club had been founded in 1893, under the patronage of the local British Consul, by a group of Englishmen and Scotsmen living in Italy. In its first rules the club only allowed membership to British citizens. This was a means of preserving the extra-territoriality of *fin de siècle* sporting circles on the continent as a sort of British reserve on foreign soil.[62] There was no possible mediation between the locals and the British footballers. Neither was there the opportunity nor the willingness to transmit the game. This was an inward-looking view of sport which lost part of its attraction by the exclusion of the crucial concept of competition.

With the arrival in 1897 of James Spensley, a doctor in charge of the British shipping crews, 'Genoa Cricket' (as it was still commonly called before World War One) decided to admit Italian, Swiss and Austrian members. The club took part in the first Italian championship a year later, winning a competition involving three other clubs. Spensley played a prominent role in the development of football in Genoa as player, director and referee, but this was not his only involvement in local public life. The marble erected in 1974 in the internal court of the house he occupied in Piazza Campetto presents him as: 'A great friend of Italy, a football pioneer and a major initiator of boy scouting'. An archetypal amateur, Spensley, who died in a Belgian hospital during World War One as a result of the injuries he suffered in the Dardanelles, was also greatly involved in philanthropic work. One obituary remembered that 'his widespread interests [were] in philosophical studies, Greek language, Egyptian papyrus, football, boxing and popular university. He even initiated an evening school in Genoa'.[63] Spensley introduced the club to the amateur spirit of football. Along with his fellow players, he would pay out of his own pocket for the one lira tickets he offered to personal guests.[64]

Football may indeed have been Britain's most durable export but it is rarely recognized that the early football clubs, even those founded by the British or with British names, were initially a mixture of different cultures.[65] In Genoa, Spensley

62. Similar examples can be found with baseball in Japan or football in India, see Donald Roden, 'Baseball and the Quest for National Dignity in Meiji Japan', *American Historical Review*, 85, 3, 1980, pp. 511–34; Tony Mason, 'Football on the Maidan: Cultural Imperialism in Calcutta', *International Journal of the History of Sport*, 7, 1, 1990, pp. 85–96.

63. Reproduction of an obituary of Spensley, 13 October 1914 in Gian Luigi Corti and Aldo Bet, *Tuttogenoa, partita per partita*, Genoa: Edizione lo Sprint, 1991, p. 45. See also, Giorgio Calcagno, 'Genoa un secolo di storia', *La stampa*, 17 January 1993, p. 19.

64. *Genoa Club*, November 1921 reproduced the financial balance of the match Genoa vs US Torino in 1898 with this reference.

65. Bill Murray, *The World's Game: A History of Soccer*, Urbana: University of Illinois Press, p. 22 regards this as a 'revisionist' approach but we would argue that this emphasis on the cosmopolitan nature of football on the continent is not incompatible with an approach which asserts the importance of the British pioneers.

was aware of football's association with modernity and quickly approached the members of local high society to join the club. Not all were Italians. The Pasteur brothers, children of a Swiss surgeon, had been born in Genoa, but studied at a business school in Bern. One of them, Edoardo, won five Italian football championship medals and was a 'genuine' sportsman rather than just a footballer. Not only was he a tennis champion and an accomplished rower, he had undertaken dangerous mountaineering expeditions in the Alps and regularly won regattas in his yacht *Azzio V.*[66] He played football with Genoa for twelve years, remaining in the game as a referee and a director until the 1950s.

Football was hardly a nationally-oriented sport in this initial phase of its international development. On the contrary, most clubs were inclined to display their links with foreigners by choosing alien names and, in many cases, foreign officials and directors. Fifteen of the twenty-five founders of the Torino FC in 1906 were Swiss citizens, and the first chairman Schönfeld, was clearly also Swiss.[67] In 1908, the founders of a new club in Milan were so proud of its cosmopolitan dimension that they could find no better name than Internazionale (better known now as Inter). Hermann Aebi, born in Milan of Swiss parents in 1892, played for Inter between 1909 and 1923. He represented Switzerland in unofficial matches before playing, as the first naturalized footballer, for Italy on two occasions in 1920.[68] His team partner Peterli played for the Swiss national side. A cover of the Italian sporting weekly *Lo sport illustrato* from January 1914 shows Peterli and Aebi having a cup of tea during the half-time break in a league match. They were Swiss, played in Italy and yet adopted English customs.[69] The Swiss fashion was at its height in Italy in 1910. Nine of the Inter players who won the league, as well as seven at Torino, five at Genoa, four at Milan and three at Juventus, were Swiss citizens.

A similar cosmopolitanism emerges from the names given to the various football clubs in the city of Barcelona around 1903. All the geographical dimensions were present, from the local *Barcelona* and *Barcelones*, the regionalist *Catalonia* and *Catalunya* and the more national *Español*, *Iberic* and *Iberia*. But identification was also international, with an *Irish Club*, an *Internacional*, a *Zurich*, a *Europa*, a *Torino* and a *Franco-Espanyol*.[70]

Many other football clubs on the continent were characterized by an international composition, with the Swiss ever-present. We mentioned in the introduction the case of Bari and the fictional Lyons side, but some clubs were even more

66. Biography of Edoardo Pasteur, *Il calcio, cronache illustrate della vità sportiva italiana*, 16 February 1924, p. 1.

67. Pierluigi Brunori, *Torino: Superga nella sua storia*, Florence: M'Litograph, 1981, p. 37.

68. Roberto Beccantini (ed.), *Dizionario del calcio*, Milan: Rizzoli, 1990, p. 3.

69. *Lo sport illustrato*, 15 January 1914.

70. Garcia Castell, *Història del futbol català*, pp. 28–30, 43.

extreme. In Naples, a pre-eminently cosmopolitan city around 1910, the two teams, Naples (pronounced with an English accent) and Internapoli, included an Egyptian fine arts student, two Swiss white-collar workers, a Belgian, a Maltese and three German clerks.[71] There were, in addition, three British middle-class professionals: James Potts, a local representative of the shipping company Cunard Line; Willy Minter, the deputy manager of the Gutteridge Department Stores; and Fred Pattison, an engineer at the Harbour's Ironworks. The clubs also included two Italian brothers, Michele and Paolo Scarfoglio, who had been educated in Switzerland. And, to consolidate the exotic image, two Norwegians signed in 1913.[72] The Swiss connection was evident almost everywhere. Swiss employees and technicians are said to have introduced football to Croatia and Corsica. Other Alpine people such as the brothers Emil and Hugo Arnstein, both Austrian citizens, founded the Black Star in Trieste in 1907 as an Austrian club.[73] Two years later, they were also involved in the creation of the Bologna Football Club. The team captain, Louis Rauch, was a Swiss dentist.[74] However, the most prolific club founder in continental Europe was undoubtedly Walter Bensemann. Son of a Jewish doctor in medicine, he had been educated at a Swiss private school and established his first club, Football Club Karlsruhe, at the age of sixteen.[75] He was instrumental in the foundation of other clubs in Karlsruhe, Strasbourg, Basle and various other German towns before moving to Britain as a schoolmaster in 1901, where he stayed until the First World War. Like Pozzo, after the war he became one of the key figures in European sports journalism and founded *Kicker*, the successful weekly football magazine.[76] Walter Aemissegger, like Gamper, was born in Winterthur – possibly the most common birthplace of club founders – and had the honour of bringing the first round ball to Venice in 1912.[77]

71. Ernest Lémenon, *Naples. Notes historiques et sociales*, Paris: Plon, 1911, p. 279 notes that a report of the French Consular Office stated that for each French clerk working in Naples harbour in 1908 there were four British and twelve Germans.

72. Roberto Ciuni, *Il pallone di Napoli*, Milan: Shakespeare and Company, 1985, pp. 16–21; Giorgio Nicolini, *La storia del Napoli*, Rome: Editrice Italiana, 1967, pp. 14–18; Elio Tramontana and Gianni Virnicchi, *Il Napoli dalle origini ad oggi*, Naples: Arte tipografica, 1970, p. 11.

73. Stefano Pivato, 'Il football un fenomeno di frontiera. Il caso del Friuli–Venezia–Giulia', *Italia contemporanea*, 183, 1991, pp. 257–72.

74. *Il resto del carlino*, 4 October 1909.

75. Eisenberg, *'English Sports' und deutsche Bürger*, p. 180; Guttmann, *Games and Empires*, p. 48; Heiner Gillmeister, 'Als die Kicker laufen lernten: Walter Bensemann und der Beginn der europäischen Fußball', *Frankfurter Allgemeine Zeitung*, 16 June 1996; J. Düblin, *75 Jahre Fußball-Club Basel, 1893–1968*, Basle: Ganzmann, 1968, p. 20.

76. Heiner Gillmeister, 'The First European Soccer Match: Walter Bensemann', *The Sports Historian*, 17, 2, 1997, pp. 1–13.

77. Gianni Brera, *Il calcio veneto*, Vicenza: Neri Pozza, 1997, p. 34.

The first footballers were enmeshed in a process which saw the expansion of major Swiss businesses into Southern Europe. The case of Barcelona was emblematic of this. All of the founders of the club were sporting amateurs who had migrated to Barcelona for other professional reasons. But playing football was a major part of their lives.[78] Gamper remembered:

> I played football in Barcelona with my friends Wild, Gaissert, Kunzle and Englers. In October 1899, we asked to be incorporated in the Tolosa Gymnasium squad. They refused to introduce us into their group because they did not intend to allow any foreigners as members. I began therefore the procedures to create a new club. This was done on 29 November 1899.[79]

The new club appeared at a moment of major social change for the city. Economically, Barcelona was emerging as the foremost city in the Iberian peninsula and the introduction of Swiss capital was instrumental to its industrial growth. Gamper, a qualified accountant himself, represented the interests of a French bank, the Crédit Lyonnais, and an international railway company, the Ferrocarril de Sarria.[80] Moreover, foreign technology and personnel were crucial to the city's automobile and electrical industries. Skilled technicians were brought in from Britain, Germany and Switzerland and carried with them new concepts of leisure and lifestyle, including football.[81]

The vitality of the Swiss club movement encouraged emigrants to form clubs abroad. In Marseilles, the Stade Helvétique, which won the French championship three times between 1909 and 1913, was formed at the same time as a Swiss business circle. The Swiss community in Marseilles represented wealth and modernity and they were instrumental in formalizing the conditions of in-migration. Potential migrants to Marseilles were advised to arrive with a good knowledge of English, typing and accountancy. Being able to play football was no doubt also an asset.

While this ideal of open membership clearly encouraged the establishment of many clubs, it also provoked exclusion. The most famous case is undoubtedly the

---

78. In fact, concluding a biographical piece on Gamper, *La Suisse sportive* wrote: 'He is an amateur from top to toe, in the very sense of the word, and a sportsman with his body and soul', *La Suisse sportive*, 25 June 1898.

79. Emilio Pérez de Rozas, 'Bar-ça, Bar-ça, Bar-ça! ou l'amour foot', *Autrement*, 'Barcelone 1888–1929', 1992, pp. 201–11.

80. See Josep Termes 'Barça y Història', in R. Besa (ed.), *Amb blau sofert i amb grana intens: Cent anys del Barça*, Barcelona: Proa, 1999, p. 32; Garcia Castell, *Història del futbol catalá*, pp. 53–61; Gabriel Colome, 'Il Barcelona e la società catalana', in Lanfranchi (ed.), *Il calcio e il suo pubblico*, pp. 60–5.

81. Eduardo Escarra, *Le développement industriel de la Catalogne*, Paris [1908], pp. 75–8.

creation of Español of Barcelona in 1900. The new club distinguished itself from FC Barcelona less through the social composition of its membership than in its opposition to the cosmopolitanism of its rival. Its founders were Spanish students and the first chairman studied engineering, later migrating to Belgium and France. A similar scenario had occurred in Paris a decade earlier. Stade Français had been established by former members of the Paris Racing Club who were exasperated by the domination of foreigners and the pervasiveness of 'English' conduct and behaviour.[82] In Marseilles, Olympique only allowed membership to French citizens; the Genoese clubs of Sampierdarenese and Andrea Doria likewise excluded all but Italians.[83] The status of foreigners remained for the first decade of the twentieth century one of the central issues of club life. Whether clubs chose to adopt a cosmopolitan practice or preferred to exclude on grounds of citizenship, they could not ignore the importance of migrants.

There is therefore little doubt that the first football players and club founders in continental Europe were migrants. Clearly they were not migrants in the sense of professionals travelling abroad to earn their money with a ball, but football was nonetheless part of their cultural baggage. Their migration traced the movement of capital. The first three countries in continental Europe to develop a football culture – Switzerland, Belgium and Denmark – were also the three with the highest GNPs. Thus an awareness of economic history may provide some explanation of the initial export of football outside the British Isles. These footballers followed the movement of capital from north to south rather than the mass flow of economic migrants from poor to rich areas of Europe. In this sense, the formation of the first clubs on the continent was an expression of *elite*, as opposed to *popular*, migratory patterns. Many of the bankers, qualified engineers and technicians retained links with home, were easily integrated, and so used football to display their status and impress the local elite.

Cosmopolitanism and the Rise of National Football

The development of these first cosmopolitan football clubs coincided with the beginnings of the national orientation of the sport, which began to place the role of foreign players, coaches and directors under challenge. The first two decades of the twentieth century marked the emancipation of non-British football, as national leagues, international fixtures and international federations were created in Europe and South America. Yet there was a fundamental tension in the existence of national leagues and national representative sides on one hand, and the preponderance of

---

82. Ronald Hubscher, Jean Durry and Bernard Jeu, *L'histoire en mouvement: le sport et la société en France (XIXe–XXe siècle)*, Paris: Armand Colin, 1992, pp. 145–8.

83. The two clubs merged in 1945 to form Sampdoria.

foreign nationals on the other. It was an issue with which administrators would struggle for the entire twentieth century.

What does 'national' football mean? Is it simply the game as played in a specific territory or does it have some more fundamental connection with national or racial characteristics, reflecting and reinforcing 'the soul of a population'? Indeed, was there a conscious attempt to adapt football to definitions of the nation and, if so, how was this achieved? Most studies of football's diffusion in Europe and South America have looked through the national lens and have regarded the national unit as the main crucible of the game's development. But as with broader political and cultural conceptions of nationalization, the process was uneven, occurring at different times in different places. Football did not become a 'game of nations'[84] as a result of one historical event, although we would argue that the impact of the First World War was crucial to this transformation and the next two decades saw its realization.

The creation of FIFA in 1904 is revealing of the problems which arise if we regard European football in its formative years as a national phenomenon. The international body which was established was not simply an amalgam of national federations. Indeed not all founder members could claim to be official representatives of their nations. Robert Guérin, the first President, was spokesman for one of three major organizations which at the time regarded themselves as the national federation of France. Spain, meanwhile, was not represented by a national body at all but by Madrid Football Club. The creation of FIFA as an *inter*national body actually sprang from national concerns: to be the single body at national level to have international recognition and the only one with a mandate to organize international fixtures and transfers. As we have noted, before World War One the national dimension of the game was not always at the forefront. This is why Stade Helvétique, a 'Swiss' team in name and composition, could win the French championship and why an annual Pyrenees Cup competition between teams from northern Spain and southern France predated similar national competitions in both countries. Early football networks were often transnational. The Lions of Flanders, a multinational selection of the best players based in northern France, played annual fixtures in Belgium but never against opponents from western or southern France. Similarly, from 1901 Milan took part each year in the Chiasso Cup in Switzerland but only played its first match against a Roman team in 1911. Even in Britain, Scottish, Irish and Welsh clubs continued to compete in the FA Cup after the creation of independent national associations. The competition was not exclusively English, as commentators often assumed, and there was no restriction in its rules which prevented non-English teams from entering. The Habsburg Empire was by

---

84. Vic Duke and Liz Crolley, *Football, Nationality and the State*, London: Longman, chapter 1.

virtue of its composition of different nationalities the closest in organization to Britain. Indeed, if the first 'international' match was between Scotland and England in 1871, and the first official 'international' match outside Britain pitted Austria against Hungary, in both cases we are talking about contests between nations which were part of the same state. As Hobsbawm has rightly stated, the early Austria-Hungary matches operated as a type of 'ritual defusion':

> They symbolized the unity of such states, as friendly rivalry among the nations reinforced the sense that all belonged together by the institutionalization of regular contests that provided the safety-valve for group tensions, which were to be harmlessly dissipated in symbolic pseudo-struggles.[85]

Some early studies attempted to apply a model to the development of national football worldwide. While the intent to clarify the path taken from an English to a world game has been useful, it has tended to over-simplify diverse and complex national chronologies. Lincoln Allison tried to trace the three major steps in the diffusion of the British game to foreign countries. In his model, football was initially exported by British engineers, tourists and seamen who played among themselves. The second phase saw the game's introduction to the local elites through inter-mediate institutions such as public schools and gentlemen's clubs. The final step was the introduction of the indigenous working class to the game.[86] While logical and initially persuasive, Allison's model is deeply flawed. First, as we have noted, it assumes a consciousness on the part of the British to disseminate football which is far from evident in many cases. Unlike men such as Spensley, who was a philanthropist and a missionary of various cultural activities, including football, most British 'exporters' had no intention of sharing their games with others.[87] We would also question the myth that British shipping crews were instrumental in sowing the seeds of football's international growth. It is difficult to imagine that these working-class seamen would have had much contact with, or could have become models for, well-educated middle-class elites in the harbours of Europe and South America. Furthermore, like many more general theories of the diffusion of sport, Allison's model takes little account of the potential for adaptation, modification and resistance towards the game and its spirit. At around the same

85. Eric Hobsbawm, *Nations and Nationalism Since 1780: Programme, Myth, Reality*, 2nd edn, Cambridge: Cambridge University Press, p. 142.

86. Allison, 'Association Football and the Urban Ethos', pp. 203–28.

87. It only tended to be administrators like Frederick Wall of the FA who regarded British footballers on tour as 'missionaries of sport' responsible for 'spreading the gospel of football to foreign parts'. Quoted in P.J. Beck, *Scoring for Britain*, London: Frank Cass, pp. 29, 53. Such interpretations of the British role were less evident amongst those who were actually involved in the founding of the first clubs and associations.

time, John Bale proposed another model which attempted to date the creation of a national association as the key moment of national football autonomy.[88] Interesting though it is, however, this theory is also contradicted by the evidence. It would be a mistake to regard the creation of national federations or associations as the necessary starting-point for the development of national football or to believe that the English chronology was replicated elsewhere. For instance, an autonomous football federation did not appear in France until 1919 and in Spain until the following year. Does this mean that playing football was a 'foreign' activity before these dates?

There are at least six moments, we would suggest, which are usually regarded as fundamental to the nationalization of football: the creation of a national federation or association; the foundation of a league championship; the *separate* establishment of a *professional* league championship; the creation of a national cup competition; the first competitive match of the national team; and finally, the translation of the 'foreign' term 'football' into the national language. We can see from Table 1.1 that the British chronology is not directly transferable and that there was little commonality in the path toward a fully national game. In Austria, France and Italy a league championship, rather than a national federation, was the initial step in the late 1890s but after this the chronology varied significantly. A national federation and international fixtures closely followed the creation of the Austrian league in 1896. France had its first international fixture in 1904 but a cup was not established until 1918 and a national federation a year later. The Italian national federation, in contrast, emerged just a month after the first league championship but the first official international fixture, against France, had to wait another decade, and a national cup – much less important than in the rest of the continent, especially England – did not emerge until 1922.

Table 1.1 Key Moments in the National Development of Football in England, Austria, France and Italy

	England	Austria	France	Italy
National Federation	1863	1897	1919	1899
Cup Competition	1871	1919	1918	1922 **
First International Fixture	1872	1898*	1904	1910
League Championship	1888	1896	1894	1899
Professional League	1888	1924	1932	1929
Translation of term 'football' into national language	n/a	1900–5	Never	1908

* Unofficial fixture

** Interrupted for a number of years

88. Bale, 'Adoption of Football in Europe', pp. 56–66.

The nationalization of European football was intimately tied to the First World War and its consequences. The 'Versailles mentality' was as evident in football as elsewhere, leading to the creation of football alliances which reproduced political allegiances, and became crucial in the construction of regional and national styles in the inter-war period. European football was divided between the victors and the vanquished. The central powers were excluded from the 1920 Olympics in Antwerp and forced to play either among themselves or against countries such as Sweden and Switzerland which had remained neutral during the war. This 'mentality' forced sporting federations to chose sides so that, for example, when the German-speaking Swiss representatives were in favour of organizing a game against Germany in 1919, the French-speaking Swiss were strongly opposed. The shackles of the wartime alliances, and the withdrawal of the British from serious international competition alongside their withdrawal from FIFA, left little scope for confrontations designed to establish a national ranking on the continent. While almost all countries adopted the British model of league championships, the application of the same model at an international level was to take the form of a revolt against the all-powerful British, expressed in the desire for autonomy and the affirmation of indigenous qualities as much as for a different concept of the game and style of play. Quotas and regulations regarding foreign players were introduced in a number of countries before the First World War and one of the consequences of the Versailles mentality in football was the complete exclusion of citizens from the Central powers in western Europe.

Football, then, was initially a game of migrants. It was only when it had become popular that restrictions were introduced limiting access to foreigners. It is important to note how early the question of quotas or full restrictions of non-nationals became central. The game's success was accompanied by the formation of national teams, which marked the end of the first cosmopolitan era. The heritage of football's early cosmopolitanism can be easily seen in the names of clubs or the colour of shirts, such as the black and white of Juventus which was borrowed from Notts County. But national football cultures were already prominent before the First World War. In this process of internationalization, the most marginalized and isolated nation of all was Britain. It is to British emigration and immigration policy, and the treatment of 'foreign' players in the home of football, which we now turn.

—2—

Britain's Splendid Isolation?

From the beginning, the relationship between British football and the wider world has been somewhat paradoxical. Britain has been perceived in popular accounts as the pioneer and the forerunner: the nation which gave the game of football to the world. There can indeed be little dispute about the primary role allocated to British individuals and organizations in the codification, bureaucratization and eventual professionalization of the 'modern' game of association football during the second half of the nineteenth century. Yet, as we have seen, the role of Britain in the subsequent international diffusion of football is less clear-cut. Despite the undoubtedly crucial role played by 'some Englishmen and Scotsmen abroad',[1] British football in the first half of the twentieth century was characterized less by a sense of its overseas 'mission' than an almost arrogant self-obsession and introversion. For many of those involved with the game in its birthplace, football outside Britain was not really considered to be *real* football at all but simply a distorted 'foreign' version of the British game.

The connections between British and overseas football could be both formal and informal. At the formal level, Britain played a marginal role in the development of the world game. The governing bodies, who considered themselves to be 'the final authority of the game',[2] nevertheless kept their distance from the first international body, FIFA, when it was established by representatives from France, Belgium, the Netherlands, Sweden, Denmark, Switzerland and Madrid (representing Spain) in 1904. Following the lead of the English FA, the British associations decided to join shortly afterwards but the relationship was never stable: the inter-war years witnessed 'a saga of separation and reconciliation' until the British associations finally re-entered FIFA for good in 1946.[3] In his history of British football, James Walvin called this the era of 'the insular game'; Bill Murray has similarly suggested that in Britain 'much of the progress on the continent was

---

1. Tony Mason, 'Some Englishmen and Scotsmen Abroad: The Spread of World Football', in Alan Tomlinson and Garry Whannell (eds), *Off the Ball: The Football World Cup*, London: Pluto, 1986.

2. For the dispute in the mid-1920s between the British associations and FIFA over their respective authority, see P.J. Beck, *Scoring for Britain*, London: Frank Cass, pp. 108–13.

3. Vic Duke and Liz Crolley, *Football, Nationality and the State*, London: Longman, p. 13.

passing unnoticed'.[4] The first World Cup Final in July 1930, for instance, heavily reported throughout Europe and South America, merited only a few lines in the English sporting weekly *Athletic News*.[5] This, however, tells only part of the story. On a less formal level British clubs, coaches and players were instrumental in the development of the administrative and playing side of football in continental Europe, the Americas and even parts of the Empire. While British clubs remained outside the network of club and international fixtures which were rapidly emerging, especially in Central Europe, the significance of touring sides from the 'home' of football and the consequent establishment of a host of long-term institutional and individual connections has been neglected in the existing literature.

At the heart of this complicated picture of formal isolation and informal contact lies the whole issue of labour migration. We will consider this phenomenon first of all *within* the nations of the United Kingdom, before looking at the relationship between Britain and the outside world. In Britain as elsewhere, players moved from club to club and from country to country even before professionalization, a situation which often caused considerable antagonism among employers. Indeed, alongside the standardization of rules and the creation of a competitive structure, perhaps the main impetus for institutional contacts between different national associations was the need to control and regulate the movement of labour. However, this was a slow and uneven process – and it was a process which became inextricably linked to broader patterns of immigration, emigration and national consciousness. Thus an interpretation which considers only Britain's 'splendid isolation' from continental and world football in institutional terms is inadequate in understanding the dynamics of the movement of football labour into and out of Britain. The restrictive barriers erected by both governmental and footballing authorities were never completely successful in insulating Britain from the world outside.

Labour Migration within Britain

Historians of sport are probably more sensitive than most to the distinction between the state of the United Kingdom and the separate nations of England, Scotland, Ireland and Wales. Alexander Grant and Keith Stringer have recently used sporting examples to outline the 'complexities and anomalies' of this relationship in their collection of essays on British history, concluding that in sport 'the concept of the

---

4. James Walvin, *The People's Game: A History of Football Revisited*, Edinburgh: Mainstream, 1994, chapter 6; Bill Murray, *Football: A History of the World Game*, Aldershot: Scholar Press, 1994, p. 93.

5. *Athletic News*, 4 August 1930.

UK is a veritable enigma'.[6] In recent years, historians have become increasingly cautious in their approach to the study of these islands. The growth of separate national historical perspectives has flourished alongside a broader conception of a 'new British history' as 'something substantively different from "English history" writ larger'.[7] There is an increasing recognition that if British history is to have any real meaning then it should incorporate both the different histories and identities of England, Scotland, Ireland and Wales and their integration within a broader British perspective: it should, in other words, be conscious both of divergence and convergence. For some historians this has meant taking an explicit 'four nations' approach, while for others the notion of 'Britain' can still act as an adequate conceptual and organizational device.[8]

Associations and competitions modelled on the English examples were soon founded in Scotland, Ireland and Wales and, with the partial exception of the latter, football in the British Isles had become firmly established on national lines by the 1890s. This structural anomaly of four separate associations and three individual (and nominally national) leagues within a single political state has naturally led most students of the game to adopt a type of 'four nations' approach and to reject as misleading the very concept of *British* football.[9] At no point, however, was the market for football talent constrained on national lines. Indeed the pattern of football migration within Britain closely followed broader trends, becoming characterized by a steady flow of talent from the poorer, peripheral nations to the richer English 'centre'. Scottish, Irish and Welsh professional footballers were no different from other workers in gravitating towards the better employment and financial opportunities available in England.

The Scottish presence in England was particularly pronounced. Whether explained by romantic notions of Scots as 'wanderers' or by a 'culture of mobility' established over many centuries, it is clear that levels of Scottish emigration in the

6. Alexander Grant and Keith Stringer, 'Introduction: The Enigma of British History', in A. Grant and K. Stringer (eds) *Uniting the Kingdom?: The Making of British History*, London: Routledge, 1995, p. 3.

7. David Cannadine, 'British History as a 'new subject': Politics, Perspectives and Prospects', in Grant and Stringer (eds) *Uniting the Kingdom?*, p. 22.

8. For the pioneering example of a 'four nations' approach, see Hugh Kearney, *The British Isles: A History of Four Nations*, Cambridge: Cambridge University Press, 1989. On an alternative approach which emphasizes the perspective of 'British' history, see Linda Colley, *Britons: Forging the Nation 1707–1837*, London: Cambridge University Press, 1992. For reflections on this see Cannadine, 'British History'; Raphael Samuel, 'British Dimensions: "Four Nations History"', *History Workshop Journal*, 40, 1995, pp. ii–xxii.

9. H.F. Moorhouse, 'One State, Several Countries: Soccer and Identities in a "United" Kingdom', in J.A. Mangan (ed.) *Tribal Identities: Nationalism, Europe, Sport*, London: Frank Cass, 1996, pp. 55–74.

nineteenth and early twentieth centuries were comparatively high. Approximately half of those who left Scotland in this period moved south of the border and, unlike in most of Europe, outward migration did not significantly decrease after 1918.[10] The impetus for this emigration is more complex than conventional economic explanations suggest. Scotland was of course 'poorer' than England in many respects and economic historians have agreed that its industrial growth was partly based on a 'low wage' economy. On the other hand, Scottish and English earnings seem to have converged in the late nineteenth and early twentieth centuries and by the First World War the central belt of Scotland was recognized as one of the four highest wage regions in Britain.[11] In fact, the most striking feature of Scottish emigrants to England, as elsewhere, has been their high level of skill and status. Industrialists, bankers, scientists and engineers were only the most recent examples of a Scottish 'brain drain' dating from medieval times. For this and other reasons, Scottish emigration has appeared to be exceptional: Scots seem to have moved for different reasons than those of other nationalities.[12] Sir Charles Dilke summed this up most famously when he suggested that whereas the Irish were forced to move, the Scottish chose to: 'The Scotch emigrant . . . leaves . . . because he wishes to rise faster and higher than he can at home'.[13]

The movement of footballers reflected this situation. English clubs recruited Scottish players even before the legalization of professionalism in 1885. The first and best known of the 'veiled professionals' of the late 1870s and early 1880s, such as James Lang and Peter Andrews in Sheffield, Fergie Suter of Turton in Lancashire and Nick Ross of Preston North End, were Scots.[14] The talent and reputation of these players was such that some English teams were staffed almost entirely from north of the border: Burnley fielded a 'Scottish XI' in the mid-1880s and when the newly formed Liverpool club needed players urgently after its split

10. T.M. Devine, 'Introduction: The Paradox of Scottish Emigration', in T.M. Devine (ed.) *Scottish Emigration and Scottish Society*, Edinburgh: John Donald, 1992, pp. 5, 11–13.

11. Keith Robbins, *Nineteenth-Century Britain: Integration and Diversity*, Oxford: Clarendon, 1988, p. 124; John Foster, 'A Proletarian Nation?: Occupation and Class since 1914', in T. Dickson and J.H. Treble (eds) *People and Society in Scotland: Volume 3, 1914–1990*, Edinburgh: John Donald, 1992, p. 210.

12. Devine, 'Paradox of Scottish Emigration'.

13. Quoted in Christopher Harvie, *Scotland and Nationalism: Scottish Society and Politics, 1707–1994*, 2nd edn, London: Routledge, 1994, p. 57.

14. J.A.H. Catton, *The Real Football: A Sketch of the Development of the Association Game*, London: Sands, 1900, p. 53; R.W. Lewis, 'The Development of Professional Football in Lancashire, 1870–1914', Unpublished PhD Thesis, Lancaster University, 1993, pp. 130–31; C.E. Sutcliffe and F. Hargreaves, *History of the Lancashire Football Association, 1878–1928*, Blackburn: George Toulmin, 1928, p. 216.

with Everton in 1892, it relied exclusively on Scotsmen.[15] Aptly known as the 'Scotch professors', these players arrived in England as highly-skilled workers who were unable to make an 'open' living from the game in their native land, where professionalism was not legalized until 1893. The majority seem to have been recruited via newspaper advertisements or more directly through football agents, club officials and, increasingly, part-time scouts. A considerable number returned north after 1893, but proportionately more continued to be attracted by the greater financial opportunities in England. While Scottish clubs were not restricted by a maximum wage rule, only Rangers, Celtic and Hearts before 1914, together with Aberdeen in the inter-war years, could afford to pay wages which matched those of the top two divisions in the English Football League.[16]

Immediately after professionalism was legalized in England, the Scottish FA reported fifty-eight registered professionals south of the border.[17] In 1910 Scots accounted for 168 (19.3 per cent) of the 870 players in the Football League and forty-five (11.7 per cent) of the 385 in the Southern League. By 1925 this figure had risen to 302 in the four divisions of the amalgamated Football League, though it represented only 15.5 per cent of the total. In view of this, the suggestion of a peak of 362 Scots in the League in 1929 seems fairly plausible. In comparison, there were only nineteen Welsh and ten Irish players in English football in 1910, although by 1925 this had increased to ninety (4.6 per cent) and thirty-eight (2 per cent) respectively.[18] The Scottish presence especially was felt as much in qualitative as in quantitative terms. The overwhelming majority of Scots played their football in the top divisions and by the 1920s English clubs were prepared to pay large transfer fees to acquire the best Scottish talent. One commentator noted towards the end of 1926 that at least seventy 'front rank players' (presumably meaning those with international or representative experience) and many more with emerging reputations had journeyed south since the First World War. Two years later the Scottish team selected to meet England at Wembley was dominated

15. Sutcliffe and Hargreaves, *Lancashire Football Association*, p. 193; Percy M. Young, *Football on Merseyside*, London: Stanley Paul, 1964, p. 44.

16. Wray Vamplew, *Pay Up and Play the Game: Professional Sport in Britain, 1875–1914*, Cambridge: Cambridge University Press, 1988, pp. 213, 224; Bob Crampsey, *The Scottish Football League: The First 100 Years*, Glasgow: Scottish Football League, 1988, p. 101.

17. Graham Williams, *The Code War: English Football Under the Historical Spotlight*, Harefield: Yore, 1994, p. 93.

18. Figures adapted from Vamplew, *Pay Up*, p. 205 (Table 13.5); Matthew Taylor, '"Proud Preston": A History of the Football League, 1900–1939', Unpublished PhD Thesis, De Montfort University, 1997, p. 289 (Table 8.2); Bob Crampsey, *The Scottish Footballer*, Edinburgh: William Blackwood, 1978, p. 32. It must be noted, however, that many of the ninety Welsh players in 1925 actually competed with *Welsh* clubs, a number of whom had been brought into the league after the First World War.

for the first time by Anglo-Scots, with only three 'home' players chosen.[19] Reciprocity was extremely rare and only served to highlight the general trend. The transfer of West Ham United's English forward Sid Puddefoot to Falkirk for a record fee of £5,000 in 1922 generated considerable interest but failed to mark any reversal in the traffic. Indeed Puddefoot returned to Blackburn Rovers three years later, apparently disillusioned with Scotland and feeling marginalized both on and off the pitch.[20]

The settlement of footballers tended to trace more general patterns. Scottish players, for instance, were not found in equal numbers in every part of England. They were concentrated in two main areas: the north-west, particularly Lancashire, and the north-east. Lancashire clubs employed all but one of the fifty-eight Scottish professionals in England in 1885 and the rapid development of the professional game from the late 1880s on Tyneside and Teeside encouraged Scottish footballers to trek the shorter distance over the border which miners and agricultural workers had been making for some fifty years.[21] Clubs like Preston North End, Newcastle United and Sunderland had already established a tradition for using Scotsmen by 1914, and regularly included as many as seven or eight in their inter-war sides. In London, the third main area of general settlement, Scots were surprisingly scarce: only Chelsea and Arsenal hired them on any regular basis.[22] Irish professionals also seem to have been drawn to cities or regions with high migrant populations. The Manchester and Liverpool clubs were noted for their tendencies to buy Irish players and London clubs also attracted a fair number. But it was Glasgow, the other major 'Irish' city in Britain, which not surprisingly became the main magnet for migrant footballers, due to Celtic's origins in, and connections with, the Irish Catholic community of the city.[23] The movement of Welsh players is more difficult to identify. Unlike the other peripheral nations, Wales was unable to establish a senior professional league and thus both its best players and its best clubs competed

19. H.F. Moorhouse, 'Blue Bonnets over the Border: Scotland and the Migration of Footballers', in J. Bale and J. Maguire (eds) *The Global Sports Arena: Athletic Talent Migration in an Interdependent World*, London: Frank Cass, 1994; p. 81; Paul Joannou, *Wembley Wizards: The Story of a Legend*, Edinburgh: Mainstream, 1990, pp. 20–3.

20. Charles Korr, *West Ham United: The Making of a Football Club*, London: Duckworth, 1986, pp. 58–61.

21. Williams, *Code War*, p. 93; R.A. Cage, 'The Scots in England' in R.A. Cage (ed.) *The Scots Abroad: Labour, Capital, Enterprise, 1750–1914*, London: Croom Helm, 1985, p. 33.

22. Crampsey, *Scottish Footballer*, p. 33; Richard Holt, *Sport and the British*, Oxford: Clarendon, p. 256. We have to disagree with Crampsey's suggestion that 'Arsenal were not noted for their fondness for Scotsmen'.

23. Tom Campbell and Pat Woods, *The Glory and the Dream: The History of Celtic FC, 1887–1987*, London: Grafton, 1987; Bill Murray, *The Old Firm: Sectarianism, Sport and Society in Scotland*, Edinburgh: John Donald, 1984.

in England. There was a definite pull of players from North Wales, where the game was more popular in its early days, to the clubs of Merseyside, Cheshire and Lancashire. Billy Meredith, born in the village of Chirk, was the most famous of Welsh internationals who spent his entire career in the north-west of England, but he was not the only one. During the depression years, however, footballers in South Wales, at least, tended to follow the general path of mass migration to the midlands or the south-east, in contrast to the northern route to professionalism favoured by rugby players.[24]

It is crucial, then, to recognize the British dimension of labour recruitment in England's dominant professional competitions from the late nineteenth century. Many Football League teams contained a mix of British nationalities; some could even be termed multinational. The Arsenal side which began the 1925/26 campaign, for instance, included seven Scots, two Irishmen and one Welshman from a total of twenty-seven whose birthplace it has been possible to trace. At the beginning of the 1933/34 season Liverpool went further by fielding a team including just two Englishmen.[25] There were of course exceptions. West Bromwich Albion and Wolverhampton Wanderers avoided non-English players, rarely having more than one or two on their books; Sheffield United's 1925 FA Cup winning side, too, was entirely English with the exception of its Irish captain William Gillespie.[26] But in general the labour force of English football clubs was genuinely *British*.

The free movement of football talent within Britain was dependent upon the establishment of administrative agreements and common regulations. The relationship between English and Scottish clubs was the most immediate concern. During the 1890s the constant movement of players across the border in both directions created considerable difficulties, especially when players were registered by clubs in both countries. These problems were partially resolved in 1897 when the English and Scottish Leagues agreed to 'the mutual recognition of players' registrations and clubs' rights in players'.[27] At the same time the International Football League

24. Robbins, *Nineteenth-Century Britain*, p. 165; John Harding, *Football Wizard: The Story of Billy Meredith*, Derby: Breedon, 1985; Martin Johnes, 'That Other Game: A Social History of Soccer in South Wales, c. 1906–1939', Unpublished PhD Thesis, University of Wales, 1998; David Smith and Gareth Williams, *Fields of Praise: The Official History of the Welsh Rugby Union*, Cardiff: University of Wales Press, 1980.

25. *Athletic News*, 24 August 1925; Young, *Football on Merseyside*, p. 131.

26. Percy M. Young, *Football in Sheffield*, London: Sportman's Book Club, 1964, p. 127; Sheffield United FC, Minutes of Football Committee, 29 April 1925. West Bromwich Albion developed a conscious policy not to sign Scottish professionals from as early as the 1900s. A thirty-year period without Scots ended in 1937 when centre-forward G. Dudley was signed from Albion Rovers. Crampsey, *Scottish Footballer*, p. 33; Maurice Golesworthy, *The Encyclopaedia of Association Football*, London: Sportsman's Book Club, 1957, pp. 138–9.

27. C.E. Sutcliffe, F. Howarth and J.A. Brierley, *The Story of the Football League, 1888–1938*, Preston: The Football League: 1938, p. 134.

Board (popularly known as the Inter-League Board) was founded in order to settle disputes and co-ordinate joint policy. An Anglo-Irish Board was established in 1914, incorporating the same recognition of club registration and transfer rights.

In practice, these developments did little to prevent the illegal poaching of professionals in different countries. Clubs in each of the four nations were habitually fined for approaching or 'tapping' players registered elsewhere in Britain, although in truth the richer English members were the main aggressors. As in politics, it was the relationship between the English and Irish authorities which generated the most dispute. Before the 1914 agreement a significant number of players who found themselves disengaged or marginalized in England crossed the Irish sea: Belfast, in particular, became known as 'a city of refuge for discontented foot-ballers'.[28] The temporary outlawing of professionalism during the First World War increased hostilities as emigrant players returned to Irish clubs without the permission of their English employers. A number of Irish clubs were accused of inducing players to move overseas with the promise of accommodation, employment or direct payment. In August 1916 the Irish FA suspended Belfast United when an English Football League player, Grimsby Town's Thomas McKenna, was revealed to have been operating as a professional under the name 'McGuiness'. In response the Football League banned its professionals indefinitely from playing in Ireland and the Irish FA, incensed by the 'hypocrisy' of the English, accused Manchester United of signing a registered Linfield player and insisted in future on sanctioning the movement of all Irish players to England.[29] Although the English veto was soon rescinded, a further dispute in 1920 over the signing by Crystal Palace of a player from the Belfast-based Distillery club led to a short breach in relations between the two leagues.[30]

The situation was further complicated by political partition in 1922 and the creation of an Irish Free State in the south of the island. The question of the recognition of two separate football associations in Ireland developed into a major and largely unresolved problem for the FA and FIFA throughout the inter-war period and beyond. Partition meant that those clubs incorporated under the aegis of the Football Association of Ireland (FAI) and the League of Ireland were no longer covered by the various league agreements.[31] Though this had limited immediate impact, it was widely recognized in England that a potential 'open

---

28. *Athletic News*, 16 January 1916.

29. *Athletic News*, 6 March, 14 August, 11 September 1916.

30. FA Archives, Minutes of Football League, 6 December 1920.

31. See Moorhouse, 'One State, Several Countries', pp. 58–64; John Sugden and Alan Bairner, *Sport, Sectarianism and Society in a Divided Ireland*, Leicester: Leicester University Press, 1993; Mike Cronin, *Sport and Nationalism in Ireland: Gaelic Games, Soccer and Irish Identity Since 1884*, Dublin: Four Courts Press, 1999.

door' had been created for discontented professionals otherwise constrained by the mutual league agreements. Neither was the longer-established migration of footballers in the other direction restricted because Free State citizens retained their status and rights as British citizens. While the majority of the traffic continued to flow west to east, the depression of the early 1930s led to a brief period of return migration which was reflected in football.[32] Free State clubs began to sign a number of top players from across the sea and by 1931 *Athletic News* could proclaim the Irish 'open door' as 'a menace, particularly to English clubs who have paid big sums of money for the transfer of players, and then find they have little control over them at the end of the season'.[33] Proposals to deter players from moving to southern Ireland proved untenable but the English authorities, at least, remained hostile to League of Ireland clubs, refusing to recognize player registrations or even organize representative fixtures until after the Second World War. Although Scotland recognized the southern authorities slightly earlier, in 1939, the Irish Free State was nonetheless left outside the formal 'British' system of player registration for most of the inter-war period.[34]

Institutional Isolation

There is little disagreement that the largely self-imposed international exclusion of the British associations in this period was motivated, at least in part, by an arrogant sense of superiority.[35] What is less often noted, explicitly at least, is that this was combined with an historically powerful distrust of outsiders. Historians such as Linda Colley have emphasized the importance of 'the Other' in defining and sustaining a common British identity, an identity which was strengthened by the fundamental insularity of an island people.[36] Institutional isolation in football was hardly surprising for a nation which not only 'defined itself over and against "Europe" as something different, something exceptional, something better'[37] but

32. David Fitzpatrick, *The Two Irelands, 1912–1939*, Oxford: Oxford University Press, 1998, pp. 215–16; Colin Holmes, *John Bull's Island: Immigration and British Society, 1871–1971*, London: Macmillan, 1988, p. 122.

33. *Athletic News*, 8 June 1931.

34. Sutcliffe *et al.*, *Football League*, p. 142; Crampsey, *Scottish Football League*, p. 251; FA Archives, Minutes of Football League, 15 December 1946.

35. For the most recent articulation of this view see, Peter J. Beck, 'Projecting an Image of a Great Nation on the World Screen through Football: British Cultural Propaganda between the Wars', in B. Taithe and T. Thornton (eds), *Propaganda, Political Rhetoric and Identity, 1300–2000*, Stroud: Sutton, 1999, pp. 265–84.

36. Linda Colley, 'Britishness and Otherness: An Argument', *Journal of British Studies*, 31, January 1992, pp. 309–29.

37. Cannadine, 'British History', p. 19.

also maintained 'a general suspicion of continental alliances and alignments and a desire to be detached from them'.[38]

The issues on which the 'home' associations parted company with FIFA in 1920 and 1928 – contacts with the defeated nations in the First World War, the question of 'broken time' payments and the definition of amateurism – masked a more fundamental perceived threat to British autonomy. Specifically, the British associations feared that their individual votes at FIFA meetings would be amalgamated and that their veto over changes in the laws of the game through the International Board would be halted. The likely loss of power along with external interference was unpalatable for the self-styled 'Motherland of football' whose representatives were not prepared 'to risk any tampering with the laws of the game from overseas pupils'.[39] The 1928 letter of withdrawal from FIFA neatly summed up the British attitude. While hoping to maintain 'friendly relations' with FIFA, the associations indicated their wish 'to conduct their affairs in the way their long experience has shown desirable', and informed the FIFA secretary that the 'comparatively recent formation' of most of the affiliated FIFA members rendered them ill-equipped to deal with the knotty issue of defining amateurism. Without the British, it was assumed that FIFA 'cannot have the knowledge which only experience can bring'.[40] Writing a month before the withdrawal, Football League official and FA Councillor Charles Sutcliffe was less diplomatic:

> I don't care a brass farthing about the improvement of the game in France, Belgium, Austria or Germany. The FIFA does not appeal to me. An organisation where such football associations as those of Uruguay and Paraguay, Brazil and Egypt, Bohemia and Pan Russia, are co-equal with England, Scotland, Wales and Ireland seems to me to be a case of magnifying the midgets. If central Europe or any other district want to govern football let them confine their powers and authority to themselves, and we can look after our own affairs.[41]

Despite sentiments of this kind, formal isolation did not mean complete severance with the outside world. In some respects it is misleading to place too much emphasis on Britain's exclusion from FIFA and the absence of her teams from the three World Cup competitions of the 1930s. National teams and club sides continued to play exhibition matches and undertake tours of continental Europe, North and

38. Keith Robbins, 'An Imperial and Multinational Policy: "The scene from the centre", 1832–1922', in A. Grant and K. Stringer (eds) *Uniting the Kingdom?*, London: Routledge, 1995, p. 248.

39. *Athletic News*, 22 February 1928.

40. FA Archives, Minutes of FA Council, Report of the Conference of the Associations of the United Kingdom, 17 February 1928.

41. *Topical Times*, 14 January 1928.

South America and parts of the Empire.[42] By the 1920s the close season continental tour had become a fundamental part of the fixture list of many leading English and Scottish clubs. West Ham United, for instance, were regular tourists, travelling to the Basque region of Spain in 1921, Austria and Czechoslovakia in 1923, Germany, Switzerland and France in 1924, the Netherlands in 1925 and Spain again a year later. Visits were sometimes reciprocated as matches with foreign teams on British grounds became more common in the 1930s. The best known series of regular matches was undoubtedly Arsenal's annual Armistice day fixture against Racing Club de Paris which began in the mid-1920s and lasted through to the 1960s.[43] While close and long-standing relationships of this kind were hardly the norm, they do indicate that beneath the surface of formal isolation there was some degree of contact with the outside world and that Britain was not so isolated as she first appeared.

The Closed Door: Football Immigrants before the 1960s

If the British did occasionally glimpse outside, they nevertheless rarely let anyone in. The labour market in British football remained closed to outsiders for much of this period, a result of collusion between the national associations and leagues, the Football Players' Union and the Ministry of Labour. Non-British footballers rarely featured in professional sides. Max Seeburg, a German forward, had a lengthy spell playing for Tottenham, Chelsea, Burnley, Grimsby and Reading between 1907 and 1914. Nils Middleboe, captain of the Danish national side, signed as an amateur for Chelsea in 1913 and stayed nine years, enjoying considerable success as captain of his side and also in his other sport of lawn tennis. Another member of the side which finished runners-up to the hosts at the 1908 London Olympics, Carl Hansen joined Glasgow Rangers for three seasons in the early 1920s.[44]

Colonial-born players, unrestricted by immigration controls, were more common. Subjects of the British Empire and Commonwealth had enjoyed a tradition of free entry into Britain from the nineteenth century and this was reinforced by the British Nationality Acts of 1914 and 1948.[45] Players from the

42. Bill Murray, *The World's Game: A History of Football*, Urbana: University of Illinois Press, 1998, p. 80.

43. George Allison, *Allison Calling*, London: Staples, 1948, p. 142; Gusti Jordan, *Football européen*, Paris: Triolet, 1947, p. 88.

44. Willy Meisl, *Soccer Revolution*, London: Panther, 1957, pp. 76, 78; Golesworthy, *Encyclopaedia of Association Football*, p. 65.

45. On the history of British immigration law, Ann Dummett and Andrew Nichol, *Subjects, Citizens, Aliens and Others: Nationality and Immigration Law*, London: Weidenfeld & Nicolson, 1990.

White Dominions were scattered across British team sheets for much of the period, although imports from the Black colonies, especially Africa, were almost unknown (see Chapter 6). In general terms, however, even recruits from the Empire and Commonwealth were rare. Certainly there was nothing approaching the 'scramble for overseas talent' which took place in cricket's Lancashire League between the wars, even taking into account the fact that football did not have the same 'imperial connection'.[46] There were as few as five players born outside Britain in England's two divisions in 1911 and just eight in four divisions by 1925.[47] Forty years later, the FA Yearbook recorded no more than fifteen players of 'foreign' origin in the top two English divisions, noting that 'the great majority [come] from South Africa'.[48]

The paucity of non-British labour clearly reflected wider prejudices towards foreigners and overseas football but it was also the result of restrictive measures passed at central government level. Before 1905 there was almost no legislative control over immigration into Britain but over the subsequent fifteen years a series of parliamentary acts placed considerable restriction on entry. The 1919 Aliens Act and the subsequent Orders in Council of 1920 and 1925, in particular, provided strict guidelines for the employment of aliens and left entry in the hands of immigration officials.[49] In this context, any attempt to import players from abroad faced significant obstacles and, in the event, few clubs tried. One or two, however, did. The best example is Arsenal's attempt in 1930 to sign the Austrian goalkeeper Rudy Hiden. Negotiations between Arsenal's manager Herbert Chapman and Vienna AC had been successful; a fee was agreed for an initial two-month contract with the possibility of renewal, and the player had even been guaranteed a supplementary job in London as a chef. Yet on his arrival Hiden was denied entry by immigration officials.[50] Some years earlier, the Belgian centre-forward Raymond Braine faced similar obstructions when he signed for Clapton Orient and was forced to return to Belgium before his League registration could be completed.[51] Both players had been refused entry according to the established Ministry of Labour criteria that their presence would have restricted the employment opportunities of British workers.

---

46. Jeffrey Hill, 'Cricket and the Imperial Connection: Overseas Players in Lancashire in the Inter-war Years' in Bale and Maguire (eds) *Global Sports Arena*, p. 52.

47. See Taylor, 'Proud Preston', p. 289 (Table 8.1 and 8.2).

48. FA Yearbook, 1964/65.

49. Holmes, *John Bull's Island*, pp. 113–14.

50. F.W. Carter and W. Capel-Kirby, *The Mighty Kick: The History, Romance and Humour of Football*, London: Jarrolds, 1933, p. 121; Arsenal FC Archives, Minutes of Board of Directors, 10 July, 28 August 1930 (We are grateful to Neil Carter for this reference).

51. Carter and Capel-Kirby, *Mighty Kick*, p. 121. Braine eventually moved to Czechoslovakia to join Slavia Prague.

The Hiden and Braine incidents prompted the football authorities into taking action of their own. Not surprisingly, British players opposed the idea of foreign imports. The Players' Union informed the Ministry of 'its disapproval of allowing Alien Professional Footballers into the country' and trusted that the Ministry would 'continue to follow its present principles'.[52] Even one of Hiden's prospective team-mates, Eddie Hapgood, later admitted that the government's action was perhaps a good thing: 'There's plenty enough good players in this country to go round without importing them from abroad'.[53] The FA similarly announced that it opposed 'granting permits for alien players to be brought into this country' and began to consider a number of measures aimed at restricting overseas professionals.[54] In October 1930 C. Wreford-Brown, a former amateur international and representative of Oxford University, proposed to the FA Council that a two-year residential qualification should be imposed on non-British players wishing to compete in the FA Cup. His primary object was to nip in the bud a possible wave of continental imports: 'with talent becoming so highly developed on the Continent no one knows what may happen in the future'.[55] But the FA actually went one step further in 1931 by extending Wreford-Brown's residential qualification to 'all clubs and all competitions', with the stated objective of preventing 'the importation of players into England from abroad'.[56] When combined with restrictive government legislation, then, the football authorities were able to erect an almost impenetrable barrier preventing any contact with continental playing talent during the 1930s.

The Second World War was instrumental in breaking down some of these barriers. Refugees from Nazi-occupied Europe, together with smaller numbers of civilian and military recruits from the West Indies, Newfoundland, British Honduras and the Indian subcontinent, contributed to making British society more cosmo-politan than it had been prior to 1939. The post-war repatriation of these groups was only partial: many remained in Britain, finding employment easily in this period of labour shortage, and were soon joined by other European and Common-wealth workers.[57] Here again football migration reflected broader migratory trends as the labour force became opened up to foreigners. Bert Trautmann is perhaps

52. PFA Archives, Minutes of Association Football Players' and Trainers' Union (hereafter AFPTU), 25 August 1930. At the time of the prospective Hiden transfer, the Ministry of Labour had contacted the Players' Union directly to ask their opinion on the question of 'alien footballers'.

53. Eddie Hapgood, *Football Ambassador*, London: Sporting Handbooks, 1944, p. 70.

54. FA Archives, Minutes of FA International Selection Committee, 25 August 1930.

55. Arsenal FC Archives, Catton Folders, B, Newspaper clipping on Wreford Brown's proposal to ban continental players, 9 October 1930, p. 174. Also see FA Archives, Minutes of FA Council, 13 October, 15 December 1930.

56. *Athletic News*, 8 June 1931; FA Archives, Minutes of FA Council (AGM), 1 June 1931.

57. Robert Miles, 'Nationality, Citizenship and Migration to Britain, 1945–1951', *Journal of Law and Society*, 16, 4, Winter 1989, pp. 426–42; Holmes, *John Bull's Island*, pp. 162–71, 210–28.

the best known of these 'displaced' footballers. A paratrooper in the Luftwaffe, Trautmann was captured near the Dutch border shortly after D-Day and transported to a prisoner-of-war camp at Ashton-in-Makerfield in June 1945. He began to play as a goalkeeper for the camp team in charity matches throughout Lancashire and so impressed the talent scouts that he joined St Helens on his release in 1948. A year later Manchester City signed him as the replacement for retiring England international Frank Swift.[58] While Trautmann's story is exceptional, other foreign footballers stationed with allied forces in Britain also began to appear for local clubs. The exiled Polish army provided a number of players, particularly in Scotland. Most played only a handful of games but some, like Alfie Lesz of St Mirren and Feliks Starocsik of Third Lanark and then Northampton Town, settled into professional careers after the war.[59]

One or two international footballers were also recruited directly as a result of British football's post-war boom, although the FA's residential qualification remained in place and meant that most could only sign as amateurs. Chelsea managed to attract Willi Steffan, a Swiss international full-back, and Orient signed the Polish national amateur goalkeeper Stanislaw Gerula, but neither lasted more than a season.[60] Albert Gudmundsson did not stay long either, making just two League appearances for Arsenal after moving from Glasgow, where he had studied marine biology and played for Rangers during the war. The Icelandic international moved to Milan in order to turn professional and went on to play for Nancy, Racing Club and Nice in France before returning home where he became a successful businessman, politician and President of the Icelandic FA.[61]

Alongside Trautmann, the most successful foreign player of the 1950s was probably Viggo Jensen. Like a number of the imports of this time, the Dane had impressed during the 1948 London Olympics. He signed for Hull City that year and enjoyed nine seasons with the club, first in a goalscoring role, netting in seven consecutive matches during 1949/50, then as a full-back.[62] Hans Jeppson made no less an impact during his brief spell with Charlton Athletic in 1951. Jeppson, who had been Sweden's centre-forward at the 1950 World Cup, came to London on a business course hoping to play for Arsenal during his stay. He was persuaded to help out Charlton instead and almost single-handedly saved the club from relegation, scoring nine times in eleven outings.[63] He then moved to Italy as a

58. Alan Rowlands, *Trautmann: The Biography*, Derby: Breedon Books, 1991, pp. 43–71.

59. Crampsey, *Scottish Football League*, p. 128.

60. On Steffen see *Sporting Chronicle and Athletic News*, 9 November 1946.

61. Fred Ollier, *Arsenal: A Complete Record, 1886–1992*, Derby: Breedon Books, 1992, p. 59.

62. *Daily Mail* (Hull), 25, 26 October 1948; Chris Elton, *Hull City: A Complete Record, 1904–1989*, Derby: Breedon Books, 1989, p. 84.

63. Jimmy Seed, *The Jimmy Seed Story*, London: Phoenix, 1957, pp. 93–7.

professional with Atalanta, later becoming the world's most expensive footballer when he was sold to Napoli for 105 million lire (just over £60,000). However, Jeppson's sojourn in south-east London was not appreciated by the football authorities. The Football League clearly felt that both club and player were abusing the system and refused Hull City's application in late 1952 to register another Danish international, Jens Peter Hansen, on amateur forms. The League stepped in to outlaw future temporary transfers involving what they considered to be 'foreign well-known players'.[64] Although a number of Scandinavians played in Scotland during the 1960s, the English door was thus effectively closed to alien football talent until the FA's qualification rule and the Football League's prohibition on foreigners were overturned in the mid-1970s.

British Players Abroad

America and France, 1921–39

British footballers were not natural travellers. Aside from the cultural and linguistic barriers to foreign settlement, most players could hardly have been inclined to leave the largest, most prestigious and, by their own accounts at least, best-quality competitions in the world. The exportation of British players in this period, then, was limited. Significantly, however, the authorities proved less able to control the outward than the inward flow of labour. Self-exclusion from FIFA for most of the inter-war years meant that the ownership rights of players did not extend beyond British shores. The first country to take advantage of this was the United States when its American Soccer League (ASL) was formed in 1921. The ASL will be considered at length in Chapter 5 but it is worth noting here that during the course of the 1920s dozens of professional players were recruited from the Scottish, English and Irish leagues to form the majority of personnel in this cosmopolitan, multinational competition. Emigration reached it peak in the mid- to late 1920s but then began to subside, foreshadowed by 'Dixie' Dean's refusal to leave Everton to join New York Giants for a reported wage of £25 per week. One English correspondent thus concluded that 'the American menace has been grossly exaggerated by the scare-mongers' and that Dean's rejection could 'be taken as a symbol of defeat for the plans of our friends on the other side of the Atlantic'.[65]

More significant than the emigration to the US of the 1920s was the emigration to France of the 1930s. This was not without precedent: British players had been involved in French 'amateur' football from its beginnings, often receiving payment in spite of strict amateur regulations. The most important figure in French football

---

64. FA Archives, Minutes of Football League, 14 December 1952.
65. *Topical Times*, 11 August 1928.

during the 1910s and 1920s was Victor Gibson. Following a tour of southern Europe as a player with the amateur club Plumstead, he signed for FC Sète in 1912 and stayed in France for the next twenty-five years. Officially employed by the club chairman in his shipyard, he nevertheless became known as the first 'professional' in French football before assuming managerial duties in 1914. Along with his team-mate Andrew Stevenson, who became responsible for British recruitment, Gibson not only helped establish a generation of talented local footballers but also signed some two dozen players from across the Channel in the years 1919 to 1926. Some of these, such as Arthur Parkes, Edward Skiller and Bill Barrett, enjoyed long and successful careers in France, with Skiller even settling in the country and assuming French citizenship.[66] In 1930 the former Rangers and Newcastle player William Aitken was recruited by Cannes from Juventus, where as an alien he had been prevented from playing for the club in official matches. With no such restrictions in France, Aitken led Cannes as player-manager to victory in the French Cup of 1932.[67]

Another interesting group of British shamateurs were drawn from the Belvedere area of Kent. Billy Cornelius was an amateur footballer who had played for, among others, Belvedere and District in the West Kent League in the early 1920s before moving to France in 1922 as one of Sète's British recruits.[68] Eventually he became player-manager of the club but was tempted to Alès, a small mining town in the Cévennes, by the industrialist owner of the local team, to become player-coach with the job of recruiting good-quality English players. He chose players he knew well and trusted, including Bob Smoker and Sid Skinner from the Erith and Belvedere club and Billy West, who had played for Bexleyheath and Welling.[69] Another former Erith player, Stan Hillier, joined nearby Cannes. None of these had established himself as a professional in Britain. Only Hillier had actually played first-team matches in the Football League, appearing thirty-six times for Bradford City in the second division and Gillingham in the third division south between 1924 and 1927; Skinner, meanwhile, only made the reserve team at Charlton Athletic.[70] No great fortunes were made in France: the money gained through football was supplemented by working in local industry. But migration did offer these players the opportunity of a better future in a place where they were more likely to be accepted and respected both professionally and socially. Many became popular local figures. In a letter home in September 1928, Cornelius described the local reaction to his newest import: 'Our football heads, as well as the crowd,

66. Y. Dupont, *Le Mecque de football ou les mémouries d'un dauphin*, Nîmes: Bène, 1973.
67. V. Caminiti, *Juventus 70*, Turin: Juventus FC, 1967, p. 163.
68. Letter from Brian Spurrell to authors, 18 August 1998.
69. *Les sports du Sud Est*, 4 July 1929.
70. Letter from Brian Spurrell to authors, 9 October 1997.

have taken to him like a duck to water, and the one topic in the town is Smoker'. Three months later Smoker was reportedly 'still doing well' on the pitch but was also 'a real favourite in our workshop and will soon be able to speak French like a froggy.'[71] Cornelius himself went one step further by becoming a naturalized Frenchman.[72] By the time shamateurism was abolished and a professional league established in 1932, Smoker and West had married local women and decided to sign professional forms with Alès. Cornelius and Skinner had moved to FC Grasse in the Côte d'Azur, continuing to work and play there, even though the club was denied membership of the new league. There was obviously no rush to return to Britain. Skinner opened a café in Grasse at the end of his career, returning to England only as a result of the German invasion in 1940.[73] Individuals of this kind hardly merit the description of *football* migrants. For most of the British shamateurs at Alès, Cannes and Sète, football served as much more than a temporary job. It was a means of integration into an alien culture and a route into a new and exciting way of life.

From its beginnings the professional league followed this tradition of importing foreign footballers. British players were regarded as particularly attractive acquisitions, partly because of their footballing abilities but mainly because no transfer fees were necessary due to Britain's absence from FIFA. In the spring of 1932 the spectre of French scouts signing up Football League professionals en masse dominated the sporting press on both sides of the Channel. French clubs at first appeared to be targeting elite players such as Chelsea's Scottish international pairing of Hughie Gallacher and Tommy Law, as well as Arsenal's David Jack, with offers of positions as player-coaches.[74] The League was clearly concerned, issuing a resolution in April intended to frighten off potential migrants and poachers. Henceforth players leaving the country without consent would be prohibited from re-registering with English clubs; continental clubs trying to sign players 'will be regarded as having committed an unfriendly act and all friendly relations will cease'. The Football League president, John McKenna, told reporters that professionals going to France 'would cease to have the right to play again in this country'.[75] 'Spotlight' agreed that if the players did decide to go overseas 'it is not *au revoir*, it's goodbye' but admitted to *Topical Times* readers that: 'I wouldn't go within 25 miles of French football as a professional player. Ask some of the continental teams about bad legs, violent spectators, rotten referees and one-man clubs!'[76]

71. *Kentish Times*, 14 September, 7 December 1928.
72. *Kentish Times*, 25 December 1929.
73. Letter from Sid Skinner's nephew to authors, 17 August 1998.
74. *Les sports du Sud-Est*, 21 April 1932; Carter and Capel-Kirby, *Mighty Kick*, p. 114.
75. FA Archives, Minutes of Football League, 22 April 1932; *Daily Mail*, 14 April 1932.
76. *Topical Times*, 30 April 1932.

These warnings and threats went largely unheeded. Nîmes's attempt to sign Gallacher and Law fell through due to a lack of financial security but the club did manage to entice two other Chelsea internationals – Andy Wilson (as player-coach) and Alex Cheyne – along with Harry Ward, an ex-England schoolboy international from Ramsgate.[77] Though not as well known as Gallacher and Law, these were valuable acquisitions for Nîmes and significant losses for Chelsea. Wilson, thirty-seven and overweight, may have been coming to the end of his playing days, having been loaned the previous season to QPR in the third division south; but he had a long and prolific career behind him, overcoming the handicap of a shattered arm sustained in the Great War and signing for Chelsea in 1923 for a then record fee of £6,500. He was in some ways an exception in professional football. Educated and literate, he regularly wrote for the London press while at Chelsea and after the Second World War found employment as a civil servant and even played bowls for England.[78] Cheyne, meanwhile, a 25-year-old current Scottish international, was at the peak of his career, having joined the London club from Aberdeen two years previously for £6,000.[79] Despite the fact that the Cheyne-Wilson transfer led to a French-English mutual agreement over contracts, a stream of British players still travelled to France in the months that followed. Hugh Vallance, a centre-forward who scored thirty goals for Brighton and Hove Albion in the third division in 1930 but had fallen out with the club, was typical. He joined Smoker and West at Alès but without any representative experience may have been surprised to find himself described in the local press as a 'regular international, twice versus Wales and once versus Ireland'.[80] Not all were professionals: some clubs still preferred to recruit amateur players. Olympique Lillois, for example, champions in the inaugural season, brought Fred Lutterloch and Jock McGowan over from the London amateurs of Tufnell Park.[81] All told, forty-three British footballers were contracted to the twenty clubs comprising the league when the first round of fixtures kicked off in September 1932.

The type of player recruited reflected French conceptions of British football as characterized by physical strength, hard work and discipline. McGowan was the archetype of the 'strong' British import: 'built like a brick house, a morphology

77. Max Soulier, *Le football gardois*, Nîmes: Bène, 1969, p. 237; Carter and Capel Kirby, *Mighty Kick*, p. 115.

78. Ralph Finn, *A History of Chelsea FC*, London: Pelham, 1969, p. 24; Douglas Lamming, *A Scottish Soccer Internationals' Who's Who,* Beverley: Hutton Press, 1987, p. 223; D. Turner and A. White, *Football Managers*, Derby: Breedon, 1993, p. 251; Soulier, *Le football gardois*, pp. 163–4.

79. Lamming, *Scottish Soccer Internationals*, p. 42.

80. Tim Carder and Roger Harris, *Seagulls!: The Story of Brighton and Hove Albion FC*, Hove: Goldstone, 1993, p. 95; *Les sports du Sud-Est*, 25 May 1932.

81. Carter and Capel-Kirby, *Mighty Kick*, pp. 117–18.

of the perfect athlete'.[82] Vallance was likened by French commentators to a 'buffalo rushing to the goal' but, in a weak team which suffered relegation, he only scored on five occasions.[83] Other players in this first batch were appreciated for their shooting and heading, aspects of the game in which the French were considered particularly weak, and more generally for their considerable workrate. Defenders were also favoured, with full backs accounting for ten and centre-halves for eleven of the first wave of migrants. By contrast, the Austrian, Czech and Hungarian imports were mostly forwards. In fact, while two Austrians and one Hungarian were the highest goalscorers, no British players featured in the top ten at the end of the season.

Despite their considerable numbers the British did not settle well. Some were signed for trial periods or on month-to-month contracts and a few, such as Bill Fraser at Marseilles, even returned home in time for the start of the English season. Certain players clearly found it difficult to adapt to the French version of football. Andy Wilson, writing shortly after his arrival in the regional sporting weekly paper owned by the Nîmes chairman, noted that 'our first training matches here may be quite difficult, as we are not used to the hot weather and the dry pitches'.[84] On his return from Marseilles in August 1932, Fraser informed British readers that the climate was 'delightful' and the pitches 'firm and easy to play on' but claimed that the ball was smaller than at home and the infrastructure – the stadia, dressing rooms and other facilities – was rudimentary.[85] More significant still, there was little evidence of integration into French culture and society. None of the initial group joined a club alone. Instead, British players congregated in small colonies, such as at Marseilles where Caiels, Jennings, Pritchard, Sherry, Trees (Fraser for a short time) and their manager Charlie Bell distanced themselves from the rest of the squad.[86] Elsewhere Britons were ostracized as they made no attempt to learn the language and brought with them alien 'traditions', such as drinking beer after the match. Yves Dupont, a Sète player in 1934, highlighted the cleavage between the two football cultures. He remembered that one of the imports, Joe Hillier, 'behaved so roughly during social events, like a savage with women, that we tried to exclude him from our dinners with directors and supporters'.[87] Later the same

---

82. Jacques de Ryswick, *100,000 heures de football*, Paris: Table Ronde, 1962, p. 32; Carter and Capel-Kirby, *Mighty Kick*, pp. 117–18.

83. *Les sports du Sud-Est*, 25 May 1932.

84. *Les sports du Sud-Est*, 19 May 1932.

85. *Topical Times*, 13 August 1932.

86. Turner and White, *Football Managers*, p. 86; Lucien Grimand and Alain Pecheral, *La grande histoire de l'OM*, Paris: Robert Laffont, 1984, p. 76.

87. Interview of authors with Yves Dupont, May 1982.

year Jack Trees had his registration with the league cancelled when it was officially noted that he had 'contracted an illness unconnected with football'.[88]

Another characteristic specific to the professionals from Britain was the complete refusal, with the exception of the Irishman Bernard Williams at Sochaux, to apply for French citizenship.[89] At the same time, the then Racing Club de Paris goalkeeper Rudy Hiden (whom Arsenal had tried to buy) along with fellow Austrian nationals Hiltl and Jordan, agreed to change citizenship on their club's request. Many of the non-British imports were further integrated by marrying French wives and remaining in France after their footballing careers had finished. No British footballers after 1932 were integrated to this extent: they failed to embrace the host culture and were unable, or unwilling, to fully adapt to French life. As one French journalist commented: 'The English are so sure of their superiority that they will not think of adapting to our rules and traditions'.[90] This provides a sharp contrast, of course, to the earlier group of British shamateurs. Whereas they were generally successful and well-liked, and tried to integrate, the post-1932 professionals remained outsiders and were not remembered so fondly by crowds, fellow players or employers.

In the first two seasons of the French first division the British were the largest non-French national grouping. Yet by the mid-1930s migration had slowed and some of the best known captures had returned home. After 1934 the majority of British players were engaged in the second rather than the first tier of French football and the British presence in the top division dwindled from 11.9 to just 1.5 per cent over the seven-year period from the creation of the league to the outbreak of war (Table 2.1). As Table 2.2 indicates, the majority of British imports played

Table 2.1 British Players in the French First Division as a percentage of all players, 1932–39

Season	No. British Players	As % Non-French Players	As % All Players
1932/33	43	40.7	11.9
1933/34	26	27.6	9.6
1934/35	15	14.3	4.5
1935/36	15	15.2	4.9
1936/37	10	9.4	2.9
1937/38	9	8.8	2.8
1938/39	5	6.9	1.5

Source: Data elaborated from *Football*, 1933–38

88. *Les sports du Sud-Est*, 6 September 1934. During his year with Marseilles, Trees' bad temper got him sent off twice. His contract was not renewed. Grimand and Pecheral, *La grande histoire de l'OM*, p. 220.

89. Gilbert Baudoin, *Histoire du FC Sochaux*, Roanne: Horvath, 1985, p. 25.

90. *Les sports du Sud-Est*, 11 January 1934.

Table 2.2 Length of Stay among British Players in French Professional Football, 1932–39

No. of Years	% of British Players
Less than 1	58.2
2	19.4
3	9.3
4	5.8
5	2.9
6	0.7
7	3.6

Source: Data elaborated from *Football*, 1933–38

in France for no more than a season. The reasons for this were varied. As we have said, even some of the most talented Britons found themselves unable to adapt to the very different culture of French society and football. Both Wilson and Cheyne re-signed for British clubs within two seasons of their move to Nîmes, the latter actually returning to Chelsea. But the best example is provided by the sojourn of Peter O'Dowd, the only fully capped English international to play in France in this period. His arrival at Valenciennes, along with George Gibson, for the beginning of the 1935/36 season apparently 'brought great hopes' to the club but they were soon to be dashed.[91] If one believes the local press, O'Dowd had a particularly bad winter in 1935. At the start of December a journalist on *Le miroir des sports* wrote that the Englishman 'has a bad attitude and wants extra money to play'. A week later, the same newspaper considered O'Dowd's contribution during a match against Lille at some length:

> On facing the Argentinian Volante, he seemed to regard the activity of his opponent with some curiosity. It has certainly been proved that this 'glory' from over the Channel is able to juggle with the ball when it is given to him but the opportunities to show his virtuosity were very rare. His impact on the match was about as significant as that of the substitutes left on the bench. O'Dowd obviously has to pay for his own cleaning; that might explain why he doesn't like to get dirty.[92]

Things had not improved by the end of the month, when O'Dowd was accused of a lack of effort and of barely meriting a place even in a veteran's team.[93] With Gibson, he was also accused, but subsequently cleared, by the French federation

91. Paul Hurseau, *L'histoire du football Nordiste*, Lille: Ligue du Nord de Football, 1977, p. 149.
92. *Les miroir des sports*, 3, 10 December 1935.
93. *Les miroir des sports*, 31 December 1935.

of being bribed to 'throw' a match.[94] O'Dowd failed to secure a regular place in a Valenciennes side which was relegated to the second division and returned to English football with Torquay United in early 1937. Experiences of this kind diminished the reputation of British players and managers, a factor which was compounded by the economic crisis in Central Europe which, as we will see in Chapter 7, allowed French clubs to acquire the very best Hungarian and Austrian players at relatively inexpensive prices.

Most of the players who had tried their luck in France were able to find an engagement when they came home. Fraser, for one, admitted that his premature return to England had been motivated by 'the danger of falling out of touch with football in this country' and, more specifically, by the FA and League warnings that players who deserted their clubs would never be allowed back.[95] However, there were no bans or blacklists: as with the American exiles, most returned to domestic football with little or no trouble. Even when complications arose, the football authorities did not bolt the door shut. When Gibson, following his problems with O'Dowd at Valenciennes, fled to England in violation of his contract with Racing Club de Roubaix in 1937, for instance, the FA urged him to return but ultimately supported the player's case when Roubaix refused either to remove his suspension or reinstate him. The FA sided with Gibson by refusing the French federation's demand for a transfer fee and allowing him to register with any English club he wished.[96] In time, the threats of 1932 were revealed as little more than bluff and bluster as numerous migrants were permitted to re-register as professionals in Britain. The outbreak of war marked the effective end of this migration with only a few Britons playing in the French League in the late 1940s.[97]

Colombia, 1950–51

Such leniency on the part of the football authorities was not to be repeated when the next migration scare occurred after the Second World War. The so-called 'Bogotá affair' has generated almost as much interest among historians as it did

---

94. Paul Taylor and Dave Smith, *The Foxes Alphabet: A Complete Who's Who of Leicester City Football Club*, Leicester: Polar Print, 1995, p. 148.

95. *Topical Times*, 13 August 1932.

96. PFA Archives, Minutes of AFPTU, 22 March 1937.

97. For a full list of British footballers in France after 1945, see M. Barreaud, *Dictionnaire des footballeurs étrangers du championnat professionnel français (1932–1997)*, Paris: L'Harmattan, 1998. The two most successful Britons of the period were the Welshman Bryn Griffiths and the Englishman John Westwood. Neither played in the Football League but both stayed at the top level of French football for over a decade. In contrast, the vast majority of post-war British migrants stayed for a matter of weeks or months.

controversy among contemporaries.[98] It has been interpreted as a key moment in the history of the profession in its place of origin: a protest against the archaic employment situation at home as well as the first major exploration of the British footballer abroad.[99] For some of the seven players who went to Colombia in 1950 the incident became the defining point of their careers. The most famous, Neil Franklin, was unable to regain his place in the England national squad on his return and five years later wrote an autobiography in which he described his time in Colombia as 'a ghastly mistake'.[100] The author of a recently published biography of Charlie Mitten based the whole book around the player's spell abroad, calling it 'Bogotá Bandit' with the subtitle 'The Outlaw Life of Charlie Mitten'. Though lasting little more than one season at most, and involving far fewer players than those of the earlier migrations to the United States and France, the significance of the episode should not be understated. As Tony Mason has argued, 'For a brief moment . . . the core of the British game appeared to be threatened'.[101]

In many respects it had little in common with the earlier examples. While the majority of players who moved between the wars were not of the highest standard, those who travelled to Colombia were all well-known stars with leading clubs. Money was clearly a motivation in each case but the sense of grievance at the lack of freedom and status accorded to the professional was much more pronounced for the Colombian migrants. The immediate post-war years was a 'boom' period for British football with attendances at an all-time high, more money being generated by clubs yet players still under tight earning and mobility restrictions and perceived, according to some accounts, as little more than 'soccer slaves'. The best footballers were increasingly coming to see themselves as highly skilled entertainers comparable with movie stars but without the same financial rewards or prestige.[102] Mitten, for one, a winger at Manchester United, apparently 'regarded himself as more than an artisan; he was an accomplished performer at the top of his profession' but felt he was not being rewarded as such in England.[103] And by the late 1940s and 1950s there seemed to be increasing opportunities for the best players to earn considerable sums abroad. The wealthiest Italian clubs were

98. See especially Tony Mason, 'The Bogotá Affair', in Bale and Maguire (eds) *Global Sports Arena*, pp. 39–48.

99. For both interpretations see Martin Polley, *Moving the Goalposts: A History of Sport and Society since 1945*, London: Routledge, 1998, pp. 49, 116.

100. Neil Franklin, *Soccer at Home and Abroad*, London: Stanley Paul, 1956, p. 102.

101. Mason, 'Bogotá Affair', pp. 39, 47; Richard Adamson, *Bogotá Bandit: The Outlaw Life of Charlie Mitten: Manchester United's Penalty King*, Edinburgh: Mainstream, 1996.

102. Ross McKibbin, *Classes and Cultures: Britain 1918–1951*, Oxford: Oxford University Press, 1998, pp. 346–7; Dave Russell, *Football and the English: A Social History of Association Football in England, 1863–1995*, Preston: Carnegie, 1997, pp. 144–51.

103. Adamson, *Bogotá Bandit*, p. 78.

prepared to pay large transfer fees and substantial contracts for foreign talent and began to broaden their gaze to northern Europe, including Britain. At the same time Santiago Bernabeu was beginning to attract players to his great Real Madrid side of the 1950s and 1960s, allegedly offering Mitten in 1951 a three-year contract worth £10,000 annually in the process.[104] Isolated instances though these undoubtedly were, playing abroad was both a more attractive and a marginally more realistic prospect for the British footballer of the 1950s compared with his inter-war counterpart.

The British 'outlaws' were part of a much larger migration to Colombia, which we will focus on in more detail in Chapter 3. An internal dispute between the newly formed professional league, the Di Mayor, and the Colombian FA led to the former's clubs, unaffiliated to FIFA, signing numerous foreign professionals without having to pay transfer fees. According to one estimate, as many as 109 foreigners were contracted to Colombian clubs in 1949. As we will see, Argentinians came in the greatest numbers but others were imported from Uruguay, Peru and Paraguay, with just a handful from Europe.[105] The method of recruitment was very much in keeping with previous footballing examples, as well as industrial employment more generally. The first approach was made via a letter from Luis Robledo, the wealthy president of Santa Fe of Bogotá, to Franklin at Stoke City in November 1949. Franklin, dissatisfied with his opportunities and rewards at Stoke, agreed to Robledo's offer and persuaded his team-mate George Mountford to sign with the club. The specific arrangements were then tied up by an agent of the club based in Switzerland. The two travelled to South America in May 1950, having misled Stoke into thinking that they were simply going to coach for the duration of the summer.[106] The other British players seem to have been recruited through a short-term form of 'chain migration'. According to his biographer, Mitten received an offer via telephone from Franklin and Robledo while on tour with Manchester United in the United States and was flown out to Bogotá immediately to consider it. Mitten was unable to persuade two of his United colleagues, Johnny Aston and Harry Cockburn, to sign with him but evidently continued to act as an agent for his new club, writing to Middlesbrough's Wilf Mannion, among others, with the initial offer of a fully paid trip to Colombia to coach and take part in six exhibition matches.[107] Stanley Matthews received an almost identical offer which included three of his Blackpool team-mates but he, too, rejected it. Roy Paul of Swansea

104. Adamson, *Bogotá Bandit*, p. 108; Rogan Taylor and Andrew Ward, *Kicking and Screaming: An Oral History of Football in England*, London: Robson Books, 1995, p. 82.

105. Tony Mason, *Passion of the People?: Football in South America*, London: Verso, 1995, p. 59.

106. Franklin, *Soccer at Home and Abroad*, p. 78–82; Mason, 'Bogotá Affair', p. 42.

107. Adamson, *Bogotá Bandit*, pp. 76–81; Nick Varley, *Golden Boy: A Biography of Wilf Mannion*, London: Aurum Press, 1997, pp. 139–40.

City and Jack Hedley of Hearts were two who actually travelled to Bogotá but eventually turned down offers to play with Millonarios, Santa Fe's city rivals.[108] They may have approached, or been approached by, the Lincoln City player Jock Dodds, who was banned by the Football League for acting as an agent for Millionarios.[109] Franklin alleges that he received 'countless letters from famous players at home', although by this time he was apparently putting potential migrants off rather than encouraging them to make the trip.[110]

The evidence of the British players' experiences in Colombia is mixed and contradictory. This is particularly so in the case of Franklin. He lasted just two months in Bogotá, playing only six matches, and does not seem to have had a good time; his autobiography presents an almost entirely negative picture of the whole venture. He apparently disliked both the game and the lifestyle in Colombia. The players, especially the Argentine imports, were resentful of the British; the standard of play was poor (although he was impressed by the training); both players and supporters were badly behaved; the climate was worse than Britain's; the food and drink was unsatisfactory; and the country was unstable, racked by political turmoil and widespread poverty amid pockets of wealth. Above all, his wife and family were unhappy.[111] However, as Tony Mason has revealed, Franklin told a rather different story to British newspapers at the time. In interviews with the *Sunday Empire News* in May and June 1950, Franklin revealed himself at ease with his new place of work: 'the climate, the people, facilities, social status – everything is better than we expected . . . and in striking contrast to the shabby treatment at home'.[112] While both versions of the story are far from reliable, it does appear that Franklin's stay in Bogotá was not the unequivocal failure which readers of his autobiography might assume.

Others shared Franklin's more negative account of Colombian football and culture. Paul was unimpressed by the place, the people and the food and stayed only ten days without even playing a match. Even Mountford, who honoured his contract at Santa Fe, indicated to the FA-Football League Inquiry on his return that 'the promises made for the negotiations for his services had not been fulfilled and that the conditions in Bogatá [*sic.*] were, in fact, very different from what they had been led to expect'.[113] Mitten was the one player who was positive about the experience, even after the English governing bodies had issued him with a

108. Stanley Matthews, *Feet First Again*, London: Nicholas Kaye, 1952, p. 86.

109. FA Archives, Minutes of Football League, 28 June 1950; Franklin, *Soccer at Home and Abroad*, p. 89.

110. Franklin, *Soccer at Home and Abroad*, p. 89.

111. See Franklin, *Soccer at Home and Abroad*, pp. 87–90, 99–102.

112. Mason, 'Bogotá Affair', p. 47.

113. Mason, 'Bogotá Affair', p. 44; FA Archives, Report of FA-Football League Joint Commission, 19 June 1951. Franklin, *Soccer at Home and Abroad*, makes an almost identical point (pp. 96, 103).

fine and suspension. According to his biographer, he enjoyed the relative status and affluence which allowed him to be 'accepted into the inner circles of Colombian social life', to live in 'a palatial, hacienda-style house' with servants and even to own a racehorse. But more importantly Mitten was impressed by the fact that footballers were regarded as professionals rather than mere workers: rather than being taken for granted, as he felt they were in Britain, the players were well looked after and well treated by the Colombians. He also appears to have made a genuine attempt to be accepted in this different cultural environment, deciding to 'wear their colours, just drop into their ways, get acclimatised, learn the language and try and absorb being one of them'. However, while Mitten claimed that he and his family made many friends, these seem to have been restricted to the British expatriate community. Indeed, so dependent were the British players upon one another that Mitten admitted feeling 'at quite a loss' when Mountford completed his contract and left Bogotá several months earlier. In the end, despite his inability to speak Spanish and his wife's homesickness, he evidently felt forced to return home mainly because there was no English school for his children.[114]

The football authorities in England used the 'Bogotá affair' as a deterrent for any professional who might be tempted to travel abroad in the future. Players suspected of being approached by foreign agents were sent a letter warning them not to consider leaving the country.[115] All four players who were actually signed to Colombian clubs – Franklin, Mitten, Mountford and Everton's Billy Higgins – were fined and suspended by a Joint FA–Football League Commission, significantly for bringing the game into disrepute by deceiving their clubs and talking to the press (in Franklin's case) as well as for the main offence of breaking their contracts.[116] Over the next few years, in press articles and player autobiographies, Bogotá became portrayed as a prime example of foreign football: uncivilized, dishonest and completely alien to the British footballer. In his 1952 autobiography, for instance, Stanley Matthews thought the whole episode was 'only a few months' wonder' and that, notwithstanding the money and the glamour, the players who went 'realized that England and English football isn't so bad after all'.[117] Franklin was keen to warn of the dangers of playing and living abroad in his autobiography:

I just couldn't live there. Neither, I venture to suggest, could the majority of my fellow countrymen . . . [I] learned that other places might not be all they seem. Wonderful, maybe, for a holiday, but a holiday and living there are two vastly different matters. I

---

114. Adamson, *Bogotá Bandit*, pp. 93–94, 106–7.

115. See Varley, *Golden Boy*, p. 140.

116. See the FA Archives, Reports of FA–Football League Joint Commissions, 17 October 1950 (Franklin), 21 November 1950 (Higgins), 19 June 1951 (Mountford), 18 July 1951 (Mitten).

117. Matthews, *Feet First Again*, pp. 86–7.

made the mistake of believing all I was told . . . I went there a happy and expectant man. I came back a sadder and wiser one.[118]

Italy, 1945–66

Bogotá excepted, there were few escape routes for the disgruntled British footballer. After the limited success of the exiles in France of the 1930s, as well as the more recent emigrants to Colombia, few Europeans clubs were prepared to pay for expensive British imports with a poor record of settling abroad. In fact, by the beginning of the 1950s only the richest Italian and Spanish teams seemed capable of matching the fees passing between British clubs, such as the £30,000 paid by Sunderland to Swansea for Trevor Ford in 1950 and the £34,500 which Sheffield Wednesday laid out for Jackie Sewell a year later. Initial attempts by the Italians to attract the cream of British talent were repelled. Wilf Mannion was scouted by Juventus in 1949 while Tom Finney was offered lucrative terms which included a £10,000 signing-on fee, monthly wages of £130, a Mediterranean villa and a continental car to sign a two-year deal with Palermo.[119] Neither of the two players' clubs, however, gave them the chance to consider the offer. Finney admitted that while the money and conditions were tempting, they may not have outweighed the risk of leaving: 'I like Preston, my home, and my friends, and it would have been no easy matter to pack up for a foreign country, where I would be playing in strange conditions and before strange crowds.'[120] Arsenal's manager Tom Whittaker was asked to coach Milan in 1948 and the Italian national team two years later but felt unable to 'make the break from England after spending a lifetime in the game here'.[121] If the big names remained unobtainable, less talented players were persuaded to try their luck in Italy. In 1948, Bill Jordan of Spurs and Paddy Sloan of Arsenal signed contracts with Juventus and Milan respectively, while the following year Frank Rawcliffe of Aldershot joined Alessandria in *Serie B*. Only Sloan, however, lasted more than a season.

By the mid-1950s the Italian raids could no longer be resisted. In 1955 Eddie Firmani, South African-born but of Italian descent, joined Sampdoria for £35,000. Two years later Juventus signed the Welsh centre-forward John Charles from Leeds United for £65,000 and Tony Marchi moved from Spurs to Vicenza for considerably less. The next swoop on British players took place after the lifting of an embargo

---

118. Franklin, *Soccer at Home and Abroad*, pp. 102–3.

119. Varley, *Golden Boy*, p. 136; Tom Finney, *Football Round the World*, London: Sportsman's Book Club, 1955, p. 98.

120. Finney, *Football Round the World*, p. 101.

121. Tom Whittaker, *Tom Whittaker's Arsenal Story*, London: Sportsman's Book Club, 1958, p. 213.

on foreigners in 1961 when Joe Baker, Jimmy Greaves, Gerry Hitchens and Denis Law were transferred to Italian clubs for fees ranging from £73,000 to £100,000. Unlike the Colombian case, of course, these were legitimate transfers between clubs whose federations were members of FIFA. But the methods employed, particularly the use of agents acting as negotiators or middlemen for Italian clubs, caused some disquiet. The best known 'agent' of the time was Gigi Peronace, described by Alec Stock, who briefly coached at Roma in 1957, as 'Italian football's man in Britain'.[122] Peronace had acted as an interpreter for Juventus' Scottish manager William Chalmers after the Second World War but soon became more closely involved in the transfer policy of a number of Italian clubs. Working as part-scout, part-agent in Britain before taking a more formal post as business manager with Torino, he was involved in most of the transfers of the 1950s and 1960s.[123] But he was not the only agent of the period. An Italian journalist acting for Milan, Roberto Favilla, made the first approach to Greaves while Firmani's transfer was initiated by a phone call from an English representative of the shipping firm owned by the Sampdoria president.[124]

What motivated these footballers to move to Italy? Greaves was unequivocal: 'I'd only got wrapped up with Milan for mercenary reasons. Money was the only motive, don't lets kid ourselves about that'.[125] The 'small fortunes' with which Greaves was lured clearly dwarfed his basic £20 wage at Chelsea. Law too was undoubtedly attracted by the financial package offered but his decision was also precipitated by his frustration at the limited opportunities for a player of his type in Britain. Firmani had not even had his own cheque-book before moving to Italy.[126] While admitting that the increase in pay was a factor, Charles played down the financial gap between England and Italy and insisted that he had been pushed to leave as well as pulled. British football was, he felt, fundamentally archaic, from the wage structure and employment conditions to the state of facilities for players and spectators. Indeed, there was 'precious little future in being a professional footballer in Britain'.[127] Neither was it so much that British players were badly paid; rather that, unlike in Italy where large bonuses were linked to success, the maximum wage ceiling meant that there was no incentive to improve. Few seem to have thought that the move abroad would improve their play. Even Charles,

122. Alec Stock, *A Little Thing Called Pride*, London: Pelham, 1982, p. 103.

123. Brian Glanville, *Football Memories*, London: Virgin, 1999, pp. 90, 112.

124. Jimmy Greaves and Reg Gutteridge, *Let's Be Honest*, London: Pelham, 1971, p. 52; Seed, *Jimmy Seed Story*, pp. 97–8.

125. Greaves and Gutteridge, *Let's Be Honest*, p. 54.

126. Denis Law with Bernard Bale, *The Lawman: An Autobiography*, London: André Deutsch, 1999, pp. 36–7; Eddie Firmani, *Football with the Millionaires*, London: Sportsman's Book Club, 1960, p. 42.

127. John Charles, *King of Soccer*, London: Stanley Paul, 1957, p. 146.

who clearly liked the style and pace of the Italian game more than most, told readers of his second British autobiography that only about five *Serie A* teams would have any chance of success in the English first division.[128] Alec Stock, by comparison, regarded the move to Roma as a welcome addition to his curriculum vitae and an opportunity to learn new coaching methods: 'I was off to Italy to further my education and give my career a new dimension'.[129]

The success of the British in Italy was mixed. After poor starts, both Firmani and Hitchens enjoyed long careers with a number of Italian clubs. Firmani's experience was no doubt eased by his Italian heritage but it was his ability to adapt and to score goals – in a league which was as unfamiliar to him as it was to the other imports from Britain – which guaranteed his success. More than most of the Football League exiles, Firmani set about becoming as Italian as possible. He went out of his way to learn the language, studying for two hours a day and keeping a vocabulary book in which he noted useful words and phrases. He also changed his eating and drinking habits, converting the taste for steak and chips which he had acquired in England to a love of wine and Italian food; he even became interested in cooking, making local dishes like *Cima alla Genovese* and spaghetti sauces.[130] Firmani remained in *Serie A* for eight seasons, moving from Sampdoria to Inter, and was even capped by Italy before he returned to his former employers Charlton in 1963. Hitchens' success was perhaps more surprising given his relative inexperience when he moved but he enjoyed nine seasons in Italy – more than any other British player to date – with Inter, Torino, Atalanta and Cagliari, making 205 appearances and scoring fifty-nine goals.

John Charles, however, made the greatest impact of all, in Britain as well as Italy. Forming a formidable striking partnership with the Argentine-born Italian Omar Sivori, he was central to Juventus's three championship winning sides in 1958, 1960 and 1961 and is still remembered as 'King John', almost an idol in this period of the club's history. He came to symbolize the Juventus motto of 'Simplicity, Seriousness and Sobriety', most notably with his 'chivalry' in helping an injured Torino opponent to his feet and staying with him while play continued during a derby clash in 1957.[131] But more than playing well, Charles settled well in Italy. His family lived in a rent-free four-bedroom flat in a fashionable suburb of Turin with a view 'worth thousands of pounds' and an apartment on the Mediterranean coast.[132] He enjoyed the weather and, like Firmani, evidently had

128. John Charles, *Gentle Giant*, London: Soccer Book Club, 1964, p. 81.

129. Stock, *Little Thing Called Pride*, p. 104.

130. Firmani, *Football with the Millionaires*, p. 95.

131. Christian Bromberger, *Le match de football: ethnologie d'une passion*, Paris: MSH, 1995, p. 150.

132. Charles, *Gentle Giant*, p. 10.

few problems adapting to the Italian lifestyle, food and culture. While disliking some aspects of the training and the game itself, Charles believed that professionals were more comfortable and better treated than in Britain. On signing, he was shocked and delighted by the fact that each player had a wardrobe and an easy chair in the dressing-room as well as a freshly laundered kit each morning for training.[133] Firmani had similarly been impressed by the fact that players had personal lockers, along with 'bathing sandals and a luxurious white robe for visits to the beautifully-appointed bathroom'.[134] Charles' main piece of advice to prospective émigrés was simple: 'it is no use trying to take England to Italy with you. When you sign you have to realize that you must accept the Italian way, even though you may not be able to understand the reason for some of their rules'.[135]

Notwithstanding the experience of Charles and, to a lesser extent, Firmani and Hitchens, the impression these migrants made was far from positive. Baker, Greaves and Law were all considered to be failures, returning to Britain within a season, a situation which when combined with Charles's move back to Leeds United, led to complaints in the summer of 1962 about the 'transfer fever' between English and Italian clubs.[136] They suffered the common complaints of the English footballer abroad: homesickness accentuated by problems with the language and the lifestyle. Off the field, club discipline caused a particular grievance, especially for Greaves who admitted feeling 'like a prisoner' from the beginning.[137] He is apparently remembered in Milan for his 'bad moods' and his dislike of coach Nereo Rocco.[138] The practice of the *ritiro*, in which the squad would go away to a hotel retreat to relax before and after matches, was especially vexing to the British, as were the stringent rules, regulations and fines which covered the overall conduct of players. On the field, the defensive tactics were less infuriating than the obstruction, impeding, diving and shirt-pulling which apparently accompanied them, all of which were regarded as alien by the British contingent.[139] In addition, the attention of the press caused discontent, particularly for Baker and Law who as young single men abroad courted controversy. The pressure was too much for Baker, who was arrested for punching a photographer in Venice and ended up, with Law, in hospital after a car accident in Turin in the early hours of the morning. Of the 1961 group

133. Charles, *King of Soccer*, p. 145.
134. Firmani, *Football with the Millionaires*, p. 46.
135. Charles, *Gentle Giant*, p. 133.
136. FA Archives, Minutes of Football League, 2 June 1962.
137. Greaves and Gutteridge, *Let's Be Honest*, p. 60.
138. Luigi 'Cina' Bonizzoni, *Calciatori stranieri in Italia ieri e oggi*, Rome: Società stampa sportiva, 1989, p. 83.
139. Law with Bale, *The Lawman*, pp. 62–3; Charles, *Gentle Giant*, pp. 70–6.

only Hitchens – 'a far more resilient and integrated personality'[140] – was prepared to follow Charles's advice by accepting 'the Italian way'.

Following the experiences of these exiles in Italy, fewer than two dozen British and Irish professionals have played in *Serie A*. The Italian ban on foreign imports which lasted from 1966 until 1980 made this impossible but even in the 1980s and 1990s past experience seemed to have taught British players and Italian clubs to be wary of committing to one another. Alongside the success of players such as Liam Brady, Trevor Francis, Mark Hateley and David Platt, who were able to adapt, there have been those who, like Greaves and Law years before, complained about the lifestyle, the press and the way the game was played and left as soon as they could. Ian Rush's earnest comment that playing in Italy was like being in a foreign country seemed to epitomize the attitude of the British footballer abroad. Italy, it seemed, would have been fine if only it was more British. Other destinations were no more popular. As Table 2.3 shows, fewer than a hundred players have been drawn from British football to the major European leagues in the half-century after the Second World War. Britain has witnessed nothing like the diaspora of native football talent which has affected most other European nations. To play abroad is still considered rather strange to the British, especially those who insist that the Football League (now the Premiership) is the best and hardest competition in the world. Kevin Keegan was accused at home of being unpatriotic and only interested in money when he left Liverpool for Hamburg in 1977.[141] And even though, after a difficult start, he won the league, reached the European Cup Final and was twice named European Player of the Year while in Germany, he was only embraced as a national hero when he returned to British football. There have been one or two players, such as Tony Woodcock in Germany and Michael Robinson in Spain, who have integrated and settled into their host society and others like Chris Waddle at Marseilles who were embraced for their sporting talent despite never really learning the language or adapting to life abroad. But many others

Table 2.3 British and Irish Footballers in the Major European Leagues*, 1945–95

	France	Germany	Italy	Spain
1945–54	4	–	2	–
1955–64	–	–	6	–
1965–74	1	1	1	–
1975–84	2	6	7	5
1985–95	16	8	12	16

* Top Divisions

140. Glanville, *Football Memories*, p. 173.
141. John Gibson, *Kevin Keegan: Portrait of a Superstar*, London: W.H. Allen, 1984, pp. 93–4.

have followed the Greaves and Law route, like Dave Watson, who played just two matches for Werder Bremen in 1979, was sent off in one and returned to England within a couple of weeks to play for Southampton.

The 'splendid isolation' of British football does not reflect the more complicated reality. The British leagues, by and large, remained the preserves of white, working-class British footballers. Those players who were recruited from abroad – South Africans and Australians – were barely visible, as they were not considered to be foreigners at all. Major foreign transfers, meanwhile, were restricted by FA regulations. Nonetheless, Britain was not absent from the twentieth-century migratory flux. Many hundreds of British players have experienced professional football abroad. Because they tended to involve the moderate rather than the star players, these instances have generated little comment. Unlike the South American and Yugoslav migrants whom we will consider in the following two chapters, British footballers have tended to be sojourners rather than settlers. In the 1999/2000 season, there were officially only three British players making their living outside the country. Playing football abroad, it seems, is simply not for the British.

—3—

The South American Artists

The quality of South American footballers was revealed to the Old World (with the exception of the British) by the victories of the Uruguayan national team at the Olympics of Paris in 1924 and Amsterdam in 1928 and at the first World Cup in Montevideo in 1930. Gabriel Hanot, a former French international and football columnist of the French weekly *Miroir des sports*, noted after the 1924 Olympic Final:

> In Paris between 25 May and 9 June there was not a single FA official, no British journalist, no British professional manager, not a single British spectator to see how other countries had adapted a proper English game to their national temperament. It was another testimony to their 'Splendid Isolation'. Nonetheless, the Olympic tournament was a prodigious success and Uruguay's matches a revelation to the world.[1]

Maurice Pefferkorn, another French journalist at the tournament wrote that 'More than its success, Uruguay's style created enthusiasm in the public. We were facing men who seemed to have found in football a second nature'.[2] A third added: 'I saw in front of me the revelation of a dream football. It had everything: ease, finesse and inspiration'.[3]

There is no doubt that some of the myths associated with South American footballers were created by the Uruguayan exhibition in 1924. Hanot, with some exaggeration, described the performance of the Uruguayans thus: 'These fine athletes are to the English professionals like Arab thoroughbreds next to farm horses'.[4] The aesthetic quality of the players was a large part of their revelation. José Leandro Andrade, the black half-back, instantly became regarded as an idol. Commentators placed great emphasis on his other passion: he was a professional tango dancer. These were the 'crazy years' of the *Ballets nègres* and Joséphine

---

1. *Le miroir des sports,* 18 June 1924.

2. Maurice Pefferkorn, *Football, joie du monde,* Paris: Susse, 1944, pp. 14–15.

3. Jacques de Ryswick, *100 000 heures de football,* Paris: Table ronde, 1962, p. 45.

4. *Le miroir des sports,* 12 June 1924. This opinion however was not shared by all French critics. Edgar Lenglet wrote: 'I am convinced that a great team like the pre-war London Corinthians, composed of the best English amateurs, would have beaten Uruguay', *Encyclopédie des sports,* Paris: Librairie de France, 1924, vol. II, p. 156.

Baker in Montparnasse and Carlos Gardel and the Argentinian tango in Paris. European specialists tried to rationalize the sudden success of these new 'strange' artists. The exotic dimension of the Uruguayan game and the fact that the team included a black player contributed to its mythology. Andrade 'loved to juggle with the ball', he was 'elegant, elastic, a wizard with the ball', descriptions not usually associated with European football players.[5] His two passions were automatically linked, creating an image of Uruguayan footballers as artists and originators of a new vision of the game.

South Americans themselves were instrumental in the development of this myth. In 1928, the journalist Ricardo Lorenzo 'Borocoto' wrote in the Buenos Aires weekly football newspaper *El Gráfico* that '[Our] football brought to Europe something unknown. In front of stronger opponents, the *criollo* player dribbled and scored. Physical strength was crushed by the talent and the quality of the *criollo* players. Argentinians and Uruguayans played the final in Amsterdam. The same players who dribbled in tango dribbled in football'.[6] In Brazil, too, the idea was prevalent that the Latin continent had created a new kind of player. In his notes on Brazilian football, Roberto da Matta remarked that '*Futebol* in Brazil is a waist-game (*jogo de cintura*) a kind of malice and swindling, which you don't find in any other football. It is the art of dodging'.[7] He considered the Brazilian players to be interpreters of a game which was less authoritarian, and more artistic, than existed in Europe. For much of the twentieth century, European clubs were equally fascinated by these South American artists and went out of their way to sign them.

European footballers had travelled to South America long before 1924. Various English, Italian and Portuguese clubs visited Brazil, Argentina and Uruguay before the First World War, often making a considerable impact. The amateur Corinthians of London in 1910, along with Southampton in 1904, Nottingham Forest in 1905, Everton and Tottenham Hotspur in 1909 and even Exeter City in 1914 all had highly successful results on the other side of the Atlantic.[8] In the same year as

---

5. Brian Glanville, *Soccer Round the Globe*, London: Sportsman's Book Club, p. 90; Luciano Serra, *Storia del calcio 1863–1963*, Bologna: Palmaverde, 1964, p. 68; Pefferkorn, *Football, joie du monde*, p. 15 speaks about the 'spicy flavour' of the Uruguayans and 'The seductive nonchalance of the elastic Andrade which instantly made him a popular idol.'

6. *El Gráfico*, 16 June 1928, quoted in Eduardo Archetti, 'Tango et football dans l'imagerie nationale argentine', *Sociétés et représentations*, 7, December 1998, pp. 117–27.

7. Roberto da Matta *Universo do futebol. Esporte e sociedade brasileira*, Rio de Janeiro: Pinakotheke, 1982, p. 28; a shorter version in French is Roberto da Matta, 'Notes sur le *futebol* brésilien', *Le débat*, 19, February 1982, pp. 68–76.

8. Tony Mason, *Passion of the People?: Football in South America*, London: Verso, 1994, pp. 15–26 entitles one of his chapters 'English lessons' and gives a detailed account of the British tourists before the War. Yet he does not mention the tours undertaken by non-British clubs. For other accounts

Exeter, Pozzo's Torino and Pro Vercelli also undertook the long journey to the River Plate.[9] The influence of these touring sides, particularly the British, was such that many local clubs adopted their names hoping, by analogy, to equal their performances and results. A club called *Corinthians* was established in São Paulo after the 1910 tour, *Everton* were formed in Viña del Mar (Chile), and *Barcelona* in Guayaquil (Ecuador). As in Europe, although for different reasons, the period of the First World War marked a major shift in outlook. The British influence largely vanished and competitions between Brazil, Argentina and Uruguay became more regular with the creation of the Copa America, the South American Championship, in 1917.[10]

With peace restored in Europe, new tourists arrived, including a Basque selection in 1922, Genoa in 1923, Español Barcelona in 1926, FC Barcelona in 1928 and Bologna and Torino again together with Ferencvaros of Hungary in 1929.[11] In 1925, Nacional Montevideo had made the reverse journey by touring Europe, as did Boca Juniors and São Paulo. Steamers were now making the transatlantic journey possible in three weeks and contributing to the intensification of these visits. In South America, the confrontations with European visitors were the most important matches of all. A history of football in the River Plate written in Argentina in 1923 dedicates its first ninety pages to the visits of European teams.[12] These encounters were expressions of a relationship marked simultaneously by friendship

---

of these British tourists see Alain Fontan, *Divin football brésilien*, Paris: La table ronde, 1963, pp. 27–9; Bill Murray, *Football: A History of the World Game*, Aldershot: Scholar, pp. 114–21.

9. V. Pozzo, *Campioni del Mondo. Quarant'anni di storia del calcio italiano*, Rome: CEN, 1960 p. 32, included various photographs of the journey in his autobiography. For him as for many others, the revelation of South American football was enormous; P. L. Brunori, *Torino: Superga nella sua storia*, Florence: M'Litograph, 1981, p. 39.

10. The opposition between English clubs and clubs emerging from the gymnastics movement such as *Gimnasia y Esgrima* led to the creation in 1912 of the Federación Argentina de Football, which affiliated to FIFA; Ernesto Escobar Bavio, *El football en el Rio de la Plata (desde 1893)*, Buenos Aires: Editorial Sports, 1923, p.11; Fernando Alonso (ed.), *Cien años con el fútbol*, Buenos Aires: Manrique Zago, 1993, p. 32; Julio D. Frydenberg, 'Redefinición del fútbol aficionado y del fútbol oficial; Buenos Aires 1912', in P. Alabarces, R. Di Giano and J. Frydenberg (eds), *Deporte y sociedad*, Buenos Aires: Eudeba, 1998, pp. 51–65. There are various accounts of the English origins of South American football in English, Allen Guttmann, *Games and Empires: Modern Sports and Cultural Imperialism*, New York: Columbia University Press, 1994, pp. 56–63; Mason, *Passion of the People?*, pp. 1–26.

11. On the Genoa tour, G. Brera and F. Tomati, *Genoa, Amore mio*, Florence: Ponte alle grazie, 1991, p. 104–5; on Bologna, Gianni Marchesini, *La storia del Bologna*, Florence: Casa dello sport, 1988, p. 107; on Español and Barcelona, J. Garcia Castell, *Història del futbol català*, Barcelona: Aymà, 1968, pp. 163–6, 183–4.

12. Escobar Bavio, *El football en el Rio de la Plata*, pp. 17–90 gives a precise account of all matches played by the tourists.

and confrontation. The symbolic dimension of these tours revealed their diplomatic importance. The winner of Genoa's match against a Northern Argentinian team received a cup offered by the local Italian-language newspaper *Giornale d'Italia*. When they played Uruguay, another trophy was presented by the director and employees of the Banco Italiano del Uruguay. For the occasion, the players received gold medals donated by a local group of Italian war veterans from José Serrato, the President of the Republic, while the Italian ambassador in Uruguay kicked off the match. A special routine was prepared for Genoa's last match on 9 September 1923, against an Argentine combination in Buenos Aires. The teams entered the field in parallel rows after which Argentina's State President Marcelo de Alvear shook the players' hands. The ball was brought to the ground by an aeroplane and President de Alvear gave the first kick.[13] Bologna's team in 1929, meanwhile, took the field in Montevideo with all players crossing a large Uruguayan silk flag 'especially made to be presented to the Uruguayan FA'.[14] The increasing role of football for the important Spanish and Italian migrant communities in South America ensured the financial success of these tours. The economic and cultural link between Italy and the River Plate was crucial given that approximately one-third of the population of Buenos Aires and Montevideo were of Italian origin.[15] Moreover, tourists such as Andrade, who crossed the Atlantic almost every year during the 1920s, presaged the transfer movement of the following decade. The main focus of this chapter will be the intercontinental migration of South American players, which initially took place in Italy as a direct consequence of the policy of autarky imposed by the fascist government.

Welcome Home!: The Ethnic Migration of the 1930s

The Argentinians

The anthropologist Eduardo Archetti has written that the Argentine style 'was the result of mixed cooking. It was neither Italian nor Spanish. A "pure style" was not only impossible, it was not required'.[16] Because of this inherent hybridity, the

13. Escobar Bavio, *El football en el Rio de la Plata*, p. 87–90.

14. *El Mundo Uruguayo*, 10 August 1929. (We are particularly thankful to Eduardo Gutiérrez Cortinas for the newspaper cuttings and biographies of Uruguayan players.)

15. On Italian emigration in Argentina, Fernando Devoto and Giorgio Rosoli (eds), *L'Italia nella società Argentina*, Rome, 1988.

16. Eduardo Archetti, 'Argentinien', in C. Eisenberg (ed.), *Fußball, Soccer, Calcio. Ein englischer Sport auf seinem Weg um die Welt*, Munich: DTV, 1997, p. 155; From the same author, 'Argentina and the World Cup: in Search of National Identity', in J. Sugden and A. Tomlinson (eds) *Hosts and Champions. Soccer, Cultures, National Identity and the USA World Cup*, Aldershot: Arena, 1994, pp. 37–63; 'Estilos y virtudes masculinas en El Gráfico: la creación del imaginario del fútbol argentino' in *Desarrollo económico*, 35, 1995, pp. 419–42.

arrival of South American players in Italy at the beginning of the 1930s has assumed many of the ambiguities attached to the concept of national identity.[17] From the Italian perspective, it was seen less as a migratory fashion than a natural and inevitable repatriation of Italian citizens who happened to be born in South America. From the Argentinian point of view, the ethnic origin of these 'Italians' had long disappeared in the face of a cultural background peculiar to the Argentines. Rather than assessing the validity of these interpretations, we would like to discuss the problems they generated.

Despite the authoritarianism of the fascist regime, Italian clubs were economically independent and run by important businessmen eager to reinforce their prestige and that of their teams. Under these circumstances, the importation of South American footballers can be read as a compromise. They were acceptable because technically they were Italians who could not only provide success for their club employers but could also enhance the standing of the national team in international competition.

The development of the game on opposite sides of the Atlantic had been very different. It generated an ambiguous situation which was considered by Gianni Brera, the most famous Italian football columnist:

In South America players dance football (*baila fútbol*) following the expectations of the crowd. Where bullfighting was forbidden, you looked for fun, for the dribbling dance (*pase de dribbling*), a pure virtuous game. In Italy it was difficult to find grounds adapted to this sort of game and even more difficult to find opponents disposed to suffer dances (*pases*), which made them look ridiculous.[18]

Some critics have argued that those who played the Argentinian game, the *fútbol criollo* as it was called, were fundamentally distinct from the European practitioners. The *criollos* (or creoles) were descendants of the original colonists: in other words, the *real* Argentinians. Their style could not be copied by Europeans; only natives were able to play *that* game. As Archetti has pointed out in his recent work, this Argentine-Italian migration proposed a logic of reciprocity as the blood of the young Europeans who emigrated to Argentina was filled with *criollo* football quality.[19] We will concentrate here on some of the aspects connected with this fundamental distinction between blood and culture, ethnicity and heritage.

This emigration of South Americans to Italy in the 1930s brought to the fore different conceptions and interpretations of citizenship and also of national roots.

17. Eduardo Archetti, *Masculinities: Football, Polo and the Tango in Argentina*, Oxford: Berg, 1999, pp. 46–76.

18. Gianni Brera, *Il mestiere del calciatore*, Milan: Baldini and Castoldi, 1994, p. 143.

19. Eduardo Archetti, 'Fútbol: imágenes y estereotipos' in F. Devoto and M. Madero (eds), *Historia de la vida privada en Argentina*, vol. 3, Buenos Aires: Taurus, 1999.

Moving from Argentina, Brazil or Uruguay, where the *jus soli* was in place, the South American footballers were transferred to a Fascist Italy run by the *jus sanguinis*. For Brera, football was a product of *jus soli*: 'Every football school depends on the ethnic background (*etnos*), the economy, the climate and the civilization (that also means the way the soil is levelled, the grounds protected and the grass sowed).'[20] Since 1850, Argentinian nationalism had built a myth around the *criollo*, who represented a rural world alien to most of these early urban footballers. A *criollo* 'would by definition represent the rural, provincial and *gaucho* interests'.[21] By contrast, most of these football emigrants were residents of Montevideo, Buenos Aires or São Paulo, two of which were ports, and all three of which had greater contact with the European world than with the pampas or Amazonia. Together with the other national myth – the *gaucho* – the *criollo* ideology became central in forging Argentinian identity. As a historian of literature writes: 'The term *gaucho* acquired particular significance in [the twentieth] century when nationalist and populist writers . . . made the gaucho the symbol of the authentic Argentina, which supposedly had been violated, betrayed, and pillaged by a rapacious, pro-European, anti-Argentine upper class and its foreign allies.'[22] Surprisingly, urban footballers of European origin were quickly associated by the Argentinian sporting press with the *criollo* and *gaucho* image. No doubt the poor social background of many players helped in the creation of the *criollo* myth because football in the River Plate had managed to seduce the working class earlier than that in continental Europe.

This was certainly true of Julio Libonatti, who became the first major Argentinian player to move to Italy when he signed for Torino in 1925. Libonatti, a former Rosario Central player from a poor Italian immigrant family originating from Genoa, had played for Argentina and scored the only goal of the South American Championship Finals of 1921. In his history of Argentinian football, Osvaldo Bayer identified Libonatti's move to Turin as the first expression of 'a colonial disease suffered by *criollo* football'.[23] Torino's chairman Enrico Maroni, an executive director of the Cinzano company, had decided during one of his business trips to Argentina to engage Libonatti. Maroni had himself discovered football during his youth in Buenos Aires and was intent on increasing the potential of his club by signing top-class players.[24] Libonatti immediately received an Italian

20. Brera, *Il mestiere del calciatore*, p. 141.

21. Nicolas Shumway, *The Invention of Argentina*, Berkeley: University of California Press, 1991, pp. 275–6.

22. Ibid., p. 70.

23. Osvaldo Bayer, *Fútbol argentino*, Buenos Aires: Editorial Sudamericana, 1990, p. 27.

24. Paul Dietschy, 'Football et société à Turin 1920–1960', Unpublished PhD Thesis, University of Lyon, 1997, p. 103.

passport and soon became the main attraction of his new team. To the fifteen caps he had received with Argentina, he added a further seventeen with the Italian national side. His technical ability and his high rate of goal scoring impressed the Italian critics while Ricardo Zamora, the Spanish goalkeeper, allegedly considered Libonatti to be the best forward in the world. He was even said by Zamora to have revolutionized the role of the centre-forward.[25] His nine years at Torino coincided with the first golden era of the club, when they won the national league for the first time ever. Off the pitch, Libonatti was known for his elegance and his profligacy. He was considered to be the best-paid player in Italy and also perhaps the best-dressed, usually sporting suede jackets. Another Argentinian had arrived with Libonatti. Arturo Chini Ludueña, nicknamed 'the lawyer', came to Italy to study but also played football for a decade as a winger for Torino and AS Roma. At the end of his playing days, he had obtained a law degree and also featured in over 200 league matches as well as international competitions for the Italian Universities team.[26]

On top of Libonatti's impact, the domination of the South American teams in Amsterdam in 1928 convinced Umberto Agnelli, the chairman of FIAT and director of the other Turinese club Juventus, to recruit Raimundo Orsi, considered to be the most influential player in the Argentinian national side. Orsi's play was said to possess 'a finesse, an ability, an ease and an elegance which the entire public admired'.[27] His 100,000 lire transfer from Independiente de Avellaneda to Turin was a reasonable sum, given that Juventus had paid double the previous year to the provincial club Casale for Umberto Calligaris, an Italian international full-back. Arriving with his wife, sister-in-law and infant, Orsi thought he had received the blessing of his federation.[28] But the Argentinian press began to make strong allegations: *El Mundo Deportivo* announced to its readers that 'It is not Juventus that pays for his transfer, it is the fascist government directly'. The same paper defined him as 'a pure Creole'.[29] The evidence suggests that following the press campaign the Argentinian FA refused to endorse the move and Orsi consequently suffered a year of 'quarantine' on his arrival in Italy. His departure was seen as a major setback for Argentinian football and indicated the possible risks if second-generation Italian immigrants began to re-establish links with the country of their parents. When a Buenos Aires newspaper complained that 'The Italians aim to

25. Guglielmo Tornabuoni, *L'ascesa del calcio in Italia*, Milan: Gazzetta dello sport ed., 1932, p. 75; Brunori, *Torino*, p. 50.

26. Pierluigi Brunori, *AS Roma: dal Testaccio alla dimensione vertice*, Florence: M'Litograph, 1981, p. 41.

27. *Le miroir des sports,* 19 June 1928.

28. *La gazzetta dello sport*, 4 October 1928.

29. *La gazzetta dello sport*, 26 October 1928.

build up a national team at the expense of Argentina. The fascist government is trying to convince *criollo* players to accept its money and transform them into Italian players', the Italian press answered: 'Orsi a *criollo*? That's a joke.'[30] On 5 October 1928, only two days after Orsi's arrival from the transatlantic steamer *Diulio, La gazzetta dello sport* published an article entitled 'Is Orsi an Italian citizen?' The newspaper referred directly to the text of national law: 'The Italian citizen born and resident in a foreign state for which he is considered to be a national by birth keeps his Italian citizenship'.[31] The article added that 'There is no question about the rights of Orsi to acquire Italian citizenship. He has always been an Italian. For this reason, we don't have sons of Argentinians in our teams.' It concluded that 'In the case of Orsi, we cannot talk about his naturalization or the renewal of his Italian citizenship, as he is somebody who has always had an Italian passport'.[32] Orsi and the other South Americans who came to Europe in the 1930s were known in Italy as the *rimpatriati*. Unlike the *oriundi* of the post-war period – with whom they are often confused – these migrants had no need to 'become' Italian or reclaim their European nationality as they were legally dual citizens.[33]

A former employee of an Argentinian railway company, Orsi was almost twenty-seven years old at the time of his move. He was described as a very normal man, 'modest and dressed modestly'.[34] But Orsi's status was to change quickly as he became wealthy, receiving a fabulous monthly salary of 8,000 lire (fifteen times the wage of a primary school teacher and eight times the average earnings of a doctor or a lawyer) with bonuses such as a car (a FIAT 509 produced by his employer) and an apartment. In the course of his seven-year contract with Juventus, Orsi proved to be a sound investment. He was part of a team which won five successive league titles (1931–35) and the World Cup in 1934. What is more, his case embodies the complexity of dual citizenship. Although his parents had been born in the province of Genoa, he was only able to speak Spanish on his arrival. This did not prevent his integration, however, and he was quickly fluent in Italian. Just a year after his arrival, he was selected for the national team, a decision opposed by the *azzurri* coach Rangone, who resigned. But for many, his arrival was seen as a means of improving the quality of the national team: 'For the good of Italian

30. *La gazzetta dello sport*, 26 October 1928; Ghirelli, *Storia del calcio in Italia*, p. 100.

31. Ferruccio Pastore, 'Droit de la nationalité et migrations internationales: le cas italien', in P. Weil and R. Hansen (eds), *Nationalité et citoyenneté en Europe*, Paris: La découverte, 1999, pp. 95–116.

32. *La gazzetta dello sport*, 5 October 1928. It is worth noting that there were still 800,000 people with Italian passports in Argentina at this time.

33. A. Papa and G. Panico make this point in their *Storia sociale del calcio in Italia*, Bologna: il mulino.

34. *Guerin sportivo*, 10 October 1928.

football, it is logical, acceptable and nationalistic (in the positive sense of the word) to look for the children of our colonies, the sons of Italian emigrants. They can always chose to become Italians'.[35] The pre-fascist governments were blamed for compelling Orsi's parents to leave Italy for Argentina; the fascist authorities were simply 'reclaiming Orsi and Libonatti, with their Italian names and Latin blood'.[36] If the success of Orsi and Libonatti accelerated the process of the reintegration of footballers from South America, Italian clubs were also aided by the world economic crash, the political instability in Buenos Aires in 1930 and 1931, and the slow process of professionalization in South American football, all of which made potential emigrants more willing to board a Europe-bound steamer.[37]

The next import, Renato Cesarini, was signed by Juventus from the Buenos Aires club Chacarita Juniors in the winter of 1929 for a monthly salary of 4,000 lire. Recommended by his friend Orsi, he was an international inside-forward. Cesarini's entire life was based around his dual identity. Born in 1906 in Senigallia, near Ancona, his family emigrated to Buenos Aires when he was just a year old.[38] He made his international debut in 1922, at the tender age of sixteen. If all talented players in Argentina quickly acquired nicknames, it was significant that Cesarini had two: *El Pelotazo* (the ball wizard) and *El Tano* (the Italian).[39] As well as playing for Argentina and Italy, he later became a famous manager in both countries, with Juventus in the 1950s and River Plate in the 1960s. His legacy to football on both sides of the Atlantic has been profound. He is one of the few players to give his name to an Italian football expression, the *Zona Cesarini*, which describes a goal scored in the last few minutes of a match. His name was also given to a professional club in Argentina, Renato Cesarini from the Rosario district.

In common with his predecessors, Cesarini's image combined an affinity with music and dancing with his football talent. According to the Italian press, Orsi too was an accordion player who practised whenever he could. When visiting a night club on one occasion he was said to have played a real Argentinian tango on his own violin because he disliked the music on offer.[40] Another press report written during preparation for the 1934 World Cup with the national team stated that: 'As soon as he wakes up, Mumò Orsi exercises his Bandoneon'.[41] Cesarini played guitar but was more admired for his dancing ability. One Juventus history noted that

35. *Il Littoriale*, 6 October 1928.

36. *Il regime fascista*, 25 June 1933.

37. H.S. Ferns, *National Economic Histories: The Argentine Republic 1516–1971*, Newton Abbot: David & Charles, 1973, pp.116–38.

38. *La stampa*, 14 February 1930; see also Dietschy, 'Football et société à Turin', pp. 272–7.

39. Bayer, *Fútbol argentino*, p. 45; Dietschy, 'Football et société à Turin', p. 277.

40. *Guerin sportivo*, 10 October 1928.

41. *La nazione*, 31 May 1934. Clearly Orsi played the bandoneon but the Italian commentators seemed not to appreciate the difference between this instrument and the European accordion.

He even managed to open a fashionable ballroom in Piazza Castello. Two orchestras played alternatively. They offered the public a series of tangos which were very fashionable at the time. Cesarini always danced himself and dressed his orchestras as *gauchos*.[42]

Cesarini was an extravagant character who was known to go out with a monkey on his shoulder, went to bed when his team-mates were waking up and took every opportunity to smoke, drink and seduce women.

Impressed by the success of its artistic imports, Juventus continued to invest in Argentina and in the summer of 1931 signed Luis Monti, the well-built defender of the Argentinian national team which had lost the World Cup Final the year before. This defeat was to become one of the two major crises of the Argentinian game in the twentieth century. The result had sent shockwaves through Argentinian football with Monti, in particular, accused of showing a lack of virility and self-control.[43] This defeat against the 'eternal rivals' accelerated the split of Argentinian football into a professional and amateur association in 1931 and led to a players' strike. In the context of a world economic crisis and financial uncertainty many Argentinian footballers preferred to seek their fortunes in Italy.[44] The political situation in Argentina after the coup d'état in 1930 was particularly conducive to emigration to Italy. The new president General Uriburu and the nationalist government in Buenos Aires shared with Italian fascism the political values of nationalism, militarism, anti-communism and anti-liberalism. Moreover, in its rhetoric and some of its policies, Buenos Aires appeared increasingly willing to collaborate with the fascist regime.[45] The image of a strong nation became essential on both sides of the Atlantic. For this reason, Monti's persona changed when he arrived at Juventus. He was said to have replaced the myth of the weak 'mandolin' Italian players with a model more suited to the strong image of the Italian fascists.[46] Monti was anything but an artist. He is still the only player to have participated in successive World Cup finals with two different teams. A loser and almost a traitor for Argentina in 1930, he had become a national model of physical strength for Italy by 1934.

42. Renato Tavella and Franco Ossola, *Il romanzo della grande Juventus*, Milan: Newton and Compton, 1997, p. 94.

43. Bayer, *Fútbol argentino*, p. 37.

44. Ariel Scher and Hector Palomino, *Fútbol: pasión de multitudes y de elites*, Buenos Aires: CISEA, 1988, p. 26–7.

45. Alain Rouquié, *Pouvoir militaire et société politique en République Argentine*, Paris: Presses de la fondation des sciences politiques, 1977, pp. 207–17.

46. Felice Fabrizio, *Sport e fascismo: la politica sportiva del regime 1924–1936*, Rimini/Florence: Guaraldi, 1976, p. 63; Papa and Panico, *Storia sociale del calcio in Italia*, pp. 158–63.

Guillermo Stabile, known as *El Filtrador* (the infiltrator), signed for Genoa at the end of 1930 after being top scorer in the World Cup. He did not come alone, encouraging his close friends Esposto, Orlandini and Evaristo to follow him.[47] A biography published in the French weekly *Match* revealed that his father was Italian by birth and his mother was born Argentinian from Italian parents. He was the fourth of ten children of a working-class family and was said to have accepted the transfer to Italy because 'he had hoped this would enable him to build a house for his parents, brothers and sisters'.[48] His transfer had been facilitated by his occupation as a customs officer at Buenos Aires harbour and with the apparent involvement of the captain of the transatlantic liner *Conte Rosso*, who happened to be a Genoa fan. At the time of Stabile's departure, *El Gráfico* was moved to comment that:

> We must not be egotistical. Orsi, Cesarini, Stabile and all those crossing frontiers in search of better horizons . . . leave to conquer other lands. The country is now a little small for us, and a good football lesson given on one of our pitches no longer dazzles anyone. For many years we have held the Chair in dribbling and in scoring goals. For that reason, it is necessary to go outside; the good players that do us proud abroad are working patriotically. Stabile goes to Italy, not to defend football in the peninsula, but to defend *criollo* football, since he is a *criollo* player.[49]

Three days after his arrival, Stabile scored three goals for his new club and quickly became a local star. Unfortunately, his Italian career was disrupted by a broken leg which kept him out for more than a year. But the flow of Argentinians continued and a trio composed of Stagnaro, *El Pirata Negro* (the Black Pirate), Guaita, *El Conejito* (the Small Rabbit) and Scopelli, *El Tano* (the Italian), signed in 1933 for Roma. Discussions about their right to represent Italy continued, with one journalist in favour of their importation commenting that 'if they couldn't play for the national team, it would be like denying them the qualities and sentiments of Italians'.[50] Three Argentinian imports – Monti, Orsi and Guaita – were among the eleven Italians who won the world title in 1934 but, interestingly, the regime did not accentuate their role in the victory. None of them, for instance, received the decoration for sporting merit from the Duce. The three footballers who *were* decorated – Meazza, Allemandi and Ferraris – were more representative of the qualities dear to Musso-lini.[51] The situation would become more difficult for the 'Romans' a year later.

47. On Stabile, see *Guerin sportivo*, 14 October 1981.
48. *Match*, 26 April, 24 May 1938.
49. *El Gráfico*, 589, 1930, p. 37 quoted and translated in Archetti, *Masculinities*, p. 65.
50. *Gazzetta dello sport*, 27 January 1933.
51. F. Gargani, *Italiani e stranieri alla mostra della rivoluzione fascista*, Rome: Saie, 1935, p. 550.

Three days before the beginning of the 1935/36 season, the Roma trio left Italy to return to South America. They were castigated in the Italian press and even accused of having illegally exported gold and money. The three had decided to leave their 'second home' to avoid taking part in the Ethiopian War. In the purest fascist style, *Il Littoriale* titled an article 'It's Disgusting' and was of the opinion that the trio had

left like robbers, head down and pale with anxiety but with wallets full of Italian money. Twice robbers in fact because they stole our money as well as our confidence. We received them as brothers coming back home, as blood from our blood. We offered them the passion of our sporting crowds, the applause of the stadiums, money and wealth and now they leave as mercenaries. They were not Italian . . . Fundamentally, we are relieved, as their departure is a kind of purification of our nation. We didn't want any sheep dressed as lions. We don't want to continue to feed these snakes. When the so-called double citizenship only serves untrue Italians, we want and we claim for a single citizenship. If they are Italian, they can't share it with anything else . . . If in South America there is somebody who doesn't want to serve his nation in the army and therefore remembers that he is Italian and goes to Italy, we don't want him. We don't want any deserters; we want true Italians. For us these deserters don't exist. It's disgusting.[52]

Bruno Roghi, the editor of *Gazzetta dello sport*, considered the case of the departed players and anticipated the future of the other *rimpatriati* in the Italian league:

Tomorrow, they will notice that something is broken in their heart. The misery of their action, the unforgettable shame which is now attached to their soul will remain . . . To Guaita, Scopelli and Stagnaro, we give the best possible passport: remorse. Regarding those 'steamer-Italians' who play in our home league, it would be inhuman to target them now. Many times we have expressed doubts about the real benefits for our football to copy and oversee their methods but this is only a sporting question. Morally, these boys need time to become like us. We don't yet need to be automatically suspicious – not all of them are like Guaita. In a sporting sense, South American athletes don't teach ours, because their style is too personal and Orsi, for example, didn't teach anything to anyone, but they have often been models in discipline and professional loyalty. The whole question, therefore, is very delicate.[53]

Guaita, in fact, was the perfect example of a hybrid Argentine. His father came from Lombardy and his mother was Spanish. After returning to South America he became a prison administrator and developed rehabilitation programmes for the inmates, many of which included football.[54] His obituaries on both sides of the

52. *Il Littoriale*, 23 September 1935.
53. *Gazzetta dello sport*, 24 September 1935.
54. Serra, *Storia del calcio*, p. 102.

Atlantic in 1959 presented him as a humanist, a great sportsman and, posthumously, as a great *Italian* footballer.[55] After this episode the number of Argentinian players in Italy diminished considerably. From the thirty-one under contract on 1 September 1935, there were only eleven a year later. This example shows how the question of the migration of footballers cannot be disconnected from its political context. It is true that from 1933 and the creation of the Argentinian Football Association (AFA), professionalism was fully recognized and more attractive for the *criollos*. But at the same time the identification of the *rimpatriati* players with fascism complicated any return to Argentina. In this context, some, like Orsi and Cesarini, did return to South America for good but Stabile and half a dozen other Italo-Argentines found contracts in France. The quantitative as well as qualitative contribution of the Argentines would remain important but low during the last decade of fascism and, significantly, no other *criollo* would play in the national team in the fascist period (see Tables 3.1 and 3.2).

Brazilians and Uruguayans

In Brazil in the 1930s, 34.1 per cent of the five million immigrants were of Italian origin. For the first time in 1870, Italian immigrants had outnumbered the Portuguese and, until the First World War, Italy supplied the greatest share of new arrivals.[56] These immigrants were mainly urban dwellers, with São Paulo and Rio de Janeiro having the largest Italian communities. That football had become a particularly popular pastime among these immigrants was testified to by the fact that the sporting club of the Italian community in São Paulo, Palestra Italia, was the largest and most prominent of all Italian associations or societies in the city. It could claim 5,000 members by the early 1930s, compared to the few hundred members of the Cultural Institute Dante Alighieri, the Republican Society Oberdan and the Italian Circle of the Fascist Party.[57] The club's influence spread far beyond the Italians themselves, reaching wider success by winning the São Paulo championship eleven times between 1909 and 1942.

The activity of Palestra Italia goes some way to explaining the overall transfer of Italo-Brazilians to Italy, as fourteen of the twenty-six registered Brazilian footballers in Italy between 1929 and 1943 were former members of the club. Unlike in Argentina, these 'Italians' used football as a means of division rather than integration. In São Paulo, a rapidly expanding urban centre whose population

55. *Il calcio illustrato*, 29 March 1964

56. E. Bradford Burns, *A History of Brazil*, New York: Columbia University Press, 1993, pp. 216, 315.

57. Angelo Trento, 'Le associazioni italiane a São Paulo', in F.J. Devoto and E.J. Minguez (eds) *Asociacionismo, trabajo e identidad étnica. Los italianos en América Latina en una perspectiva comparada*, Buenos Aires: Cemla, 1992, pp. 31–57.

quadrupled between 1850 and 1920, the immigration of the Italians reached impressive levels. Around 1920 there were allegedly more Italians in São Paulo than in Venice. The community had maintained strong links with Italy. It was Emmanuele Carta, a pasta salesman from São Paulo, who wrote to Juventus in 1931 to suggest the acquisition of the Palestra Italia player Sernagiotto.[58] He was one of thirty-nine players who crossed the Atlantic in the summer of 1931, although only about half of these found contracts in Italy.[59] Sernagiotto cost Juventus only 20,000 lire, one-twelfth of the most expensive move of the year, Colombari's 250,000 transfer from Torino to Naples, thus revealing the economic advantages of the South American market. In 1933, at the peak of the Brazilian emigration (and the world economic crisis) Lazio, under the patronage of General Vaccaro, head of the Milizia and chairman of the Italian federation, recruited some twelve Italo-Brazilians, including the coach Amilcar Barbuy. The team was known simply as *Brasilazio*.

Yet as Tables 3.1 and 3.2 indicate, apart from the 1931–35 period, Brazilian-born professionals played only a marginal role in Italian football compared with that of the Argentines. This can be explained first of all by the recurring problem of the *saudade*, or homesickness, suffered particularly by Brazilians transferred to Europe. The Italian winter, although hardly cold by northern European standards, represented a particularly difficult period for those migrants who were missing home. The death of Ottavio Fantoni, Lazio's half-back, on 8 February 1935, had a major impact on the attitude of the Brazilian exiles. He had played in Rome with his two cousins, featuring once in the Italian national side. His Italian origins were unquestionable as both of his parents had been born in Tuscany, and he was described by the press not as an artist but a professional – 'serious, brave and correct'. Fantoni had sustained what looked like a minor nose injury in early January, which subsequently became infected. A team-mate, Silvio Piola, remembers that Fantoni contracted septicaemia and died in a matter of weeks under indescribable pain.[60] Ten days later Frione, a young Uruguayan centre-half with Ambrosiana-Inter, also died, three weeks after a match against Naples in which he had contracted pneumonia.[61] In both cases, the Fascist rhetoric emphasized the love these players had exhibited for their teams and the pride they had felt to be back in Italy. They had even been prepared, it was suggested, to die with the club badge close to their heart. In reality, of course, these incidents made the South Americans uneasy. They

58. *Guerin sportivo*, 20 June 1984.

59. Waldenyr Caldas, *O pontapé inicial: Memória do futebol Brasileiro (1894–1933)*, São Paulo: Ibrisca, 1990, p. 202–3.

60. Marco Barberis, *La leggenda di Silvio Piola*, Milan: Sugarco, 1986, p. 29; *Gazzetta dello sport*, 9–10 February 1935.

61. *Gazzetta dello sport*, 19 February 1935.

The South American Artists

Table 3.1 The *Rimpatriati* in the Italian Professional League, 1929–43

Year	Argentina	Brazil	Uruguay	Total
1929–30	6	2	–	8
1930–31	12	5	1	18
1931–32	17	13	4	34
1932–33	15	15	11	41
1933–34	22	19	10	51
1934–35	21	11	13	45
1935–36	31	7	11	49
1936–37	11	4	9	24
1937–38	11	4	14	29
1938–39	11	2	13	26
1939–40	19	2	11	32
1940–41	19	1	8	28
1941–42	16	–	7	23
1942–43	16	–	4	20
Total	**60**	**26**	**32**	**118**

Note: The table only includes those who played in Divisions One and Two and came from a South American club. We counted around sixty other South Americans who arrived in Italy but never played in the league.
Source: R. Barlassina, *Agendina del calcio*, vol. 1 to 11, Milan: Gazzetta dello sport, 1933–1942; Carlo F. Chiesa and Alessandro Lanzarini, 'Il grande libro degli stranieri', special insert, *Guerin sportivo*, 1, 1995.

Table 3.2 Contribution of the *Rimpatriati* to the Italian National Team, 1929–43

Players	Country of Origin	Caps with Italy	Main Honours
Orsi	Argentina	35	World Cup 1934
Andreolo	Uruguay	26	World Cup 1938
Monti	Argentina	18	World Cup 1934
Libonatti	Argentina	17	Central European Cup 1927/28
Demaria	Argentina	13	World Cup 1934
Cesarini	Argentina	11	Central European Cup 1931/32
Guaita	Argentina	10	World Cup 1934
Guarisi	Brazil	6	World Cup 1934
Faccio	Uruguay	5	
Sansone	Uruguay	3	Central European Cup 1931/32
Fedullo	Uruguay	2	
Mascheroni	Uruguay	2	
O. Fantoni	Brazil	1	
Puricelli	Uruguay	1	
Scopelli	Argentina	1	

Source: Data from Fabrizio Melegari (ed.), *Almanacco illustrato del calcio 1999*, Modena: Panini, 1998

were more than willing to earn their living in Italy but were certainly not prepared to die away from home. The second reason for the marginalization of the Brazilians was the difficulty they experienced integrating into Italian society. Brazilians were accused of making little effort to speak the Italian language, which led to increased dressing-room tensions and rivalries. As a result, club directors and supporters were distrustful of the real identity and quality of these Brazilian 'wonders'. By no means all the Brazilian *rimpatriati* succeeded in Italy. Four players from Palestra Italia arrived in February 1933 in Naples, introduced as true champions. They left under less triumphant circumstances. Ragusa and Goliardo played only one league match, Santillo two, while Barilotti did not feature once in the team. They are still remembered in Napoli club histories as *i bidoni brasiliani*, the Brazilian fakes.[62]

On both sides of the Atlantic there was considerable debate about the true Italian origins of these Brazilians. At Torino, for instance, Bertini was sent back to Brazil in order to prove his Italian citizenship because 'the federation had received whispers from South America which called into question the real Italian identity of the player'.[63] Certain players may indeed have changed their names to make their Italian roots seem more plausible and improve their chances of a move to Italy but the majority had no need to do so as they had been active in the Italian movement before coming to Europe. This emphasis on the true Italianness of the Brazilians effectively excluded those non-whites who were becoming increasingly significant in Brazil's multiracial football.[64] Interestingly, the migrating players were not known under the same name in the two countries. Players who in Brazil were only known by their footballing 'stage names' were compelled in Italy to use their Italian surnames. Thus Filò in Brazil was Guarisi in Italy, Ratto was Castelli and Pepe became Rizzetti. This twin personality is emblematic of the complex position of these second-generation immigrants. From the mid-1930s the import of South Americans had its critics in Italy. 'We are fed up with "Italians" who are unable to speak Italian, and do not assist their team-mates. It may seem xenophobic, but we prefer national products.'[65] When in 1941 Brazil entered the war on the side of the allies, the Italian organizations and societies were dismantled. Palestra Italia became Palmeiras and the few remaining Italo-Brazilians were expelled from Italian football.

62. G. Nicolini, *La storia del Napoli*, Rome: Editrice Italiana, 1967, p. 52.

63. *Gazzetta dello sport*, 22 January 1933.

64. Sergio Leite Lopes and Jean-Pierre Faguer, 'L'invention du style brésilien. Sport, journalisme et politique au Brésil', *Actes de la recherche en sciences sociales*, 103, June 1994, pp. 27–35.

65. Ermanno Santorro, 'Dei calciatori di importazione', *Milano*, 19 March 1934 quoted in Felice Fabrizio, 'Funzione e strumentalizzazione dell'attività ginnico-sportiva dilletantistica e professionale in Italia nei contesti del regime fascista: dalle olimpiadi del 1924 a quelle del 1936', Unpublished Doctoral Thesis, Università Cattolicà Milan, 1973, p. 196.

Along with the Argentinians and Brazilians, the third main strand of this South American emigration consisted of Uruguayans. As shown in Table 3.1, their transatlantic journeys began later but can be interpreted as the most durable of the three. Like Juventus and Genoa with their Argentines and Lazio and Napoli with their Brazilians, certain clubs decided to specialize in Uruguayan imports. Fedullo then Ochiuzzi, Sansone, Albanese, Andreolo, Porta, Liguera and Puricelli all played for Bologna while Pedro Petrone, the centre-forward of the Uruguayan national team, chose Fiorentina and was quickly followed by Laino, Gringa, Sarni and Antonioli. At Inter, two other World Cup winners, Mascheroni and Scarone, were accompanied by the Frione brothers, Faccio, Porta and Tambasco. Their import was of some significance to Italian football. While Andreolo became the only *rimpatriato* member of the Italian World Cup winners of 1938, for Bologna the contribution of the Uruguayans was essential and enduring. Sansone was a first-team regular for ten seasons, Fedullo and Andreolo for nine and Puricelli for five.[66] In 1989, Raffaele Sansone explained the circumstances of his recruitment by Bologna at the age of twenty-one:

> In 1929 and 1930, there was still no recognized professionalism in Uruguay. I played then for Peñarol and worked at the building of the Centenario Stadium for the World Cup. The club gave me extra cash for the matches, but no real salary. At that time my friend Fedullo played for Bologna. He mentioned my name to the Bologna directors who were looking for new Uruguayan signings and had a kind of agent who lived in Montevideo. He came to offer me a contract. I accepted immediately and arrived a month later via Genoa . . . I had no real problem with the Italian language. At home, with my parents, we used a mixture of Italian and Spanish. And in Bologna, Fedullo introduced me to all the other players.[67]

All the Bologna players showed an obvious attachment to their second home. With the exception of Fedullo, they all married Italian women and stayed in the peninsula after their careers.[68] Ettore Puricelli trained various professional clubs including Milan and Foggia in *Serie A* before retiring in Rome where he was able to buy a comfortable house,[69] while Andreolo, the most successful of all, had to accept a less prestigious coaching job in the poor southern town of Potenza where he died in 1981. Petrone, by contrast, one of the most popular and best-paid players of his

---

66. Pierre Lanfranchi, 'Bologna, the team that shook the world!', *International Journal of the History of Sport*, 8, 3, 1989, p. 342.

67. Interview of authors with Raffaele Sansone in Bologna, 21 July 1989.

68. Rafael Bayce, *100 años de fútbol*, Montevideo, 1970, p. 509; *Il calcio illustrato*, 26 April 1964.

69. *Guerin sportivo*, 24 September 1986.

day, finished his life selling vegetables in Montevideo's open market after being employed as a hotel waiter.

The contribution of the South Americans during this period has been summarized by Giuseppe Meazza, captain of the 1938 Italian national side: 'We had a temperamental affinity with the South Americans; their superiority in ball control and juggling techniques helped us immensely'.[70] A more recent account added: 'Rare were the flops. The majority of them were a clear class above. They were very superior champions'.[71] As we can see from Table 3.2, these migrants were not only instrumental in the development of club football, but also strongly influenced the national team. The significance of their legacy was apparent during the 1978 World Cup in Argentina. The Italian national team invited Orsi and Monti, two elderly men still living in South America, to their hotel and as special guests to all their matches in recognition of the links which they had established with Italian football.

From this point on, the footballer from abroad had a new and exciting resonance. Directors and supporters began to treat the arrival of every steamer as the promise of a saviour, a player who could change the fate of their club. At the same time, there was a risk and anxiety associated with these artists who, suffering from *saudade*, might leave in the night on the return boat to South America. Thoughts of expectation and disillusionment automatically accompanied the recruitment of overseas players.

The Italian experience may have been unique but some South Americans were also to be found in France and Spain during the 1930s. Sochaux, the club owned by the car company Peugeot, followed the example of Juventus and began to recruit South Americans of French origin. Five Uruguayans and three Argentinians played for the club between 1934 and the Second World War. One, Conrad Ross, was initially player-manager, while Pedro Duhart and Hector Cazenave were successful enough to be selected for the French national team. In contrast, Irrigaray and Ithurbide, two players with Basque roots, and Miguel Angel Lauri, a regular in the Argentinian national side, made a less significant impact. Reports alleged deep rivalries between the South Americans and the rest of the team.[72] Some two dozen other Argentinians figured in the French league during the course of the 1930s. Half of them, including Scopelli and Stabile, arrived from Italy at the time of the Ethiopian expedition.[73] Another Argentinian who had started his career in Morocco

---

70. *Lo sport illustrato*, 5 August 1954.

71. Angelo Rovelli, 'Il romanzo degli stranieri', in L. Giannelli (ed.), *100 anni di campionato di calcio*, Florence: Scramasax, 1997, p. 52.

72. Alfred Wahl and Pierre Lanfranchi, *Les footballeurs professionnels des années trente à nos jours*, Paris: Hachette, 1995, p. 96.

73. M. Barreaud, *Dictionnaire des footballeurs étrangers du championnat professionnel français (1932–1997)*, Paris: L'Harmattan, 1998, pp. 23–4.

was to become particularly famous. Helenio Herrera played for Second Division Charleville and Roubaix before beginning his managerial career in France (see Chapter 7). Brazilians were rarer still, with only two employed by French clubs at the time. One, the mulatto goalkeeper of Marseilles in the 1930s, was known in Brazil as Jaguare and in France as Vasconcellos.[74] On balance, the South American influence in France during the 1930s was marginal when set against that of the British and Eastern Europeans, something which may be explained by the negligible French emigration to South America.

The same could not be claimed of Spain. In the years preceding the Spanish Civil War a number of famous South American footballers came to Spain, although not all were accepted with open arms. The Uruguayan Scarone was boycotted by his team-mates at Barcelona in 1926. His immense talent with a football was not enough in the eyes of his colleagues to compensate for his inferior colonial accent and working-class background.[75] Circumstances also conspired against Enrique Fernández, a member of the Uruguayan World Cup winning squad of 1930, who played for Barcelona from 1934 to 1936. While he was on holiday in Uruguay during the summer of 1936, the club asked him not to return because of the Civil War.[76] Jaguare/Vasconcellos, before going to Marseilles, and Dos Santos, famous in Brazil under the stage name Fausto, recognized as the first black stars of Vasco De Gama,[77] also stayed for a short period with Barcelona while another compatriot, Giudicelli, moved from Torino to Real Madrid. In general, however, the impact of South American players in Spain before 1939 was also fairly limited.

The disruption of the Spanish Civil War and the Second World War undoubtedly affected some of Europe's South American migrants. In a few cases, this led to the unusual phenomenon of reverse migration from Europe to the Americas. Isidro Langara and Angel Zubieta, two Basque players from Bilbao, were republicans who chose, in the wake of Franco's victory, to settle in Argentina while with a Basque touring party. They became star attractions for San Lorenzo, Langara even going on to top the Argentinian goal-scoring list in 1942. Not to be outdone, River Plate also had its Basque, Cilauren. The majority of the Basque squad remained in Latin America, generally in Mexico and Chile, with only two players agreeing to return to Franco's Spain.[78] The Second World War had the effect of pushing the

74. L. Grimaud and A. Pécheral, *La grande histoire de l'OM*, Paris: Robert Laffont, 1984, p. 204 have written that 'the Jaguar was almost a mythical hero in Marseilles'.

75. A. Closa and J. Blanco, *Diccionari del Barça*, Barcelona: Enciclopèdia catalana, 1999, p. 345; José Luis Marco and Antonio Hernaez, *CF Barcelona Campeones*, Madrid: Mirasierra, 1974, p. 62.

76. Closa and Blanco, *Diccionari del Barça*, p. 142.

77. Leite Lopes, 'L'invention du style brésilien'.

78. Joseba Gotzon Varela Gómez, *Historia de la selección de fútbol de Euskadi*, Bilbao: Beitia, 1998; Patxo Unzueta, 'Fútbol y nacionalismo vasco', in S. Segurola (ed.), *Fútbol y pasiones políticas*,

majority of South Americans out of France. In the autumn of 1939 and the spring of 1940 many opted for the calm of Portugal to continue playing football. Jaguare/ Vasconcellos, once again, left Marseilles for Porto together with Hermes Borges from Antibes. The Argentinians Raul Sbarra, the brothers Hector and Horacio Tellechea, plus Oscar Tarrio and Scopelli, remained in Portugal for some years as players and then managers. The immigration of South Americans before 1939 was thus concentrated in the Latin countries of the south, barely affecting the rest of Europe at all.

The 1940s and 1950s: The Strike, the Colombian Episode and Migration to Europe

The Second World War, in which Argentina remained neutral, marked the high point of Argentinian football. Following the introduction of professionalism, average attendances rose from 7,696 in the five years from 1931–35 to 11,736 between 1941 and 1945. This was a time of Argentinian hegemony over South American football.[79] Players from a host of South American countries acquired professional contracts with clubs from Buenos Aires. The Argentinian league produced outstanding players such as River Plate's forward line of Muñoz, Moreno, Pedernera, Labruna and Loustau, which is remembered as *la máquina* (the machine) and has acquired an almost mythical status in Argentina.[80] In 1947, the Argentinian Players' Union was founded and during the following autumn the players went on strike, leading to the longest and most serious industrial dispute in world football history, only resolved in May 1949. By that time, more than fifty players had left for Colombia.

The official history of Argentinian football described the strike as a massive loss of football blood. Another study saw it as marking the beginning of the degeneration of Argentinian football: 'From that moment on, migration to other latitudes – with the accompanying financial gains this implied – became the natural aspiration for a good number of Argentinian footballers.'[81] Almost every club was

Madrid: Debate, 1999, pp. 147–67; Manuel Leguineche, Patxo Unzueta and Santiago Segurola, *Athletic 100: Conversaciones en La Catedral,* Madrid: El País Aguilar,1998, pp. 37–38.

79. Scher and Palomino, *Fútbol: pasión de multitudes y de elites*, p. 46.

80. Pablo A. Ramirez, 'Alzas y bajas en el fervor por el fútbol', *Todo es historia*, 23, 272, 1990, pp. 88–96; Carlos Peucelle, *Fútbol todo tiempo e historia de 'la Máquina'*, Buenos Aires: Axioma, 1975.

81. Alonso, *Cien años con el fútbol*, pp. 68–9; Scher and Palomino, *Fútbol: pasión de multitudes y de elites*, p. 49; Armando Ramos Ruiz, *Nuestro fútbol: grandeza y decadencia*, Buenos Aires: LV Producciones, 1973; Rodolfo Chisleanski, 'La huelga del 48', *La Razón*, 28 January 1985 gives a full list of the players who migrated to Colombia.

touched by the flight to Colombia: River Plate lost five players, whereas San Lorenzo, Rosario Central and Independiente each lost three. Colombia was not, however, the only destination. Moreno, one of *la máquina*, chose to emigrate to Chile. Juan Carlos Hohberg went to Montevideo's Peñarol, while the Boca star Boye, San Lorenzo's Aballay and many others opted for Italy, which had by this time officially reopened its borders to foreigners. France received a handful, like Cisneros from Gimnasia y Esgrima (via Club Loyola Caracas in Venezuela) and Alberto Muro, who travelled to Sochaux via Nacional Montevideo. Argentinians were also to be found in Mexico and Central America. Only Racing managed to hang on to its entire squad. The economic motives which pushed other players to leave the country seem in Racing's case to have induced them to remain. In 1951, the club offered its professionals excellent salaries and major bonuses, such as the latest model Chevrolet, after their third consecutive league success.[82]

The Colombian rebels were some of the most prestigious players in Argentina. Alfredo Di Stefano, a promising forward who had won the league with his club River Plate in 1947, scoring twenty-seven goals in the process, was part of the Colombian expedition, recruited together with Néstor Rossi by his former team captain Adolfo Pedernera.[83] Years later, Di Stefano recalled his experience at Bogotá where he had signed for Millonarios:

> In Bogotá the Millonarios players were really living a life of . . . millionaires. Every day they went to training at the end of the morning, then everybody was invited for lunch at the club's headquarters. The Colombian cuisine, based on rice, manioc, pork meat and fried bananas was a discovery for us. They drank a special kind of beer, the Bavaria, which was fantastic. And after that, we had a Colombian coffee, rightly considered the best in the world. Later, a siesta, and sometimes the cinema and a quick visit to the dancing. When you come from the country of the tango, you aren't ashamed to show that you possess the art of dancing.[84]

The contrast with the experience of the British migrants, discussed in the previous chapter, is striking. Four months after Di Stefano's arrival, Millonarios were champions and the club offered him a ticket to spend time in Buenos Aires, where he married before returning to Colombia with his wife. In his recollections, he tends to idealize his Colombian period. Supporters named the team 'the blue ballet' because they were considered not only athletes but players who could elevate

82. Pablo A. Ramírez, 'Política y fútbol', *Todo es historia*, 21, 248, 1988, pp. 34–43.

83. FIFA Archives, Ban on Argentinian Players 1950 (otherwise undated). Following Article 18 of the FIFA statutes, all Argentinian players signed by Colombian clubs without paying a transfer fee were banned from playing in all FIFA countries. These included Gorzo, Giudice, Pedernera, Néstor Rossi, Di Stefano, Fasciones, Navarro, Perucca, Benegas and Ferreyro.

84. *Miroir du football*, March to October 1961, June 1961.

football to an art. Their strategy was very simple: there were no defensive tactics, all the emphasis was on the attack. Apparently the directors left the players free to pick the team and decide how to play. They liked to win but never intended to humiliate their adversaries, sometimes beginning 'the ballet' when they were a few goals ahead but consciously choosing to score no more. As Bill Murray has noted, for the English (especially Franklin) this 'ball playing and exhibitionism' was evidence of a lack of discipline and an aversion to hard work.[85] For Di Stefano and others, Colombian football offered the freedom to play as artists.

Other outlaw clubs and leagues spread throughout Central America. More than sixty players had emigrated to Mexico's Liga Mayor in 1945 and 1946, while others went to Peru.[86] And when in May 1952 a group of entrepreneurs decided to create a professional club in Guatemala, independent of the national association, it was to Buenos Aires that they travelled to 'contract good players'. With the mediation of José Alberto Cevasco, an Argentinian citizen and the former manager of the Municipal de Guatemala club, they signed fifteen professionals for the new club which they called 'Palermo'. The expedition travelled back in a matter of days, with the exception of one new signing who, when the group stopped off in Santiago, changed his mind and returned to Buenos Aires. All the others continued the long journey despite having no clearance documents from their former clubs. Because they were not recognized by the national association, the outlaws were only allowed to play exhibition matches. On 22 June 1952, wearing identical colours to those of River Plate (a white shirt with a red diagonal stripe and black shorts), Palermo of Guatemala, a team composed entirely of Argentinians, met Cartago from Costa Rica in front of a full house, in what was the first professional football match in Guatemala. In the following weeks they played against a Mexican side and the Spanish club Celta Vigo.[87] It is difficult to say with any accuracy who these players were. No one on the list seems to have made any previous impression as a professional in Argentina. Most were probably reserves who, in this time of constant disputes between the AFA and the players' union, were keen to improve their low wages abroad.

In Europe, meanwhile, the rules regarding access to South American players had changed. From 1947, the Italian federation permitted its clubs to recruit five players from foreign associations, three of whom could be foreign citizens.[88] In March 1949, the Italian Football League introduced a further rule which stated

85. Murray, *Football: A History of the World Game*, p. 141.

86. Alonso, *Cien años con el fútbol*, p. 65.

87. José Antonio Guzmán, *Historia del fútbol de Guatemala*, Guatemala: Federación Nacional de Football, 1952, p. 222.

88. Rules of the Italian Federation, *Almanacco del calcio illustrato 1948*, Milan: Corriere della sera, 1947, p. 9.

that: 'Every team can have a maximum of three players from foreign associations. These must include the *oriundi* as well as the foreigner.' This document marked the appearance of a new word and a new concept.[89] The *oriundi* – the term means 'originally from' in Spanish – were South American players of Italian or Spanish origin who were able to have their 'original' citizenship reinstated. Crucially, for the Italian authorities the *oriundi* were not the same as the *rimpatriati* of the pre-war years, who had been regarded legally as Italians. For the first time, these South American imports were classified alongside foreign players rather than Italians. Although regulations alternated between defining them as 'foreigners' and 'Italians' for the next two decades, footballers were now effectively divided into three distinct categories: nationals, *oriundi* and foreigners. In Franco's Spain, a reformed constitution in 1954 made possible the establishment of dual nationality agreements with South American countries. This new policy was legitimized by the suggestion that 'Spain shares a spiritual mission with the countries with which she is inexorably linked'.[90] As a result, the number of *oriundi* arriving in the Spanish league increased, as did the possibility of South American players receiving Spanish citizenship. It is no coincidence that the transfers of Di Stefano and Héctor Rial to Real Madrid took place in the same season.

The case of Alfredo Di Stefano is instructive of the subtle changes in migration patterns from the 1930s to the 1950s. Di Stefano was the product of a multicultural immigration. Each of his grandparents had been born in a different country: one in Italy, one in Argentina, one in France and one in England. In Argentina his nickname was *El alemán* (the German) on account of his blonde hair and sturdy physique. After his sojourn in Colombia, he settled in Spain, acquired Spanish citizenship and played for the Spanish national side. His transfer from Millonarios to Real Madrid in 1953 marked the end of the Colombian mirage but also the integration of Franco's Spain through its chief ambassador, Real Madrid, and signalled the importance of foreign stars in the creation of the European Cup. From the early 1950s, the major Spanish clubs were keen to show their ability to compete in the international market place and buy the best 'products' available. Di Stefano's Real was said to have been used by Franco (a Di Stefano admirer himself) as evidence of Spain's re-emergence as a normalized European country.[91]

---

89. For a chronology of the regulations regarding foreign players in Italy, Bonizzoni, *Calciatori stranieri in Italia ieri e oggi*, pp. 224–5.

90. Francisco Javier Moreno Fuentes, 'La migration et le droit de la nationalité espagnole', in P. Weil and R. Hansen (eds), *Nationalité et citoyenneté en Europe*, Paris: La découverte, 1999, p. 129.

91. On this subject see the well-documented chapter on Di Stefano's transfer to Spain in Julián García Candau, *Madrid–Barça: Historia de un desamor*, Madrid: El País Aguilar, 1996, pp. 173–88; C. Fernández Santander, *El fútbol durante la guerra civil y el franquismo*, Madrid: San Martín, 1990, pp. 151–9.

In Italy, the pattern of South American recruitment had also changed. The thirty-five players recruited by Italian clubs in Brazil between 1949 and 1964 were no longer drawn from a single club as they had been in the 1930s, but from thirteen different ones. Moreover, the main exporting clubs were also the most successful ones: Botafogo Rio with seven players, Palmeiras (the former Palestra Italia) with four, Santos and Portuguesa with three. Black players also began to cross the Atlantic more frequently. The Uruguayan La Paz had moved to Naples in 1950 as the first black player in Italian professional football but he remained the exception for most of the decade. Black footballers only really became popular in Italy after the Brazilian World Cup victories of 1958 and 1962 and as a result of the Pele phenomenon. Amarildo, for example, who had replaced Pele in the 1962 World Cup Finals, moved from Botafogo to Milan. Cane arrived from the small Rio club Olaria to Naples, Jair moved from Portuguesa to Inter and Nene from Santos to Juventus. Another Black Brazilian featured in the society pages of the press more than the sporting section. Germano was transferred from Flamengo to Milan in 1962. He was rarely picked for the first team but his romance with Princess Agusta created a scandal which forced him to relocate to Genoa for a season before marrying the Princess and fleeing with his new wife and child to Standard Liège. Many of these players enjoyed long and impressive careers in Italy. Sergio Clerici and José Altafini played for eighteen seasons in the Italian league. The first had been transferred from Pele's Santos in 1960, and the second, a Palmeiras player, was Pele's substitute in Sweden. Angelo Sormani stayed for fifteen years, Luis Vinicio, Nene, Da Costa and Cane for thirteen while Amarildo, Cinesinho and Jair all played for a full decade in Italy.[92] All but one were strikers, a position which became synonymous with the Brazilian game. For Italian agents, South America provided a pool of attacking and creative talent.

Black Brazilians went to France as well. Brandaozinho played for each of the clubs of the Côte d'Azur – Cannes, Monaco and Nice – between 1952 and 1957. Another Brazilian, Yeso Amalfi, became famous in France as 'an artist, a poet and a whimsical footballer'.[93] In Spain, Didi moved from Brazil to Real Madrid in the late 1950s at the age of thirty-one. At Real he 'spent a season of bitter frustration' – some allege because of the colour of his skin, others because he was unable to get on with Puskas and Di Stefano – and returned to his former club Botafogo in time to pick up his second World Cup winner's medal with Brazil.[94]

On the South American scene, the Argentine national team had dominated the 1957 South American Championship in Peru. Their main attraction were the three

---

92. There were, of course, some cases of *saudade*, like Julinho, the Fiorentina star who was called 'Signor tristezza' in Florence and could not stand more than three years in Europe.

93. Ryswick, *100 000 heures de football*, p. 321.

94. Brian Glanville, *The Puffin Book of Footballers*, Harmondsworth: Penguin, 1978, p. 46.

central forwards – Angelillo, Maschio and Sivori – labelled 'The Angels with Dirty Faces' after the Hollywood movie. All twenty years of age at the time, they came from the popular suburbs of Buenos Aires and were perceived as football's 'bad boys'. The team of which they were a part scored some twenty-four goals in their five matches in Peru and were widely expected to repeat this success in Sweden a year later. Unfortunately, all three had by then left for Italy where they immediately received Italian citizenship. Omar Sivori, *El Cabezón* (the big head), was paid £91,000 by Juventus to forge an attacking partnership with John Charles. Angelillo, meanwhile, went to Inter and Maschio opted for Bologna. The goalkeeper of the team, 'Flaco' Domínguez, left at the same time for Real Madrid. Sivori, in particular, enjoyed phenomenal success in Italy, encouraging comparisons with his predecessors:

> The anecdotes regarding Sivori are rich and diverse even if he is not as excessive as Libonatti who used to buy twenty-five shirts at a time, or Cesarini who arrived one day to a training session wearing only a dressing-gown. In general, the *oriundi* are extravagant. Before every match Sivori bets with Juventus' Chairman Mr Agnelli, FIAT director: that if he scores a goal, he is allowed to smoke a cigarette as soon as he comes back to the dressing room. If not, the chairman himself lights his cigarette. Sivori is lazy. He likes to sleep until lunch time. He has missed training more than once, and has had to be woken up to get ready for matches. [95]

The freedom of the market allowed the directors of their Argentinian clubs to make a quick profit from the unexpected triumph of 'the Angels'. The national team, however, whose appearance at the World Cup Finals was the first since 1934, but still figured as one of the favourites, were fatally weakened. They crashed to defeat against Germany and were humiliated 6–1 by Czechoslovakia, with a team which actually included some of the previous generation of Argentine migrants, such as the 35-year-old Nestor Rossi. It was felt by some that the spoliation of the promising talent of Argentina by rich European clubs was destroying the very essence of the game. A British football magazine could claim that: 'There seems to be an unending flow of South American stars to the Old World; "Fame in South America – Fortune in Europe" has become the motto of many players born on the other side of the Atlantic'.[96] Football once again reflected the weakening of the South American economy. After 1950 Uruguayan clubs were unable to compete with the major Italian clubs and could do little to keep their best players. Pepe Schiaffino, Uruguay's best paid player, increased his salary three times over when he signed for Milan in 1954 earning seven times as much as Didi, the best-paid player in Brazil, and twice as much even as Di Stefano at Real Madrid.[97]

95. *Miroir sprint*, 15 February 1960.
96. *World Soccer*, May 1961.
97. Les cahiers de l'Equipe, *Football 1956*, Paris: L'Equipe, 1956, p. 99.

The 1960s and 1970s: Transcontinental and Transatlantic Migration

Migration within South America

Football assumed a new political dimension for the unstable military regimes in South America in this period. In Argentina the crisis of 1958 had major repercussions. As a French journalist observed of Argentinian football: 'At the moment they have lost all faith. For the first time, they doubt their "superiority". Two forward lines of international standard composed of young Argentinians are currently playing in Italy. The new generation has already gone.'[98] For Bayer, Argentinian football in the 1960s was in 'total disorientation'.[99] This climate of deep despair touched all forms of Argentinian culture, including its literature. 1962's best-selling books were *La crisis Argentina* by José Rodriguez Tarditi, *¿Que pasa en la Argentina?* (What has happened to Argentina?) by Eduardo Triscornia and *Me duele la Argentina* (Argentina causes me pain) by Octavio Gonzáles Roura.[100] This pessimism convinced the national association and the government to place restrictions on the freedom of movement of the best players. From the summer of 1961, all members of the national squad were required to remain at home. Wealthy clubs, particularly Boca Juniors and River Plate, became closely associated with the political establishment and were encouraged to invest in keeping their best players and buying other South American stars from Peru, Brazil and Uruguay.[101] In 1960, River's chairman, Antonio Liberti, even planned to buy European stars, signing a pre-contract agreement with French and Spanish national team players such as Roger Piantoni and Ladislao Kubala and actually signing a Spanish international. Because foreign players had only played a marginal role, the Argentinian league had never placed restrictive measures on their importation. The situation changed in 1960 when ten Uruguayans, nine Brazilians and four Peruvians played in the Argentinian league. River Plate's attack, for instance, did not feature a single Argentinian. The sports section of the Buenos Aires daily *El Mundo* printed under the headline '¡Invasión!' the faces of two smiling black Brazilian imports, Mauro and Edson. The next page showed a photograph of a desperate young Argentinian player sitting in the dressing room, with an accompanying text: 'An exasperated young man meditates'.[102] Did such attacks suggest

---

98. *Football Magazine*, May 1961. Its rival *Miroir du football*, March 1961, entitled its regular column on Argentina 'After Euphoria now Affliction'; Amilcar Romero, *Deporte, violencia y politica (crónica negra 1958–1983)*, Buenos Aires: CEAL, 1985, p. 22.

99. Bayer, *Fútbol argentino*, p. 89.

100. Rouquié, *Pouvoir militaire et société politique en République Argentine*, p. 519.

101. Ramírez, *Politica y fútbol*, p. 39.

102. *El Mundo*, 20 March 1961.

that black Brazilians and Peruvians such as Edson and Benítez at Boca and Paulinho, Joya and Gómez Sánchez at River Plate, had to suffer racism in a country with no black minority? This must remain a matter of conjecture at present, especially as the Argentinian literature is silent on this point.

How did this intracontinental migration affect the Brazilians and Uruguayans? A French history of Brazilian football published in 1963 provided a table of all Brazilians playing abroad that year. Of about one hundred in total who were earning their living abroad, the eighty-four in the top divisions included: eleven in Argentina; four in Colombia; ten in Mexico; three in Peru; and one each in Ecuador, Uruguay, Venezuela and Jamaica. In Europe, there were twenty-one in Portugal, eighteen in Italy, twelve in Spain, and one each in France and Austria. The author concluded, however, by playing down the significance of this emigration, noting that the most talented players had not been considered for export.[103] Uruguay suffered particularly from this intracontinental migration. Rafael Bayce counted 625 professional football players who left the country in the period 1958 to 1983 (see Table 3.3) of whom only one in six went to Europe. He commented on the reasons behind this mass exodus:

For professional sportsmen, emigration has become a logical decision resulting from the political difficulties, the economic crises and the devaluation of the Uruguayan peso. For foreign clubs, it is always easy to buy Uruguayan players. The domestic clubs are in such a precarious state that they are asking low prices on the international market for a group of well-prepared players, who are both cosmopolitan and favourable to emigration.[104]

The Uruguayan manager Pepe Sasia added that 'the best Uruguayan players play here as little boys, when they are just beginning, and as veterans when they are finishing. Their [whole] youth and their peak athletic years are spent abroad'.[105] Neither did Uruguay experience significant in-migration. Throughout the 1960s and the early 1970s, the leading goal-scorers in the Uruguayan league may have been foreigners such as the black Ecuadorian Spencer for Peñarol or the Argentinian Luis Artime for Nacional, but the number of foreign players never exceeded sixteen and generally stayed below a dozen.

103. Fontan, *Divin football brésilien*, p. 259–61.

104. Rafael Bayce, 'Deporte y sociedad', in *El Uruguay de nuestro tiempo 1958–1983*, Montevideo: CLAEH, 1983, pp. 49–72.

105. José Sasia, *Al dondo de la red*, Montevideo: Signos, 1989, quoted in Joseph L. Arbena, 'Dimensions of International Talent Migration in Latin American Sports', in John Bale and Joseph Maguire (eds), *The Global Sport Arena: Athletic Talent Migration in an Interdependent World*, London: Frank Cass, 1994, p. 104.

Table 3.3 Uruguayan Professional Footballers Abroad, 1958–1983

Place	Number	%
Argentina	162	25.9
Brazil	41	6.6
Other American	310	49.6
Europe	112	17.9
Total	**625**	**100**

Source: Rafael Bayce, 'Deporte y Sociedad', in *El Uruguay de nuestro tiempo*, Montevideo: CLAEH, 1983, p. 60.

Migration to Europe

In spite of these developments, European eyes were still set on South American football. The Brazilian government faced requests from the millionaire Milan clubs, along with the Spanish giants, Barcelona and Real Madrid, to buy the 'new king', Pele. More than any other member of the World Championship squads, Pele received the favours of the Brazilian authorities. He was treated as a national hero on his return from Sweden in 1958 but was also pressurized into remaining in Brazil. His club, Santos, were in a position to offer extremely lucrative contracts and benefits for him and his family. Santos gained a new-found popularity after 1958 and were now able to attract vast crowds all over the world, receiving contracts for at least fifty exhibition matches a year. In the spring of 1959, Pele played twenty matches in thirty days with Santos, in Bulgaria, Belgium, Holland, Germany, Switzerland, Spain, Portugal and Italy. The whole world had discovered the phenomenon the previous year on television screens and evidently wanted to see him in the flesh. The impact of television helped him to become the first world football star. Santos, meanwhile, became a travelling circus with Pele as *the* attraction; contracts for matches often required his participation for at least sixty-five minutes. After initial success in South American competitions and the World Club Championship, by the early 1970s Santos were often accused of being interested only in gate receipts and of becoming 'the Harlem Globetrotters of world football'.[106]

The closure of the French and Spanish borders in 1962 and the Italian in 1966 largely explain the reduction in transatlantic migration during the 1960s. In each of the three cases, the presence of foreign players was made responsible for the poor results of the national team. In Spain, the South Americans in general, and

---

106. Mason, *Passion of the People?*, p. 89; Ryswick, *100 000 heures de football*, p. 318.

the Argentinians particularly, were stigmatized.[107] Clubs in France and Portugal were now looking to Africa where they could acquire adequate players at much lower prices (see Chapter 6). More importantly, FIFA's 1964 decision to prevent footballers representing more than one national side was a crucial factor in the re-evaluation of importation policies.[108] A new conception of *sporting* nationality was enacted. Dual citizens and players who had changed citizenship were no longer eligible for their second nation. The measure had been intended to prevent players leaving Eastern European clubs illegally and playing for a country in the West. Examples such as Ferenc Puskas, who played for Spain at the age of thirty-five in the 1962 World Cup after fleeing Hungary in 1956, had led the Communist countries to promote this motion to the FIFA assembly, where they gained the support of the South Americans, long afflicted by the *oriundi* rule. Henceforth, the attraction of South American stars for Southern European clubs was consider-ably diminished.

Moreover, throughout Europe Argentinian footballers had become less fashion-able in the late 1960s as a result of the violent and defensive game identified with club sides such as Estudiantes and Racing. The *criollo* game was no longer associated with virtuosity but with the image seen on television during the finals of the Inter-Continental Cup where Argentinians were sent off and committed aggressive acts against opponents. To add to the negative picture, the national team failed to qualify for the 1970 World Cup Finals.

But the phenomenon of the *oriundi* did not stop for good. Spain may have closed its borders to foreigners but not to *oriundi*. Their status, however, had changed. To become an *oriundo*, one had to have Spanish parents but also not to have been previously selected for the national team of one's country of birth. In France, it was the limit of two foreign professionals at each club for the majority of the 1970s and 1980s which impelled directors to import players who could receive a national passport. César Auguste Laraignée, a central defender from River Plate with an obvious French lineage, signed for Stade de Reims in 1972 and could through the *jus sanguinis* (having proved to have French ancestors) automatically acquire French citizenship. The same summer José Montagnoli signed a French contract for Nice. He had been born in Paris in 1953, when his father was playing professional football for CA Paris. Although his family returned to Argentina when he was a child, the fact that he had been born on French soil, irrespective of his inability to speak French, made him eligible for a French passport (*jus solis*).

The Spanish borders were opened once more in 1973, allowing each club to sign two foreigners. This decision was in fact a direct consequence of a series of

---

107. Vicente Verdú, *El fútbol: mitos, ritos y simbolos*, Madrid: Allianza editorial, 1980, p. 18.
108. FIFA Archives, Minutes of the Players' Status Committee, 20 October 1963.

scandals involving the method of recruiting *oriundi*. In 1972, Barcelona signed three – Cos, Leguizamon and Heredia – but the league refused to validate the transfer of Heredia, as well as Echecopar who had signed for Granada, claiming that their Spanish descent could not be proved. To demonstrate the inequity of this *oriundi* regulation, Barça's lawyer travelled to South America. He came back with documents proving that the majority of the *oriundi* birth certificates were false. One case became particularly infamous in Spain. An Argentinian player wrote in his claim for a Spanish passport that his father was born in a city called 'Celta de Vigo'. Cos himself, an Argentinian, had crossed the border to Paraguay, where it was easy during the Strossner regime to acquire unchecked birth certificates. As a consequence of these scandals, the league decided to re-open the borders but continued to accept the existence of *oriundi*.[109]

Of the fifty-four foreign players recruited by Spanish professional clubs in 1973, forty were South Americans from former colonies and nineteen of these were Argentinians (Table 3.4). The cultural links, the question of language and the relatively low cost of the players combined to determine the near monopoly of South America. For a decade there was little change, with a clear sense of continuity in the place of origin of foreign players (see Table 3.5b). Atlético Madrid signed three Argentinians in 1973 from San Lorenzo: Ayala, Heredia and Panadero Díaz. While the first two were regarded as foreigners, Panadero signed a Spanish licence. The sporting daily *Marca* interviewed him on his arrival at Madrid airport to introduce him to the readers and clarify his cultural and ethnic background. The curious discussion which followed, in which he had to justify his Spanish ancestry, is testimony to the suspicion surrounding the *oriundi* in Spain during the 1970s:

Q: What is your name?

A: Rubén Osvaldo Díaz.

Q: Why are you always referred to as 'Panadero' then?

A: It is because my father was a baker [Panadero means baker in Spanish], and I often helped him at work.

Q: How can you claim Spanish citizenship?

A: It's clear! My 'old man' [*mi 'viejo'*] was born in Lugo and went to Argentina aged seventeen. My mother is Argentine by birth.

Q: Do you have any relatives in Spain?

A: It is possible, but the truth is that I don't know.[110]

---

109. Closa and Blanco, *Diccionari del Barça*, p. 273, Verdú, *El fútbol: mitos, ritos y símbolos*, p. 18.

110. *Marca*, 2 August 1973.

Table 3.4 Recruitment of Foreign Players in the Spanish League, 1973

Division One			Division Two		
Athletic Bilbao	–	–	**Baracaldo**	–	–
Atlético Madrid	Ayala	Argentina	**Betis**	Olmeda	Argentina
	R. A. Heredia	Argentina	**Burgos**	–	–
	Panadero Díaz	Argentina	**Cadiz**	Bocoya	Chile
Barcelona	Cruyff	Holland	**Córdoba**	D. Onega	Argentina
	Sotil	Peru		Dominicchi	Argentina
Castellón	Dumat	France	**Dep. la Coruña**	–	–
Elche	J. C. Heredia	Argentina	**Hércules Alicante**	Aicart	Peru
	Hiller	Germany		Nagy	Hungary
Español	Cino	Paraguay		Rey	Uruguay
	Ortiz Aquino	Paraguay	**Levante Valencia**	Caszely	Chile
Gijon	Doria	Argentina	**Linares**	–	–
	Landucci	Argentina	**Mallorca**	Urquia	Honduras
Granada	Echecopar	Argentina		Bran	Honduras
	Montero	Uruguay	**Orense**	Pasternak	Argentina
	Castillo			Fonseca	Portugal
Las Palmas	Carnevali	Argentina	**Osasuna**	–	–
	Verde	Argentina	**Rayo Vallecano**	Abellan	Chile
Málaga	Guerini	Argentina		Cordo	Chile
Murcia	Taverna	Argentina	**Sabadell**	Djordjevic	Yugoslavia
	Verza	Paraguay	**Salamanca**	Galleguillos	Chile
Oviedo	Djoric	Yugoslavia	**San Andrés**	Roth	Germany
Real Madrid	Mas	Argentina	**Sevilla**	Biri-Biri	Guinea
	Netzer	Germany		Esparrago	Uruguay
Real Sociedad	–	–		Fleitas	Paraguay
Santander	Martínez	Argentina	**Gim. Tarragona**	Pelezinho	Brazil
	Zuviria	Argentina		Toto	Brazil
Valencia	Jara	Austria	**Tenerife**	Ferreiras	Argentina
	Keita	Mali		Kraus	Chile
Celta Vigo	Aguerre	Uruguay	**Valladolid**	–	–
	Aparicio	Uruguay			
Zaragoza	Arrua	Paraguay			
	Blanco	Uruguay			

Source: Marca, 29 May 1974 (Division One); *Marca*, 26 August 1973 (Division Two)

An average player, 'Panadero' Díaz was able to profit from his dual citizenship by signing a lucrative contract, even if his links with his father's native country were tenuous at best.

The position of Argentine migrants during the years of dictatorship, coinciding with the countries' first World Cup victory, was less favourable. To prepare for the event, forty players were included on a list of possible selections for the World Cup squad and members of this group were forbidden from moving abroad. There could be no repeat of the experience of 1957. Menotti, the national coach, was reluctant to select players registered abroad and so renowned internationals, such as Bargas, Piazza, Wolf, Carnevali, Ayala and Carlos Bianchi, who had signed for Spanish and French clubs before the beginning of the dictatorship, were never seriously considered for the squad. The composition of the national squad reflected the autarkic views of the regime. Their best player, Mario Kempes was the only expatriate recalled for the national cause, while playing for Valencia in Spain. All the others were required by Menotti and the federation not only to stay in the country but also to remain completely at the disposal of the federation for half a season prior to the competition. This was to be a domestic affair. One of the slogans of the military dictatorship was 'Twenty-five million Argentinians will play for the World Cup' and thus the whole nation had to make sacrifices. The people transformed this quotation to read 'Twenty-five million Argentinians will *pay* for the World Cup'.[111]

The departure of four of the 1978 squad immediately after the Finals, namely Osvaldo Ardiles and Ricardo Villa to Tottenham Hotspur, Alberto Tarantini to Birmingham City and Daniel Bertoni to Seville, marked a relaxation of this defence of the national team, although it only lasted a year. The experience of those who moved to England was particularly interesting. Ardiles and Villa were the first foreign professionals to play in the Football League after the lifting of a ban which, as we saw in the last chapter, had stood on the statute books of the governing bodies for some forty-six years. Tottenham chose these first foreign imports carefully. The decision was not based on nationality but on quality, reflecting their intention to be seen buying the best in the world, while also enabling them to satisfy the stringent requirements of the Department of Employment. Ardiles, particularly, was considered apposite for the English game. Not only had he impressed in his role behind Kempes and Luque as a play-maker for the World Champions but it was felt that he would blend well with Tottenham's own 'artist', Glenn Hoddle, and with the tradition of the team. One article specifically compared him with Danny Blanchflower, 'the intellectual of Tottenham's League and FA Cup winning team' of 1961.[112] Moreover, as a middle-class, English-speaking former law student, it was thought that Ardiles would have less trouble adapting to England than most 'Latins'. The transfer, orchestrated by former Argentinian captain Antonio Rattin, as well as Sheffield United manager Harry Haslam and his Argentinian coach Oscar Arce, proved highly successful, with Ardiles and Villa helping Tottenham lift the FA Cup in 1981 before the Falklands War complicated the football relationship between the two nations.

111. Alejandro Turner, '25 miliones des Argentinos: Fútbol y discurso en el Mundial 78', in Alabarces *et al.*, (ed.), *Deporte y sociedad*, pp. 143–50.

112. *The Guardian*, 12 July 1978.

Table 3.5a Return Migration of Argentinian Footballers, 1981

Argentinos Juniors	Lorenzo (Man.)	Peru
Boca Juniors	Brindisi	Spain
	Morete	Spain
	Trobbiani	Spain
	Carniglia (Man.)	France
Colón	Alonso	USA
	Méndez	Spain
Estudiantes	Pachame (Man.)	USA
Ferro Carril	Saccardi	Spain
Huracan	Babington	Germany
	Marangoni	England
Independiente	Trossero	France
Newell's Old Boys	Santamaría	France
	Yazalde	France
Platense	Anzarda	Spain
	Oviedo	Spain
River Plate	Heredia	Spain
	Kempes	Spain
	Tarantini	England
	Di Stefano (Man.)	Spain
Rosario Central	Carnevali	Spain
	Chazaretta	Spain
	Finaroli	Spain
San Lorenzo	Ceballos	Spain
	Scotta	Spain
Talleres Córdoba	Bravo	France
Vélez Sarsfield	Bianchi	France
	Piazza	France

Source: Data elaborated from 'Diego Maradona e l'Argentina', Calciomondo, 17, supplement to *Guerin sportivo*, 30 September 1981

Between 1979 and the next World Cup Finals in 1982, the export of Argentinian players to Europe was strictly prohibited. This was pre-empted by a new series of scandals over false birth certificates, which had led the Spanish authorities to limit the number of *oriundi* at each club to one.[113] As a result clubs such as Boca Juniors and River Plate called back a significant number of nationals playing in Europe (see Table 3.5a). Mario Kempes was signed by River Plate, but the club was never able to pay the transfer fee. In this case, the political aims of the regime exposed the financial weakness of the club.

This authoritarian method was considered the only possible way to keep the established players and rising stars playing at home in preparation for the next

113. 'Los internacionales: otro escandalo', *Don Balón*, 11 December 1979.

Table 3.5b South American Players in the European Professional Leagues 1980–81

	ARG	BRA	CHI	COL	PAR	PER	URU
Austria	–	–	–	–	–	–	2
Belgium	2	5	1	–	–	1	–
England	4	–	–	–	–	–	1
France	12	2	–	–	–	–	4
W. Germany	–	1	–	–	–	–	–
Greece	8	1	–	–	–	1	–
Italy	2	4	–	–	–	–	–
Portugal	–	19	–	–	1	–	–
Spain	39	4	–	–	15	–	10
Switzerland	–	1	–	–	–	–	–
TOTAL	67	27	1	–	16	2	17

Source: Data elaborated from various European Almanacs

World Cup. The dictatorship treated the retention of players' contracts as a matter of prestige. The presence of South American players in European leagues at the beginning of the 1980s was thus relatively marginal. As before, the destination of these players reflected the legacy of colonial histories and cultural links (Table 3.5b). The Spanish league accounted for 62 per cent of the migrants from its former colonies (Argentina, Uruguay and Paraguay) while Portugal employed the majority of the Brazilians. Similarly, half of the Argentinians in Greece were so-called 'ethnic Greeks' such as Oscar Bistakis, Riccardo Kontogeorgakis and Alfredo Glasmanis, who were not considered to be foreigners.[114] Italy had just reopened its borders, allowing only one foreign player for each of the sixteen elite clubs. Of the 22-man Argentinian squad for the World Cup in Spain, return migrants outnumbered expatriates: Ardiles (Tottenham), Valdano (Zaragoza) and Bertoni (Fiorentina) were contracted to European clubs but Kempes, Santamaria, Tarantini and Trossero had already come home. As a comparison, at the same tournament Brazil had two expatriates and no return migrants and Peru had two of each (Table 3.6).

Maradona and Di Stefano

The transfer of Diego Maradona to Barcelona in 1982 outlined the contrasting attitudes towards South American players. The *Pibe de oro* (golden boy) failed to gain consent or win sympathy in the Catalan capital. The hepatitis he contracted in Catalonia, along with his injuries and the problems in adapting to European football, may provide some explanation. But other historical and cultural factors linked to the contrasting importation policies of Barcelona and Real Madrid could

114. *Greek Football Panini Album 1981*, Modena: Panini, 1981.

Table 3.6 South American World Cup Finals Squads' Place of Employment, 1978–98

	1978	1982	1986	1990	1994	1998
ARGENTINA						
Home	21	19	15	8	10	6
Europe	1	3	6	12	9	16
Latin America			1	2	1	
Elsewhere					1	
Not Registered					1	
BOLIVIA						
Home					19	
Europe					1	
Latin America					2	
BRAZIL						
Home	22	20	19	10	12	9
Europe		2	3	12	10	11
Elsewhere						2
CHILE						
Home		21				18
Europe						1
Latin America						2
Elsewhere		1				1
COLOMBIA						
Home				20	18	10
Europe				2	2	3
Latin America					2	8
Elsewhere						1
PARAGUAY						
Home			15			3
Europe						3
Latin America			7			15
Elsewhere						1
PERU						
Home	21	16				
Europe		1				
Latin America		5				
Elsewhere	1					
URUGUAY						
Home			16	9		
Europe			2	10		
Latin America			4	3		

be advanced to explain his early departure to Naples. Although his purchase was initially represented as a dream and ideal of *Barça* and its chairman Mr. Nuñez, who were proud to be able to buy the biggest talent and the most expensive player in the world, Maradona was very quickly regarded as a second-class foreigner. His artististic footballing qualities but, perhaps more importantly, his cultural and ethnic background, were antithetical to the requirements of the Catalan ideal. 'As a virtuous, facetious, even wily player, a lover of glorious feats, moving about with his family and friends, now a wealthy man but with the culture of the pauper he used to be' he did not have the rational and modern characteristics preferred at Barcelona.[115]

In fact, much of the history of the opposition between Barcelona and Real Madrid can be seen in the Spanish adventures of the two Argentine champions, Di Stefano and Maradona. Observers eager to find antithesis and contrast, between centralism and autonomy, democracy and Francoism, colonial economy and capitalist progress, have often looked at the character and quality of footballers. International football stars encourage affiliation and partisanship and, as such, can become extraordinary vehicles for the creation of opposition.[116] The glory of Real Madrid is associated with a community of players born in a former colonial empire which had formed the basis of the city's power. From Di Stefano to the Mexican Hugo Sánchez, from the other *criollos* Roque Olsen and Héctor Rial in the 1950s and Jorge Valdano and Fernando Redondo more recently to the Uruguayan José Santamaría, these sons of the great kingdom of Spain have often been instrumental in important periods of the club's history. By contrast, the only South American artists who succeeded in Barcelona were Brazilians (Jaguare, Romario, Ronaldo, Rivaldo) and even they feature far behind the Europeans Cruyff, Kubala and Koeman, or even Schuster, in the collective memory of the club. Indeed, the attitude to foreign players in the Spanish league could be analysed as a concrete representation of the geopolitical aspirations of the elites in Barcelona, Madrid and Bilbao. From this perspective, Maradona could not possibly have succeeded at the Camp Nou.

Even today, the heritage of Di Stefano is essential in understanding Real's foreign recruitment policy. The *saeta rubia* (the blond arrow) was irreplaceable. In fact, when the borders reopened to foreign players in 1973, Real's directors seemed to want to replicate the qualities of their former star with the combination of two foreign recruits. To find an equivalent in his style and physiognomy, they signed elegant blond German midfield player Günther Netzer. Di Stefano had,

115. Christian Bromberger, 'Foreign Footballers, Cultural Dreams and Community Identity in some North-western Mediterranean Cities', in Bale and Maguire (eds), *Global Sports Arena*, p. 177; Alicia Dujovne Ortiz, *Maradona c'est moi*, Paris: La découverte, 1992, pp. 38–40.

116. Bromberger, *Le match de football*, p. 165–71.

after all, been known as *El alemán*. To reproduce his Argentinian heritage, they chose Oscar 'Pinino' Mas, a small winger from Di Stefano's first club River Plate, who was as quick as an 'arrow'. Not surprisingly, the result was disastrous, as the two never managed to combine these qualities or even to communicate properly. As a further tribute to Di Stefano, over the years Real have signed a number of sturdy, 'blond' Argentinians: Guerini, Wolf, Roberto Martínez, Ruggeri, Esnaider, Redondo and Bizarri. After the failure of Mas, however, not a single small, dark Argentinian *pibe* winger wore the white shirt.[117]

More than four hundred Argentinian footballers have moved to Spain since 1973.[118] Their locations provide a virtual history lesson. Argentinians have been ignored by almost every Basque club (who rejected non-Basques anyway) while most of the Catalan clubs also refused to apply to football what they considered to be an imperialistic rationale (see Table 3.4). In contrast, the clubs from Castilla, Andalucía, Valencia, Aragón and the islands have concentrated on Argentinians in their foreign recruitment.[119] One of these migrants, Jorge Valdano, has highlighted the important role of Las Palmas and Tenerife over the years for the players from across the Atlantic. 'That Carnevali, Brindisi, Morete and Wolf in Las Palmas [and later Redondo, Pizzi, Ojeda and Dertycia in Tenerife] were major figures was beside the point. The Canary Islands became a first step towards a career in continental Europe in a kind of continuous Atlantic stream.'[120] In this sense, we should recognize the element of fidelity which seems to have determined foreign recruitment at many clubs, allowing Barcelona to ignore Argentinians for fifteen years after Maradona and to continue to follow the Dutch model begun by Cruyff.

The attitude towards Diego Maradona in Naples epitomizes the impact foreign players can have under certain circumstances in particular cities. On the day of his arrival in 1984, 60,000 spectators turned up see him at the San Paolo stadium and, over the next seven years, Maradona reached a popularity and a success never previously recorded in Naples. His behaviour, his countenance and the rituals he adopted, like kissing the head of the physiotherapist before every match, transformed him into a symbol of the city. Obviously his footballing talent was essential

---

117. Verdú, *El fútbol: mitos, ritos y simbolos*, p. 30; on the question of the *pibe* see Archetti, *Masculinities*, pp. 182–8.

118. This figure, relating only to those players in Division 1 and Division 2A, is based on the data on club squads presented in the annual almanacs of *Don Balón* (Barcelona) 1978–1999 and various other sources, particularly *Marca* between the years 1973 and 1979.

119. The clubs with the highest number of Argentinians between 1978 and 1999 were: Valencia (17), Atlético Madrid (16), Las Palmas (16), Mallorca (16), Seville (16), Málaga (12), Zaragoza (12), Real Madrid (12), Tenerife (12), Valladolid (11), Betis (11), Elche (11), Murcia (11), Oviedo and Santander with ten Argentinians were the first clubs from the north, Español had eight (same data as previous note).

120. Jorge Valdano, *Sueños de fútbol*, Madrid: El País Aguilar, 1994, p. 60.

in the formation of the myth that surrounded him: 'a champion like Maradona with his tactical sense is an excellent team-mate, a charismatic leader and a virtuoso'.[121] But, as Vittorio Dini has pointed out, other elements contributed to his adoption.[122] Napoli had never been Italian champions before his arrival but during his time at the club they won the *scudetto* twice, as well as the Italian Cup and the UEFA Cup. In a city stigmatized as a model of disorganization, he managed to win and to win with style. Pride was also essential. When Maradona agreed to come to Naples, he was seen as rejecting the prejudices associating the city with the Mafia and accepting the challenge. The nickname given to Garrincha in Brazil in the 1960s – 'The Joy of the People' – may be reasonably used for Maradona's Neapolitan period. The parallel with the Brazilian winger can be drawn from his style of play, his life off the field and the intense passion he generated.[123] Leite Lopes has described Garrincha as an 'anti-athlete', with incomparable and unstoppable dribbling skills. Maradona, too, hardly looked like an athlete. He was too small and fat to represent a national football style.[124] In the Italian language extraordinary football actions have become 'Maradonian'. A cult devoted to Maradona developed in Naples after 1987, and is still present almost a decade after his departure, when the supporters chant 'Diego! Diego!' at every home match. If his original background marginalized him at Barcelona, he quickly lost the label of 'foreigner' in Naples to become an adopted local. We could even ask how far Maradona's move to Naples was a genuine migration, given that the geographical distance was reduced by shared cultural and religious values. The climate, the food and a tolerant attitude towards his transgressions certainly seemed to contribute to Maradona's integration. There was no vast cultural block between Villa Fiorito, where he grew up, and Soccavo, the place where he trained daily in Naples; the inhabitants and their habits were similar.

For the last twenty years or so, Maradona has polarized opinion between the good and the bad, the civilized and the rough, the fair and the unfair, the legal and the illegal, the creative and the mechanical, the south and the north. His legal problems, his addiction to drugs, his attacks against the establishment, the illegitimate son he left in Naples, his continuous disaffection for training sessions,

121. Alessandro Dal Lago and Roberto Moscati, *Regalateci un sogno*, Milan: Bompiani, 1992, p.22.

122. Vittorio Dini, 'Maradona, héros napolitain', *Actes de la recherche en sciences sociales*, 103, June 1994, pp. 75–8.

123. On Garrincha, Sergio Leite Lopes, 'La disparition de "la joie du peuple": notes sur la mort d'un joueur de football', *Actes de la recherche en sciences sociales*, 79, September 1989, pp. 21–36; on the passion generated by Maradona in Naples, see Bromberger, *Le match de football*, pp. 39–43, 138–44; Vittori Dini and Oscar Nicolaus (eds), *Te Diegum: Genio, sregolatezze e bacchettoni*, Milan: Leonardo, 1991.

124. Leite Lopes, 'La disparition de "la joie du peuple"', p. 27; Archetti, *Masculinities*, p. 188.

his recent friendship with Fidel Castro and, of course, the goal he scored against England with 'the hand of God' have transformed him for most of the media into an 'anti-hero': a good footballer but a bad man.[125] He has constantly been compared with Pele, who was much more successful in his post-football years. However, Maradona has kept his popular support in Naples, Buenos Aires and elsewhere. As one of his Argentinian devotees told Archetti: 'now our problem is that we had Maradona, and we will always expect to get another one'.[126]

Towards Globalization?: South American Footballers in Europe since the late 1980s

With the proliferation of players' agents and agent networks, the movement of young players has increased. South American nations have suffered major economic crises in the last fifteen years, leading to diminishing gate receipts. Transfers, now conducted in US dollars, generally represent the major source of income for club sides. In 1989 Platense, a small club from Buenos Aires, received $400,000 from Grasshoppers of Zurich for the transfer of their striker Néstor de Vicente. This represented more money than the gate receipts of the entire season.[127] Since the devaluation of the Argentinian Austral in 1989, almost every player good enough to be exported has left the country. From this moment on, even the national teams of Argentina and Brazil have been mainly composed of players registered abroad (see Table 3.6).

The career patterns of South American players have changed fundamentally in the last fifteen years. Moving to Europe when still young, they now have a dual existence as employees of European clubs and representatives of their national teams. This change has undoubtedly been associated with the emergence of the player's agent, who has been extremely important in transforming the relationship between players, their initial employer and national associations. From the transfer of Bertoni in 1978 – an agent himself today – to that of Batistuta in 1991, agents have been essential in organizing transfers to Europe (see Table 3.7).

Table 3.7 shows the most significant Argentinian imports in Europe since the late 1970s. Two main points emerge from this. First of all, the continuity in the destination of players from earlier periods is striking. Latin countries are still the

---

125. A view shared by the authors of various books. Juan José Sebrelli, *La era del fútbol*, Buenos Aires: Editorial sudamerica, 1998, pp. 119–53; Jimmy Burns, *The Hand of God: The Life of Diego Maradona*, London: Bloomsbury, 1996. For another interpretation see Maria G. Rodríguez, 'El Football no es la patria (pero se parece)', in P. Alabarces and M.G. Rodríguez (eds), *Cuestión de pelotas*, Buenos Aires: Atuel, pp. 37–25, who insists on the political use of Maradona in Argentina.

126. Archetti, *Masculinities*, p. 188.

127. Sergio Levinsky, *El negocio del fútbol*, Buenos Aires: Corregidor, 1995, p. 99.

Table 3.7 Significant Argentinians in Europe since the late 1970s

Year of Arrival	Name	Age	Clubs	Left
1978	**Bertoni**	23	Seville, Fiorentina, Napoli, Udinese	1987
1982	**Maradona**	22	Barcelona, Napoli, Seville	1993
1982	**Díaz**	22	Napoli, Avellino, Fiorentina, Inter, Monaco	1991
1989	**Balbo**	23	Udinese, Roma, Parma, Fiorentina, Roma	2000*
1989	**Sensini**	23	Udinese, Parma, Lazio	2000*
1990	**Chamot**	21	Pisa, Foggia, Lazio, Atlético Madrid, Milan	2000*
1990	**Esnaider**	17	Real Madrid, Zaragoza, Atlético Madrid, Español, Juventus	2000*
1990	**Redondo**	21	Tenerife, Real Madrid, Milan	2000*
1990	**Simeone**	20	Pisa, Seville, Atlético Madrid, Inter, Lazio	2000*
1991	**Batistuta**	22	Fiorentina, Roma	2000*

(*) still under contract in Europe

main targets. In 1998/99, there were sixty-eight South Americans in Spain, fifty-five in Italy, ten in France and only eight in Germany and England.[128] If the volume of migrants has increased, their relative distribution throughout Europe remains much the same. Secondly, the careers of the most talented South Americans have developed within a European context. The European experience starts earlier and lasts longer than in previous decades. It is interesting to note that, with the exception of Simeone and Chamot, the majority of Argentinians mentioned in Table 3.7 moved straight away to *elite* European clubs and have remained within this prestigious circle for most of their careers.

In recent years Japan has also emerged as an alternative market to Europe for Brazilian footballers. Once again, the movement of these footballers reflected wider political developments, including the labour shortage and changes in immigration laws in the early 1990s. Foreigners of Japanese origin (the so-called *Issui*) were permitted and encouraged to find work (mainly unskilled) in Japan. The historical migratory links between the two countries, which meant that in 1988 there were some 530,000 *Issui*, along with 110,000 Japanese citizens in Brazil, contributed to the volume of migration across the Pacific.[129] It is hardly surprising then that when the full-time professional J-League began in 1993, Brazilians were conspicuous from the start. There seems to have been little of the opposition to foreigners in Japanese football which has affected other parts of Japanese society, and

128. Paolo Piani, 'Gli stranieri nei principali campionati europei', *News Letter del settore tecnico della FIGC*, 1, 1999, p. 2.

129. Raisul Awal Mahmood, 'Labour Crunch, Foreign Workers and Policy Responses: The Experience of Japan', *International Migration*, 34, 1, 1996, pp. 97–114.

Brazilians from Zico onwards have maintained a strong and permanent presence in the J-League. Although foreign players have been limited to three per club, at the start of the 1999 season half of these (twenty-three of a total of forty-six) were Brazilians. Four clubs – the champions Kashima Antlers, Kyoto Purple Sanga, Shimizu S-Pulse and Verdi Kawasaki – had a full quota of Brazilians and only three had none at all.[130] Although Europe continues to be the principal stage for the South American artists, the rise of the professional game in Japan has offered a viable alternative for Brazilians at least.

The careers of the four major South American stars of the last half century are symptomatic of broader patterns of South American migration. Di Stefano, Pele, Maradona and Ronaldo marked the changing modes of migration in the history of football and thus defined their respective eras. Di Stefano left Argentina at the age of twenty-three and made his name outside his native land. Of the twelve national championship medals he won, only one was achieved in Argentina. The others were won during his time in Colombia (three) and Spain (eight). His international career revealed the dominance of the Spaniard over the Argentine. He played seven times, scoring seven goals, for Argentina, and competed unofficially twice for Colombia; but his greatest impact was with Spain, for whom he played thirty-one times and scored twenty-three goals. He even received the highest of Spanish honours, being decorated from the Isabel Catholic Order in 1960.[131] Other stars of the era, such as Sivori and Santamaría, followed similar career paths. Their reputations were made through their European success: the South American public never saw them playing for domestic sides or their national team after their departures to Europe. During the 1950s, South American football was not capable, economically or legally, of keeping its best players. International regulations made no requirement that club sides freed their players for national team matches, and footballers were not regulars on the first transatlantic flights.

Pele, on the other hand, remained with his first professional club for eighteen years. His first transfer, to New York at the age of thirty-four, came after he had officially retired. The 1960s witnessed a distancing of the two continents. In a period of unsettled politics, South American clubs prevented their best players from moving to Europe. The fame and success of Brazil, and the regular European tours of Pele's national and club sides, helped to cement his image on both sides of the Atlantic. What is more, his aura profited immensely from the spread of television and the development of air travel. Santos was only able to retain his contract as a result of the US dollars received for exhibitions and tours abroad. Twenty years later, Maradona was emerging as a precocious talent. He began his career with Argentina Juniors at the age of fifteen and although he left his country

---

130. *Calcio 2000*, December 1999.
131. García Candau, *Madrid–Barça*, p. 143.

relatively young, at twenty-two, he had already managed to play over 200 league games in Argentinian football. He played in Europe for eleven years but, unlike Di Stefano, this did not prevent him from playing for the nation of his birth, which he represented nearly one hundred times. FIFA's more stringent citizenship rules precluded him from representing any other nation even if he had wanted to. Eventually Maradona returned home, finishing his career in Buenos Aires. Unlike Ronaldo, his early talent was not converted into an early transfer as the national authorities impeded the movement of players to Europe.

Ronaldo played only a dozen matches in the Brazilian league before his transfer to PSV Eindhoven at the age of seventeen. His experience conveys more than that of anyone else the hegemonic position of the Western European leagues in world football. The recruitment of South American talent today is highly speculative. Because there are no longer restrictions on the number of contracted foreigners, the clubs of southern Europe are able to increase their South American quota annually, with fewer and fewer returning. Theories of globalization can hardly explain the trends we have tried to analyse. The continuity in the direction and the destination of player migration from the 1930s to the 1990s is salient. While there have rarely been any transfers of professional footballers from Europe to South America, Italy and Spain have been the constant magnets for South American stars. In all the talk about Europe's position at the centre of football's global economy, it should not be forgotten that players tend to move to *particular* countries – for economic, legal, historical and cultural reasons – rather than to 'Europe' as a single, unstructured entity.

The Yugoslav Wanderers

In 1998, more than 2,000 professional footballers from the former Yugoslavia played abroad. The impact since 1992 of the civil war and the break-up of the nation only partly explains the dissemination of Yugoslav footballers across the globe. In fact, the phenomenon has deep historical roots, beginning during the second half of the 1920s, the same period when players from Austria, Czechoslovakia, Hungary and the first South Americans began to move across Europe to play football. Over the last four decades in particular, players from Yugoslavia have been employed in all the major European leagues and have played for 'ethnic' clubs in Australia, Canada and the United States. Possibly more than any other nationality, Yugoslavs have wandered across the European continent and beyond to play professional football.

As we have observed of other cases, the chronology, scale and direction of Yugoslav migration has not been indiscriminate. The outflow of players has been conditioned by the changing nature of domestic politics and economics and by international diplomacy, which have themselves heavily influenced the regulations of the national football federation. It is impossible to understand the movement of Yugoslav footballers since 1945 without being aware of the politics and ideology of the Tito regime, its relationship with Western and Eastern Europe and the internal nationalist tensions of the recent past. However, the history of the migration of Yugoslav footballers begins much earlier than this.

The Student Footballers, 1925–35

Although the case we will consider in this section involved no more than two dozen individuals, we would argue that its singularity and its resonance in a key period of the development of European football justifies the attention given to it. Football in Yugoslavia had shown significant advances by the middle of the 1920s, particularly in three urban centres: Belgrade, Zagreb and Sarajevo. Although a newly-constituted state, Yugoslavia was quick to join FIFA and become involved in international competition, sending a team to the 1920 Olympics. However, its football remained backward when compared with the game of Central European neighbours Austria and Hungary. Contact with foreign countries was sporadic. There were no Yugoslavian players in any of the major European leagues and

Yugoslav teams were not in the habit of touring southern Europe for Armistice Day, Easter or Christmas as did the Swiss, Belgians and British. The years 1925 and 1926 marked the beginnings of the internationalization of Yugoslav football. In June 1926, the national team played against France for the first time and the following season two Yugoslav players signed contracts with the French club Montpellier. There was a diplomatic context to these decisions, as they coincided with the French attempt to maintain its strategic position in Europe through the 'little entente', a defensive agreement with Czechoslovakia, Romania and Yugoslavia as well as the signing of a separate cooperation agreement with Yugoslavia.[1] It is therefore reasonable to assume that these contacts between footballers were related to improving political relations. Moreover, these Yugoslavs were fundamentally different from the contemporary examples of the British footballers who travelled to France and the South Americans who moved to Italy, in that they were part of a pattern of elite migration. As a historian of the Balkans has written: 'During the interwar years, the Serb intelligentsia suffered a massive attack of *French flu* (as a British ambassador ironically called it). The French avant-garde and the Jacobean conception of the state fascinated the elites . . . Writers, artists and lawyers went to study in France.'[2]

The first Yugoslav to play for Montpellier was Veljko Culic, a law student who had previously turned out for Jugoslavija Belgrade. He had not been recruited specifically by the club but was in Montpellier to finish his studies. In February 1927 two of his friends arrived in the city. Unlike Culic, Dusan Petkovic and Branko Sekulic were well-known sportsmen at home, having participated in the previous three Yugoslav Championship Finals, winning twice. They were also regulars in the national team. Petkovic was an elegant inside-forward and Sekulic a quick, skilful winger. Both were middle-class Francophile 'gentlemen' from Belgrade.

At a time when professionalism was prohibited and shamateurism rife, the French authorities were weary of granting registrations to most footballers but placed no barriers in the way of these Yugoslavs.[3] As a brilliant student who had already received his BA and was at Montpellier writing his PhD, Petkovic could have been the ideal amateur sportsman. Sekulic was a different case entirely. He had spent a few months the previous year playing football in Switzerland for Urania Geneva and there is little doubt that he made his living from the game. Like Petkovic, however, he was registered as a student at Montpellier University. Petkovic and Sekulic played for two teams, Montpellier University Club (MUC)

1. Jacques Néré, *The Foreign Policy of France from 1914 to 1945*, London: Routledge, 1975, pp. 42–43; Fred Singleton, *Twentieth Century Yugoslavia*, London: Macmillan, 1976, pp. 80–1.

2. Joze Pirjevec, *Serbi, Croati, Sloveni: Storia di tre nazioni*, Bologna: il mulino, 1995, p. 48.

3. Alfred Wahl, 'Le footballeur français: de l'amateurisme au salariat (1890–1926)', *Le mouvement social*, 135, 1986, pp. 7–30.

and the Sports Olympiques (SO) Montpellier. MUC competed in the national university championship but had few supporters and little money, and was run like any other student society.[4] As a society which kept close to the original aristocratic values of football, one would have thought that MUC would have defended such a principle within its own team. Yet while it was respectful of amateur rules in its internal functioning, the club saw no problems in having foreign players; even foreigners who were paid to play football by another club. Indeed, these foreign 'shamateurs' were not just accepted, they were embraced. Culic was chosen to be the captain and manager of the team and to organize it in an effective and rational way.[5] Success was quick in coming. With its three Yugoslavs, MUC easily won the university championship and then, in a friendly match in Paris, drew against a full-strength Red Star Paris team which had just won the French Cup. Thus a team which was totally unknown to the public and had no prominent French players found itself at the very top of the national football hierarchy. Lucien Gamblin, a former international, wrote after the final of the university championship:

> Even though the Montpellier team easily dominated its Paris counterpart, we can't be proud of its success. What does this mean for French university football? A championship won by foreigners who came to France not to study but to play football.[6]

But for the club itself there was no contradiction in this. Playing football was coming to be regarded as a sensible way of paying for a student's studies and combining the two seemed to be a logical solution. This was a more pragmatic take on amateurism than the doctrinal approach of Gamblin. At the end of the season, SO Montpellier also won its regional league. In a short space of time, the three Yugoslavs had become popular and successful sporting figures in this pocket of southern France.

Montpellier's success had a direct influence on its neighbours. During the summer of 1928 Sète recruited a young Yugoslav international player called Ivan Beck. Milorad Mitrovic and Milan Becic signed in the spring of 1929, the first for Montpellier, the second for Sète. Two more Yugoslavs, Ferante Kolnago and Milan Bonacic (both Croats) arrived at Marseilles the same summer. To justify their recruitment, the five newcomers all registered at local universities. It is interesting to note that while this fashion for Yugoslavs was popular in Montpellier and Sète, only thirty kilometres apart, and Marseilles, their regional rival on the Mediterranean coast, there were no other Yugoslavians in the French leagues. This was a

4. Willy Monnier, the son of Henry Monnier, was also a member of MUC. All the documentation regarding the club comes from its minute books, MUC, Section de football association, comptes-rendus des réunions 1928–1931, Private manuscript collection.

5. AGM of the MUC, 7 June 1928, MUC, Section de football association.

6. Quoted in 'Le crime du Montpellier Université Club', *Les sports du Languedoc*, 3 April 1928.

small and closely-bound community of student-footballers. In their first year, Petkovic and Sekulic lived together in a small apartment situated in the university old town. The following year, Beck and his friend Mitrovic rented a villa together next to the river in Montpellier.[7] The case of Beck is particularly instructive. He was a young man of only nineteen when he arrived but had already represented his country at the Amsterdam Olympics. The Sète directors had clearly taken a risk in recruiting him. He knew none of his new team-mates, had never lived in a foreign country and did not speak a word of French. But for a number of reasons Beck settled well and became extremely popular. First of all, there was already a model for the success of Yugoslavs at Montpellier. Secondly, the two groups of Yugoslavs at Sète and Montpellier offered an immediate site for rivalry between the players and supporters of the clubs. Thirdly, the presence of his four compatriots considerably eased the potential problems of acclimatization.

At the end of the season, for the first and only time, the French Cup Final pitted Sète against Montpellier, while MUC with its four Yugoslavs easily won the French University League for the second year running. As a consequence of their defeat in the Cup, Sète disposed of two British players and hired two Yugoslavs in their place and finally, in 1930, won the French Cup with two of its Yugoslav imports on the field. A few weeks later, Beck, Sekulic and Stevanovic, one of the new arrivals at Sète, boarded the boat for the first World Cup Finals in Uruguay. The diplomatic connotations of the European participation in the World Cup are particularly revealing. France, two of the signatories of the 'little entente' – Yugoslavia and Romania – and France's traditional allies Belgium, were the only European competitors. And of course three of the Yugoslavian team played in southern France.[8] With the introduction of professionalism to France in 1932, the role of the Yugoslavs diminished. Because Yugoslavian football was not yet professional and its players were generally not as advanced as those of Britain, Austria, Hungary and Czechoslovakia, only a further dozen players moved to France in the course of the 1930s.

But transient though it was, it would be wrong to underplay the significance of this group. The combination of students and Yugoslavs brought rapid success to an area with little footballing pedigree. But these student-footballers also represented a particular type of foreign player, one who, despite the protests of Gamblin and others, was clearly there for more than football itself and was able to understand and appreciate French culture. Petkovic possibly illustrated this best of all. He left Montpellier in 1930 when he had completed his doctorate. Two years later, when the French national team toured Yugoslavia, he wrote articles for a French sporting

7. MUC, Section de football association, List of the club members 1928 and 1929.
8. *World Soccer*, May 1961.

paper in which he indicated how much he missed French cultural life, the people and his friends, finishing his second article with the clear statement: 'Vive la France!'[9] Financially, the acquisition of the Yugoslavs was also beneficial to the French clubs. In 1931 Sète became the first French team to be invited to Yugoslavia, where they played in Belgrade, Novi Sad and Split and also encountered the Yugoslav national team.

Although he had already represented Yugoslavia, Ivan Beck later captained Sète, chose French citizenship and was capped by France. In 1934 he became the first non-national to captain a French Cup winning side. Beck was undoubtedly the most famous of all Yugoslavian footballers in France between the wars.[10] During the Second World War, he became leader of a partisan group in the Alps, with the nickname 'Tito'. He never returned to Yugoslavia, and died at the age of fifty-three on Sète harbour, where he worked as a docker. He stayed in the setting of his footballing glory long after his playing days and is still remembered fondly as a local hero. But Beck's case provides only the most salient example of the assimilation of these Yugoslavs. In 1958, almost thirty years after his career ended, Sekulic had his testimonial match in Montpellier[11] and for almost sixty years, Mitrovic, who had returned to Split in 1934, continued to correspond regularly, in French, with Yves Dupont, one of his former French team-mates. Writing about his Yugoslav colleagues, Dupont said: 'Their human qualities were superior to the Swiss and British. I owe a lot to Petko, Sekou, Yvan Beck and Mitro'.[12]

Mitrovic had been forced to leave French football because his native country refused to adopt professionalism. A major dilemma was posed to all Yugoslavian footballers. If they wanted to sign as professionals abroad, they would be banned at home. This situation remained unchanged until the 1950s. Although only a handful of Yugoslavs played football in Switzerland or France during the 1930s, some followed the same routes as their South American colleagues. With the outbreak of war, the Croat Slavko Kodrnja left France for Portugal, where he became a top goal-scorer with Porto. Ivan Petrak, a railway employee followed the same path, settling in the distinguished seaside resort of Cascais and marrying a wealthy Portuguese woman.[13]

9. *Les sports du Sud-Est*, 16 June 1932.

10. For a biography of Beck, see 'L'homme sportif du jour: Yvan Beck', *Le miroir des sports*, May 1934.

11. Roger Rabier, *Allez SOM: cinquante ans de football montpellierain (1919–1970)*, Montpellier: private edition, 1985, shows a photograph of the event.

12. Letter from Yves Dupont to the authors, 5 November 1987.

13. Fredi Kramer (ed.), *Hrvatski nogometni savez 80. obljetnica*, Zagreb: HTZ, 1992, p. 115.

Footballers and Tito's Yugoslavia

During World War Two, fascist Italy annexed Dalmatia. In 1942, two of the best footballers in the region, Manola and Matosic, were recruited by Lazio and Bologna respectively. In Rome emphasis was placed on the geopolitical dimension of their recruitment: Dalmatia was a part of the new Italy and the presence of Dalmatian players in the Italian league was testimony to the new allegiance of the province. After the war, however, emigration from Yugoslavia to the West was made virtually impossible. Only a handful of footballers were able to leave their country to become professionals in the late 1940s. Vinko Golob first emigrated to Prague before becoming a professional in Toulouse and Venice; Vinko Trskan also effectively cut his ties with Yugoslavia when he played in Austria and France. Both players were banned by the national federation, Fudbalski Savez Jugoslavije (FSJ), and were stripped of Yugoslav citizenship.[14]

The early years of Titoism heralded an orthodox socialist vision of society and football antithetical to the professional game in the West. Players became amateurs employed by big factories, and club names were transformed. Zagreb's club Grandjanski was replaced by Dinamo, a side connected to the Croat army.[15] In Belgrade, Jugoslavija was dismantled and supplanted by Partizan, the club of the militia and the federal army; Red Star became a symbol of communism and the club of the party.[16] New clubs took on the terminology of socialist realism: *Sloboda* (Freedom) in Tuzla, *Proleter* in Zrenjanin, *Radnicki* (Workers) in Nis and Kragujevac, *Buducnost* (Future) in Titograd and *Jedinstvo* (Union) in Bihac.

The split between Tito and Stalin in the spring of 1948 initially had little impact on the status of footballers. Yugoslavia kept its distance from the Soviet model, but in football the first visible distinction came with the choice of opposition for the national team and the destination of tours. Between 1949 and 1957, the Yugoslavian team was not invited to play a single friendly match against a communist country in Europe but instead toured Egypt, Israel and Indonesia, and in the late 1950s and early 1960s played against new opponents such as Morocco, Tunisia, Japan, Hong Kong and Ethiopia.[17] In 1949, Hajduk played in France, Saarland, Belgium and toured Australia; Dinamo, meanwhile, went to Switzerland

14. FIFA, Players Transfer Files 1947–1950. In these two cases, the Yugoslav federation tried to stop the players signing professional licences in France.

15. On the 'Dinamo' name in Eastern Europe, see Vic Duke and Liz Crolley, *Football, Nationality and the State*, London: Longman, 1996, p. 93.

16. Ljubomir Vukadinovic, *Yugoslav Football*, Belgrade: Jugoslovenska Knjiga, 1950, pp. 10–13.

17. *Almanah yu Fudbal 88–89*, Belgrade: Tempo, 1989, pp. 123–31; Ron Hockings and Keir Radnedge, *Nations of Europe. A Statistical History of European International Football 1872–1993*, Vol. 2, Emsworth: Articulate, 1993, p. 396–400.

and Austria, Red Star to Malta and Partizan to Sweden.[18] In this period of new alliances, Tito's Yugoslavia was involved in creating a new position of political non-alignment and in the establishment of diplomatic links with Nasser and Nehru which offered the possibility of a 'Third Way'. Such an approach was becoming visible in football too. The Yugoslav national side was also proving highly competitive after finishing second at the London Olympics in 1948 and qualifying for four consecutive World Cup tournaments between 1950 and 1962. But as in other Eastern European countries, Yugoslav players were considered to be 'state amateurs' and were thus not permitted to play abroad.[19]

The introduction of semi-professionalism in the wake of the Budapest coup was the first significant step towards wholesale migration. It led in 1957 to Bernard Vukas, forward and captain of Hajduk Split and the national team, being allowed (perhaps even encouraged) to sign a professional contract with Bologna in Italy. This provided further evidence of the Yugoslav peculiarity of mixing socialism with the opportunity for some of the most renowned scientists and artists to travel and work abroad. For footballers, it meant that the opportunity to go abroad and make money would be granted to the most accomplished and experienced, provided they received the sanction of the state. Managers were the first to be invited to display their talent in foreign leagues. Bencic accompanied Vukas to Bologna in 1957, while Brocic and Ciric were permitted to join Juventus and Lazio respectively the following year. But in spite of these examples, the outflow was still relatively limited: during the late 1950s, no more than two dozen players went abroad.

It was with the Belgrade conference of non-aligned countries in 1961, however, that a new ideological approach created the basis for a more extensive model of professionalism. In a series of economic reforms, the government gave more freedom to domestic business, while on the foreign trade side the number of products subject to restrictions was reduced. In parallel with this, an increasing number of the nation's senior players were freed to finish their careers abroad. To name just a few, Vujadin Boskov and Todor Veselinovic went to Sampdoria, Vladimir Beara and Branco Zebec to Alemania Aachen and Milos Milutinovic to Bayern Munich and then Racing Paris. Up until 1965, some fifty Yugoslav professionals were signed by Western European clubs, particularly those in Holland, Germany and Austria.

18. Vukadinovic, *Yugoslav Football*, pp. 12–13.

19. Rare exceptions, however, were made. After playing for Red Star, Branislav Vukosavljevic acquired a passport and moved to Zurich where he studied philosophy at university. An injury seemed to have stopped his career when he was in Belgrade, but he recovered and managed to win the Swiss league in 1956 and play over 100 matches with the Grasshoppers. His playing days over, Vukosavljevic returned to Belgrade in the 1960s to run a travel agency. J. Ducret, *Le livre d'or du football suisse*, Lausanne: L'âge d'homme, 1994, p. 163.

The new economic reforms of 1965 heralded dramatic changes in the Yugoslav economy and employment structure. With a further shift towards liberalism and the renouncement of a policy of full employment, workers were not only allowed but encouraged to seek work abroad and send money home. The system proved economically successful and 'life became prosperous not only for the Communist elite but also for the middle class social segments, especially in comparison with the rest of Eastern Europe'.[20] This was particularly evident in football after 1966. In that year Partizan Belgrade reached the final of the European Cup. Three years later, ten of the eleven players who featured in the final were employed abroad. The goalkeeper Soskic played in FC Cologne; of the defenders and midfielders, Jusufi was at Frankfurt, Mihajlovic in Lyon, Becejac in Austria, Rasovic at Dortmund and Vasovic at Ajax. Of the forward line, Bajic was at Lille, Kovacevic at Nantes, Galic at Liège and Pirmajer at Nîmes. Only Hasanagic remained at home.[21] Even their manager, the Bosnian Abdullah Gegic, signed a contract with the Turkish club Fenerbahçe. Milan Galic's signing for Standard provoked a response by other Belgian clubs. A Belgian journalist commented that: 'What has been most surprising during the close season is the growing trust given by Belgian football to Yugoslav players, despite last year's experiences with Drazen Jerkovic at Gent and the fiasco of Veselinovic at Union Saint-Gilloise. Gent has purchased three new Yugoslavs this season, Beringen two and Standard has tried to realize the transfer boom by buying Galic.'[22] Notwithstanding those like Jerkovic and Veselinovic who performed below expectations, the Yugoslavs were hot property. Ten started the 1966/67 season in Belgium while seventeen of the twenty-eight foreign players registered in Austria were Yugoslavs.[23] In that one summer an astonishing total of 122 professional players (the equivalent of eleven teams) left the country to sign contracts abroad. In addition, twenty-five players signed up to the National Professional Soccer League (NPSL) in North America, which was outside FIFA regulations and therefore provided no transfer fees for their donor clubs (see Chapter 5).[24] Under new regulations, players were considered to be free agents and organized their own transfers with only 10 per cent of the transfer

---

20. Dimitrije Djordjevic, 'The Yugoslav Phenomenon', in J. Held (ed.), *The Columbia History of Eastern Europe*, New York: Columbia University Press, 1992, p. 332.

21. *Football magazine*, March 1968.

22. *Miroir du football*, September 1966.

23. Hans Molenaar, *Top Voetbal '67–'68*, Baarn: de Boekerij, 1969, p. 118.

24. *De Telegraaf*, 1 November 1967; Molenaar, *Top Voetbal*, pp. 13–14, 202; Colin Jose, *NASL: A Complete Record of the North American Soccer League*, Derby: Breedon Books, 1989, pp. 41–6. In America, the players were concentrated mainly at three clubs: six joined the Los Angeles Toros, while the Oakland Clippers and the St Louis Stars had eight each. Former internationals Sekularac, Kostic and Vidinic were part of this expedition.

fee going to the selling club.[25] This sudden outflow of footballers reflected changes in all sectors of employment. The number of workers temporarily abroad was zero in 1950, 50,000 in 1960 and 783,000 by 1970, a total representing 9.8 per cent of the entire Yugoslav workforce.[26]

In the wake of this liberalization and in an effort to reduce the haemorrhaging of football talent, an emergency meeting of the FSJ was called in April 1967 to regulate transfer movement and to provide a formal stucture for the migration of players abroad. A series of measures was introduced which accorded with the prevailing economic trend yet compensated the clubs by consistently enhancing their incomes through transfers. To emigrate in future, players had to have reached their twenty-eighth birthday, to be free of military obligations and to have the agreement of their home clubs. The transfer fees were now divided in a proportion more satisfactory for selling clubs: 65 per cent of the transfer fee went to the club and 35 per cent to the player.[27] With one or two rare exceptions, the national team chose not to use the services of these exiled players. At the same time, full-time professionalism was finally recognized, although only in the top division.

Politically and economically, this system once again placed Yugoslavia outside the Eastern European Comecon model. It was the only non-capitalist country to accept professionalism, the transfer of players abroad and, from the 1970s, the only one to build up its football industry systematically through the international transfer system.[28] There is nothing surprising in this if one considers that the Yugoslav economy as a whole depended on interaction with Western Europe. Tourists came in, Western capitalists invested and workers emigrated: this was not communism as it would have been recognized in Moscow or Sofia.[29] But, as in industry, the departure of skilled footballers led to a decline in productivity at home and Yugoslavia failed to qualify for the 1966, 1970 and 1978 World Cups.

By 1971 more than 300 of the Yugoslav workers abroad were footballers. Faced with a large demand from the professional leagues in Germany, France, Belgium, Holland, Switzerland and Austria, the major Yugoslavian clubs began to develop

25. Molenaar, *Top Voetbal*, p. 202.

26. Harold Lydall, *Yugoslav Socialism: Theory and Practice*, Oxford: Oxford University Press, 1984, p. 160, Table 8.2.

27. Molenaar, *Top Voetbal*, p. 203.

28. There was some attempt to imitate the Yugoslav approach in Czechoslovakia and Romania in 1968, in the context of the Prague Spring and the Ceaucescu dissidence. Senior players were allowed to finish their careers in Western Europe as professionals but structural differences remained. Professionalism was not introduced officially at home and the transfer of players was organized directly by the national federation with no direct club involvement. In the event, few players were affected and the export of players lasted no more than three years.

29. Duncan Wilson, *Tito's Yugoslavia*, Cambridge: Cambridge University Press, 1980; Joseph Krulic, *Histoire de la Yougoslavie: de 1945 à nos jours*, Brussels: Editions Complexe, 1993, pp. 107–16.

systematic policies for the formation and exportation of players. Footballers had become a good currency for the economy. We shall focus next on one specific club over two decades to highlight in more detail how this policy operated.

Hajduk Split: An Export Company

Named after a group of Dalmatian outlaws, Hajduk Split was formed in 1911. Successful in its early years, the club then failed to win a single championship between 1955 and 1971. Yet in the next decade, Hajduk were by far the most successful Yugoslav team and the only one capable of challenging the Belgradese supremacy. Between 1971 and 1987 the club won four league and seven cup titles and, perhaps more importantly, dominated the national junior championship. From the early 1970s youth coach Tomislav Ivic began to formulate a policy of recruiting players early in an effort to establish a strong youth structure. On graduating to first team manager he used this reservoir of junior talent to secure domestic success. As Table 4.1 indicates, these players were then systematically transferred to foreign clubs. This constant outflow was contained by the parameters of the 1967 regulations and the continuous policy of youth development. For almost twenty years, there were no major exceptions to the rule. Only one player, Slavisa Zungul, left Hajduk and Yugoslavia before the stipulated age (he was twenty-four), to sign a foreign contract without the club's agreement. As a consequence, Zungul was automatically banned by FIFA but as his new club, the New York Arrows in the Major Indoor Soccer League (MISL), was not under the jurisdiction of the international governing body, he could continue a prolific goal-scoring career.[30] The other two players (Bonacic and Bucan) who left before the cut-off age of twenty-eight were both amateurs who had rarely played for the Hajduk first team.

The regulations could be liberally interpreted in some cases. Ivica Hlevnjak left the club in 1973 to sign for Strasbourg just before his twenty-eighth birthday as a reward for his contribution as a loyal first-choice player over the previous ten years. His career abroad was very different from his experience in Yugoslavia. In France, he spent two years at an anonymous club struggling in the first division before moving to Epinal, a semi-professional second-division side, where he enjoyed the status of a local hero. He was thirty-four when Epinal abandoned professionalism and freed him to finish his playing days in America's MISL. Dragan Holcer was an exception to Hajduk's policy. He had been recruited from the Serbian club Radnicki Nis in 1968 and in the eight years he spent at the picturesque Mediterranean city of Split he reached footballing fame, accumulating forty-five

---

30. In the twelve years he played in the MISL, Zungul scored 652 goals in 423 matches, making him by far the most prolific player in the whole league; *Major Soccer League Official Guide, 1990–91.*

1. Fanstiaho Jarbas (Cané), A Brazilian.

2. Guaita, Stagnaro and Scopelli arrive in Rome railway station, 1933.

3. Montpellier Université Club, with Mitrovic (5th from right, standing).

4. The marriages of football migrants Jeppson and Vinicio to Italian women.

5. In ídolos – page 17. The marriage of the Portuguese footballer Freitas (discussed in Chapter 6) to a local girl.

6. Harry Ward – one of the British migrants to France.

7. Andy Wilson (with Scottish international cap) – one of the British migrants to France.

8. Football Magazine (page 11) – Team photo of Partizan Belgrade – finalists in 1966 European Cup. Within 3 years, all of the team had moved abroad, with the exception of Hasanagic (bottom, extreme left). Mentioned in Chapter 4.

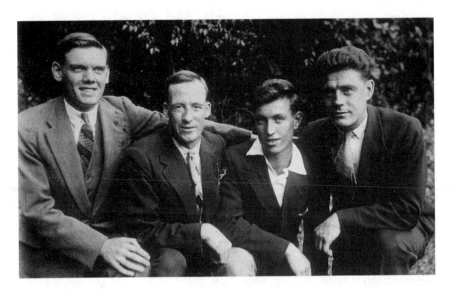

9. The 'Bexleyheath' group of British football migrants. Left to right: Bob Srioker, Billy Cornelius, Billy West, Sid Skinner.

10. The South American artist Raimundo Orsi, star of the Juventus and Italian teams of the 1930s.

11. Two generations of migrants to Italy. A training session at Juventus with manager Cesarini (second left) and John Charles (far right). The other players are the Italians Boniperti (far left) and Nicole (second right).

The Yugoslav Wanderers

Table 4.1 Hajduk Split's Exports, 1972–92

Season	Player	New club	Country
1971/72	Ivan Pavlica	FC Metz	France
1972/73	Pero Nadozeva	SC Lokeren	Belgium
	Ivica Hlevnjak	RC Strasbourg	France
	Ratomir Vuckovic	AC Ajaccio (div. 2)	France
1973/74	–		
1974/75	Miroslav Boskovic	SCO Angers	France
	Dragan Holcer	VfB Stuttgart (div. 2)	Germany
	Branko Oblak	FC Schalke 04	Germany
1975/76	Tomislav Ivic (Manager)	Ajax Amsterdam	Holland
	Vanco Balevski	Karlsruher SC	Germany
	Rizah Meskovic	AZ'67 Alkmaar	Holland
1976/77	Ivan Buljan	Hamburger SV	Germany
1977/78	Jure Jerkovic	FC Zurich	Switzerland
	Luka Bonacic (*)	Grasshoppers Zurich	Switzerland
1978/79	Mario Boljat	FC Schalke 04	Germany
	Vilson Dzoni	FC Schalke 04	Germany
	Ivan Katalinic	Southampton	England
	Slavisa Zungul (**)	Golden Bay Earthquakes	USA
1979/80	Tomislav Ivic (Manager)	RSC Anderlecht	Belgium
	Drazen Muzinic	Norwich	England
	Luka Peruzovic	RSC Anderlecht	Begium
1980/81	Borisa Djordjevic	Hamburger SV	Germany
	Mikun Jovanic	RSC Anderlecht	Belgium
	Sime Luketin	FC Sochaux	France
	Milorad Nizetic	Linares CF (div. 2)	Spain
	Ivica Surjak	Paris Saint-Germain	France
1981/82	–		
1982/83	Zoran Jelikic	Standard Liège	Belgium
	Boro Primorac	Lille OSC	France
1983/84	Josip Cop	Sturm Graz	Austria
	Dusan Pesic	Fenerbahçe Istanbul	Turkey
	Zoran Simovic	Galatasaray Istanbul	Turkey
1984/85	Nikisa Cukrov	SC Toulon	France
	Vedran Macan	CD Malaga	Spain
	Dzevad Prekazi	Galatasaray Istanbul	Turkey
	Nenad Salov	Viktoria Aschaffenburg (div.2)	Germany

Table 4.1 (Continued)

Season	Player	New club	Country
1985/86	Ivica Kalinic	Tirol Innsbruck	Austria
	Vatroslav Petrinovic	Admira Wacker Vienna	Austria
	Blaz Sliskovic	Olympique Marseille	France
	Zlatko Vujovic	Girondins Bordeaux	France
	Zoran Vujovic	Girondins Bordeaux	France
1986/87	Josip Skoblar (Manager)	Hamburger SV	Germany
	Ivo Jerolimov	Cercle Bruges	Belgium
	Mladan Pralija	Hamburger SV	Germany
	Vedran Rozic	Sydney Croatia	Australia
1987/88	Branko Miljus	Real Valladolid	Spain
	Zoran Vulic	Real Mallorca	Spain
1988/89	Frane Bucan (*)	RC Genk	Belgium
	Nenad Gracan	Real Oviedo	Spain
	Branko Karacic	Cercle Bruges	Belgium
	Jerko Tipuric	Cercle Bruges	Belgium
1989/90	Stanko Poklepovic (Man.)	APOEL Nicosia	Cyprus
	Aliosa Asanovic (**)	FC Metz	France
	Bernard Barnjak (**)	CD Castellón (div. 2)	Spain
	Dragutin Celic	Hertha BSC Berlin (div. 2)	Germany
	Nikola Jerkan (**)	Real Oviedo	Spain
	Ivan Pudar	Sporting Espinho	Portugal
	Josko Spanjic (**)	Austria Klagenfurt (div. 2)	Austria
1990/91	Josip Skoblar (Manager)	Famalicão	Portugal
	Luka Peruzovic (Man.)	SC Charleroi	Belgium
	Alen Boksic (**)	AS Cannes/ Ol. Marseille	France
	Darko Drazic	Fortuna Dusseldorf	Germany
	Predag Erak (**)	Iraklis Salonica	Greece
	Robert Jarni (**)	Bari	Italy
	Radovan Krstovic	Alpine Donawitz	Austria
	Dragan Setinov	Ethnikos Pireo	Greece
	Ivica Vastic (**)	First Vienna FC	Austria
1991/92	Goran Alar	Alpine Donawitz	Austria
	Spjepan Andrijasevic (**)	AS Monaco	France
	Marin Lalic (**)	Paços de Ferreira	Portugal
	Goran Vucevic (**)	FC Barcelona	Spain

(*) As amateur allowed to leave the country before the age of 28
(**) Professional player under 28

international caps and diversifying his income by opening a pub.[31] His first season in Stuttgart in 1975 coincided with his new team's return to the German top flight and he played there as a *libero* for six more seasons. When he finally left it was to Schalke, whom he helped gain promotion to the top division. Both Hlevnijak and Holcer managed to carve themselves very successful, profitable and relatively long careers in spite of the fact that they had left Yugoslavia at an age when other players may have begun to think about retirement.

At Hajduk, Ivic replaced the departing players with apprentices from within the club and so invested the proceeds from international transfers into the youth team infrastructure. As a result, twenty-five youth team players between 1967 and 1982 made the path to the professional team and fifteen of these played for the national side.[32] Of the 1974 Yugoslav World Cup squad, Buljan, Muzinic, Jerkovic and Surjak had all graduated from the Hajduk youth set-up. In 1985, a modern 50,000 all-seater stadium called Poljud and a sports complex including an Olympic-size swimming pool with a number of gymnasiums were built, largely from the money made through these international transfers. The Hajduk model became recognized across Europe, Ivic even being head-hunted by Ajax Amsterdam and Anderlecht, later to become two of the continent's key actors in the formation of young players (see Chapter 7).

The 1970s were the 'golden years' of the Hajduk model. More often than not, the players who moved abroad were successful in their new environments. They adapted easily, caused few problems and, of course, learnt the language. The clubs who bought them were generally pleased to have acquired good players at reasonable prices and many came back for more. It is true that they did not get young players who could then be sold on for a large profit, but what they did receive was an employee with a secure profile, experienced on the field and generally settled domestically, with a wife and children. For their part, Hajduk and other clubs who adopted similar policies benefited financially from the exchange. The players of Hajduk Split, Partizan and Red Star Belgrade and Dinamo Zagreb became trademarks of football quality at an affordable price.

The transfer of Ivan Katalinic to Southampton in February 1980 indicates the potential benefits all parties could receive from the migration of Yugoslav footballers. In a letter from Ante Zaja, Hajduk's secretary general, to the player's prospective employers, Katalinic was described as 'a firm character leading a very solid private life'; as a footballer he was 'very disciplined and laborous [*sic*]'. Katalinic was given a glowing reference which highlighted his contribution to Hajduk's domestic success and outlined his experience in European club and

---

31. *Kicker Sportmagazin*, 12 June 1975.
32. Zdravko Reic, 'Hajduk', *Guerin sportivo*, 16 October 1985, pp. 74–7.

international football.[33] With some exaggeration, he was described as 'among the five best goalkeepers in Europe'. For Southampton, Katalinic was a goalkeeper with an international pedigree at a reasonable price. The leading English goalkeepers were much too expensive. The club had made an offer for QPR's Phil Parkes but at £500,000 he was 'out of our price range'; Katalinic cost less than half of that. And for the player himself, the deal represented a sizeable financial sum which was a reward for his commitment to the game at home. He was to receive a minimum of £20,000 per annum plus bonuses, a figure far in excess of his previous salary.[34] This was the type of reward which Yugoslavs were coming to expect as a result of their export at twenty-eight to Western Europe.

Ethnic Clubs and Football Immigrants

Throughout the twentieth century, playing football was a way for the Croatian communities in particular to meet in their new country of residence, especially in North America and Australia.[35] The official history of the Croatian federation has observed that from 1922 there was a Croatian immigrant team in Milwaukee and another one the following year in Chicago. In 1964 the Croatian Soccer Federation of the USA and Canada was founded as an ethnic league with headquarters in Cleveland. It involved the following sixteen clubs from all over North America: Croatia Toronto, Croatia Windsor, Croatia London St Thomas, Croatia Norval, Croatia Vancouver, NK Zagreb-Toronto, Croatia Hamilton, Adria Oshawa, Jadran Chicago, Hrvat Chicago, NK Zagreb-Collinwood (Cleveland), Croatia Detroit, Croatia Milwaukee, Croatia Cleveland, Croatia Los Angeles and Hrvatski Milwaukee. In Australia, Napredak became the first Croatian club in 1939. A Croatian Soccer Association was formed in 1974 while Melbourne Croatia (founded in 1953) has been one of the most successful of all Australian club sides. Matches opposing Serb and Croat clubs could be particularly violent affairs in Australia: Wray Vamplew has commented that 'in such circumstances cynical tackles and off-the-ball incidents could be seen as political rather than professional fouls'.[36]

33. PFA Work Permit File, 1980–84, Ante Zaja to Southampton FC, 6 August 1979.

34. PFA Work Permit File, 1980–84, Southampton FC Application to the Department of Employment for a work permit for Ivan Katalinic, 18 December 1979.

35. Ivan Cizmic, 'Nogometni sport medju hrvatima izvan domovine', in Kramer (ed.), *Hrvatski nogometni savez 80. obljetnica*, pp. 260–7 gives a precise account of the Croatian clubs abroad.

36. Wray Vamplew, '"Wogball": Ethnicity and violence in Australian soccer', in J. Williams and R. Giulianotti (eds), *Game Without Frontiers: Football, Identity and Modernity*, Aldershot: Arena, 1994, p. 212; Phil Mosely, 'Balkan Politics in Australian Soccer', in J. O'Hara (ed.), *Ethnicity and Soccer in Australia*, Sydney: ASSH, 1994, pp. 32–43.

Table 4.2 Composition of the Toronto Metros-Croatia Squads 1975–1978

	Squad	Croats	Prof. in Div 1. Yugoslavia
1975	25	13 + Manager	2
1976	26	9 + Manager	1
1977	23	14 + Manager	4
1978	25	14 + Manager	3

Source: Data elaborated from Colin Jose, *NASL, A Complete Record*, Derby: Breedon, 1989, pp. 140, 162, 182, 207

It is interesting to note that ethnic rivalries between Serbs and Croats were more evident in Australian soccer from the 1960s than in Yugoslavia itself. The federalist regime created by Tito tried to minimize the conflict between nationalities and prohibited the prefix 'Serb' or 'Croatia' for football clubs. Similarly, the FSJ was not keen to allow the transfer of leading players to American, Canadian and Australian ethnic clubs. As shown in Chapter 5, Toronto Metros became Toronto Metros-Croatia between 1975 and 1978. Over this period, the club employed thirty-seven Yugoslavian-born players and managers, all but three of whom were Croats. However, if Croatian players were the most important group, the squad was mainly composed of semi-professionals from division two in Yugoslavia and Croatian-Canadians (Table 4.2). And the club's major success was achieved when the Croatians were in the minority.

The most famous player the Croatian team ever employed was the Portuguese star Eusebio, who scored sixteen goals in twenty-one matches in 1976, the year Toronto won the NASL trophy. Three full Yugoslav internationals played for the side. Filip Blaskovic was already thirty-one years old when he was given a free transfer from Dinamo Zagreb in 1976. Drago Vabec came on loan for four months from the same club in 1977 and the third Yugoslav international to play for the club was the Bosnian Sead Susic, brother of the more famous Safet, who came from Red Star Belgrade via the Colorado Caribous. On the other hand, the club recruited seven amateur internationals from division two clubs.[37] The same occurred in Australia a decade later. Of the eighteen Yugoslavs playing in the national league, only the Croatia Sydney player-manager Vedran Rozic was a former international. All the others had been reserve choices or division-two players at home.[38] The Yugoslav federation and the clubs preferred to arrange transfers with established European sides and remained reluctant to become entangled with these 'ethnic' clubs.

37. Tomislav Markovic, *1976–77 Godisnjak Fudbalskog Saveza Jugoslavije*, Belgrade: FSJ, 1977, pp. 184–90.
38. Data from *Australian Soccer Annual 1989*, pp. 29–45.

Yugoslav Players Abroad

During the 1970s, the French monthly *Football Magazine* dedicated a series of articles to the daily lives and peculiarities of the Yugoslavs employed in the national league. Here we shall use this source to provide clues to the experience and lifestyle of these migrants. More than anything else, the articles emphasized the ability of the group to adapt. Vladimir Kovacevic, for one, admitted that 'I feel contented in France. The Yugoslavs feel almost at home here. It must be a question of temperament. We are not homesick'.[39] Vahidin Musemic added that 'Our mentalities and lifestyles are similar'.[40]

Most of these migrant players were married, and in general had a good education and a cultured background. Like their predecessors of the 1920s, the majority had studied at university. Ivica Osim had a degree in mathematics, Musemic was a dentist, Petkovic and Dzajic were economics graduates, Kovacevic had studied physical education and Vojislav Melic, Kiril Dojcinovski and Dusan Galic had all been law students at Belgrade University before becoming professional footballers.[41] Their wives were also mostly well-educated working women. Mrs Kovacevic was an architect, Mrs Musemic and Mrs Savic were trained language teachers while Mrs Petkovic had studied physics. The wife of Marco Mlinaric was an actress in Zagreb's national theatre.[42] In their reports, the French journalists were impressed when they compared these educated players with the less cultured background of the average French footballer and his spouse. They were also portrayed as living respectable middle-class lives. Osim rented 'a quiet apartment with his wife and children' and slept thirteen to fifteen hours a day; Katalinski, too, was said 'to love comfort'. Melic's hobby was filming his children, Musemic loved chess and horse-riding while Pantelic preferred hunting and playing *pétanque* (boules), the French bowls game. Ivan Curkovic apparently spent three hours a day reading books and journals on economics and politics.[43] Slobodan Topalovic was a talented painter who exhibited his work while Dusan Savic was said to live the normal life of a professional footballer, except that he 'spent time in art galleries, and with his great friend the surrealist painter Ljuba Popovic' and was 'a frequenter of second-hand bookshops'.

39. Jacques Touffait, 'Kovacevic: la douceur angevine lui réussit', *Football Magazine*, November 1970.

40. Victor Peroni, 'Les deux amours de Musemic', *Football Magazine*, September 1974.

41. Jacques Etienne, 'Melic: le langage de la vérité', *Football Magazine*, January 1972; Gérard Ernault, 'Petko-Gavroche', *Football Magazine*, May 1974; Jacques Touffait, 'Osim: l'hirondelle qui ne fait pas le printemps', *Football Magazine*, February 1971.

42. On Savic and Mlinaric, *L'Equipe*, 17 August 1988.

43. *France football*, 4 December 1979.

As we noted of Katalinic's application to Southampton, the attitude and behaviour of Yugoslavs off the field was considered an important part of their success. A club history of Sochaux noted that: 'Since 1962, strong links have been woven between Sochaux directors and Yugoslav clubs. They are based on confidence and respect. In Sochaux we have appreciated the morality and the professional behaviour of the southern Slavs.'[44] The choice of France was in many cases determined by the presence of compatriots. This could have negative consequences, however. In Nice, Bjekovic and Katalinski were initially ostracized because they were always together and spoke Serbo-Croat with the manager. But when they decided to learn the language and send their children to French schools, most of these problems were solved. During his first year at Strasbourg, Osim spoke German with his manager and his two German team-mates, which led to deteriorating relations with the majority of the players who spoke only French. After a year, he had improved his French and as recognition of his willingness to integrate was designated team captain. The term 'integration' was often used by French journalists to sum up the Yugoslavs, the majority of whom signed three-year contracts and fulfilled all their duties. This symbolic integration and coopera-tion between the two nations was acknowledged at the very highest level. In October 1977, a number of Yugoslav footballers in France, including Ivan Curkovic and Limoges's semi-professional Slobodan Stojovic, were invited by president Giscard d'Estaing to a black-tie dinner at the Palace of Versailles on the occasion of a state visit of Marshall Tito.[45]

Although the fitness and dedication of the Yugoslavs at training sessions impressed their employers, one peculiarity which was often reported was their tendency to smoke. Josip Katalinski, nicknamed 'Skija' after a popular brand of Yugoslav cigarette, told a reporter that, like many in Yugoslavia, he 'did not dislike tobacco. Like Johan Cruyff he drags at least twenty a day'.[46] Ilija Pantelic, too, was pictured smoking in a short biographical piece.[47] Dragan Dzajic, a non-smoker who did not drink alcohol was described by his French manager as 'intelligent, polite, friendly and modest';[48] in the same way, Vahidin Musemic, 'educated, calm, friendly and scrupulously honest'[49] was representative of the kind of player managers liked to work with.

44. Frédéric Vial and François Ruffin, *FC Sochaux Montbéliard*, Lyon: La manufacture, 1988, p. 101.

45. *France football*, 18 October 1977.

46. Victor Sinet, 'Josip Katalinski: le démon de l'attaque', *Football Magazine*, February 1976.

47. Gérard Ernault, 'Ilija Pantelic, le comte de Saint-Germain', *Football Magazine*, September 1974.

48. Tony Arbona, 'Dzajic', *Football Magazine*, September 1975.

49. Jovan Velitchkov, 'Vahidin Musemic: il marque des buts avec les yeux!', *Football Magazine*, July 1974.

When the most popular and successful Yugoslav import of all, Josip Skoblar, left Marseilles in November 1974, he had scored more than 200 goals in a little over five years.[50] He detailed his future ambitions: 'I plan to manage the hotel chain I have opened on the Dalmatian coast. I studied business, which will be very useful. I also opened a clothes shop this month here in Marseilles. In the meantime I will continue to play football for Rijeka and try to get my coaching diploma'.[51] A famous coach in Yugoslavia ten years later, he made an unsuccessful comeback as general manager of Marseilles but his feelings had not changed: 'I often come back to Marseilles, where I still own a clothes shop and have kept some very good friends.'[52] When their playing careers finished, a number of migrants returned to Yugoslavia as football managers. A few, however, remained in France. After seven years with Lyons, Ljubomir Mihajlovic took the opportunity to buy and manage a hotel in the French town; Josip Katalinski ran another hotel in Antibes but invested part of his money in Sarajevo. More impressively still, Ivan Curkovic had become a very rich man after nine years with Saint-Etienne. He owned houses in Belgrade, Mostar (his home town) and in France. He had invested on the stock exchange in diamonds and in shares in a health clinic. He was also one of the directors of a multinational fashion factory and lived a millionaire's life jetting between Belgrade and the Côte d'Azur. He is now one of the executive directors of the FSJ and continues to run businesses in different countries, while Milan Galic, another former migrant to France, is the legal adviser to the federation in Belgrade.

Those who migrated to Belgium have shown a similar attachment to their second homes. Standard Liège employed twelve Yugoslav players between the mid-1960s and the early 1980s. Seven became football managers while one is now a gardener in Sarajevo and another, the reserve goalkeeper Zdravko Brkljacic, runs a tourist village in Croatia. His daughter chose to stay in Belgium after finishing school and opened a restaurant in Liège. Brkljacic now spends a month a year in Belgium, and, like many return migrants, is 'very proud when Belgians come to visit me in Croatia'.[53] Another Yugoslav who played in Belgium and France, Silvester Takac, is now a football manager living in France but kept the house he bought in Belgium. Antwerp's goalkeeper, Ratko Svilar was said to be 'calm and concentrated', which

50. On Skoblar in Marseilles, Christian Bromberger, *Le match de football: ethnologie d'une passion*, Paris: MSH, 1995. In a survey of supporters in 1987, Skoblar remained the most popular choice of all the club's players and many boys born in Marseilles in the early 1970s were called 'Josip' or 'Yosip'.

51. Victor Sinet, 'L'adieu de Skoblar à Marseille' *Football Magazine*, December 1974.

52. *France football*, 8 November 1983. He insists, in his French autobiography, on the durable friendships he made in Marseilles; Josip Skoblar, *Chasseur de buts*, Paris: Olivier Orban, 1977, p. 116.

53. Pascale Piérard and Michel Dubois, *Standard, une épopée*, Alleur-Liège: Le Perron, 1992, p. 183.

no doubt helped him to play for the club until the age of forty-five. Significantly, his son has kept his name alive as a professional with Antwerp.

There were some failures of course. Salih Durkalic, a rare case of an unmarried migrant, never adapted to life in Sochaux. He socialized in the evenings with the local Yugoslavs who worked in the Peugeot factory and was dismissed after two years.[54] In Belgium and Germany especially, the Yugoslav immigrant communities were seen as a potential danger, capable of marginalizing the players and slowing down their integration. Mario Boljat at Schalke 04 and Boris Djordjevic in Hamburg failed in their first year and were given no second chance, although Djordjevic remained in Germany, running a pub and playing amateur football in Berlin. In general, the French press presented Yugoslav players as 'exceptional footballers, very adaptable but lacking cohesion and psychologically weak'. Like the South Americans, they were seen as 'ball lovers' and artists, but 'over-individualists strongly opposed to productive football'.[55] If they managed to settle well abroad, they rarely achieved the highest recognition. No Yugoslav has ever won the European Footballer of the Year award and, like their national team, have tended to be regarded as underachievers at international level. Indeed the poor results of the Yugoslav national team have often been seen as a consequence of the migration of so many of its footballers. It has sometimes been perceived as a side of mercenaries, more interested in the individual ability to charm international recruiters than in physical strength, team spirit and solidarity.[56]

Finding New Markets

For most of the 1970s, France, Belgium, Germany, Austria, Holland and Switzerland were the exclusive European destinations for Yugoslav professionals. Yet from the late 1970s, a number of new and potentially lucrative markets began to open up. In the first two years after the lifting of the ban on alien players in England, twelve Yugoslavs were registered with Football League clubs. However, strict limits were placed on new arrivals. The British Department of Employment would only grant the necessary work permits to players from non-EEC countries if they had been capped by their country and were regarded as having 'a distinctive contribution to make to the national game'.[57] Quite surprisingly, the British were mainly interested in defenders. Three goalkeepers – Borota at Chelsea, Avramovic at Notts County and Katalinic at Southampton – and seven defenders represented the core

54. Vial and Ruffin, *FC Sochaux Montbéliard*, p. 100.
55. 'Yougoslavie: ces mercenaires qui ne manquent pas de talent mais de cohésion', *La dernière heure, les sports*, 29 May 1982.
56. *Miroir du football*, November 1973.
57. PFA Archives, Work Permit File, 1980–84, A.J. Gulliver to Cliff Lloyd, 8 June 1979.

of the Yugoslav migrants to Britain. In other countries, they were present in every position on the field.[58] The return to democracy in Greece coincided with the adoption of professional football. From 1979, each club in the top division was authorized to employ two foreign players, and for the next eleven years, twelve Yugoslavs on average were employed annually by Greek clubs. From 1983 the Turkish borders were also opened to foreign players. Finally, imports to Spain increased as the peninsula ceased to be the preserve of South American players (Table 4.3).

There were two main reasons behind this search for new markets. First, competitors began to appear on the European transfer market to challenge the Yugoslav dominance. Players from Poland and Hungary with excellent international experience were increasingly available for cheaper prices from the late 1970s. Sixty Polish players, for example, moved to France between 1975 and 1985, mainly to semi-professional second division clubs (thirty-four of the total) and clubs in the top division with limited budgets, like Auxerre and Valenciennes. In the 1980/81 season, there were more Polish than Yugoslav players in the French second division.[59] At the same time, eight Yugoslavs and five Poles were under contract in Belgium. The Poles abroad included members of the 1974 and 1978 World Cup squads, like Boniek (Juventus), Zmuda (Verona), Deyna (Manchester City), Szarmach (Auxerre), Gadocha (Nantes), Lato and Lubanski (Lokeren, Belgium), goalkeeper Tomaszewski (Beerschot Antwerp) and the sweeper Gorgon at the Swiss semi-professional club St Gallen. In 1981, Hungary gave foreign transfer opportunities to a dozen of its senior internationals, a move which was soon followed by Czechoslovakia. Yugoslavia's monopoly over experienced but economical players was under challenge, particularly as the Polish federation began practising a dumping policy. The German market for Polish players had been restricted to opponents of the Communist regime or those Poles with German roots who could acquire a German passport. For the first time in 1984, German clubs began to buy players from Poland, leading to increased competition and a considerable reduction in transfer prices. But there was no corresponding change in international regulations. In the majority of Western European countries, clubs were still allowed to employ only two foreign players and, with this increased supply, the contractual power of potential migrants, their clubs and the agents was proportionately reduced.

The second reason for this search for new markets was internal. The Yugoslav economy suffered a major recession in the 1980s. The self-management dream

58. In 1981, the Yugoslavs in France were mainly forwards (fourteen out of twenty) and in Germany the different positions were well balanced, with eight defenders, six midfielders and six forwards.

59. M. Barreaud, *Dictionnaire des footballeurs étrangers du championnat professionnel français (1932–1997)*, Paris: L'Harmattan, 1998, pp. 201–14.

and the regulated market economy proved unsuccessful and by 1983 foreign debt amounted to $20 billion. This crisis culminated in 1989 with a record inflation of 2,500 per cent and an average living standard inferior to that of thirty years earlier.[60] The degradation of the national economy had a profound influence on the football market. The first sign of this came in 1982, when the FSJ blocked the international transfers of three Yugoslav internationals who had performed poorly at the World Cup in Spain. Vladimir Petrovic, Dusan Savic and Safet Susic were punished by being forced to continue to play at home. Petrovic and Savic had signed from Red Star for Arsenal and Sporting Gijon respectively, while Susic, a highly-rated player from FK Sarajevo, had been engaged by Paris Saint-Germain after signing *two* contracts in Italy (for Torino and Inter), both of which were invalidated. The ban, however, was short-lived, mainly due to Red Star's desperate need of foreign currency. By Christmas 1982, the players had been permitted to join their new clubs abroad. In the face of the national economic crisis, the federation had been unable to impose restrictions and clubs had to face a new transfer logic. To remain viable, the only solution was to acquire foreign currencies by selling as many players as possible abroad. As the federation did not intend to change the twenty-eighth birthday rule, club directors had to find new solutions.

For the previous twenty years, the 'big four' clubs – Red Star, Partizan, Dinamo and Hajduk – had prioritized the development of young players. As we noted of Hajduk, they kept their best talents until the age of twenty-eight and invested the transfer income in the youth sector (youth coaches were rewarded as much as first-team coaches) or in rewards to players. The national transfer market had remained largely limited to lower-division players, with a maximum wage restricting earnings at the top end. *Modus vivendi* and self-regulation among clubs helped to create a system which functioned smoothly and out of which all parties profited. The directors of Red Star Belgrade, led by managing-director Dragan Dzajic (the former star of the 1970s who had studied economics during his playing career), decided to invest their valuable foreign money in the domestic market. In the summer of 1983, with the money received from Arsenal and Gijon, Red Star signed four internationals from rival first division clubs: Ivkovic from Dinamo, Elsner from Olimpija, Mrkela from OFK and Krivokapic from Sutjeska. This new policy had a dramatic effect on the organization of Yugoslavian football. When the dinar lost its value on international exchanges, Red Star had a decisive advantage. Its rivals, in precarious financial situations, were rarely able to refuse the small sums offered for domestic transfers, which increased the discrepancy

60. Branka Magas, *The Destruction of Yugoslavia: Tracking the break-up 1980–92*, London: Verso, 1993, pp. 94–7; Stefano Bianchini, 'La transizione post-communista in Jugoslavia, Albania e Romania', in R. Spanò (ed.), *Jugoslavia e Balcani: una bomba in Europa*, Milan: FrancoAngeli, 1992, p. 138.

between Yugoslav clubs. This also underlined the failure of Yugoslavia's alternative approach to professional football. As the *Financial Times* noted in June 1984, it was an example of 'the country's acceptance of capitalist economic principles – exclusive reliance on monetary principles – implying that the West is ahead ideologically'.[61] Red Star's reputation and its international network effectively guaranteed its players a contract and a good deal abroad when they turned twenty-eight.

From, this point on, Red Star curtailed its investment in the youth sector and chose to buy players aged between twenty-four and twenty-six, who were then sold on to the international market. In six years the club acquired the contracts of twenty-four under-21 and full-internationals, before selling their rights to foreign clubs. Over the same period, Red Star contributed only two players to the national market (Goran Milojevic and Djurovski), both of whom were signed by local rivals Partizan. Acquiring players such as Prosinecki, Pancev, Savicevic and Dragan Stojkovic, Red Star established a hegemonic position over the national labour market and Yugoslav football in general. In response Hajduk intensified its youth policy while Partizan, remembering the theory of the third way, innovated by investing in two Chinese internationals in 1988, Liu Haiguan and Jia Xhuchen. Dinamo tried to compete with Red Star through imitation but with less success at national level, although the club consolidated its position in Croatia. For all the other professional clubs, the elite international market, already limited, was effectively closed.

If we compare the exports of a middle-sized top division club over ten years, the effect of these changes becomes evident. Velez Mostar, a club from South Bosnia, transferred seven players from its 1974 squad to premier-division European clubs; only one player, Boro Primorac, was transferred domestically to one of the 'big four' (Hajduk).[62] Of the 1984 squad, seven professionals signed contracts abroad but none went to a major club. Second-division clubs in Germany and Spain and second-rank Turkish, Greek and Swiss clubs became the most common destinations.[63] The economic benefit of these transfers was minimal. Velez's two best players, Goran Juric and Drazen Prskalo, went to Red Star and Dinamo as a

61. *Financial Times*, 18 June 1984.

62. The destinations of the 1974 Velez squad were as follows: Dusan Bajevic and Franjo Vladic (AEK Athens), Ahmet Glavovic (1860 Munich), Alex Ristic (Eintracht Braunschweig), Enver Maric (Schalke 04), Dzemal Hadziabdic (Swansea), Vahid Halilhodzic (Nantes). Data elaborated from Mladen Delic, *Enciclopedija jugoslavenskog nogometa*, Zagreb: Spektar, 1974.

63. The destinations of the 1984 Velez squad were as follows: Sead Kajtaz (Nuremberg, Germany), Vladimir Skojacic (Kalamaria Greece), Misa Krsticevic (Oberhausen, German Division Two), S. Tanovic (Eskisehirspor, Turkey), N. Bijedic (Bursaspor, Turkey), Semir Tuce (Lucerne, Switzerland), Hamel Karabeg (Burgos, Spanish Division Two). Data elaborated from Milos Marinkovic, *Almanah Fudbalskog Saveza Jugoslavije 1978–1986*, Vol. 2, Belgrade: FSJ, 1988, pp. 278–9.

logical consequence of the Yugoslav 'new deal'. With the further shift towards a more liberal economy, the minimum age for international transfers was finally reduced in 1989 to twenty-six, allowing the main clubs to face their financial difficulties by increasing the introduction of foreign money at a time of massive inflation.

The War and its Consequences

This economic chaos was echoed by a tenuous political situation and both were reflected on the football scene. The antagonism between Croatian and Serbian football became more pronounced in the late 1980s. There had always been some distinction. Under the dictatorship of Ante Pavelic and the pro-Nazi Croatian state during the Second World War, Croatia had a national team which played nineteen matches between 1940 and 1944 while Dinamo Zagreb has had a Croat flag on its blazon since the 1960s. Even the term 'football' was expressed differently: *Nogomet* in Croatian and *Futbal* in Serbian.

Ivan Colovic has studied the changing attitudes of supporters, press and players and the role of football at the beginning of the civil war. The original Partizan-Red Star and Dinamo Zagreb–Hajduk Split rivalries evolved into a nationalistic conflict between the Croats and the Serbs.[64] The matches between teams from Belgrade and Zagreb became demonstrations of nationalist violence. Dinamo Zagreb's links with the HDZ (Croatian Democratic Union), the nationalist Croatian party of Franjo Tudjman, became increasingly evident. Zvonimir Boban, the young star of Dinamo, found himself at the centre of the dispute after a match against Red Star in May 1990, when he attacked opposition players and officials in the name of Croatia and its leader, followed by hooligans of the club who fought with the Red Star supporters. The Belgrade press stigmatized those 'bad sportsmen' whom it saw as predicating nationalism: Arapovic, the basketball star of Cibona, the Croat Boban, the Kosovar Salja (or Shala) and the Slovene Skerjank who also played for Dinamo Zagreb. Dinamo had just recalled Zelko Adzic, a former youth team player, who had spent three years with Croatian ethnic clubs in Minnesota and Sydney. Significantly, the club recruited players of different ethnic nationalities (Albanian Kosovars, Muslims from Bosnia, Slovenes) but no Serbian players. At the end of 1990, the Dinamo directors decided to revert to the old name of the pre-communist period, HASK Gradjanski. The Yugoslav national team, on the other hand, became a mosaic of ethnic nationalities under the guidance of Ivica Osim, himself a Bosnian with Serb links married to a Croat. Through the national

---

64. Ivan Colovic, *Campo di calcio, campo di battaglia: il calcio dal racconto alla guerra. L'esperienza iugoslava*, Reggio Calabria: Mesogea, 1999, pp. 23–65.

team, the existence of a unified Yugoslavia and the role of its emigrants were promoted. For the 1990 World Cup, the squad of twenty-two players was composed of eight Croatians, six Bosnians, three Montenegrins, two Serbs, two Macedonians and one Slovenian. It was also a mixture of professionals abroad and young home-based players.[65] But domestically, Yugoslavian football was becoming increasingly nationalistic. The links with nationalist extremists became particularly evident when Zeljko Rajznatovic 'Arkan' became the leader of the Red Star supporters group and used football grounds to recruit his 'tigers', who would become famous for their crimes in Vukovar and in Bosnia.[66] The club that had represented Yugoslav communism and national unity for decades slowly became a symbol of Serbian identity.

In this troubled context, the increased emigration of players outlined in Table 4.3 can be explained by an economic crisis that pushed players, clubs and agents – who become crucial in this period – to look for fresh money and better contracts. Football was deeply affected by political changes at international and domestic level. The disintegration of the communist model in the late 1980s forced the FSJ in 1990 to bring an end to restrictions on international transfers. Age limits and military obligations were struck from the regulations. The impetus for these changes came from Eastern Europe and on this occasion the Yugoslavs were obliged to follow so as to keep a grip on the international market. But migration was also stimulated by renewed interest in Yugoslav players as a result of victory in the Under-20 World Championship in Chile in 1987.

The model proposed by Guy Hermet to explain the nationalist explosion in Yugoslavia applies perfectly to the football situation.[67] First, the dominant but contested nationality (Serbia) profited from circumstances (incidents during the Red Star–Dinamo match, under-representation of Serbs in the national team, the attitude in the internal transfer market) to re-establish its hegemony, provoking in turn a separatist reaction from the other nationalities. Secondly, the communist elites turned to nationalist movements. Once again, the changes at Red Star, Partizan

---

65. The eight Croatians were Ivkovic, Vulic, Jarni, Panadic, Prosinecki, Zl. Vujovic, Boksic and Suker; the six Bosnians were Omerovic, Jozic, Hadzibegic, Baljic, Susic and Sabanadzovic; the three Montenegrins, Lekovic, Brnovic and Savicevic; the two Macedonians were Stanojkovic and Pancev; the two Serbians were Spasic and Stojkovic; and Katanec was the lone Slovenian. The nine professionals abroad consisted of Ivkovic (Portugal), Jozic and Katanec (Italy), Vulic (Spain), Hadzibegic, Brnovic, Vujovic and Susic (France) and Bajic (Switzerland).

66. On Arkan see Colovic, *Campo di calcio, campo di battaglia*, pp. 46–52; Misha Glenny, *The Fall of Yugoslavia*, London: Penguin, 1992, p. 39; Paolo Rumiz, 'Armi, droga, mafia: la guerra come affare', *Limes*, 1–2, 1993, pp. 117–23.

67. Guy Hermet, *Histoire des nations et du nationalisme en Europe*, Paris: Seuil; 1996, pp. 219–20.

and Dinamo Zagreb are cases in point.[68] Thirdly, the intellectuals reinforced this division. The intellectual Milan Dzadzic observed that in the late 1970s 'my friends and myself identified four institutions representative of the social life of the Serbians today: the Serbian Academy of Arts and Sciences, the daily paper *Politika*, the publishing house Prosveta and Red Star Belgrade'.[69] For many intellectuals, football clubs became the ideal forum for popular nationalism.

To reflect this nationalism, migrant members of national communities were included in the teams. Miodrag Belodedic (or Belodedici in the Romanian orthography), a Romanian international from Steaua Bucharest emigrated illegally to Belgrade in 1989 to play for Red Star. Two years later, he explained to Belgrade's weekly sports journal *Tempo* the motives behind his move:

> Five years ago, on his death-bed, my father told me that my only fatherland was Serbia. He told me that I had to go to Serbia and play for Red Star where a big future was awaiting me . . . It is true I played for the Romanian national team, but only as a representative of the Serbian minority. Now my only will is to play for my national team, Yugoslavia, but I cannot. FIFA refused my request because I have changed citizenship. But this is not fair. I have not changed nation; I have simply returned to my fatherland. I took risks to do it. When I left, Ceaucescu's son condemned me to the death penalty for desertion.[70]

At the time of the interview, Belodedic lived a comfortable life with his mother and sister in Belgrade. The club paid him a monthly salary of $5,000 and bonuses such as a car and an apartment. But with the beginning of the war in Bosnia, this symbol of Serb nationalism left (along with most of the Red Star team), in his case to play for Valencia. The new Romanian government returned his passport and he rejoined the Romanian national side for the 1994 World Cup. Two of his team-mates in the Red Star side that won the European Cup in 1991 became symbols of the nationalist conflict. Sinisa Mihajlovic was born in Vukovar in Krajina of a Serbian father and a Croatian mother. While playing for Red Star, he took the side of the Serbians and told a *Tempo* reporter: 'Our supporters are at the front, my people give their blood and I have to play football. If I continue to do it, it is just to defend the honour of my land'.[71] At twenty-three, he left Yugoslavia to play (and then marry) in Italy. Now a dual citizen, he still plays for Yugoslavia,

---

68. Colovic has insisted on the changing discourse of the Red Star directors. In 1992 their chairman stated that the club had never been connected with the communist elite, although every director since the foundation has been a party dignitary. Colovic, *Campo di calcio, campo di battaglia*, p. 37.

69. Quoted in Colovic, *Campo di calcio, campo di battaglia*, p. 38.

70. *Tempo*, 25 December 1991, interview translated in *Guerin sportivo*, 26 February 1992.

71. *Tempo*, 11 December 1991.

and recently expressed on Italian television his friendship with the deceased Arkan. Robert Prosinecki, meanwhile, was born in Germany but grew up in Croatia. He was only eighteen when he was signed by Red Star. Forced to choose in 1991, he opted to emigrate to Spain and two years later finally decided to 'become' Croatian.

In Croatia after the declaration of independence, Franjo Tudjman himself suggested a new name for the former Dinamo (now HASK Gradjanski) – Croatia Zagreb. As a part of his foreign policy, Tudjman placed significant emphasis on the organization of the national team and strengthening of Croatia Zagreb. Football had been a symbol of the Croatian diaspora much earlier, with the recruitment by Dinamo Zagreb in 1982 of the young 'ethnic Croatian' Australian Edward Krncevic from Marconi Sydney, the first foreigner to play in the Yugoslav league.[72] After Croatian independence, Hajduk Split imported other Australian Croatians, including Mark Viduka, Josip Skoko and Steve Horvath.

Bosnia faced the most critical situation of all. During the siege of Sarajevo, three apprentices at FK Sarajevo were killed. The former team captain, Zelimir Vidovic, who had returned home in 1989 after five years as a professional in Austria, was another victim of war. A Muslim married to a Serbian, Vidovic ran a public house in the Serbian area of the city but, after refusing to put a *cetnik* flag in the window of his premises, he was arrested and killed by the Karadzic paramilitary troops.[73] Historically, FK Sarajevo had always been an ethnically mixed club, but with the outbreak of war, the FSJ allowed the Serbian players to leave the club without transfer fees. Vidakovic went to Red Star, Nedic and Raickovic to German second division clubs, Lazic and Slijvic to France. The Bosnian players abroad, meanwhile, decided to create a national team, with Faruk Hadzibegic and Mesa Bazdarevic at Sochaux in charge of the organization of fixtures. Between 1992 and 1995, thirty professional players from Bosnia migrated to Turkey, the only European country that expressed official support for Bosnia Herzegovina. Radmilo Mihajlovic, playing for Schalke 04 during the siege, sent help to Sarajevo, while one of the best players, Emir Vazda, was injured by a grenade on his way to a training session.

As Table 4.3 shows, it is clear that the war accelerated migration from the former Yugoslavia to a number of European countries, particularly Germany, Greece, Austria, Belgium, Cyprus, Portugal and Turkey. Some questions need to be asked about this most recent outflow of players. How are the transfers organized? How are so many players able find clubs? Most importantly of all, does the different destination of the various Yugoslav nationalities reflect the diplomatic relations of

---

72. Wray Vamplew *et al.*, *The Oxford Companion to Australian Sport*, Oxford: Oxford University Press, 1992, p. 200.

73. Fabio Sfiligoi, 'L'Odissea del Sarajevo', *Guerin sportivo*, 17 March 1993.

Table 4.3 Professional Footballers from former Yugoslavia in Europe, 1979–1996

Year	AUT	BEL	CYP	ENG	FRA	GER	GRE	ITA	POR	SPA	TUR
79/80	4	13	–	6	20	25	12	–	–	5	–
80/81	19	17	–	12	21	23	13	–	–	12	–
81/82	26	11	–	9	17	23	12	–	1	6	–
82/83	20	11	–	8	25	22	10	1	2	9	–
83/84	18	12	n.a	4	23	22	14	1	1	5	2
84/85	24	15	n.a	2	26	27	17	–	3	4	8
85/86	18	18	n.a	1	35	31	15	1	3	5	6
86/87	23	15	2	1	35	20	16	1	1	3	11
87/88	27	13	2	1	44	27	14	3	2	11	17
88/89	42	26	1	–	54	24	6	4	2	12	12
89/90	42	27	3	–	63	26	10	6	1	19	8
90/91	42	18	4	–	61	28	10	4	3	21	15
91/92	42	19	8	–	54	33	24	6	15	31	17
92/93	35	57	12	–	37	44	58	11	23	42	23
93/94	26	39	21	–	37	46	56	9	34	31	17
94/95	23	29	n.a	2	28	41	62	10	39	37	n.a
95/96	29	31	n.a	5	29	60	61	9	41	31	n.a

Source: Data from various European football alamanacs

recruiting states? Only partial answers are possible. What can be said, however, is that we need to understand this migration in terms of the movement of different nationalities and not just as Yugoslavian footballers generally.

The predominance of the migration to Germany reflected the general flow. Of the 820,000 former Yugoslav asylum-seekers in Europe in 1994, 340,000 went to Germany, a country with an established Yugoslav migrant population.[74] As we can see from Table 4.4a, although every nationality is represented, the Croatians constitute the majority of the former Yugoslavs in German football. Diplomatic and linguistic connections have helped to develop this affinity further. Thus in 1992 a song called 'Danke, Deutschland!' was constantly played on Croatian radio after the recognition of the Croatian nation by the Bonn government.[75] It is important to note that every third Yugoslav in Germany migrated *before* playing professional football or, like the Kovac brothers (current Croat internationals), were born in Germany but never acquired citizenship. By contrast, the Yugoslav migration to Spain can be explained mainly by economic considerations (Table 4.4b). The embargo on Serbia and the low salaries required by its players have

74. 'Les réfugiés de l'ex-Yougoslavie', *Le monde diplomatique*, January 1994, pp. 10–11.
75. Misha Glenny, *The Fall of Yugoslavia*, p. 193.

Table 4.4a Professional Footballers from former Yugoslavia in German Divisions 1 and 2, 1997–98

	Total *	%
Bosnia	6 (1)	11.6
Croatia	29 (8)	55.8
FYRM **	6 (2)	11.6
Slovenia	3 (1)	5.7
Yugoslavia ***	8 (4)	15.4
TOTAL	**52 (16)**	**100.1**

* In brackets are the players who arrived in Germany before their professional career
** Former Yugoslav Republic of Macedonia
*** Includes Serbia, Vojvodina, Montenegro and Kosovo
Source: Data elaborated from *Kicker Sportmagazin*, 'Bundesliga 97/98'

Table 4.4b Professional Footballers from former Yugoslavia in Spanish Divisions 1 and 2A, 1997–98

	Total	%
Bosnia	3	6.2
Croatia	12	25
FYRM (*)	–	–
Slovenia	–	–
Yugoslavia (**)	33	68.8
TOTAL	**48**	**100**

(*) Former Yugoslav Republic of Macedonia
(**) Includes Serbia, Vojvodina, Montenegro and Kosovo
Source: Data elaborated from Don Balón, 'Extra Liga 97/98'

persuaded many Spanish clubs to chose Serbs ahead of the more expensive Croatian migrants.[76]

Yugoslav footballers also moved en masse to minor European professional leagues such as Greece. In 1991, the Greek authorities allowed its lower-division clubs to engage two foreigners each. The majority of these jobs were taken by Yugoslavs, leading to a massive increase in numbers. In Belgium, semi-professional clubs with low budgets who had not been able previously to pay transfer fees to Yugoslav clubs profited significantly from the arrival of Yugoslavs who, because of the war, were suddenly free of contracts. In a matter of months, the Yugoslav

76. For the effect of the UN embargo on Yugoslav athletes more generally, see Borivoje Lecic, 'Participation of Yugoslav Athletes in International Competitions, 1992–95', *Yugoslav Survey*, 37, 2, 1996.

league received 3,500 emigration demands. Under these circumstances, Red Star lost fifty players between 1993 and 1996. As Dragan Dzajic complained: 'In the past we were able to keep our players for six or seven years, now we cannot keep them more than two seasons. A good player like Ognjenovic earns only £100 a week here. This is ridiculous compared with western salaries.'[77] Only England seemed to remain disinterested in Yugoslav footballers, although this has changed somewhat in recent years.

During the 1990s, most major European clubs acquired young players from the former Yugoslavia. At Milan, the Croatian Boban played for some years with the Montenegrin Savicevic, the same national combination of Suker and Mijatovic performed at Real Madrid, while Lazio has a Croatian (Boksic) and a Serb (Mihajlovic). All these players were part of the same Yugoslavian youth teams but are now rivals in international competition. Both the Croatian and Yugoslavian national sides now rely almost entirely on emigrant players and clubs in both countries continue to release young talent into the international market each year.

The changing patterns of Yugoslav football labour migration provide a good example of the complexity of the overall phenomenon. From the student-footballers of the mid-1920s, Yugoslavs have moved abroad to play football but have done so under fluctuating economic and political circumstances. For the last forty years, the structure and economy of Yugoslav football has been geared toward the export of domestic talent. A move to Western Europe has long been considered a reward for senior professionals, especially at the leading clubs. But despite the relatively close diplomatic and economic links between Yugoslavia and the capitalist West, the outflow of players remained until the late 1980s subject to restrictions, most significantly on the basis of age. The dramatic events of the civil war have thus simply intensified a process already well established. Citizens of the former Yugoslavia, it seems, can be found today in almost every European country, but their specific destinations are the outcome of a myriad of economic, political and historical factors. The Croatians, Bosnians, Serbs, Slovenians and Montenegrins are maintaining the tradition of the Yugoslavs as Europe's foremost football wanderers.

77. *France football*, 23 April 1996.

—5—

Rediscovering America

North America has always stood at the periphery of the football world. Despite the close relationship which both the United States and Canada, as former colonies, maintained with Britain, and the apparent popularity of the game in certain schools and universities in the late nineteenth century, association football was unable to break through as a national sport capable of challenging the popularity of baseball, gridiron football, basketball and (in parts of the continent) ice hockey. This has perplexed historians. For a society as ethnically diverse as North America's, built on the old and new immigration of Europeans, and thus in many respects ideal for the mass diffusion of the game, football's relative marginalization has required some explaining. It has been argued that, in the United States particularly, during the second half of the nineteenth century the kicking game was effectively 'crowded out' of the available sporting space by baseball and gridiron, which were able to invent themselves as genuinely American activities. Like socialism, football was considered inappropriate for Americans in an era when advocates of nativism were attempting to bind together a heterogeneous population and create a collective national identity.[1] While baseball became the game of the masses, and gridiron served the requirements of those higher up the social scale, football became the sport 'of immigrants, aliens, "outsiders" and youngsters'.[2]

If football was 'crowded out', however, it did not simply go away. It survived, and in certain areas flourished, on the edge of North America's sporting culture. In New York, Philadelphia, Chicago, St Louis, Milwaukee and parts of California

1. See Andrei S. Markovits, 'The Other "American Exceptionism": Why is there no Soccer in the United States', *International Journal of the History of Sport*, 7, 2, September 1990, pp. 230–64; Andrei S. Markovits and Steven L. Hellerman, 'USA', in C. Eisenberg (ed.), *Fußball, Soccer, Calcio. Ein englischer Sport auf seinem Weg um die Welt*, Munich: DTV, 1997, pp. 185–212; John Sugden, 'USA and the World Cup: American Nativism and the Rejection of the People's Game' in J. Sugden and A. Tomlinson (eds), *Hosts and Champions: Soccer Cultures, National Identities and the USA World Cup*, Aldershot: Arena, 1994, pp. 219–52. For criticisms of this view, Nathan D. Abrams, 'Inhibited but not "crowded out": The Strange Fate of Soccer in the United States', *International Journal of the History of Sport*, 12, 3, December 1995, pp. 1–17; Ivan Waddington and Martin Roderick, 'American Exceptionalism: Soccer and American Football', *The Sports Historian*, 16, May 1996, pp. 42–63.

2. Abrams, 'Strange Fate of Soccer', p. 3.

and in Canadian cities such as Toronto, Montreal and Winnipeg, football clubs were established and competed for years in local leagues and cups.[3] Yet in its professional guise, football has been considered an unequivocal failure, mainly due to the absence of a permanent league structure. The history of the professional game in North America has been marked by short periods of success followed by internal conflict and the withering away of interest. First in the early 1890s, then in the 1920s and, once again, in the late 1960s to the early 1980s, major professional leagues were created, although only the last of these, the North American Soccer League (NASL), could claim to be national in scope. Common to all these ventures was the proliferation of 'foreign' players, whether imported directly from overseas football, recently-arrived immigrants or 'naturalized' North Americans. More so than in any other part of the world, professional football in North America has been shaped by migration and by its dependence on a non-national labour force.

It is a truism that immigration has played a central role in the construction of US society. According to Oscar Handlin in his seminal work *The Uprooted*, immigrants were not just a key factor in understanding American history: rather 'immigrants *were* American history'.[4] For Maldwyn Allen Jones, immigration 'has been the most persistent and the most pervasive influence in her [America's] development'.[5] Between 1820 and 1987, 54 million people migrated to the United States, with a peak of 30 million in the period 1861–1920. Yet what has marked both the United States and Canada out from other countries of immigration has not been the scale of immigration so much as its diversity. Whereas other countries such as Australia and Argentina had populations with higher proportions of foreign-born peoples at various times, none could boast a population drawn from so many different places across the globe. Even from its colonial days, the USA had been host to a range of ethnic and national groupings. The 'old immigrants' of the 1820 to 1880 period came mainly from north-western Europe, especially Ireland, Germany and Britain, whereas the 'new immigrants' who arrived after 1880 were largely south-eastern Europeans, particularly Italians, Slavs, Hungarians, Poles and Jews from Russia and Germany. In addition, smaller but still significant groups of Mexicans, Japanese and Chinese came to live and work in US cities. It is hardly

3. See John C. Pooley, 'Ethnic Soccer Clubs in Milwaukee', in M. Marie Hart (ed.), *Sport in the Socio-cultural Process*, Dubuque: William C. Brown, 1976, pp. 328–45; Gary Ross Mormino, 'The Playing Fields of St. Louis: Italian Immigrants and Sport, 1925–1941', *Journal of Sport History*, 9, 2, Summer 1982, pp. 5–19; Alan Metcalfe, *Canada Learns to Play: The Emergence of Organized Sport, 1807–1914*, Toronto: McClelland & Stewart, 1989, pp. 74–80.

4. Oscar Handlin, *The Uprooted: From the Old World to the New*, Boston: Watts and Co., 1953, p. 3.

5. Maldwyn Allen Jones, *American Immigration*, Chicago: University of Chicago Press, 1960, p. 1.

surprising, then, that the United States has been portrayed historically as the classic country of the immigrant and of immigration.

Yet the conception of the United States as 'a nation of immigrants' has not been left unchallenged.[6] For some, the immigrant has acquired an almost legendary status which has contributed to an overstating of social diversity at the expense of unity.[7] In contrast, early studies of immigration focused a great deal on the process of assimilation, whereby new arrivals gradually, often over generations, shed their Old World identities and become Americanized. According to such a view, assimilation and integration are inevitable, and US society is likened to a 'melting pot' of ethnicities and nationalities. More recently, however, historians have recognized that assimilation and ethnic identity are not necessarily polar opposites but could in fact complement one another.[8] Traits, values, and beliefs brought over from Europe could facilitate the adjustment of immigrants to a new environment: 'becoming American often entailed growing more self-consciously Polish or Italian, not less'.[9] It seems that the identity of individuals and groups in North American society are more subtle and complex than the simple models of assimilation or pluralism suggest.

Any understanding of immigration and the immigrant experience needs to consider the situation in both the donor and the host country. This involves an analysis of the classic push-pull factors but also needs to take account of the role of the state, informal networks between migrants and non-migrants and prior links between sending and receiving countries. Above all, one must recognize that migration involved choice, a variable often overlooked in the North American case. As Alan Kraut has commented, migrants were never the passive objects of impersonal forces but were individuals who faced decisions at every stage: for all those who chose to migrate, there were many others who chose not to.[10] Professional footballers probably enjoyed more choice than most. Few of those who travelled to the United States and Canada from the late nineteenth century were anything like the impoverished 'huddled masses' of popular accounts. But neither

---

6. As expressed by St John de Crevecoeur in the 1770s and John F. Kennedy in his posthumous book *A Nation of Immigrants* (1964). See John Higham, *Send These to Me: Immigrants in Urban America*, Baltimore: Johns Hopkins University Press, rev. edn, 1984, pp. 3–4.

7. Higham, *Send These to Me*, pp. 4–5.

8. Peter Kivisto, 'The Transplanted then and now: the reorientation of immigration studies from the Chicago School to the new social history', *Ethnic and Racial Studies*, 13, 4, October 1990, pp. 455–80; James P. Shenton, 'Ethnicity and Immigration', in E. Foner (ed.), *The New American History*, Philadelphia: Temple University Press, 1990, pp. 251–70.

9. Michael Perman (ed.), *Perspectives on the American Past: Volume 2*, Lexington: DC Heath, 1990, p. 110.

10. Alan M. Kraut, *The Huddled Masses: The Immigrant in American Society, 1880–1921*, Arlington Heights: Harlan Davidson, 1982, p. 4.

were they completely separate from the more general story of migration to North America. This chapter will attempt to analyse the process and the nature of football migration in the context of both North America's immigrant and sporting history.

The First Football Immigrants, 1894–1921

The first professional football league in the United States, the American League of Professional Football (ALPF), was launched by a group of National League baseball club owners in October 1894. Founded in the game's initial base in the north-eastern states, the league included clubs from Baltimore, Boston, Brooklyn, New York, Philadelphia and Washington. Possibly because it operated for less than a month, historians have tended to pay it scant regard. In terms of its labour force, however, the ALPF was an important precursor of later events. The evidence here is admittedly rather patchy. David Waldstein and Stephen Wagg have recently suggested that 'most of the players were foreigners' but this is imprecise and potentially misleading.[11] The term 'foreigner' is open to considerable interpretation and fails to address the important distinction between 'voluntary' and 'imported' immigrants which began to preoccupy US workers from the mid-1880s.[12] If Waldstein and Wagg are suggesting that the majority of the ALPF's workforce was 'imported' then they are surely wrong. Only one club, the Baltimore Orioles, looked overseas, bringing in five players from professional clubs in England. The others seem to have relied on the established immigrant communities, drawing mainly on 'English and Irish players from local leagues'.[13]

The demise of the ALPF was prompted by a proposed investigation of Baltimore's imported players by the immigration authorities. The club owners cut their losses, turning back to baseball; the English players returned home. A few professional leagues continued to operate over the next two decades but they were localized in the game's strongholds of New England, New York and St Louis. Initially none of these clubs were wealthy enough to consider the importation of overseas players. In time, however, a number of powerful teams drawing on the talent of mainly immigrant workers were established by company owners on the east coast. At the forefront was Bethlehem Steel, a large industrial concern in

11. David Waldstein and Stephen Wagg, 'Unamerican Activity: Football in US and Canadian Society', in S. Wagg (ed.) *Giving the Game Away*, London: Leicester University Press, 1995, p. 75.

12. A.T. Lane, 'The British and American Labour Movements and the Problem of Immigration, 1890–1914', in K. Lunn (ed.) *Hosts, Immigrants and Minorities: Historical Responses to Newcomers in British Society*, Folkestone: Dawson, 1980, p. 344.

13. Steve Holroyd, 'The First Professional Soccer League in the United States: The American League of Professional Football (1894)', US Soccer Archives, http://www.sover.net/-spectrum/alpf.html [Accessed August 1999]. Abrams suggests that Baltimore imported eight foreign players in all, 'Strange Fate of Soccer', p. 13.

Pennsylvania, which pioneered the system of bringing in professionals who worked in the company while playing football for the company team. The majority of the team who won the 1916 National Challenge Trophy were apparently recruited in this way from Scotland, although most clubs, including Bethlehem's main rivals Fall River Rovers, continued to rely on native and immigrant players.[14]

The American Soccer League, 1921–31

The creation of the American Soccer League (ASL) has been regarded as a watershed in the history of the game across the Atlantic. For many, these were the 'golden years' of US soccer.[15] Without doubt, it was the first attempt to create a competition comprising the best teams in the country. Its clubs were also far more ambitious in their recruitment policies than previously. The ASL was effectively a multi-ethnic and multinational league, drawing on American-born European personnel but also importing significant numbers of Austrian, Hungarian, Swedish, Irish, English but, above all, Scottish footballers. The timing of this flood of foreign imports was somewhat ironic, coinciding as it did with the passing of the 1921 Immigration Act, described by one historian as 'the most important turning-point in American immigration policy'.[16] For the first time numerical restrictions were put on immigrants of each nationality and, with the subsequent passing of the 1924 Johnson-Reed Act, a ceiling was placed on total immigration and a quota assigned to each nationality.[17] A door was opening for European professional footballers at the very time when the USA was bringing an end to unlimited immigration.

In its initial seasons the clubs, mainly company teams on the eastern seaboard, were still staffed predominantly by immigrant employees who had been brought to the area for industrial work rather than football. Scots were conspicuous from the start, especially in teams such as J & P Coats, a Scottish-owned firm based in Pawtucket, Rhode Island, and those of Holyoke and Fall River, Massachusetts, whose mills had long-established Scottish links.[18] The Bethlehem Steel and Fall River teams, in particular, were composed almost exclusively of former Scottish

14. Bill Murray, *Football: A History of the World Game*, Aldershot: Scholar Press, 1994, p. 261.

15. The statistical history of the ASL is covered in Colin Jose, *American Soccer League, 1921–31: The Golden Years of American Soccer*, Lanham, Maryland: Scarecrow Press, 1998.

16. John Higham, *Strangers in the Land: Patterns of American Nativism*, New York: Antheum, 1975, p. 331.

17. Thomas J. Archdeacon, *Becoming American: An Ethnic History*, New York: Free Press, 1983, pp. 171–2; Elliott Robert Barkan, *And Still They Come: Immigrants and American Society, 1920s to the 1990s*, Wheeling, Illinois: Harlan Davidson, 1996, pp. 9–15.

18. Bernard Aspinwall, 'The Scots in the United States', in R.A. Cage (ed.) *The Scots Abroad: Labour, Capital, Enterprise, 1750–1914*, London: Croom Helm, 1985, pp. 96–7.

professionals. Most, either injured or out of favour at home, had moved to the States voluntarily but increasingly the major clubs were prepared to 'raid' British teams directly. Backed by wealthy companies and free-spending owners, clubs such as Bethlehem certainly had the resources to do so. They were estimated to have been able to pay imports such as Walter and Alex Jackson between double and three times their earnings at home. By 1923, according to one writer, 'a clever player could earn £20 a week; substantially more than he could hope to make in Britain'.[19]

It was with the expansion of the ASL in 1924 that clubs seriously began to tempt British professionals across the Atlantic. Although both the United States and the British associations were now affiliated to FIFA, ASL clubs continued to sign players free of charge and without reference to the British clubs with whom they were registered. In England the activities of US scouts and agents caused a minor panic, especially when the first prominent international player, Manchester City's Irish forward Mickey Hamill, was signed by the Boston Wonder Workers in the summer of 1924. The Football League's vice-president Charles Sutcliffe, however, was unperturbed, believing that the so-called 'American menace' would be shortlived and the players would come to realize 'that to leave England with its definite benefits for America with its promises is taking a leap in the dark'.[20] In Scotland the menace was more real. As we have noted, there was already an existing link with the USA, with Scots numerous in the towns and factories in which the ASL was based. Perhaps of more importance, however, were the poor conditions and wages of professionals at most Scottish clubs. Few were recruited from the richer clubs whose wages matched those available in England but, even so, America could attract a number of players of international status who had relatively poor contracts at home. Alec McNab, an international winger, had been offered a weekly wage of £4 at Greenock Morton before deciding to join Boston on £12 a week 'to work and play football'; Dunfermline goalkeeper Willie Paterson saw his earnings quadruple when he signed for the same club. For professionals like this the attraction of the ASL was clear. Talking to a Scottish journalist, another Boston signing, Johnny Ballantyne, put it starkly: 'I want to improve my position. Who doesn't? I hope to make 12 pounds a week in America. What chance have I got of doing that here?'[21]

Between 1924 and 1928, the height of the American recruiting campaign, the British associations could do little to check the drain on playing talent. Though members of FIFA for these four years, they were unable to force US clubs to recognize their registration and contractual rights. The signing of Ballantyne in the spring of 1924 particularly infuriated the Scottish FA as the player had already

19. Brian Glanville, *Soccer Round the Globe*, London: Sportsman's Book Club, 1961, p. 87.
20. *Sports Pictures*, 31 May 1924.
21. Jose, *American Soccer League*, pp. 7–8.

received summer wages from Partick Thistle. Subsequent signings soured relations between the Scottish and the US associations and led to a special meeting of the former body to deal specifically with the 'American menace'. Deterrent measures were also enacted in England. At the end of 1926 it was ruled that players leaving for a club in the United States or the continent could not be re-registered until the Football League 'has had ample opportunity to investigate the circumstances under which the player left and the reasons for and the conditions attendant on his return'. A few months later the League suspended a former Bradford player for alleged inducements to contracted English players and issued the warning that it would 'entirely prohibit all Tours to the United States so long as any American Club improperly attempts to interfere with any of our League clubs'.[22]

This was not just a British problem: clubs and associations in other parts of Europe faced the prospect of losing their best players to the ASL. The tours made by Vienna Hakoah in 1926 and 1927, regarded as successful in the States, were ultimately disasters for the Austrian champions. Following the first tour, Hakoah lost almost its entire team to the Jewish-owned ASL clubs Brooklyn Wanderers and New York Giants. More players defected a year later and the Vienna club were forced to compete in domestic competition with a virtual reserve side, which led eventually to their relegation from the Austrian first division.[23] In response to these and other losses, the Austrian, Hungarian, Czechoslovakian and Yugoslavian associations issued a motion in early 1927 to expel the United States Football Association (USFA) from FIFA at that year's congress in Finland. Accusing 'certain American clubs' of 'continually enticing European players to break their contracts', the Central European nations hoped that the threat of expulsion would lead to a change in importation policy across the Atlantic. Faced with similar complaints from Scotland and Ireland, the USFA and the ASL agreed on an immediate end to negotiations for foreign players until the congress but indicated that if restrictions were placed on European recruitment it might be necessary to leave FIFA 'in order to have an untied hand in developing the game in this country'.[24] In the event the Europeans backed down before the congress began, although Article 17, ensuring the international observation of national suspensions, was tightened up so as to avoid the problems of players jumping contracts. After the British withdrawal from the world body a year later, the USFA established a 'working agreement' with the English and Scottish associations to respect each other's registrations and suspensions.[25]

---

22. FA Archives, Minutes of Football League, 13 December 1926, 7 March 1927.

23. Roman Horak and Wolfgang Maderthaner, *Mehr als ein Spiel: Fussball und populare Kulturen in Wien der Moderne*, Vienna: Locker, 1997, pp. 190–1; Leo Schidrowitz, *Geschichte des Fußball-sports in Österreich*, Vienna: ÖFB, 1951, pp. 151–2.

24. *New York Times*, 25 January 1927.

25. *New York Times*, 25 June 1927; 5 January 1929.

It is difficult to be precise about the numbers of European players who migrated to ASL clubs in these years. Colin Jose's research has been crucial in establishing the basic pattern of migration, but there are still gaps in the data and problems of interpretation. The birthplaces of many players are unknown and in the North American context birthplace is a particularly flawed indicator of nationality. In many cases there is little means of distinguishing between immigrants who arrived with their families some years earlier and those recruited directly from European clubs in the 1920s. For this reason, it has been necessary to consider birthplace alongside club of origin, where this is known. As Table 5.1 shows, Scottish footballers dominated the ASL almost from the start. The number of British players reached its peak between 1926 and 1929, after which the disruption caused by America's internal 'soccer' war, together with the agreement to respect contractual rights on both sides of the Atlantic and the financial impact of the Wall Street Crash, caused a decline in migration. While nobody matched the Scots for sheer numbers, the Central Europeans who began to arrive after 1926 were certainly of a higher quality. The concentration of national and ethnic groups at particular clubs was a feature of the ASL. We have already seen how the Jewish imports were initially targeted by two New York clubs. In 1928 one group of former Vienna Hakoah players left these clubs to establish Brooklyn Hakoah while another had already set up New York Hakoah in the rebel Eastern Professional Soccer League.[26] A year later the two merged to form Hakoah All Stars, a side composed exclusively of Austrian, Hungarian and Czech Jews. Other clubs flirted with an overt ethnic

Table 5.1 Nationality of European Players in the ASL, 1921–31

Season	Scottish	English	Irish	Hungarian	Austrian	Swedish	Other
1921/22	19	7	1	–	–	1	1
1922/23	30	9	1	–	–	–	1
1923/24	47	9	2	–	–	–	1
1924/25	63	12	6	–	–	7	3
1925/26	78	13	9	–	–	7	4
1926/27	82	17	9	5	6	3	4
1927/28	83	10	14	6	6	2	3
1928/29	80	14	6	6	2	4	3
1929/30	73	10	6	12	5	5	5
1930 (Fall)	52	6	4	8	2	2	6
1931 (Spring)	50	7	3	6	2	1	4
1931 (Fall)	34	7	3	5	3	2	5

Source: Complied from data in Jose, *American Soccer League*

26. *New York Times*, 28 October, 3 November 1928.

identity but were less successful. Philadelphia Celtic, with a side dominated by players recruited from the Irish League, lasted just over a month in 1927; Bridgeport Hungaria, whose name betrayed their national roots, achieved little more two seasons later. It was indeed hardly surprising that club owners with European backgrounds relied on imports from their former homelands. This certainly explains why Ernest Viberg recruited a number of fellow Swedes, including former internationals Herbert Carlson, Caleb Schylander and Thore Sundberg, when he took over New York's Indiana Flooring club in 1924.

What were the experiences of these football emigrants to the United States? For some, it was literally life-changing, offering them and their families a chance to enjoy a more prosperous lifestyle in a new country. Harold Brittan, for instance, moved to the United States in 1920 after spending a number of seasons playing mainly reserve team football at Chelsea. He then enjoyed eight years as a leading ASL player, bought a car dealership and was even involved in buying the Providence franchise. Others settled in the States after the demise of the league in 1931 and continued their careers in football management or administration. Malcolm Goldie was one of many who assumed US citizenship, played for his adopted national team and never returned home, in his case working as a soccer coach at the Massachusetts Institute of Technology.[27] Indeed, six of the 1930 World Cup squad who travelled to Uruguay had been born in Britain though only one, George Moorhouse, had played professionally before emigrating. Moreover, whereas they had often been struggling on low wages on the fringes of their teams back home, many were now well-paid sportsmen with a rare talent. The moderate players were probably lauded for the first time in their professional careers; the better players became stars. Alex Jackson, a young outside-right with Dumbarton when he moved to Bethlehem Steel in 1923, later admitted that he had settled well in the States and made friends, and had not intended to return home for good when he accompanied his brother to Scotland for his wedding and signed for Aberdeen while he was there.[28] In January 1927 the Austrian newspaper *Der Professional* could comment, with considerable exaggeration, that the Hungarian international winger Jozsef Eisenhoffer had become 'a super-hero for all Americans – bigger even than Jack Dempsey and Johnny Weissmueller'.[29]

The picture was not so rosy for everyone. The problems of adapting to life and work in an alien culture were considerable. Even the relatively successful Jewish

---

27. Jose, *American Soccer League*, pp. 470, 476–7.

28. *Athletic News*, 11 August 1930; Brian Glanville, *Soccer: A Panorama*, London: Eyre and Spottiswood, 1969, p. 66. Within five months of his return, Jackson was in the Scottish national team. He was a member of the 'Wembley Wizards' who beat England 5–1 in 1928 and went on to become one of the leading Football League players of the inter-war years with Huddersfield Town and then Chelsea.

29. Cited in Horak and Maderthaner, *Mehr als ein Spiel*, pp. 191–2.

migrants from Vienna faced difficulties. In letters home, they complained of being overworked by an authoritarian boss who treated them 'like robots'. The New York players also suffered financially: Bela Guttmann was initially forced to teach popular dance to dock workers in order to subsidize his income. They were obliged to spend much of their spare time promoting the game in theatres, nightclubs and public houses, leading some to describe football in the US as 'a cabaret game'.[30] A New York correspondent for an English newspaper was more worried by the cosmopolitanism of ASL teams: 'There is quite a mingling of Continental players, scarcely one of whom speaks English . . . all sorts of complications are likely to result'.[31] For these and other reasons, some players found it impossible to settle and were quickly on the return ship home. In 1927 the Austrian inside-forward Carl Jinda completed a three-month contract with Brooklyn Wanderers before returning to Vienna. A year before, Irish international Mick O'Brien had returned to England after playing just seven matches for the same club. In an article for *Topical Times*, O'Brien was highly critical of all aspects of the ASL, concluding that 'my experience has proved that the conditions, the grounds, the refereeing and the manner in which the game is governed are so bad that I never want to see any British player any nearer America than this side of the Atlantic'. O'Brien's dissatisfaction was undoubtedly fuelled, however, by the fact that the club owner Nathan Agar had suspended and fined him for breaking his contract by refusing to play and for insubordination when he refused to leave the dressing-room.[32]

Although most European imports stayed much longer than this, remigration was the norm. Indeed, it can be argued that most of the footballers who travelled from Europe to the USA in the 1920s were in essence temporary migrants, or sojourners, who never intended to make a new home across the Atlantic. In this respect, they were hardly unique among industrial workers in this period. From 1880 to 1930, the repatriation of European immigrants stood somewhere between one-quarter and one-third.[33] Return migration was facilitated by a relatively moderate attitude to emigrants in Europe, despite the widespread fears of players being suspended or banned for life. The majority of footballers were able to resume their professional careers in Europe, and some even returned to their former clubs. Ballantyne, who jumped contract in 1924, re-signed for Partick Thistle four years later and played a further 248 times for the club; Tommy Muirhead, who had been player-manager at Boston and was instrumental in persuading Ballantyne,

30. Horak and Maderthaner, *Mehr als ein Spiel*, pp. 192–4.

31. *Athletic News*, 11 October 1926.

32. *Topical Times*, 25 December 1926.

33. Mark Wyman, *Round Trip to America: The Immigrants Return to Europe, 1880–1930*, London: Cornell University Press, 1993, p. 6; Herbert G. Gutman, *Work, Culture and Society in Industrializing America: Essays in American Working-Class and Social History*, Oxford: Blackwell, 1977, p. 40.

McNab and others to leave Scotland, was similarly able to resume his career at Glasgow Rangers just one year after leaving the club in dispute.[34] Eisenhoffer, Guttmann and Leo Drucker, meanwhile, moved to France after the disintegration of the ASL. Drucker finished his career in Malta while Guttmann continued his globe-trotting as a coach, managing club sides in Portugal, Hungary, Austria and Uruguay (see Chapter 6).

Migration was a two-way process. Alongside return migration, some British clubs reversed the trend by purchasing North American nationals. Many were in fact British-born, having moved to Canada or the United States as teenagers: their return to Britain representing a long-term process of remigration. This partial opening of the North American labour market was no doubt facilitated by close-season tours: Glasgow Rangers visited the United States twice, and Preston North End, Kilmarnock and Celtic once, between 1928 and 1931.[35] Celtic attempted to sign New York Yankees forward Billy Gonzales following his hat-trick against the Glasgow club during a fixture on the 1931 tour.[36] Fall River goalkeeper James 'Joe' Kennaway so impressed Celtic officials on the same tour that he was signed to replace regular John Thomson after he died in an Old Firm clash a few months later. Kennaway won two championship and three cup medals and remained the first choice goalkeeper until the Second World War when he returned to Canada, later moving back to the United States and coaching university teams before becoming, in 1948, an US citizen. Kennaway had already represented Canada and Scotland, gaining his only cap for his adopted country in a match against Austria at Hampden Park in 1933. Scottish-born Barney Battles was another dual international who played for Scotland in 1931 during his time with Hearts after he had represented the United States six years earlier.[37]

The Years In Between, 1931–67

The collapse of the ASL effectively led to the demise of professional football in the USA, although largely amateur competitions and leagues continued in pockets of the country. Most accounts of football in the States pass over this period entirely,

---

34. Jose, *American Soccer League*, pp. 321, 487–88. Interrupted only by this brief spell in the United States, Muirhead played 352 games for Rangers between 1917 and 1930 and won eight Scottish caps. He went on to manage St Johnstone in Scotland and Preston North End in the Football League before settling into a journalistic and media career after the Second World War.

35. Jose, *American Soccer League*, pp. 11, 13–14, 467–95.

36. Murray, *World's Game*, p. 57; Waldstein and Wagg, 'Unamerican Activity', p. 77.

37. Eugene MacBride, Martin O'Connor and George Sheridan, *An Alphabet of the Celts: A Complete Who's Who of Celtic FC*, Leicester: ACL and Polar Publishing, 1994, pp. 212–13; FA News, April 1976; Colin Jose, *Keeping Score: The Encyclopedia of Canadian Soccer*, Vaughan, Ontario: Soccer Hall of Fame, 1998, p. 157; Jose, *American Soccer League*, p. 11.

aside from a brief mention of the 1950 World Cup victory against England. Bill Murray is therefore probably right to describe the game in the 1940s as 'a non-event'.[38] During 1946 and 1947, however, there was an attempt to create a new regional league, with teams drawn from Chicago, Detroit, Pittsburgh, St Louis and also one from Toronto in Canada. The North American Soccer Football League (NASFL), as it was called, also followed the ASL in its desire to attract foreign talent. According to the English press, the NASFL, under the direction of Ferdinand Weiszmann and Phil Wrigley, 'the chewing gum millionaire', had intended to establish a scouting network in England to lure stars with offers of the equivalent of £25 per game, significantly more than the new £9 maximum in the Football League. Concerned by the possible threat to the English game, the FA stepped in to regulate a scheme with one of the NASFL clubs, the Chicago Maroons, which would allow 'good young players' who were out-of-contract to play for the club while receiving sponsorship in their chosen profession.[39] No Englishmen seem to have been tempted, but the following March six players – four Poles and two Scots – were attracted to Chicago.[40] Others, like Les Medley, did not arrive specifically to play football. A Londoner, Medley had joined Tottenham Hotspur in 1939 but his experience with the RAF in Canada during the war persuaded him to emigrate in 1946. He played for Toronto Greenbacks the following season but returned to Tottenham in 1948 where he stayed for five years, even being capped on six occasions by England, before crossing the Atlantic again to settle.[41] Financial problems caused the NASFL to shut down after its second season but in April 1950 the FA Bulletin carried an offer for either British professionals or amateurs to join teams in New York, Chicago or Philadelphia. Recruits, ideally 'single men not over 27 years of age', would receive one year contracts and have their return trips paid in full. Applicants were selected and interviewed by the 'resident American representative in London'.[42] The agents, scouts and middlemen of earlier years were absent. This was a more formalized method of recruitment, similar to the acquisition of student-athletes from abroad.[43]

In 1960 a more collective method of foreign recruitment was attempted when the sports promoter Bill Cox formed his International Soccer League (ISL). While often dismissed as an oddity, the ISL's hiring of entire clubs from abroad to compete

38. Murray, *Football: A History of the World Game*, p. 265.

39. *Sporting Chronicle and Athletic News*, 21 December 1946; FA Bulletin, No. 4, 19 December 1946.

40. *New York Times*, 22 March 1947.

41. Jose, *Keeping Score*, p. 164; Sam Bartram, *His Autobiography*, London: Burke, 1956, p. 70.

42. FA Bulletin, No. 21, 4 April 1950.

43. John Bale, *The Brawn Drain: Foreign Student-Athletes in American Universities*, Urbana, University of Illinois Press, 1991, pp. 100–10.

during their close season in New York was a logical extension of the importation principle which would continue to dominate professional soccer. European associations were willing to allow clubs to play as long as there was no threat to domestic football and the English Football League, for one, initially had no shortage of clubs eager to compete.[44] Alongside the foreign clubs, the organizers included an 'All-Star team' to represent the home country. Called the New York Americans, the team was actually made up of mainly imported players. In 1961 the Americans were managed by Newport County's Alf Sherwood and included ten Britons and one Argentinian. The same season Montreal Concordia reportedly fielded a team consisting of imported 'world-class players . . . together with an already well-stocked local nucleus',[45] including England's Alan Mullery, just nineteen years old at the time, and the Welsh international Ken Leek. In Canada, moreover, an Eastern Canadian Professional Soccer League (ECPSL) had been established in 1961 and attracted experienced professionals from Britain and elsewhere. Coached by the former Scottish international goalkeeper Tommy Younger, Toronto City managed to recruit players of the calibre of Stanley Matthews, Danny Blanchflower and Johnny Haynes.[46] Montreal Cantalia, meanwhile, was dominated by little known Argentinian professionals like Walter Ormeno, Giuseppe Tufano and Ishmael Ferreira while another member of the league, Toronto Italia, had been formed by Italian immigrants ten years earlier and continued to include a number of immigrant, and occasionally imported, Italians. In November 1964, *World Soccer* featured Nigel Sims, who had kept goal for Aston Villa in the 1957 FA Cup Final, but moved to Toronto City for a summer sojourn in 1963 before returning to England. He was joined at Toronto by coach Malcolm Allison and five former Football League players but found himself in a league of 'many different nationalities'. Nonetheless, Sims evidently enjoyed the experience and recommended 'the life to any player who gets a free transfer from his club'.[47] For others, the Canadian way of life was more than a temporary experience. Hector Marinaro came to Canada in 1961 after playing for Racing Club in his native Buenos Aires for nearly a decade and a further four years in El Salvador. He signed for Montreal Concordia in the ISL, then played for Toronto Italia in the ECPSL, before going on to coach various Toronto franchises. A native South African, Ted Purdon had spent eleven years as a professional in England when he joined Toronto Roma in 1962. Three

---

44. FA Archives, Minutes of International Football League Board, 23 September 1959; 21 February 1960. Burnley played in the first competition but were left unimpressed by the organization of the Americans and delivered a 'catalogue of complaints' to the Football League on their return. See Bob Lord, *My Fight for Football*, London: Stanley Paul, 1963, pp. 51–9.

45. *World Soccer*, February, June 1961.

46. Jose, *Keeping Score*, p. 124.

47. *World Soccer*, November 1964.

seasons in Toronto with Roma and then City, and one with New York Ukrainians followed before Purdon decided to stay in Canada for good.[48]

The ISL finished, at the same time as the ECPSL, in 1965 but two years later the idea was revived when the United Soccer Association (USA), having to operate its league at short notice, decided to bring in European and Latin American teams. On this occasion, the teams were assigned to specific cities and given new names; some effort was even made to align them with appropriate ethnic communities. The venture, however, failed to pull in sufficient spectators and in 1967 the USA merged with Bill Cox's rival National Professional Soccer League (NPSL) to form the North American Soccer League (NASL).[49]

The North American Soccer League, 1968–1984

Commentators have often related the fortunes of the NASL to its labour-recruitment policies. The league faced the perennial dilemma that while there were insufficient North American players of the required quality, an over-reliance on foreigners would reinforce the notion of football as an 'unamerican', or foreign, game. As with previous ventures, practical and financial considerations forced NASL clubs to base their sides mainly around imports but for the first time there was a conscious, if belated, effort to 'Americanize' the league. Pele's arrival in 1975 was an important turning-point, as it encouraged the signing of better foreigners and further marginalized the North Americans. In the end, the NASL's efforts at 'Americanization' were at best half-hearted and the tension between the policies of importing aliens and using native talent was never resolved.

At first the domination of the foreigner was all but absolute. Before the NASL, the NPSL had operated for one season as an 'outlaw' league using foreign imports to fill its team rosters. This freed it from international regulations regarding contracts and transfers but meant that any player who joined risked punishment on his return. English players, for instance, were given a twelve-month ban while the Yugoslav authorities placed a life ban on defectors. Despite these sanctions, the NPSL still managed to entice over one hundred players from across the globe, including internationals like Vidal and Santisteban from Real Madrid, the Argentinian Cesar Menotti, the Yugoslav Bora Kostic and a 40-year-old Ladislao Kubala, who arrived from Español to play briefly in Toronto in the same team as his son.[50]

48. Jose, *Keeping Score*, pp. 163–4, 171.

49. For a detailed account of the various attempts to form professional leagues after 1965, the USA–NPSL dispute and the origins of the NASL, see Paul Gardner, *Nice Guys Finish Last: Sport and American Life*, London: Allen Lane, 1974, pp. 214–39; Murray, *Football: A History of the World Game*, pp. 266–8.

50. Gardner, *Nice Guys Finish Last*, p. 224; Glanville, *Soccer: A Panorama*, p. 236.

Most of the imports who played alongside the handful of North Americans, however, were of much poorer quality. At Philadelphia Spartans, for instance, John Best joined on a free transfer from Tranmere in the English fourth division and found himself playing with the former Argentinian centre-half Ruben Navarro and the Austrian goalkeeper Fraydl.[51] The trend was set for the early years of the NASL. The percentage of home players slowly increased, from 8.5 per cent in the first season to 36.3 per cent by 1973 (Table 5.2), but the relative weakness of grass-roots and college recruits made it essential to continue to look abroad. Many clubs focused on Latin American and Caribbean talent: Brazilians, Jamaicans and Trinidadians were common throughout the NASL in the early 1970s. In addition, the potential difficulties of obtaining European players were soon eased by taking them on loan for the duration of the NASL season. This, it was hoped, would avoid the messy business of transfers and contractual disputes.

The data in Table 5.2 shows that in all but one season after 1973 over 35 per cent of NASL players were North Americans. Yet only a small proportion of these actually appeared on a regular basis. The 1975 Championship final between Tampa Bay Rowdies and Portland Timbers, for instance, featured neither an American nor a Canadian.[52] Notwithstanding the growth of soccer as an intercollegiate sport, and the increasing use of the college system to draft young recruits, natives found

Table 5.2 Citizenship of Players in the North American Soccer League, 1968–80

Season	North American		British		Other European		Latin American		Rest of World		Not Known	
1968	34	(8.5)	84	(21.1)	174	(43.7)	71	(17.8)	35	(8.8)	–	
1969	30	(32.6)	15	(16.3)	19	(20.7)	12	(13.0)	11	(12.0)	5	(5.4)
1970	24	(20.5)	25	(21.4)	20	(17.1)	25	(21.4)	21	(17.9)	2	(1.7)
1971	34	(19.0)	45	(25.3)	42	(23.6)	26	(14.6)	20	(11.3)	11	(6.2)
1972	36	(24.1)	48	(32.2)	21	(14.1)	27	(18.1)	15	(10.1)	2	(1.4)
1973	64	(36.3)	48	(27.3)	29	(16.5)	14	(7.9)	20	(11.4)	1	(0.6)
1974	104	(36.1)	86	(29.9)	36	(12.5)	30	(10.4)	28	(9.7)	4	(1.4)
1975	133	(31.2)	136	(31.9)	68	(16.0)	37	(8.7)	33	(7.7)	19	(4.5)
1976	161	(35.9)	156	(34.7)	63	(14.0)	36	(8.0)	17	(3.8)	16	(3.6)
1977	147	(36.5)	159	(39.5)	67	(16.6)	12	(3.0)	17	(4.2)	1	(0.2)
1978	194	(33.8)	214	(37.3)	117	(20.4)	23	(4.0)	24	(4.2)	2	(0.3)
1979	230	(37.7)	178	(29.2)	124	(20.3)	41	(6.7)	31	(5.1)	6	(1.0)
1980	211	(39.2)	148	(27.5)	107	(19.9)	43	(8.0)	23	(5.2)	–	

Source: Data elaborated from Colin Jose, *NASL: A Complete Record of the North American Soccer League*, Derby: Breedon Books, 1989

51. Glanville, *Soccer: A Panorama*, p. 237.
52. *New York Times*, 31 August 1975.

it difficult to break into NASL sides.[53] In 1979, for example, only twenty-nine of the ninety-seven youngsters signed in the annual draft played that season. Even national team players such as Ricky Davis and Gary Etherington were not guaranteed a regular match at New York Cosmos; Dan Ebert, meanwhile, New York's first pick in the 1979 draft, failed even to appear as a substitute.[54] This did not go unnoticed. In the course of the 1970s the league authorities constructed various regulations designed to limit the number of foreigners and encourage the use of home talent. Initially teams were only required to include a minimum number of nationals on their rosters (rising from three in 1973 to five in 1975, with three for the new franchises). From 1976 this 'American quota' was applied to the actual line-up on the field. No more than ten foreigners were allowed to play at any one time, a figure which was to be reduced by one each season. By 1979 only thirteen non-North Americans were permitted on each club roster.[55] There was also some degree of governmental restriction. As with all alien workers, footballers required the Department of Labor to issue them with visas. For the most part, the government was not obstructive, granting the visas requested by the league authorities. Yet under pressure from the newly-formed Players' Association in 1979, the Labor Department reduced the league's foreign allowance from 245 to 220, or ten imports per year.[56] Later the same year, the Immigration and Naturalization Service (INS) threatened to deport any foreign player who failed to observe a strike called by the Players' Association. In the event, the INS withdrew their threat, probably after advice that such action would send the professional game into turmoil.[57]

Of the foreign players, Britons dominated from the start. Of all nationalities, it was the British, and particularly the English, who established a permanent presence in the NASL. Not only was 'the NASL . . . launched with a heavy stock of British manpower'[58] but its administration also betrayed a strong British connection. Phil Woosnam, for example, was a key figure in the NASL as Commissioner from 1969 to 1983. The former Welsh international had arrived as player-coach for Atlanta Chiefs in 1966 and, along with fellow Briton and former journalist Clive Toye, was responsible for most of the policy decisions of the 1970s. Was it not

53. Bale, *Brawn Drain*, pp. 55–7; Sugden, 'USA and the World Cup' pp. 243–4.

54. *Football sélection*, October 1980; *Miroir du football*, 25 April 1979.

55. *New York Times*, 31 August 1975, 10 October 1977, 17 October 1979; *World Soccer*, December 1977.

56. PFA Archives, American Soccer Files (hereafter AS Files), Letter from Aaron Bodon, Chief, Division of Labor Certifications, US Employment Service to Ralph Kramer, Acting Associate Commissioner, Examinations, Immigration and Naturalization Service, 23 January 1979; *New York Times*, 25 January 1979.

57. *New York Times*, 15, 16, 18 April 1979; PFA Archives, AS Files, Letter from John Kerr, North American Soccer Players' Association (NASPA) to Cliff Lloyd, 13 June 1979.

58. *World Soccer*, March 1977.

natural that these men should look towards their homeland for coaches and players? Woosnam certainly targeted British clubs and associations throughout the 1970s, regularly circulating details of engagements in the NASL. On the donor's part, encouragement was received from the Professional Footballers' Association, which provided contacts and advice for prospective migrants, while clubs seem to have been prepared to write North American summer engagements into player contracts.[59] The Italian magazine *Guerin Sportivo* felt that the 'British invasion' of North American football was a logical phenomoneon; the result of a shared language, cultural similarities, business connections and the ease of recruitment.[60] By the late 1970s, however, a trend away from British imports was being observed. The British were still the largest group by far but their influence was now under challenge from the importation of large numbers of West German, Dutch, and Yugoslav footballers. Some nationalities were not so easily lured to America. The two major footballing nations in South America, Argentina and Brazil, rarely contributed more than a dozen players a season, even as the league expanded during the mid- and late 1970s. The Argentinian national goalkeeper Hugo Gatti, for instance, wrote in his autobiography that while he was flattered to have been contacted directly by Pele to join New York Cosmos, he wanted to continue to play 'real' football rather than the sanitized NASL version.[61] Italians were also rare. With the exception of Giorgio Chinaglia, there were just three Italians, among 380 non-North Americans in the NASL in 1979, whose combined appearances that season amounted to sixteen. And in general, those who decided to emigrate, like San Jose's Antonio Cestarollo, were unknown at home. For Italian footballers, one commentor thought, 'the real "America" is still to play in Italy'.[62]

The national profile of immigrants differed from club to club and changed over time. The discontinuity in ownership and coaching meant that few teams drew players consistently from the same source. Nor does there seem to have been any pattern in the residence of migrants. Clubs do not seem to have gone out of their way to buy players who would appeal to local ethnic communities. The obvious exception to this was the Toronto Metros-Croatia which lasted from 1975 to 1978, and which we considered in the previous chapter. In 1975 the struggling Toronto Metros club was bought by Croatian business interests, who added the 'Croatia' label to become the first specifically 'ethnic' club in the NASL. The composition of the squad changed drastically, with Croatian and other Yugoslavian players brought in. Some were Canadian-born but the club also acquired a number of

---

59. See, for instance, PFA Archives, Minutes of PFA, 14 March 1971, 24 March 1974, 21 January, 9 September 1979.

60. *Guerin sportivo*, 25 July 1979.

61. Hugo Gatti, *Yo, el único*, Buenos Aires: Abril, 1977, p. 24.

62. *Guerin sportivo*, 25 July 1979.

professionals directly from Croatia on permanent or loan deals similar to those established between NASL and British clubs.[63] In general, however, it was more likely for the complexion of club rosters to reflect the identity of the coach than the local ethnic community. When Rinus Michels arrived as coach of Los Angeles Aztecs in 1979 he brought in five fellow Dutchmen, including Johan Cruyff, and transferred thirteen British players who had played under his predecesor, the Englishman Peter Short. In this way, it is not hard to see a connection between the prevalence of British coaches and the prevalence of British players: one reinforced the other. Nonetheless there were still some clubs who managed to be more cosmopolitan. Perhaps to satisfy the cities' diverse population, the New York Cosmos fielded multinational sides under a series of coaches of different nationalities throughout the 1970s. In 1979 the Cosmos squad which started the season was composed of citizens from eleven countries; Chicago, San Diego and Tampa Bay were all close behind with eight.[64]

The attitude towards the NASL's policy of importation from outside North America was mixed. Initially there was little objection to NASL clubs purchasing players who were unable to forge a career in their home countries or taking others on loan during the European close season. However, as the NASL became more ambitious and progressed financially, foreign clubs and associations became increasingly suspicious of this new 'American menace'. Problems were caused when better players began to migrate and the NASL's extended season started to interfere with the game elsewhere. The North American authorities were regularly accused of ignoring FIFA regulations by acquiring contracted or banned players: the Football League chief executive, Alan Hardaker, warned in January 1978 that if this continued the North Americans would be 'cut out of international football altogether'.[65] These specific objections were often expanded into a more general critique of the NASL. The British journalist Brian Glanville, a persistent critic of the North American approach to football, thought that the reliance on foreign talent was 'parasitic' and called the league 'a curiously half-baked, lop-sided affair'.[66] FIFA secretary Helmut Käser believed that 'it is not normal that a first division team is composed of foreigners . . . the approach to the game in the United States is purely money. The sport has no value at all. It is show, it is a commercial approach'.[67] These comments were prompted by the potential conflicts over the availability of players in World Cup years, and further aggravated by Commissioner

63. Jose, *Keeping Score*, p. 141.
64. *Guerin sportivo*, 25 July 1979.
65. *The Times*, 17 January 1978.
66. *World Soccer*, June 1977.
67. *Sunday Times*, 22 January 1978.

Woosnam's provocative statement that the NASL was ready to monopolize the world's elite football talent.

More concrete action was taken to protect European football from the supposedly predatory North Americans. In West Germany, the departure in April 1977 of national captain Franz Beckenbauer, at the age of thirty-one, to New York Cosmos convinced the federation to place an informal ban on all transfers abroad until after the following year's World Cup competition.[68] Britain, who stood to suffer the most from the ambitions of North American clubs, established a series of measures towards the end of the 1970s aimed at regulating and containing the flow of players across the Atlantic. In 1978 an agreement was reached between the Football League and the NASL which set out exact guidelines for the transfer of players and for loan arrangements. Henceforth international clearance certificates were needed before any move could take place.[69] For many British clubs, this did not go far enough. Pressure was mounting for the prohibition of loan transfers altogether, especially after a well-publicised conflict between Fulham and Los Angeles Aztecs over the registration of George Best.[70] Derby County's manager Tommy Docherty, for one, complained that transatlantic loans were likely to increasingly disrupt the English game, leaving teams to begin the season 'with half their players in America'.[71] The following season the loaning of players from English and Scottish clubs was banned.[72] The decision had been prompted by the collapse of Charlton Athletic's partnership with NASL club New England Teamen, which was to have allowed the two clubs to exchange players on a more regular basis. An advocate of the financial benefits of the loan system the previous year, Charlton chairman Mike Gliksten led the calls for its abolition at the 1979 Football League annual meeting. In his view, players could not be shared and, for all their friendly words, the North Americans could not be trusted: 'the rule book has meant nothing'.[73] His fellow directors agreed.

Who were the NASL migrants and what were their expectations? Such a question can hardly be answered comprehensively but a few possibilities suggest themselves. Much of the existing literature has focused on particular 'types' of football migrant, which seem to overlap, if not to fit precisely, with our formulation of the 'itinerant', the 'mercenary' and the 'settler'. Paul Gardner divided the first

68. *World Soccer*, May 1977; *New York Times*, 27 April 1977.

69. Football League Handbook, 1978/79; *The Times*, 17 January, 7 February 1978; *The Guardian*, 17 January 1978.

70. On the Best case see Alan Hardaker, *Hardaker of the League*, London: Pelham, 1977, pp. 188–90.

71. *The Times*, 7 April 1978.

72. FA Archives, Minutes of the Four British Associations and the Football Leagues of England, Scotland and Ireland, 20 December 1979.

73. *The Times*, 18 February 1978; *The Guardian*, 3 June 1978; *Daily Telegraph*, 2 June 1979.

wave of British migrants into three categories: the 'opportunists' who were interested only in money; the 'has-beens' whose careers at home had all but finished; and the 'mediocrities' who hoped that they could succeed in the lower standard of football. [74] Woosnam was rather more explicit when he wrote to the managers of all Football League clubs in January 1972, outlining 'the type of players we would like to recruit'. They fell into four categories:

1. The experienced professional, perhaps with previous international experience, who, by example would raise the standard of play and have great impact. We would hope to attract a number of players in this category.
2. The experienced professional, with ambitions to go into coaching and/ or management, who, by spending a few months on the North American sport scene would gain tremendous experience and help our clubs in development work in the cities.
3. The professional player, of all ages, who is being granted a free transfer, and, having obtained a club for the following season in England, could spend the summer in North America.
4. The young professional, who, by having the opportunity to travel and play in North America for 3–4 months, with and against players of varied styles and temperament, would mature into a better player.[75]

The post-Pele era arguably introduced a further 'type' – the high-profile star international such as Beckenbauer, Cruyff, Best, Eusebio and Carlos Alberto. Underpinning each of these categories was the assumption that playing football in North America was like the parenthesis within a professional career: an aside from the *real* game in Europe or South America. It is surely no coincidence that commentators, and players themselves, often referred to the experience of North American soccer as a break or a holiday.[76] Hardaker believed that for English

74. *World Soccer*, March 1977.

75. PFA Archives, AS Files, Circular from Phil Woosnam to Football League Club Managers, 19 January 1972.

76. See, for instance, Jeff Powell, *Bobby Moore: The Life and Times of a Sporting Hero*, London, Robson Books, 1993, pp. 230–2; Colin Jose, *NASL: A Complete Record of the North American Soccer League*, Derby, Breedon, 1989, p. 14; Sugden, 'USA and the World Cup', p. 244. Paul Breitner, who never played in the NASL but apparently watched matches while on holiday in the States, was scathing of what he called this 'American operetta league' and those who played there, although he admitted to liking the stadiums and the spectating experience. Paul Breitner, *Ich will kein Vorbild sein*, Munich: Copress, 1980, p. 62. Peter Beardsley, who moved to the NASL with the Vancouver Whitecaps at the beginning of his career, was criticized for 'taking an easy football option' and 'lacking ambition' but regarded it as a more valuable experience than most. He argued that few of the foreigners were there to make easy money and that most 'took it just as seriously as if they were playing for big prizes at home'. Peter Beardsley, *My Life Story*, London: Collins Willow, 1985.

players loan periods in the NASL were no more significant than 'making a bob or two in their holidays' and the apparent lack of effort from certain imports led North American observers to the same conclusions.[77] Certainly, few migrants felt any real commitment to the NASL, or to North America itself. The NASL encouraged the type of seasonal migration which had existed for many years in cricket and rugby league, or in relation to baseball in the USA and the Dominican Republic, although in this case it was mainly one-way.[78] Many of its players were 'birds of passage', travelling to and from the United States as part of a regular pattern of migration.

The material benefits of playing in North America could be considerable. At the upper end of the scale, the NASL imports were among the best-paid footballers on the planet. Pele's deal with New York Cosmos, worth between $4 and $5 million for eighty-five matches over three years, made him, according to the *New York Times*, 'the highest-paid team athlete in the world'.[79] The player himself admitted that this was 'more money than I had been paid in eighteen years with Santos'.[80] For Dutch international Johan Neeskens, New York's 1979 offer of $2 million annually over five years was too good to ignore. No European club could offer him anything like the same financial package.[81] Pele and Neeskens, however, were hardly representative. Only a small elite reached this level of pay, and only then during the NASL's boom years between about 1975 and 1981. The highest-paid footballer in the United States in 1970, one-armed Argentinian Victorio Casa, received just $15,000 per year in comparison.[82] British players on loan could expect to earn a reasonable sum of between £75 and £125 per week in 1972 but three years later the average salary in the NASL was only $3,500 for the four-month season, a figure dwarfed by the earnings of even journeymen baseball and basketball players.[83] As a group, footballers were undoubtedly the poor relations of American professional sport. But even the more modestly rewarded players enjoyed a lifestyle and a standard of living which was unattainable at home. There

77. *The Guardian*, 17 January 1978.

78. On Dominican baseball see Alan M. Klein, 'Trans-nationalism, Labour Migration and Latin American Baseball', in Bale and Maguire (eds) *Global Sports Arena*. For an interesting comparison with the migration of American basketball players to Europe, see Jim Patton, *Il Basket d'Italia*, New York: Simon and Schuster, 1994.

79. *New York Times*, 4 June 1975.

80. Pele with Robert L. Fish, *My Life and the Beautiful Game*, Oxford: Oxford University Press, 1979, p. 93.

81. *Guerin sportivo*, 28 June 1979.

82. *New York Times*, 26 April 1970.

83. PFA AS Files, Woosnam to Football League Clubs, 19 January 1972; Jason Grief, 'Major League Soccer versus North American Soccer League: The Improvement of the American Player', Tufts University Student Essay, http://www. sws. bu.edu/palegi/jason.html [Accessed May 1999].

were plenty of rags-to-riches stories. Ronnie Sharp, for one, had moved as a part-time player, allegedly making just £8 per week at Scottish club Cowdenbeath, to Fort Lauderdale Strikers in 1975. Within two years his earnings had increased to £295 a week and he was living 'a luxurious life' including 'a huge car and an expensive home'. In August 1978, Patrick Barclay of *The Guardian* reported that 'at the average club your average former First Division "name" player, the wrong side of 30' could make between £15,000 and £20,000 a year in the NASL. Colin Waldron, who had moved from Sunderland to the NASL in 1977, thought that, taking account of fringe benefits such as car, apartment and medical care, he was receiving three times as much as at a top English second division club.[84] Although the French newspaper *Miroir du football* thought he was relatively poorly rewarded, the Ghanain national captain Abdul Razak still received $50,000 a year, together with a house and car, in the deal which brought him to New York Cosmos. His more illustrious team-mate Giorgio Chinaglia, meanwhile, owned a house with twelve rooms, a swimming pool, a tennis court and two limousines. In addition to endorsing a range of products, he also had his own office in the Warner Communications Building in Manhattan.[85] North America was clearly a land of opportunity for some.

Even so, the fundamental problem faced by migrants of adapting to a new culture was particularly evident in the North American case. François Van der Elst found it especially hard to integrate when he arrived at the Cosmos from Anderlecht in 1980. He complained of a failure to understand the US mentality and a difficulty in adapting to NASL rules. The matches, he felt, were like 'a film scenario with everything planned in advance' and the artificial turf was akin to playing on glass.[86] Even Pele commented that the pitches were 'not proper football pitches' and that the league lacked an effective infrastructure[87]; Gordon Hill, a British NASL referee, agreed that the quality of some grounds was 'pitiful, small, bumpy with poor changing rooms'.[88] The European players seem to have been particularly bothered by the travelling, which was aggravated by the frequency of matches. The diversity of languages affected some. In an article on the NPSL in 1967, France's *Football magazine* noted the confusion caused by the polyglot nature of the teams. As a result team-mates rarely talked to each other and players of certain nationalities became isolated. Marcel Nowak, for instance, a French import in Chicago Spurs' multinational team, had no means of communicating with fellow players or management, which led to misunderstandings on and off the field.[89] At times,

84. *Sunday Times*, 27 March 1977; *The Guardian*, 17 August 1978.
85. *Miroir du football*, 8 August 1979; *Football sélection*, January 1981.
86. *Guerin sportivo*, 5 August 1980.
87. François Thébaud, *Pele: une vie, le football, le monde*, Paris: Hatier, 1975, p. 43.
88. *World Soccer*, April 1977.
89. *Football magazine*, August 1967. Also see Gardner, *Nice Guys Finish Last*, pp. 225–6.

linguistic and cultural differences could lead to tensions within NASL sides. New York Cosmos, by far the most successful team of the late 1970s, were nevertheless riven by internal divisions. There were consistent reports of conflict between players and even suggestions that the team was split into an English and non-English camp. According to the Yugoslav midfielder Vladislav Bogicevic, the Cosmos players remained for the most part strangers to one another.[90]

In the end the collapse of the NASL was the result of financial mistakes made by the league administration and the club owners. Both overstretched themselves in an attempt to expand and to attract and retain high-quality imports.[91] By the early 1980s the favours which had been extended to the NASL by the European associations, particularly over the loan system, had been withdrawn and North America took its place as another competitor in the international market for football labour. With falling attendances and revenues it was no longer able to compete. Had the United States been chosen to host the 1986 World Cup it is conceivable that crowds would have increased and the league would have been able to reconstruct itself as a stronger magnet for international talent. In the event, however, the NASL suffered from an inability to Americanize quickly enough. The quota system proved ineffective in undermining the reliance of most clubs on foreign imports. Few had the type of tradition of local football talent which allowed St Louis to field sides consisting largely of North American players, until low crowds led to the franchise being moved in 1978 to California. Likewise, the policy of Chicago Sting under the German-born US coach Willy Roy of promoting indigenous players found few imitators among the predominantly non-North American coaching staff of the NASL.[92] A belated programme of Americanization was attempted in 1983, principally with the establishment of the Team America franchise as an entirely native team and an official training camp for the national side. The experiment failed, as many national team players refused to leave their existing NASL clubs; a similar plan to transform the Montreal franchise into Team Canada did not even make it to the starting gates.[93] This coincided with an alleged attempt to weaken the grip of British and Irish managers and administrators, through the forced resignation of commissioner Phil Woosnam and of coaches such as Alan Hinton, Terry Hennessey and Johnny Giles.[94] This failed too, and the British

90. *Sunday Times*, 16 April 1978; *World Soccer*, May 1977.

91. See PFA Archives, Work Permit File, 1980–84, J.D. Reed, 'It's Time For Trimming Sails in the NASL', 1980 (otherwise unsourced and undated), p. 22. Also Simon Kuper, *Football Against the Enemy*, London: Phoenix, 1995, p. 160.

92. *Miroir du football*, 25 April 1979; David Barnes, *The Game of the Century*, London: Sidgwick & Jackson, 1982, pp. 134–5.

93. Jose, *NASL*, pp. 15, 301; *New York Times*, 17, 21 April 1983.

94. *The Times*, 17 December 1983.

soon came back to dominate playing, coaching and administration in the final days of the NASL as they had from the beginning.

The importation of alien footballers did not cease with the demise of the NASL in early 1985. Perhaps because it was literally a different game, indoor soccer has been largely ignored in previous accounts. Significantly, however, the Major Indoor Soccer League (MISL), established in 1978, served as an important source of employment for many NASL players during the winter off-season and for those who had not made the grade in the conventional game. In certain respects, the MISL represented a more thorough attempt at Americanization, through a modification of the environment and rules of football to suit domestic sporting tastes. Played in ice hockey stadiums, the indoor game was a more open, high-scoring affair which acquired a physical dimension similar to that associated with hockey. The consequent threat of injury was considered too risky for the technically-gifted international stars of the NASL and even an American such as NASL goalkeeper Bob Rigby considered the MISL 'a kind of circus . . . closer to rollerball than football'. For these reasons, and possibly because it could not afford the higher salaries of the outdoor game, the MISL included fewer foreign players. *Football sélection* estimated in May 1980 that about three-quarters of the professionals were born in the United States or Canada.[95] As Table 5.3 shows, the percentage of North Americans in the MISL between 1978 and 1990 was at least 53. In contrast with their dominance in the NASL, only 12.4 per cent were British, many of whom had stayed on after the demise of the outdoor league. Of the MISL's own imports, the Yugoslavs were the most significant, accounting for 6.3 per cent of the league's entire personnel, a development largely explained by the fact that the league was Yugoslav-owned.

Table 5.3 Citizenship of Major Indoor Soccer League Players, 1978–90

Citizenship	No.	%
North American	567	(53.0)
British	133	(12.4)
Yugoslav	68	(6.3)
Rest of Europe	94	(8.8)
Latin American	60	(5.6)
Rest of World	35	(3.3)
Not Known	113	(10.6)

Source: Compiled from data in the MISL Official Guide, 1990–91

95. *Football sélection*, May 1980.

Professional football in the United States and Canada continues to be deeply affected by the distinction between the 'foreigner' and the 'native'. It took eleven years before a professional league competition was created in the United States to match the scope and ambition of the NASL. Established in 1996, from the very beginning Major League Soccer (MLS), a US rather than a broader North American competition, included as the central pillar of its recruitment policy a strict limit on foreign imports. Each franchise was permitted to field a maximum of four, subsequently increased to five, foreign players in each match, thus ensuring a majority of United States personnel in every fixture. A forced policy of Americanization was no doubt more plausible by the mid-1990s due to the improving quality of the top national team players, many of whom were recalled from European leagues, and the maturation of college soccer in the States, which provided a larger pool of talent than had existed during the 1970s and 1980s. The imports chosen by the MLS executive (rather than the clubs themselves) seemed to reflect the changing ethnic complexion of US society. The proliferation of British players and coaches in particular, and Europeans in general, which had characterized the NASL was not to be repeated. MSL preferred to contract Latin Americans who were not only more likely to appeal to Hispanic spectators but were also cheaper. Thus the first season of MSL was dominated by individuals such as DC United's Bolivian Marco Etcheverry, Tampa Bay's Colombian veteran Carlos Valderrama and the LA Galaxy trio of Mauricio Cienfuegos of El Salvador, Ecuador's Eduardo Hurtado and the flamboyant Mexican goalkeeper Jorge Campos.[96] Just twelve Europeans were included among the forty-four foreigners in the rosters for the 2000 season. In comparison, there were five Colombians and four players each from Bolivia and El Salvador.[97] It is surely ironic that MLS now has a smaller percentage of imported players than most of the major European leagues and that there are, for example, more North Americans in the English Premiership than Britons in MLS. At the same time as British club sides are beginning to resemble the polyglot outfits of the North American professional leagues of the 1920s and the 1970s, the football authorities in the United States have seriously attempted to limit the impact of outsiders and prevent the continued stigmatization of football as a 'foreign' sport.

Football is played by many North American girls and boys but has failed at a professional level to gain popularity and financial viability. It has always been considered as an ethnic sport, concerning only restricted communities. As in the case of the Croatians in Toronto and the Mexicans in San José, the football qualities of foreigners mattered less for recruiters than their possible links with a target

96. *When Saturday Comes*, December 1996.
97. Major League Soccer Website, http://www.mlsnet.com/news/rosters [Accessed February 2000].

−6−

Africans in Europe

The story of the migration of African footballers to Europe is in many respects a very different one from those we have previously considered. With few exceptions, football in Africa is not professionalized and so a move to Europe has traditionally been the *only* way of becoming a recognized international footballer. The accepted chronological distinctions between colonial and post-colonial periods are certainly crucial but we also need to be aware of specific factors which have affected migratory patterns in football. Football is Africa's most popular male leisure activity and from an early date African footballers in Europe have become important symbols of international recognition and achievement. The particular skills required have allowed individuals with relatively low levels of 'Westernization' to become successful on both continents. Like music, football has created popular figures and role models who have progressed without denying their difference or requiring training to adapt to Western standards. The enduring problem for African football is that the organizational weakness and the fragility of the professional sporting economy at home has precluded any alternative to the emigration of the best performers. Footballers, like other technical and qualified professional migrants, have faced the dilemma that '[w]hile Africa needed their expertise, they became positive evidence that Africa had arrived'.[1]

Africa is often perceived as a single continent rather than a collection of independent states. There are sensible reasons for thinking in this way. Subordination to, and dependency upon, Europe from slavery to the colonial era and beyond was an experience common throughout the continent. Since the 1950s at least, pan-Africanism has been a powerful force for regional integration, emphasizing the political but also the economic, social and cultural connections between African states. The organization of football on the African continent has been unified and distinct since the creation of the Confédération Africaine de Football (CAF) in 1957. Competitions − such as the Cup of Nations, the Champions Cup and the Cup Winners Cup − have reproduced the European model of national and club

---

1. Joseph E. Harris and Slimane Zeghidour, 'Africa and its diaspora since 1935', in A.A. Mazrui and C. Wondji (eds), *General History of Africa Volume 8: Africa since 1935*, Oxford: Heinemann/ UNESCO, 1993, p. 707.

championships, while domestically every African nation has adopted a European rather than an American structure of sporting competition.[2]

Yet for all its attractions, it would be misleading to ignore the obvious complications which arise from analysing the African continent as a single, undifferentiated unit. In many respects, the idea of 'Africa' is a simplification. Geographic, linguistic, religious and cultural divisions are manifold while economic development has revealed a clear split between richer and poorer areas. Football has also developed unevenly. No East African nation, for example, has ever qualified for the World Cup. North African countries, particularly Algeria, Egypt and Morocco, dominated African competitions for a long time while clubs, national teams and players from six countries on the West coast – Senegal, Ivory Coast, Ghana, Nigeria, Cameroon and the Democratic Republic of Congo (the former Zaire) – have monopolized black African football. Likewise, the European destinations of African footballers cannot be disconnected from the colonial experience. The British situation, where professional football was socially exclusive and confined to members of the white working class, differed from that in France and Portugal. Here footballers from the colonies were allowed, even encouraged, to play in the national team of the colonial power. What better than the best indigenous colonials representing the national team to demonstrate the stability of colonial links? Notwithstanding this, African migration has also followed fashions and trends. After the success of George Weah, European clubs discovered the flavour of Liberian footballers; two decades earlier, players from Mali arrived en masse in the French league after the success of Salif Keita.

As in other economic sectors, there has also been a reverse migration of skilled technicians. Coaches from Europe have taken some of the most important jobs, as national and club managers. Africa as a whole has suffered a lack of skilled managers and the European migrants have often used their position to recruit the best African products for their European clubs. Under these circumstances, football mirrors the neo-colonial trends in which raw materials are traded without genuine investment in infrastructure and training.

African football in general, and the migration of its players in particular, is often perceived in terms of its 'dependency' upon Europe or its 'exploitation' by Europeans. Yet it is surely a simplification to regard African migrants merely as passive tools of European club owners. Poor employment conditions and low pay may appear common but should not be regarded as the generic experience of the African footballer in Europe. Africans have in fact constituted a mixed, hetero-

---

2. Indeed, it is telling that the idea for the creation of CAF had its origins in Europe, following a meeting of representatives of the Egyptian, South African and Sudanese federations in the Hotel Avenida in Lisbon in August 1957. Mustapha Fahmy, 'Organizzazione amministrazione', in *Proceedings of the Conference 'Africa 2000'*, Florence: FIGC, 1991.

geneous group from the very beginning. On top of the general categories we outlined in the introduction, the migration of African players can be divided into four main areas. First, those who were stars in Africa have often accepted unstable conditions in Europe, playing at semi-professional level and hoping to climb the European career ladder. Secondly, for a large group of established players in Africa who came to Europe, football alone could not explain their migration. These individuals attempted to advance simultaneously at university or in another job; some remained active and successful in European football but others stopped playing entirely and settled into other occupations. Thirdly, some economic migrants to Europe have taken up football professionally in their host country. Finally, aspirant professionals are increasingly recruited in their early teens and spend the beginning of their careers in European club youth teams. Although they do not move as professionals, their football talent is the reason for their recruitment. A fifth group further complicates the status of African migrants: those second-generation immigrants who have no direct link with the African birthplace of their parents, but nonetheless represent African countries in international competition. Such distinctions are necessary in order to understand the complexity of the connection between football and African migration. If making a living from football requires migration to Europe, football has not always been the sole reason to leave Africa.

The Colonial Period

The European powers did not of course approach their African territories or their colonial populations in the same way. There is little doubt that Tropical Africa, especially West Africa, was less central to British imperial power than it was to the French. In terms of strategy, prestige and even overseas trade, most of Africa was marginal compared with other parts of the empire over which the British exercised direct and indirect rule.[3] Although they were free to enter Britain, a practice confirmed by the 1948 Immigration Act, there was neither a major attempt to import large numbers of Africans, nor to assimilate them into metropolitan society. The French, in contrast, regarded all colonies as part of a 'greater France'. The notion of 'Overseas France' was revealing of the ideal of assimilation which determined French imperial relations. According to the academic Arthur Girault, assimilation meant 'an increasingly intimate union between the colonial and metropolitan territory . . . The colonies are theoretically considered to be a simple extension of the soil of the mother country'.[4] More specifically, Algeria maintained

3. P.J. Cain and A.G. Hopkins, *British Imperialism: Innovation and Expansion, 1688–1914*, London: Longman, 1993, pp. 381–91.

4. Quoted in Raymond F. Betts, *France and Decolonisation, 1900–1960*, London: Macmillan, 1991, p. 17.

a special relationship with France. As a *colonie de peuplement*, it was the one colony with a large residential French population and an established tradition of labour migration to the metropolitan centre. Algeria's special status was confirmed in 1947. Henceforth all Algerians automatically became French citizens and the principle of free movement between the two territories was formalized. Within two years, the number of Algerians migrating to France had soared from 65,000 to 265,000.[5]

In common with the French, Portugal regarded its African territories not as colonies but as 'Overseas Provinces'. They too adopted a policy which permitted indigenous Africans to become 'black Portuguese', although in practice relatively few were assimilated in this way. By 1950, for instance, fewer than one in every hundred Africans from Angola and Mozambique were classified as 'assimilated persons'.[6]

Such distinctions provide a fundamental backdrop for the contrasting attitudes to the recruitment of African footballers. This being said, it would be mistaken to attempt simply to read off the pattern of football migration from more general colonial perspectives. Even if we agree that footballers have resembled economic migrants in certain ways, we must admit that they are hardly representative of this broader group. The relative ease with which they could move to Europe contrasts sharply with the tightening of immigration controls which has affected the bulk of Africans, especially since the 1970s. The notion of 'Fortress Europe' has clearly impacted upon skilled professionals such as footballers less than it has upon most African migrant workers.[7]

France and its colonies

> Along with the school education, sporting education of our black brothers must give marvellous results. Initiation to football is less arid, I think, than initiation to literature or rhetoric, but sporting education is highly civilising, without a doubt.[8]

This quotation from an article in the French press in 1929 clearly indicates that the French authorities showed some interest in football. It was a reference to the game in the black African colonies, a sport as yet played only by a small number

5. Sarah Collinson, *Europe and International Migration*, London: Royal Institute of International Affairs, 1993, p. 48.

6. Fola Soremekun, 'Portugal, Mozambique and Angola: Trends Towards Future Relationships', in A. Sesay (ed.), *Africa and Europe: From Partition to Independence?*, London: Croom Helm, 1986, pp. 86–103; Basil Davidson, *Modern Africa: A Social and Political History*, 3rd edn, London: Longman, 1994, p. 159.

7. Panikos Panayi, *Outsiders: A History of Minorities in Europe*, London: Hambledon, 1999, pp. 146–60.

of 'natives'. The situation was much different in North Africa, where football had already reached high standards. The French did not ignore these developments. African players were to be found in the French professional league from its creation in 1932. In addition, by the Second World War three Muslims from Algeria and Morocco had played with the national team, as had a black player from Senegal.

Indeed, despite the same type of prejudice which existed in all the colonial nations, the French authorities encouraged a policy of integration, if not in domestic life then on the football field. More than any other European country, France was prepared to give Africans access to professional football. How can this be explained? One important point to remember is the role of football in French society. In contrast with that in England, football never became an important element of the national character, an activity which helped to define the French and Frenchness. The notions of a 'French game' or a 'French style' were much later developments than elsewhere in Europe. As such, football could be shared with sons of the colonies and sons of immigrants without compromising the soul of the sport. A comparison with other sports is particularly revealing here. Rugby and cycling, sports which were closely in tune with the concept of *la France profonde* (the deep France) and rural French life, were virtually closed to the African population. In athletics and boxing, however, as in football, the participation of Africans was common and relatively unproblematic. Racism may not have been absent but formal discrimation was rarely so evident as in other European countries. In 1922, 'Battling' Siki, a black boxer born in Senegal, became world champion after defeating national hero Georges Carpentier, while in 1928 Ahmed El Ouafi, a Muslim Algerian, became the first non-white African to win an athletics gold medal at the Olympic Games.[9]

For these reasons, we cannot agree with the assumption that the British were wholly successful and the French unsuccessful in 'the diffusion of soccer to the African continent'.[10] Providing access to the elite and the professional market was an important aspect of the diffusion process in which Britain showed relatively little interest until the end of the twentieth century. On the contrary France and, after the Second World War, Portugal and Belgium adopted a more open policy.

---

8. *Match*, 20 August 1929.

9. On Battling Siki, Bernadette Deville-Danthu, *Le sport en noir et blanc*, Paris: L'Harmatthan, 1997; Edouard Seidler and Robert Parienté, *Dictionnaire des sports*, Paris: Seghers, 1964, p. 28; Pierre Naudin, *La foire aux muscles*, Paris: Editeurs Français Réunis, 1961, p. 264; E. Gerald, 'Battling Siki: The Boxer as Natural Man', *Massachusetts Review*, 29, 3, 1988, pp. 451–72; on El Ouafi see *Athletic News*, 13 August 1928 and on a comparison with the composition of the British athletics team at the same Olympics, see H. B. Stallart, 'The Olympic Games', in Amateur Athletic Association, *Fifty Years of Progress 1880–1930*, London: Amateur Athletic Association, 1930, p. 102.

10. Allen Guttmann, *Games and Empires: Modern Sports and Imperialism*, New York: Columbia University Press, 1994, pp. 63–9.

The implications of this are crucial in the debate about sporting migration, a discussion which in Britain and the United States has tended to ignore the experiences of other imperial powers.

The first stream of footballers to France was dominated by North Africans. One notable exception was Raoul Diagne, a Senegalese, born in French Guyana. His father, Victor Diagne, was a member of parliament and his mother a middle-class Parisian woman. Educated in the Parisian Lycée Louis le Grand, he had a long and prolific professional career. He played from the creation of the league to the war years and was a member of the national team before deciding in the 1950s to return to Senegal to become a sports director.

The other African migrants were mainly Algerians and Moroccans. Algeria, in particular, was becoming an increasing force in French football. In the 1930s, there were more registered players in Algeria than in the Paris region.[11] Indeed French football was closely connected with its Algerian counterpart. From 1932, the French Champions toured Algeria every year, while an annual match between a French 'B' team and the Algerian national side had begun some years before. There were even calls for Algerian clubs to be included in the French league and cup but this was resisted until the 1950s. Members of both the Muslim and European communities were involved in football, often in the same clubs, although all-Muslim teams were also common.[12] The two most famous Algerian footballers of the inter-war period were undoubtedly Albert Camus, who played in goal for the junior team of Racing Union Algiers, and Ahmed Ben Bella, the first president of the Algerian Republic in 1962, who even played one match in the professional team of Marseilles in 1941.[13]

The early 1930s marked the first arrival to France of large groups of Algerian immigrant workers as well as an increasing number of Algerian students attending French universities. The first professional footballers fitted these categories neatly.[14] When Ali Benouna signed for Sète in 1932, recruited from US Orléansville (now Skikda), he combined his football activity with a manual job at the docks. Kouider

---

11. In June 1934, Paris had 13,448 registered players and Algeria 13,494. However facilities were very unequally distributed. Paris had 110 equipped stadiums while Algeria had twenty. AGM of the FFFA (French Football Association) 1934, reported in *Les sports du Sud-Est*, 21 and 26 July 1934.

12. Benjamin Stora, 'Algérie, années coloniales: quand le sport devient un facteur de mobilisation politique', in *Jeu et sports en Méditerrannée. Actes du colloque de Carthage, 7–9 novembre 1989*, Tunis: ACIF, 1991, pp. 143–53.

13. A photograph of Camus as a footballer has been choosen by the editors for the front cover of his recently published diaries. On Ben Bella, L. Grimaud and A. Pécheral, *La grande histoire de l'OM*, Paris: Robert Laffont, 1984, pp. 102–4.

14. Abdelmalek Saïd, 'Les trois âges de l'émigration algérienne en France', *Actes de la recherche en sciences sociales*, 15, January 1977, pp. 59–79.

Daho, a medical student born in Oran, came to France to play professional football and complete his studies. Emile Zermani was already working in Marseilles as a shopkeeper when he was signed by Olympique Marseille while Abdelkader Ben Bouali, from a wealthy Algerian family, was signed by Montpellier in 1933.

With the arrival of Larbi Ben Barek to Marseilles in 1938, a new type of African import emerged. Ben Barek was an instant star. Just four months after his arrival he was selected for the national team and quickly became a French icon. Born in Casablanca in 1917, he had worked as a cleaner at a gas company for twenty francs a day; his first contract at Marseilles multiplied this income fifty times over.[15] Ben Barek was hardly a marginal player. He became a key figure in the French national side and the first French player to be transferred to a major foreign club when he moved to Atlético Madrid for one million pesatas in 1948. The highest transfer fee at the time in the Spanish league, Ben Barek's move was viewed as a sign of the 'fraternal relations between Spain and the Arabs'.[16] In the 1950s, three Moroccan players – Chicha, Mahjoub and Salem – followed him to France and then Spain, courted by clubs hoping to find the new 'Black Pearl'.

North Africans were increasingly involved in the French professional league after the Second World War. Between 1945 and 1962, seventy-six Muslim Algerians, thirty-four Moroccans and seven Tunisians played in French professional football. Of these, eight Algerians and four Moroccans were selected to represent France.[17] With the uprising of 1954 and the beginning of the Algerian War, the place of football in French-Algerian relations was further complicated. The final details of the armed struggle were planned when representatives of the Algerian Liberation Front (FLN) met in Switzerland, during the latter stages of the 1954 World Cup.[18] Henceforth, football came to be associated with the integration of all communities in France. From 1956, Algerian clubs took part in the French cup and the following year the modest amateur club El Biar caused a sensation by knocking Reims, European Cup finalists six months earlier, out of the tournament. The final itself also became a defining moment of the war, as the President of the Algerian Assembly, Ali Chekkal, an opponent of independence, was assassinated at the end of a match won by a Toulouse side fielding the Algerians Said Brahimi and Ahmed Bouchouk. In this context, the departure of eight professionals from their French clubs in April 1958 to join the team of the Algerian Independence

15. Larbi Ben Barek with Jean Eskenazi, 'Les mémoires de la perle noire', *But et Club, Le Miroir des sports*, issue 486, 1 November 1954.

16. C. Fernández Santander, *El fútbol durante la guerra civil y el franquismo*, Madrid: San Martín, p. 97.

17. M. Barreaud, *Dictionnaire des Footballeurs étrangers du championnat professionnel français (1932–1997)*, Paris: L'Harmattan, 1998, pp. 68–82, 183–91, 240–3.

18. Charles-Henri Favrod, 'La Suisse des négociations secrètes', in J.P. Rioux (ed.), *La guerre d'Algérie et les français*, Paris: Fayard, 1990, p. 397.

Movement in Tunis placed football migrants at the centre of the war for independence. In its editorial, *Le Monde* wrote that 'The French public is more sensitive to the disappearance of Algerian footballers than Algerian politicians'. These were wealthy professionals in a competition which was closely followed in Algeria and which was regarded by both Muslims and Europeans as a potential force for unity and integration. The FLN's official communication described the players as fighters for independence: 'As patriots seeking the liberation of their country above all else, our footballers have given the youth of Algeria an example of courage, rectitude and unselfishness'.[19]

At the same time, *The Times* published a series of articles depicting these footballers as political activists.[20] Banned immediately by FIFA, these outlaw footballers provide a unique but important example of the involvement of professional footballers in political struggle. Yet it would be wrong to reduce them to revolutionary fighters: once independence was achieved, most rejoined their clubs in France in order to continue their professional careers and to ensure that the Algerian federation could join FIFA.[21] Rachid Mekhloufi provides a particularly potent symbol of this displaced group. In April 1958, he was preparing for the World Cup with the French national team after being a part of the French army side which won the world military championship in Buenos Aires a year earlier. Shortly afterwards, he was a rebel, spending the years between 1958 and 1962 touring with the FLN as ambassadors of the revolution. Yet unable to follow his career in a new country where professionalism in sport was banned, Mekhloufi migrated once more back to France. He was, in the phrase of Abdelmalek Saïd, part of a second wave of emigrants pushed back to France by their ambiguous status in Algeria.[22] By 1964 Mekhloufi was once again a French champion and as captain of his team receiving the French cup from the hands of De Gaulle in 1968, he was told by the general that 'La France c'est vous'. Too political to be accepted by the sporting establishment in France, he was at the same time too professional and Westernized for the newly independent Algerian authorities.

From the early 1950s, footballers from Francophone West Africa began to migrate to France. A handful around 1955, there were some forty-three by 1960.

19. *Le Monde*, 17 April 1958.

20. *The Times*, 15, 16 April 1958.

21. The Algerian government subsequently took the step of prohibiting the export of its best talent: 'We regret to tell you that following the decision of our state secretary of Youth and Sport, the Federation has decided to take every step to terminate the departure of our young players abroad and therefore we will not give any clearance certificates'. FIFA Archives, Nation Files, Algeria (To 1983), Letter from Algerian Football Federation to FIFA, 24 November 1964.

22. Saïd, 'Les trois âges de l'émigration algérienne en France' notes that emigrants aged between twenty and thirty-five made up 60 per cent in 1954.

All, however, were French citizens from colonial territories. Their recruitment can be explained by three factors: the poor finances of French clubs; the closure of the French border to 'foreign' players in 1955; and, as in other cases, the presence of colonial footballers as students. One such arrival had a significant impact on the status of all players in France. Eugène N'jo Lea was hardly a poor unskilled African immigrant. A promising talent in Cameroon, he was sent to France to complete his baccalauréat in Roanne and initially played only at amateur level. He later combined a football career with university study, moving to Lyons to read law and signing professional forms with Saint-Etienne, where he became a prolific goalscorer. A fan of Dizzy Gillespie, he played the trumpet, loved reading Kafka and managed to receive his PhD in law as well as a league title with Saint-Etienne. A magazine of the time portrayed him as the archetypal modern footballer, combining a conscientious study regime with the ascetic life of a sportsman: 'I almost never go out in the evenings. Between my training, my reading and my music I have no time left to go to the movies or to a bar'.[23] Yet at the age of twenty-nine, N'jo Lea chose to forgo football for a career in law and later became Cameroon ambassador to the UN. Perhaps more significantly, he was instrumental in the creation of the French Players' Union in 1961. Ironically, by that time Cameroon had achieved independence and so, as a foreigner, N'jo Lea was ineligible to take office in the union.

This was a long-term form of migration, which often outlasted a relatively short football career. Twenty years later, N'jo Lea's son, who had been born in France, followed in his father's footsteps when he became a professional footballer. The son of another Cameroonese player of the period was to become a world-famous tennis player. Zacharie Noah was a defender with Sedan and married a French Physical Education teacher. In 1961, the year his club won the French cup, his son Yannick was born. The national identification of such second-generation migrants was complex. When Yannick won the French Open in 1983 as a Frenchman, he wore the colours of Cameroon to display his dual nationality. Camille Passi was an apprentice at the Congo Railway Company when during a match for the local representative side against the crew of *Le Jeanne d'Arc* naval vessel he was approached to sign for Béziers in the French second division. He enjoyed a moderate career at the lower level but through his footballing contacts was able to find a good job as an insurance broker when he stopped playing. For Passi, football enabled him to improve his social status, to meet his French wife and together to have two sons who became professionals, one even reaching international status for France.[24] For these West African migrants, playing professional football was certainly an important means of integration but it seems

23. *Football Magazine*, March 1961.
24. Letter from Camille Passi to authors, 31 May 1989.

to have been only one of a number of considerations in moving to Europe in the first place.

The apparent openness to African talent in colonial France had its limitations. At times there was public rejection of the idea of French football as a 'melting pot'. Take the reaction of a journalist in 1937 to the request of Nice's Tunisian import Boudejemaa for a pay rise:

> The Tunisian is unable to write but is evidently good at counting! The football world is criticized enough from all parts and cannot afford to accept ridiculous requests from primitives. He must consider himself happy enough to earn good money with his feet, given that the other extremity, his brain, is of little help to him.[25]

Descriptions of African footballers revealed a more subtle form of discrimination. From early on, the discourse on African players was binomial: gift and immaturity. Representations of African footballers focused on their 'natural' characteristics. Their success in sport was not the result of their hard work, of their abnegation. They become stars of the sporting show only with their innate talent. Their biographies refer to supernatural elements to explain their success. Mahjoub, the Moroccan midfielder of Racing Paris, 'spoke with arabesques' with his feet, Salif Keita 'recalled conjuring' and Ben Barek, the 'Black Pearl' of French football, 'gave to Madrid spectators, who loved to see it, a recital of feints like a juggler'.[26] This irrational dimension attached to the coloured players is given as the only plausible explanation for success – a divine origin.

Players are always categorized into different types. In every team you will find some physically strong players, some team players, some runners, some technical players. Yet Africans were considered, almost unfailingly, as instinctive players. They played the game but easily gave up. They were nice to watch but not really efficient. Workers with little skill, they were unsuited to tactical schemes. Such attitudes were reflected in the positions and responsibilities given to Africans on the field of play. Most were employed as wingers or full-backs, two positions on the margins of the field said to require 'natural' qualities rather than thought, vision and reflection. Benouna, Zermani and Derdour were all wingers while Ben Bouali was a full-back. The central positions of goalkeeper, centre-half and inside-forward were rarely filled by Africans. Indeed, of the eighteen Muslim Africans employed in the top two French divisions in 1937, none occupied any of these key positions.

25. Jean Allègre, 'Que vont faire les Aiglons', *Les sports du Sud Est*, 19 August 1937.
26. F. Majoub, *Trente ans de Coupe d'Afrique des nations*, Paris: Jeune Afrique, 1988; Ben Barek, 'Les mémoires de la perle noire'.

Britain and its colonies

As with France, the earliest African footballers arrived in Britain primarily to further their education or learn a trade, a common means of entry for African migrants more generally.[27] Egyptians were among the first African imports. Hassan Hegazi, for instance, joined Fulham as an amateur from Dulwich Hamlet in 1911 while attending London University. He played only a couple of matches – for Fulham and Millwall – before enrolling to study Arabic and history at Cambridge in 1913. Similarly, Tewfik Abdullah arrived in England in 1920 to learn 'something about the engineering trade'[28] but also to play football, which he did professionally for Derby County, Cowdenbeath, Hartlepools United and Bridgend Town before moving to the United States to play in the ASL. Other Egyptian student-footballers, like Mohamed Latif of Jordanhill College and Glasgow Rangers, and Mohamed el Guindy and Abdul Kerin Sukr, who both attended Leeds University and signed as amateurs for Huddersfield Town in the mid-1940s, were recruited following recommendations from James McCrae, who had previously coached in Egypt.[29] The presence of these players seems to have generated more curiosity than criticism. Abdullah was depicted wearing his Derby shirt in front of a pyramid on the front cover of *Topical Times* in November 1920.[30] Guindy, who never reached the Huddersfield first team, was portrayed as a Westernized Egyptian who 'speaks English fluently and perfect French ... Although almost ebony-coloured, [he] dresses well, and his suits would do credit to Saville Row'.[31]

White South Africans, however, were undoubtedly the most popular imports. One small town, Boksburg, was said to have produced nine players for the English and Scottish leagues between the wars.[32] Liverpool, in particular, recruited a number of South Africans from the mid-1920s, including goalkeeper Arthur Riley and inside-forward Gordon Hodgson, and by the early 1930s had six on their books.[33] Like Liverpool earlier, Charlton Athletic established a significant colony of South African footballers in the decade after 1945. Frustrated by the lack of cheap young talent at home, Charlton's manager, Jimmy Seed, successfully exploited his contacts and made personal visits to persuade some thirteen 'Springboks'

27. Colin Holmes, *John Bull's Island*, London: Macmillan, 1988, p. 34.

28. Quoted in Phil Vasili, *Colouring over the White Line: The History of Black Footballers in Britain*, Edinburgh: Mainstream, 2000, p. 64.

29. Ibid., pp. 65–6.

30. *Topical Times*, 13 November 1920.

31. Alec E. Whitcher, *The Voice of Soccer*, Brighton: Southern Publishing, 1947, pp. 39–40.

32. Robert Archer and Antoine Bouillon, *The South African Game: Sport and Racism*, London: Zed Press, 1982, p. 99.

33. Percy M. Young, *Football on Merseyside*, London: Stanley Paul, 1964, pp. 116, 130–1.

to make the trip to London in ten years. Some failed to make the grade but others enjoyed long careers, including those like Eddie Firmani and John Hewie who even received international recognition, with Italy (as we have seen) and Scotland respectively.[34] Black South Africans were far less common, marginalized, as Phil Vasili has powerfully observed, by the cultural prejudice of British scouts and agents as well as the introduction of domestic restrictions on their movement. It was not until the late 1950s and early 1960s that the first Black South Africans, such as Stephen Mokone, Gerry Francis and Albert Johanneson, were being brought to Britain to play professionally.[35]

West Africans were no more common. In many respects the story of the Ghanaian Arthur Wharton, who became the first Black footballer in Britain when he played for various clubs including Preston North End and Sheffield United in the 1880s and 1890s, is exceptional.[36] Yet his arrival in Europe as a student from a relatively wealthy African family underlines the secondary role ascribed to football among many of these migrants to England, France and the rest of the continent. The first Nigerians to play in the Football League during the late 1950s and early 1960s all arrived with the twin purpose of earning money from football and acquiring training in a profession or a trade. Tesilimi Bagolun joined Midlands League Peterborough United and took a position at a local printing company; Francis Feyami intended to learn carpentry while at Cambridge City but stayed for just four months. Elkanah Onyeali, meanwhile, played for Tranmere Rovers while a student of electrical engineering at Birkenhead Technical College but informed the local press that 'study comes first', and was prepared to miss matches which clashed with his academic timetable.[37] These players competed sparingly and did not stay long. Football enabled them to travel and acquire experience and training but it is doubtful whether it was envisaged as a profession in its own right.

Portugal and Belgium: The Colonial Resource

No country more than Portugal has built its football reputation upon sons of its colonies and former colonies. Portuguese football, relatively slow and late to professionalize, had employed players from South America and Eastern Europe

34. Jimmy Seed, *The Jimmy Seed Story*, London: Phoenix, 1957, pp. 53–61.

35. Vasili, *Colouring over the White Line*, pp. 100–11.

36. On Wharton, see Phil Vasili, *The First Black Footballer: Arthur Wharton, 1865–1930*, London: Frank Cass, 1998; Ray Jenkins, '"Salvation for the Fittest?": A West African Sportsman in Britain in the Age of the New Imperialism', *International Journal of the History of Sport*, 7, 1, May 1990.

37. Vasili, *Colouring over the White Line*, pp. 111–17.

since the 1940s. Clubs began to recruit players from the African colonies in the 1950s, largely as a consequence of the defeats experienced in propaganda tours to Angola and Mozambique.

As in the French case, the initial African migrants to Portugal can be separated into two main groups, distinguished by social background, wealth and career pattern. Miguel Arcanjo, born in 1933 in Nova Lisboa (Angola), was a central defender who played nine times for Portugal. An educated black, he was the son of a colonial civil servant employed in the agricultural division office. He had learned football when studying at a seminary and was recruited by FC Porto at the age of eighteen to play football but also continue his studies.[38] Lucas Figuereido 'Matateu', born in Lourenço Marques (now Maputo), Mozambique, was capped twenty-seven times for Portugal. He arrived in Portugal in 1951, the same year as Arcanjo, but his background was much different. A working-class child, Matateu began playing football for the club João Albasini, a side exclusively composed of native Africans. At the moment of his transfer, he was already a football star in Mozambique, as striker of his local club Primo de Mayo and the Mozambique national side. At twenty-four, he had also experienced professional advantages through football when Primo de Mayo offered him a better job to sign for them. In September 1951, the Lisbon club Belenenses flew Matateu over to join them and he was immediately included in the first team, receiving his first cap twelve months later. By contrast, the young Arcanjo was considered too light and inexperienced to play first-team football and had to wait two years to join Porto's starting eleven. Whereas for Matateu such inactivity would have been a major career setback, Arcanjo was still able to continue his education while struggling to make his name in football.

Matateu's impact on Portuguese football has tended to be forgotten outside his country. Yet he was instrumental in Portugal's first victory over England in Oporto and topped the league scorers' lists in 1953 and 1955.[39] Like the Italian clubs who acquired South Americans in the 1930s, Portuguese teams, after the success of Matateu, began to recruit large numbers of both black and white players on the African market. Hence in 1958 Sporting Lisbon signed Hilario, a mulatto from Mozambique, who played forty times for Portugal and thirteen years for his club.[40] Benfica, the other major club from Lisbon, whose rules only allowed the inclusion of Portuguese citizens, nevertheless recruited a number of players from the colonies, like the white Angolans Aguas and goalkeeper Costa Pereira. Mario Coluna, a black from Mozambique, signed in 1954 and stayed for sixteen years. By the early

---

38. *Idolos*, December 1980, pp. 16–19.
39. Brian Glanville, *Soccer Round the Globe*, London: Sportsman's Book Club, 1961, p. 71.
40. *Idolos*, December 1980, p. 14.

1960s the importation of Africans had reached almost the same level as in France, with thirty employed by first-division clubs.[41]

Eusebio da Silva was born in 1942 in Lourenço Marques. He arrived at Benfica in 1961, a few weeks after the club's first European Cup victory. Eusebio became unquestionably the most successful Portuguese footballer of all time, winning ten league championship medals and finishing top of the national scorers' list on seven occasions. He was capped sixty-four times for Portugal and scored 317 goals for his club. In the 1966 World Cup in England, the first time Portugal had qualified, he scored nine goals to win the Golden Boot and was widely considered as Pele's only serious challenger as the world's best player. In fact in many ways Eusebio's career was comparable to Pele's. European Footballer of the Year in 1965, and soon acquiring the status of a national hero in Portugal, the 'Black Panther', as he was nicknamed on account of his African origins and his style at the time of Malcolm X and Angela Davis, was clearly a symbol less of rebellion than of integration.

Bela Guttmann, a migrant himself as both player and manager (see Chapter 5), signed Eusebio for only £7,500. Yet within a matter of weeks, he had been capped for the national team and been instrumental in Benfica's second European Cup triumph.[42] In the context of 1960s Portugal, a closed society with little contact with the rest of Europe, Eusebio became the hope for a better future. The emigration of Portuguese workers to other European countries (particularly France) was rapidly on the increase. A living example of social mobility, success and integration in a Salazarist Portugal where opportunities were so limited that 100,000 workers left the country annually, Eusebio's popularity among Portuguese workers abroad was phenomenal.[43] He personified a proud and confident Portugal, and his popularity in the country has not been matched since. Indeed, Eusebio was not even fifty when Benfica's directors decided to erect a sculpture of him at the entrance to the Stadium of Light. Since the 1980s Eusebio has had various duties at Benfica, from youth coach, to public relations officer and team manager. Yet he remains an uneasy symbol. A monument of Portuguese football and society, and an official ambassador for the national team two decades after the end of his career, Eusebio's links with Mozambique and Africa have become increasingly tenuous over the years. He was described in 1964 as

41. José Torre, 'Mario Esteves Coluna: Schwungard der Benfica Elf' in K.H. Hubu (ed.) *Die Großen am Ball*, Munich: Copress, 1972, pp. 44–7.

42. Brian Glanville, *The Puffin Book of Footballers*, Harmondsworth: Penguin, 1978, p. 50.

43. Patrick Weil, *La France et ses étrangers: l'aventure d'une politique de l'immigration 1938– 1991*, Paris: Calmann-Lévy, 1991, p. 375. His table 5 shows that from 50,000 Portuguese immigrants in France in 1962, there were 300,000 Portuguese in 1968 and by 1974, at the apex of the phenomenon, 750,000 immigrant workers. Also see Maria Beatric Rocha Trindade, 'Portugal', in R.E. Krane, *International Labor Migration in Europe*, New York, Praeger, 1979, pp. 164–72.

A poor boy who suddenly became rich and admired. With football, he has been able to buy a house for his parents in Mozambique and two buildings, which have made great profits for him. But he has remained down-to-earth and friendly. He loves records, cinema and considers his car as a toy. He has refused to sign for an Italian club because his mother wanted him to stay in Lisbon.[44]

If Eusebio finished his career in North America and Mexico, but came back to Lisbon, Mario Coluna chose to return to Mozambique after independence and develop coaching programmes there.

Many of Portugal's African immigrants had similarly ambiguous relationships with their old and new homes. Carlos Alhinho, originally from Cape Verde, signed a contract with Academica de Coimbra in 1966. The sixth of fifteen children, he came to Portugal to study agrarian engineering and to play football in division one with the university club. He succeeded at all levels, managing to get his degree, be capped by the Portuguese national team, ensure a transfer to a leading club, Sporting Lisbon, and marry a young student from Coimbra. His professional career continued in Spain with Real Betis and in Belgium with RWD Molenbeek. While in Belgium, however, he and his family suffered the life of displaced immigrants:

Everything was different and the relations between people were extraordinarily cold. It was a difficult time in my life. I didn't integrate in the team or make friends in the squad. I prefered to spend my time with students from Leuven University who were originarly from Cape Verde. Fortunately, I also had relatives living in Rotterdam, 140 km away from Brussels. I could not possibly have stayed there for more than a season.[45]

He returned to Portugal to play for Benfica, at the same time opening a sportswear shop in the Portuguese capital and obtaining his coaching degree. Well established in Portugal, he returned part-time to Africa and later coached the national teams of Cape Verde and Angola. Another player who reflected the dual identity of African migrants was Fernando Freitas, born in 1947 in Lobito, Angola. He began playing indoor football (*futebol de salão*) before signing for the local club Lusitano de Lobito. From there he moved to Portugal in 1967 together with two of his teammates, Arlindo Leitão, who also signed for Porto and Chipenda, who joined Belenenses. Success at Porto led to his selection for the national team. After independence in 1975, Freitas, an Angolan citizen, was entitled to claim dual citizenship as a resident in Portugal for the previous five years. From Angolan origins, Freitas' migration to Portugal had brought him wealth and fame in both Africa and Europe. With the money he made from football, he was able to buy a

44. Cahiers de l'Equipe, *Football 1964*, Paris: L'Equipe, 1964, p. 156.
45. *Idolos*, January 1979, pp. 22–3.

house and secure his future, buying a hair-dressing salon run by his wife.[46] After the independence of the Portuguese African colonies, the migration of footballers became more complicated legally but continued at a similar pace and rhythm.

The Belgians did not welcome foreign players before the late 1950s. Initially, only professionals from Hungary and Britain were recruited but by 1960 around thirty players from the Belgian Congo were employed by Belgian clubs, ten of whom were in the first division. The most famous, Joseph Kialunda from Anderlecht, was described as 'The Puskas from Leopoldsville'. Another leading import from Congo, Paul Bonga Bonga, a powerful defender, played with Standard Liège for many years. These players arrived at the time of Zairian independence, before the movement of footballers was prohibited by the Zairian authorities in 1962 and they remained the only Africans in Belgian football for some years.[47] In fact, of the Zairian team which qualified for the 1974 World Cup, the only player with foreign experience was their manager Kalambay, who had been part of this initial cohort. The position of Zaire was symptomatic of the general reticence of African nations to let their players leave for Europe.

As Table 6.1 shows, the neo-colonial model applies perfectly to the links existing between players from Zaire and their former colonial ruler. After the liberalization of Belgian import regulations in 1978, Zairian exiles returned to their previous destination. If the second half of the 1980s witnessed a general diversification of African recruitment in Europe, the traditional migration routes remained largely unaffected. Of the Africans who played in Belgium between 1985 and 1995, 40 per cent came from Zaire (Table 6.1). Yet Belgium was also developing more generally into a magnet for African football talent: a favourite first stop for other African migrants in search of good contracts in Europe. The bilingualism of Belgium probably persuaded clubs in Flanders to look to English-speaking Africans, especially Nigerians. The most successful, like Stephen Keshi and Daniel Amokachi, regarded Belgium as a stepping stone to the richer leagues. By the 1990–91 season, there were more Nigerians (twenty) than Zairians (fifteen) in the top two divisions.[48] Other players from former British colonies, such as the Ghanian Nii Lamptey and the Zambian Kalusha Bwalya, similarly began their European careers in Belgium. With Britain uninterested in its colonial resource, Belgium was happy to accommodate these players. The specific regulations regarding

46. *Idolos*, April 1979, p. 18. On the legal status of dual citizens from the former colonies, Rui Manual Moura Ramos, 'Mouvements migratoires et droit de la nationalité au Portugal dans le dernier demi-siècle', in P. Weil and R. Hansen (eds), *Nationalité et citoyenneté en Europe*, Paris: La découverte, 1999, pp. 221–38.

47. For biographical sketches of this group, *Miroir du football*, November 1960.

48. *Afrique football*, November 1990.

Table 6.1 African Players in Belgium Divisions 1
and 2, 1985–1995

Zaire	48
Nigeria	25
Morocco	8
Ghana	7
Sierra Leone	5
Senegal	4
Tunisia	4
Cameroon	3
Guinea	3
South Africa	3
Zambia	3
Algeria	2
Ivory Coast	2
Rwanda	2
Congo	1
Gabon	1
Kenya	1
Liberia	1
Malawi	1
Togo	1
Zimbabwe	1
Total	126

Source: Various Belgian Sporting Almanacs, 1985–95

foreign signings allowed Belgian clubs who had contracted Africans before the age of seventeen to treat them as Belgians for football purposes. Conversely, the relative lack of competition for places in Belgian club sides made them particularly attractive for Africans seeking an early experience of elite European football. The success of unknown African players such as Jules Bocandé and Eugène Kabongo, who after short spells with Seraing, a first division club in the suburbs of Liège, signed lucrative contracts with Paris St Germain and Racing Paris respectively, convinced agents and players of the soundness of this strategy.

Indeed Belgian football provided an early indication of the changing attitudes of European clubs towards the African market. Diversifying their recruitment, clubs began to contract professionals from hitherto untapped nations such as Sierra Leone and Zambia. The reasons for this were purely economic. As with the Danes in the late 1970s and the Eastern Europeans in the late 1990s, Belgian clubs have considered young foreign players as an investment, to be bought cheaply (with the help of agents whose activities were recognized much earlier here than in the rest of the continent) and sold abroad for a significant profit. It is possible to detect a change in the career patterns of Africans in Europe from the mid-1980s. If Seraing recruited Kabongo from Zaire at the age of twenty-three as a full international, Anderlecht have since 1988 barely engaged a single African over the age of eighteen. Belgian clubs have pioneered the trend for buying young and thus ensuring many African footballers an exclusively European playing career.

The New Image of Africa

In 1982, a new image of African football emerged in the eyes of the world. The two African representatives at the World Cup in Spain narrowly failed to qualify for the second stage. Neither Algeria nor Cameroon fitted with the image of a gifted but immature amateur team representing a poor, underdeveloped continent. Both were composed mainly of players earning their living as professionals in France. The Algerian squad, in particular, was a mixture of second-generation immigrants with dual citizenship and a few of the best amateurs in the Algerian league. Mustapha Dahleb, for instance, was the captain of Paris St Germain and had only ever played in Algeria during his military service. The defenders Mansouri and Kourichi played their first match in Algeria the previous year, after the Algerian Sports Ministry changed its rules to allow the children of exiles to represent the nation. The Cameroonese situation was slightly different. Their most famous player, Jean-Pierre Tokoto, had played for over a decade in France and was finishing his career in the NASL in Boston. A decade earlier, he had been captain of the only 'African' selection to compete internationally, at the Copa Independencia Do Brazil. Roger Milla and Thomas N'kono were the other key figures in the team. The first had joined a French professional club at the age of twenty-five and was enjoying considerable popularity; the latter challenged the prejudice against African goalkeepers by signing his first professional contract with Español at the end of the competition.

The inclusion of European-based professionals in African national sides was made possible by the FIFA ruling of 1981 which obliged clubs to release players for all World Cup qualifying and finals matches. As a consequence, fifteen players in the French professional league and one from the Belgian league were included in the Algerian and Cameroonese squads. Four years on, the Algerian and Moroccan World Cup squads had a total of fifteen players based in France, along with one each in Spain, Portugal, Switzerland, Belgium and England. The Cameroon squad which reached the quarter-finals of the 1990 competition had eleven professionals employed in Europe. This trend towards squads based around European exiles reached its high point at the African Nations Cup of 2000, when the entire squad of finalists Nigeria worked in Europe.

Despite this trend, there was a continued resistance to Africans in a number of European countries. The old colonial ties were still very much in place in 1982. Only one African footballer had ever played in Germany and one in Italy, both countries with marginal ties to Africa for most of the twentieth century. Moreover, the Africans playing in France came exclusively from former colonies, as did those in Portugal. Belgium aside, the migratory routes established prior to independence continued to operate. What is more, many football migrants continued to be drawn to Europe for more than money. A full international in Cameroon, Eugène Ekéké left in 1976 to seek fortune in France. Like N'jo Lea two decades earlier, he admitted that he 'played two cards simultaneously' by continuing his football at non-league level and studying economics at university.[49] Progressing to the top divisions in France and Belgium, Ekéké was selected for the 1990 World Cup squad and scored in his only appearance in the quarter-final defeat by England. Milla saw the beginning of his professional career interrupted by a one-year ban resulting from his club in Cameroon refusing to give him clearance to play with Valenciennes. In his first full season of 1978/79, he was instrumental in helping the club to avoid relegation and was rewarded with a transfer to Monaco. He went on to win two successive French cups with Monaco and Bastia before helping Saint-Etienne and Montpellier regain their top division status. Contrary to certain accounts, Milla was unquestionably a star at each of his French clubs.[50] He arrived in Europe relatively late in his career and although he finished at the age of thirty-eight, he did not make the fortune he might have expected.

By the 1980s the concept of 'African' players had become particularly complicated. The generic term 'African' could conceal various categories of players. In France especially, the distinction between the 'nationals' and 'foreigners' was far from straightforward. If we look closely at the French league in the 1986/87 season (Table 6.2), we can get some idea of this complexity. In column one (French citizens born in Africa) are players such as Jean Tigana who was born in Bamako (Mali) but had arrived as a child to Marseilles, received French citizenship and played for France. The first time the young professional Marcel Desailly, born in Ghana, migrated was when he joined Milan in 1994. Basile Boli, born in the Ivory Coast, followed his elder brothers and sisters to France. His father sent him to Paris at the age of thirteen to qualify in general mechanics 'to get a job . . . and to stop concentrating on football'.[51] Although each of these players maintained links with Africa, they were French citizens and *not* football migrants.

The 1982 World Cup placed a spotlight on a second group of Africans playing in France – the dual citizens whose football careers in France began at amateur or

49. *L'Equipe*, 22 November 1983.

50. Simon Kuper, *Football Against the Enemy*, London: Phoenix, 1985, pp. 112–33 gives an unflattering account of Milla and his status in France. An indication of his popularity is provided by his appearance on the cover of the official history of Montpellier. Dominique Grimault and Eric Champel, *Montpellier La Paillade SC: Histoire d'une passion*, Montpellier: Montpellier PSC, 1988.

51. Basile Boli, *Black Boli*, Paris: Grasset, 1994, p. 69.

Table 6.2 African Players in French Divisions 1 and 2, 1986/87

Country	French citizens born in Africa	African or dual citizens recruited in France	African or dual citizens recruited abroad	Dual citizens born in France
Algeria	–	8	2	16
Benin	–	1	2	–
Burkina Faso	–	–	1	–
Cameroon	–	3	6	3
Congo	–	5	6	2
Gabon	–	1	1	1
Ghana	1	–	1	–
Guinea	1	–	–	1
Ivory Coast	2	–	8	–
Madagascar	2	–	–	–
Mali	1	–	1	–
Morocco	–	4	4	–
Senegal	1	4	8	–
Zaire	–	1	4	–
TOTAL	8	27	43	23

junior level (column two). Almost every case was different but in general they too were not strictly football migrants. Abdallah Liegeon was born in Algeria as the son of a French father and Algerian mother. His family migrated to France when he was a child. A holder of two passports, Liegeon's performances at Monaco attracted the Algerian selection committee. His dual identity was outlined by the fact that he played internationally as Medjadi (his mother's maiden name) but was Liegeon in France. Karim Maroc, the son of Algerian parents, was born in Tunisia during the Algerian War. He grew up in the Bordeaux area and signed his first professional contract with Lyons at the age of eighteen. The possibility to play at a World Cup for Algeria was a reward of being a second-generation immigrant but his life and career were located in France.

The genuine football migrants are those in column three. These players moved to France as professional footballers. Joseph Antoine Bell, for example, the Cameroonese goalkeeper of Marseilles, had previously experienced professional football in Egypt in the early 1980s while Abedi Pele, a star in Ghana, was recruited from Qatar by the anonymous second division club Niort in 1986. The first English-speaking African in French football, Pele's situation was precarious as he was considered a foreigner in a way that the French-speakers were not. At a time when clubs could only employ two foreign players, few were prepared to consider African professionals who could not easily receive a French passport. There were still remnants of a colonial perspective but from the arrival of Pele, and George Weah two years later, French recruiters began to regard Africa as a foreign market comparable to Argentina or Yugoslavia. Not all African migrants were employed at the highest level in France. Isiaka Ouattara had already played for the national team of Burkina Faso when a club chairman recruited him for his club in division one in France. Unfortunately, Loudun competed in the top division of the regional rather than the national league. Yet after a year Ouattara was promoted to the real division one and following three years as a foreign amateur when he rarely played, the acquisition of a French passport transformed his career.

The final column features French-born citizens who were entitled to receive another passport by virtue of the country of origin of their parents. Cherif Oudjani was born in Lens, the son of a professional Algerian footballer who had migrated to France in the 1950s and was part of the FLN rebel team. His country of birth, education and employment was France but he played for Algeria. Indeed like the Jamaican internationals in the English Premiership, these footballers could be considered migrants only in terms of their international careers. Algerians represent the majority of this last group, due to the freedom of movement agreed between the two countries following independence in 1962, which allowed children of Algerians born in France to receive both passports.[52] Such intricate distinctions reveal the complexities of the terms 'African' and 'immigrant' in the context of post-colonial European society and the rigidity of sporting conceptions of citizenship which permit a player to compete for a *single* national team.

The importance of Africans in the European football market is increasingly difficult to ignore. In 1994, *France Football* published a photograph of the Lens side of the 1950s alongside the current team underneath a caption announcing 'The Return of the Black Faces'. Lens, situated at the centre of the mining district of northern France, had for decades based its team around miners from the Polish immigrant community, nicknamed 'The Black Faces'. By the end of the 1970s, the pits had closed and the football club's recruitment policy had to change. While the miners and Polish surnames had gone, there were now seven players born in Africa: two each from the Ivory Coast and Cameroon, one from Benin, one Nigerian and one from Madagascar.[53] Moreover, Lens was hardly exceptional. A survey by *L'Equipe* in 1991 on all professionals in France revealed that every tenth player had been born in Africa, a higher proportion than in any single French region.[54] Since 1988, a monthly magazine called *Afrique Football* has been published in Paris, which looks exclusively at African football but significantly focuses more on the African migrant in Europe than on the domestic game. By 1998, African

52. Collinson, *Europe and International Migration*, p. 53.
53. *France Football*, 1 August 1994.
54. *L'Equipe*, January 1991, *passim*.

footballers played professionally in twenty-nine European countries, including those of Scandinavia and Eastern Europe. Quantatively, Belgium, France and Portugal remain, together with Germany, Holland, Switzerland and Turkey, the main importers.[55] Some characteristics of the African market make it particularly attractive for the poorer European leagues who are prominent exporters of talent within Europe. Africans are generally cheap, often successful and are used to replace emigrants. As with the South Americans, there has been a shift in the career patterns of African imports, with the young spending their entire career in Europe but continuing to play for their national side in Africa. It is no longer absurd to regard African footballers as 'normal' professionals, given that many follow the same occupational routes as their European counterparts.

The African market has not, however, remained unchanged. Success at World Youth and Olympic competitions has led West African nations – especially Nigeria and Ghana – to supplant the North Africans as the dominant exporters. There has been a diversification of African migrant talent: almost every nation in the continent now supplies one or two players to Europe. Moreover, the European market for Africans now works in two distinct phases. The best players do not move to the premier leagues immediately, only progressing to England, Italy and Spain once they have settled on the continent. The career of George Weah, one of the biggest African stars of all – who moved from Liberia to Cameroon, from Cameroon to Monaco and then on to leading clubs in the continent's major cities, Paris St Germain, Milan and Chelsea – has provided a model of progress. Weah's career has been similar to that of the best European stars except that he continues to turn out in international competition for Liberia.

Yet if Africans increasingly resemble 'normal' European professionals, we should not ignore the peculiarities of the African experience. Racism, 'exploitation' of young players, the mishandling of transfer monies and poor labour rights continue to afflict these imports. 'For the four years I have played in the *Bundesliga*, I often heard "Blacks, go home!" and I never managed to get used to it', commented the Senegalese international Souleyman Sané in 1993.[56] Born in Dakar, Sané spent his youth in France. He was a dual citizen who came to Germany during his military service for the French army and found a contract with the division-two club SC Freiburg. During a match against FC Cologne, his marker, the German international Paul Steiner, was accused in the popular press of having said to him: 'Hey, you! Black sheet! what are you doing in Germany? Go home!'[57] Recent cases in Italy

55. For meticulous quantative data on Africans in Europe in recent years, see Filippo Maria Ricci, *African Football Yearbook 1999*, Fornacette: Mariposa, 1999.

56. Souleyman Sané interviewed in *Fußball und Rassismus*, Göttingen: Werkstatt, 1993, p. 23.

57. Kathrin Weber-Klüwer, 'Fußball und Rassismus in Deutschland', in *Fußball und Rassismus*, p. 54.

and Germany have indicated the continued prevalence of racism. During the 1999/ 2000 season, alleged racist comments by players and supporters provoked these leagues to establish the type of anti-racism campaigns that have been long established in Britain. The opportunities provided by European football have to be balanced against the continued tendency to stereotype, exploit and marginalize the African player.

Post-colonial Africa has remained economically dependent upon Europe. Success and achievement for African footballers can only be attained abroad. The African example shows how established links and colonial routes remain essential in contemporary migration patterns. Despite the evident improvement in perform- ances in international competition – including victories for Nigeria and Cameroon in the last two Olympic Games – Africa in general is still considered a source of cheap labour. There is no doubt that the colonial economy continues to apply to the European football industry: French clubs still consider themselves to have a monopoly over the best Cameroonese players as do the Portuguese over their former colonies of Angola, Mozambique and Cape Verde. The migration of African footballers is certainly not a post-colonial phenomenon. The experiences of Weah and Yeboah are therefore probably not so dissimilar from those of N'jo Lea and Eusebio. Heroes in their country of birth, they could only win on European terms and so became displaced heroes.

—7—

National Styles, International Stars

This chapter looks at the links between national teams, national styles and the use of, and restrictions placed upon, 'foreign' players. Debates concerning the role of non-nationals have often been connected with the results of national teams during major competitions, while the prohibition of foreign players is frequently justified as a safeguard measure to protect the quality and development of young 'local' talent. Thus it took a goal scored by a Korean dentist, Park Dok Hoo, against Italy in the 1966 World Cup to convince the Italian federation to close its borders for some fifteen years. Since the 1930s the football industry has been organized in a way that has complicated the international migration of personnel and generated problems which have not been experienced by competitors in other migratory sports such as golf and tennis. Players have been employed and paid by club sides but their fame was dependent on performance and achievement with their national team, a selection based, in theory at least, on citizenship irrespective of the location of the player's club. This has created considerable tension, especially when club and nation are seen to have divergent interests.

The way in which a football team plays is rarely determined only by the qualities of its players or the application of scientific tactics. At clubs and national teams, a new coach invariably has to work in the shadow of 'history' and 'tradition', whether characterized by success or by failure. This often involves an engagement with a particular way or 'style' of playing. It need not bear much relation to reality. In practice, playing styles change regularly as players and coaches come and go or modify their tactics. But the perception of a constant style is nonetheless powerful, corresponding to 'a stereotyped image, vested in tradition, that the community gives itself and wishes to show to others'.[1] At the national level, the idea of distinct playing styles is particularly potent. National teams in an international sport such as football are much more than just a selection of eleven of the best players in a given territory. They are symbolic representatives of the nation, a focus for national identification. According to Eric Hobsbawm's well-known interpretation of Benedict Anderson: 'The imagined community of millions seems more real as a

---

1. Christian Bromberger, 'Foreign Footballers, Cultural Dreams and Community Identity in some North-Western Mediterranean Cities', in J. Bale and J. Maguire (eds), *Global Sports Arena: Athletic Talent Migration in an Interdependent World*, London: Frank Cass, 1994, p. 181.

team of eleven named people.'[2] As such, a national style of play must also say something about the nature of a people, what they are like and how they want to be seen.

Discussions of playing style can, of course, degenerate into crude national stereotypes based on assumed, and often implicitly racial, characteristics. The Brazilians, we are often told, are flamboyant and inventive, the Italians and Spaniards skilful but temperamental, while the Africans display raw talent but are naive and unrefined. The Germans, meanwhile, are ruthlessly efficient and the English stoical, phlegmatic and predictable. The British tabloid press is not the only party guilty of this. Recent studies have noted the similarity of the images, metaphors and vocabulary associated with specific nations throughout the European media, alongside the prevalence of particular 'national obsessions'.[3] As Matti Goksøyr and Hans Hognestad have pointed out, there is a danger here of conceiving playing styles 'as nothing less than a transfer of alleged national virtues and vices'.[4] Yet for all this, the idea that nations, regions or even specific teams have, or can have, distinct footballing styles raises a number of questions concerning the migration of footballers. Are foreign players necessary? Are they able to play football in the same way as it is played in the host country? Do they strengthen or damage the game? Does their presence modify the very essence of the game?

The Emergence of National Styles

National styles developed in tandem with international competition. The Olympics of 1908 and 1912 were the first opportunities for nations to compete against one another in an international tournament and to express their own particular conceptions of the game. But national styles were consolidated during the inter-war years, a period which witnessed the construction of a European football network. Throughout the continent, international football matches were used as symbolic commemorations of international friendships and diplomatic alliances.

2. Eric Hobsbawm, *Nations and Nationalism Since 1870: Programme, Myth, Reality*, Cambridge: Cambridge University Press, 1990, p. 143; Benedict Anderson, *Imagined Communities: Reflections on the Origin and Spread of Nationalis*m, London: Verso, 1983. For a similar application of Anderson's maxim to football see Vic Duke and Liz Crolley, *Football, Nationality and the State*, London: Longman, 1996, pp. 4–5.

3. Neil Blain, Raymond Boyle and Hugh O'Donnell, *Sport and National Identity and the European Media*, London: Leicester University Press, 1993; Liz Crolley, David Hand and Ralf Jeutter, 'National Obsessions and Identities in Football Match Reports', in A. Brown (ed.), *Fanatics!: Power, Identity and Fandom in Football*, London: Routledge, 1998, pp. 173–85.

4. Matti Goksøyr and Hans Hognestad, 'No Longer Worlds Apart?: British Influences in Norwegian Football', in G. Armstrong and R. Giulianotti (eds) *Football Cultures and Identities*, London: Macmillan, 1999, pp. 201–10.

Fixtures were often arranged to coincide with national days (such as Armistice Day), were accompanied by festivities, and became a focus for the celebration of national unity. They were regularly attended by presidents, royalty and other state dignitaries. The construction of national stadia in the 1920s and 1930s – Prater in Vienna, Centenario in Montevideo, Wembley in London – can be seen as a physical expression of the emerging role of the national football team as an ambassador of the nation.

Football's inter-war renewal was to be initiated in Central Europe. Until the mid-1920s, teams from Austria, Hungary and Czechoslovakia (particularly from the capital cities), precluded as they were from competing with Western European selections, played against each other on a regular basis, establishing a strong network of football relations and rivalries. Unlike the British, who were miserly in their continental appearances, these teams showed themselves ready to confront each other and demonstrate their talents. This was made possible by the creation in 1927 of the Mitropa Cup, an annual competition involving the top two Austrian, Czechoslovakian, Hungarian and Yugoslavian club sides. The changing balance of European diplomacy was closely traced in the pattern of international football competition. The bilateral agreements with Austria and Hungary, arranged by Mussolini and his Foreign Minister Grandi, which signalled Italy's diplomatic *rapprochement* with Central Europe coincided with the introduction of the Mitropa Cup and undoubtedly prefaced Italy's inclusion in the competition when Yugoslavia withdrew in 1929.[5]

Roman Horak and Wolfgang Maderthaner have suggested that 'the true contribution of the Mitropa Cup lay in the final crystallisation of a specifically Central European playing style'.[6] Alternately referred to as the 'Vienna' or 'Danubian School', or the Austrian 'system', this style owed much to the cosmopolitan mixture of footballers who played in the major cities of Central Europe at the time. Frequent competition allowed the major city clubs to establish 'a sort of Central European internationalism' which encouraged a vibrant interchange of ideas and personnel between Vienna, Budapest, Prague, and other cities such as Berlin and Bologna. The game which emerged was considered both to be more technical, with the emphasis on control and ball skills, and to embody a more tactical and systematic approach, in contrast to the rather haphazard English

---

5. On the diplomacy of the period see, J. Rotschildt, *East Central Europe between the Wars*, Seattle: University of Washington Press, 1977, pp. 163–77. Particularly on football, see Diego Cante, 'Propaganda e sport negli anni trenta. Gli incontri di calcio tra Italia e Austria', *Italia contemporanea*, 204, 1996, pp. 521–44.

6. Roman Horak and Wolfgang Maderthaner, 'A Culture of Urban Cosmopolitanism: Urdil and Sindelar as Viennese Coffee-House Heroes', in R. Holt, J.A. Mangan and P. Lanfranchi (eds), *European Heroes*, London: Frank Cass, 1996, p. 150.

'kick and rush' game which eschewed preparation and coaching. It reached its apogee in the success of the Austrian *Wunderteam* of the early 1930s. During a short period in 1931 and 1932, the Austrians beat Germany and Switzerland twice and Hungary once, and drew against the Czechs. Scotland were defeated 5–0 in Vienna, a victory which was proclaimed as 'a tribute to Viennese aesthetic sense, imagination and passion'[7] but it was the narrow 4–3 defeat by England at Stamford Bridge in December 1932 which was arguably the team's greatest triumph. Despite a poor start, the Austrian team came back to dominate the match with a type of 'intellectual football' which received plaudits in the British as well as the domestic press.[8] More than anybody else, the centre-forward Matthias Sindelar personified this new style of play. Known as *der Papierene* or 'the Wafer' because of his slight build, Sindelar avoided physical contact, relying on intelligent movement, accurate distribution and technique. Reflecting the artistic and creative culture of the Viennese coffee-house, his spontaneous use of feints and tricks baffled less inventive opponents and he apparently preferred 'to walk, or rather to dance the ball not only towards the goal, but literally into the net'.[9]

In Vienna, Budapest and Prague, capital cities without hinterlands, football was transformed into an export product. The endemic economic crises which characterized the nations of Central Europe in the 1920s, the weakness of domestic markets, and the difficulties which these 'new little nations' encountered on the international scene further accentuated the importance to them of football. Since they were becoming masters of their craft at a continental level, these teams sought to make real gains from the hitherto symbolic gains achieved on the field of play. The introduction of professionalism in all three countries at the end of the 1920s made it possible to create a market linked to football. Professionalism not only meant that players were paid but also that they represented assets and thus a potential source of profit. By transferring them to foreign teams, their clubs could secure substantial revenues which were otherwise limited.

Although conceived in isolation, then, this Central European style was not nurtured independently; it was rapidly diffused through the constant movement of players, coaches and teams across Europe. Even in the early 1920s Hungarian footballers, in particular, had become models of a new and distinct style of play. Alfred Schäffer, a 'shamateur' who made his name with MTK Budapest, played in Munich, Basle, Prague and Vienna, becoming widely known throughout the region as 'the Football King'. One of Schäffer's MTK team-mates, Kalman Konrad, lived and played for a time in Vienna, where he was said to have influenced the

---

7. Horak and Maderthaner, 'Culture of Urban Cosmopolitanism', p. 151.

8. Willy Meisl, *Soccer Revolution*, London: Panther, 1957, p. 60.

9. Meisl, *Soccer Revolution*, pp. 56–7. Further on Sindelar see R. Horak and W. Maderthaner, *Mehr als ein Spiel: Fussball und populare Kulturen in Wien der Moderne*, Vienna: Locker, 1997.

play of the young Sindelar.[10] The 1930s witnessed a diaspora of Austrian and Hungarian players throughout the continent. The French league certainly received the most. Some sixty-one Austrians, fifty-nine Hungarians and forty-three Czechoslovakians were registered with French clubs between 1932 and 1939, figures matched only by the large British contingent (see Chapter 2). Coaches or trainers were, if anything, even more widespread. In Italy, Central Europeans dominated coaching positions at the top clubs, effectively rationalizing and professionalizing the game. All six of Bologna's coaches between 1921 and 1942 were from *Mitteleuropa* and even at a minor club like Udinese, each of the twelve coaches employed between 1920 and 1940 was Hungarian.[11] By the Second World War, the Central Europeans had certainly eclipsed the British coaches, whose influence was on the decline. Most important of all, perhaps, Central European teams were eager to demonstrate their footballing prowess through constant tours and performances abroad. The circle in which the best Austrian, Hungarian and Czech clubs competed was constantly expanding. The connection with Bologna, for example, was established as early as 1921 when Rapid Vienna visited Italy and beat the local side 4–1. Two years later, Rapid returned along with Ujpest of Budapest and in 1924 Nemzeti of Budapest and WAC of Vienna played in Bologna.[12] Foreign tours and international tournaments had always been essential in securing the financial well-being of these clubs but by the early 1930s the trend had reached dramatic proportions. The leading Austrian clubs, such as Austria and Rapid Vienna, spent much of their time playing abroad.[13] Between January 1931 and March 1932, for instance, Austria Vienna played sixty-nine matches abroad, winning fifty-six and losing only six.[14] The list of the visiting clubs to Barcelona between 1921 and 1925 is a good indicator of the centrality of the emerging *Mitteleuropa* teams in the rest of the continent:

1921–22   Sparta Prague (Cze), Viktoria Zizkov (Cze), Rapid Vienna (Aut), Gradjanski Zagreb (Yug), Servette Geneva (Swi), Crook Town (Ire), St. Mirren (Sco),

10. Meisl, *Soccer Revolution*, pp. 56, 72.

11. Raffaele Meroi, *Storia dell'Udinese calcio*, Udine: Campanetti, 1989, p. 323.

12. See Roberto Lemmi Gigli and Giancarlo Turrini, 'La lunga linea Rossoblu', in *Il Mezzosecolo del Bologna*, Bologna: Poligrafia del Resto del Carlino, 1959, pp. 79ff.

13. For Rapid, see Fonje Lang, *Das ist Rapid. Der Weg der Grünweissen Meistermann-schaft*, Vienna: Josef Faber, 1952, p. 10.

14. J. Wendt, 'Grundzüge der Geschichte der Deutschen Fußball-Bundes und des bürgerlichen deutschen Fußballsports in Zeitraum von 1918 bis 1933', Unpublished PhD Thesis, University Halle/Witteberg, 1975, pp. 125–32.

1922–23   Pro Vercelli (It), SpVgg Fürth (Ger), Notts County (Eng), Ilford (Eng), Vienna FC (Aut), MTK Budapest (Hun), Ferencvaros (Hun), Servette (Swi), Gradjanski (Yug), Maccabi Brno (Cze)
1923–24   Cracovia (Pol), Fürth (Ger), Vasas Budapest (Hun), Sparta Prague (Cze), Slavia Prague (Cze), MTK Budapest (Hun), Newcastle Utd (Eng).
1924–25   Austria Vienna (Aut), Hungaria Budapest (Hun), Viktoria Zizkov (Cze), CS Prague (Cze).[15]

Italy was particularly important in the creation of this football network in continental Europe. As we have noted, the influence of the British in Italy declined as a consequence of the First World War and a new flow of sporting immigrants came from Central Europe. From 1922, almost every Italian club recruited Hungarian and Austrian players. These Danubian footballers had profited from the policy of reconciliation in Central Europe initiated by Mussolini.[16] The Italians, too, capitalized on the economic crises which contributed to the emigration of skilled middle-class footballers and managers from Central Europe. The number of Danubian football migrants in Italy doubled annually: there were twenty in 1923, forty in 1924 and eighty by 1925.[17] The importance of these migrants became such that the Italian federation, now run by the fascist leader Arpinati[18], decided in the renewed football charter signed in the seaside resort of Viareggio in August 1926, to ban foreign players in order to adapt football to the new autarkic policy of the regime.[19] Symbols of this kind were important for the fascist government.

Although it could not have emerged *without* a mixture of *Mitteleuropean* and South American input, the development of an Italian style of play was the outcome of a distinctly national conception of football. The role of the fascist regime in the promotion of Italian football is a vast and complex subject. At first glance, the fact that the two fascist decades coincided with the major successes of Italian football suggests a clear state involvement in the development of the game. On

15. Pierre Lanfranchi, 'Die Entwicklung eines europäischen Netzwerks, 1920–38', in R. Horak and W. Reiter (eds), *Die Kanten des runden Leders*, Vienna: Promedia, 1990.

16. Pierre Lanfranchi, 'Bologna: The team that shook the World!', *International Journal of the History of Sport*, 8, 3, 1991, pp. 336–47.

17. Vincenzo Baggioli, *Storia del calcio italiano*, Rome: De Carlo, 1943, p. 150; A. Papa and G. Panico, *Storia sociale del calcio in Italia*, Bologna: il mulino, 1993, suggested a maximum total of forty Danubian players, underestimating a phenomenon which extended far beyond the first division. In the regional division two Tuscany-Emilia group, there were seventeen in 1926 and a match 'Hungarians of Italy' vs Tuscany was organized in Florence, *La nazione*, 26 June 1926.

18. On Arpinati see Stephen B. Whitacker, 'Leandro Arpinati, anarcoindividualista, fascista, fascista-pentito', *Italia contemporanea*, 196, 1994, pp. 471–89. On his links with Bologna FC, Lanfranchi, 'Bologna', pp. 336–47.

19. For the complete text of the Viareggio Charter see *Il mezzogiorno*, 4–5 August 1926.

closer inspection, however, the situation does not appear so simple. Mussolini himself had no particular affection for the game. He was indeed portrayed as the first sportsman of the nation, and was photographed on motorbikes, horses, swimming and shooting, even once on a bicycle; but he was never pictured kicking a football. In fact, some party dignitaries were strongly opposed to football as an alien game, preferring *tamburello*, an indigenous racket sport reminiscent of real tennis, or even the British game of rugby, which though foreign at least encouraged participants to show strength, determination and physical vigour. Within the party, however, others understood the importance of football as a means of creating consent. The construction of large stadiums and the visibility of international competition was actively promoted by the regime. Stadiums, more than any other place, became key arenas of consent and the choice of names and symbols exemplified the links between sport and fascism. In Florence, the stadium built for the World Cup in 1934 was named after Berta, a fascist activist murdered by socialist militants. The Littoriale stadium opened in Bologna in 1927 was a vast multi-sport construction, with a swimming pool and several tennis courts, topped by a statue of the Duce on horseback.[20] The work of Francesco Varrasi has shown the impact of the futurist architecture in the construction of new stadia: their style embodied modernity and solidity but there was also an unequivocal link with the Roman Empire.[21]

Similar sentiments were used to describe the style of the 'fascist' athletes in the press. Although the two main daily sporting papers survived the fascist period, the tone of writing changed fundamentally. Their main aim was to assert the differences with other 'national' interpretations of football and express the superiority of the Italian game, the Italian people, and ultimately the fascist regime. The physical image of Italian athletes became essential. They had to be strong, quick and clever. While the king, Victor Emmanuel III, was slight and barely over five feet tall, and Italians had the reputation of being in poor health and underweight, the footballers were lauded as 'new' Italians. Newspaper advertisements were important in the creation of this national style. Meazza, the national team captain, promoted the Argentinian gel 'that leaves the hair as tidy after the game as before'. Others advertised toothpaste, razor blades and aftershave.[22] They were portrayed as examples of the modern, clean, successful Italian fascist. Photographs showing them doing the fascist salute, or being received by the Duce after matches, reinforced this image. The significance of this modern Italian style was reflected

20. See Sauro Onofri and Vera Ottani, *Dal Littoriale allo Stadio: Storia per immagini dell'impianto sportivo bolognese*, Bologna: CCC, 1990.

21. Francesco Varrasi, *Economia, Politica e Sport in Italia, 1925–35*, Florence: Fondazione Franchi, 1999.

22. See Paolo Fachinetti, 'Sport e pubblicità', *I Problemi di Ulisse*, special issue, 'Lo Sport', May 1982, p. 47.

in the reaction to the success of Bologna, winners of the Mitropa Cup in 1932 and 1934 and of the international Paris Exhibition Tournament in 1937. Nicknamed 'The Team that Shook the World', Bologna's defeat of Chelsea in the final of the Paris tournament was interpreted as a vindication of fascist ideology and style. The local paper, *Resto del Carlino*, celebrated the victory in the following terms:

> Bologna won a hard battle, using the virile style and irresistible attacks that characterise Fascist athletes. These are athletes who put all their efforts to a single end and a single goal: to offer sporting Italy the most glorious trophies. They present themselves before the crowds of the whole world in the image of their nation: young, valiant, and combative everywhere, at every moment in every action.[23]

Interestingly it was a *rimpatriato*, Miguel Andreolo, who embodied this style better than any other. Andreolo was a strong, virile hero, one of the new Italian athletes who was capable of beating the English at their own game. 'Powerful in his charges, a veteran kicker of free-kicks like cannon balls, unbeatable in the head game, he was above all a cunning tactician, full of guile.'[24] As the best *centro-mediano metodista* of his generation, he occupied a strategic position which displayed the progress of the regime and the physical vitality and strength of its representatives on the international stage. In addition to the Parisian triumph, Andreolo played in the Italian side which won the 1938 World Cup, the Central European selection which beat Western Europe in Amsterdam in June 1937 and a year later led Europe against England in London.

In the rhetoric of commentators and the press, tactics were essential. The style of play expressed Italian identity as much as the physique. Journalists emphasized the intrinsic differences between the English 'kick and rush', the Central European 'system' and the Italian model, *Il metodo*. In continental Europe, comparisons between national styles became unavoidable. René Dedieu, one of France's most successful coaches, observed after Bologna's 1937 triumph that 'The English applied the WM [formation]; it proved effective against the Austrian System, but useless against the Italian *metodo*'.[25] It may have thus reached the top of football's hierarchy by the late 1930s, but the Italian model easily outlasted the fascist period and the tactical discourse surrounding it continues to this day. While it originated for political reasons, the vital significance of a distinctly Italian way of playing continued (and continues) to be articulated and defended. *Il metodo* involved a

23. *Il Resto del Carlino*, 8 June 1937.

24. Alfio Biagi, 'L'Arte di Michelone', *Il Guerin Sportivo*, 46, 1981, p. 75.

25. *Les sports du Sud-Est*, 10 June 1937. More generally on the distinction between national styles from a linguistic point of view, see F. Marri, 'Metodo, sistema e derivati nel linguaggio calcistico', *Lingua Nostra*, 44, 2–3, pp. 70–83.

specialization of the playing roles far beyond the simple defence, midfield and attack. There has been a continuity, for example, in the definition of the two distinct types of full-back, with specifically prescribed duties: the *terzino marcatore*, a marking full-back such as Gentile in the 1982 World Cup winning side, and the *terzino fluidificante*, a fluid full-back such as Facchetti in the 1960s or Cabrini (also in 1982) and Maldini in the late 1980s and 1990s. Terms describing the playing roles could be extremely precise, indicating the expected duties as well as the position on the field. In the 1960s Inter team Domenghini was *mezz'ala di sostegno*, a holding half-wing back, a description which would be immediately understood by the majority of the Italian sporting public.

Notwithstanding the specific 'national' elements ascribed to the Italian system from the fascist period, its development in the course of the twentieth century was also bound up with the evolution of a cross-national 'Latin' playing style and with the import of foreign players and coaches. The Central European game brought to Italy by Austrian and Hungarian coaches was adjusted to suit the dry pitches of the Mediterranean area, with a style based on short passing and intensive technical training. As a tactical approach, it relied on a strong defensive trio, with the centre-half taking a less creative role than in the existing 2–3–5 formation. Significantly, this approach had been pioneered by the South Americans Monti, who played for Argentina in the World Cup Final of 1930, and Andreolo when he played for Uruguay. Monti went on to play the new 'destructive' centre-half role for the Italian side which won the 1934 World Cup. At club level, it was a particular feature of Monti's team Juventus, and other Italian clubs brought it to the attention of northern Europeans through participation in the Mitropa Cup. The style was successfully deployed all over Europe by Italian and Spanish teams, at both club and national level. The 1934 World Cup semi-final pitted Italy and Spain, the main exponents of the Latin style, in one of the tensest matches of the inter-war period. Played in Florence, it went to a replay, which Italy won 1–0 after a 1–1 draw in the first match.

After the Second World War, the development of a more technical, tactical and defensive style continued and was personified by one man: Helenio Herrera. An Argentine by birth, Herrera had been a professional footballer, and subsequently a team manager in France during the 1930s. In 1949, he moved to Spain and coached various clubs before joining Atlético Madrid and then Barcelona. Herrera's approach was the antithesis of the Hungarian 'Golden Team' of the 1950s, for whom the objective was to score one more goal than the opposition. He chose instead to build his sides around a strong defence, reinforced by a fifth player – the *libero* or free defender – and to concede one goal less than the other side. Arriving at Inter in 1961, he created one of the most consistently successful teams of all time. Inter frequently won 1–0 and Herrera's tactical approach, now called *catenaccio* or 'the lock', was stoutly defended by the Italian press. Gianni Brera called it *Il gioco all'Italiania*, 'the Italian game'. This style, originating with Juventus and Inter, was often expressed as the Three S's: Simplicity, Seriousness and Sobriety. Italian clubs concerned themselves with the result rather than the show offered to the public; they were, after all, likely to prefer a winning team that played badly to a losing one that played well.[26] The terms themselves, like the style of play, were open to export. The *libero* and *catenaccio* are Italian terms now recognized internationally as descriptions of a particular defensive tactical approach. The 'Italian' style, then, was in reality permeable to foreign input: those who implemented it, such as Monti, Herrera and Suarez, had formed their football vision elsewhere.

The sporting press in Europe and South America played a key part in the recognition of national styles of play.[27] The discussion of tactical approaches to the game became a claim for national identity and superiority in the journalism of individuals such as Gabriel Hanot in France, Hugo Meisl in Austria, Herbert Chapman in England, Vittorio Pozzo in Italy and Borocoto in Argentina, all of whom were actively involved in international football as players, managers and administrators. Yet the articulation of specifically 'national' styles often cut across the strictly technical differences in the way in which players lined up on the pitch and the tactics they employed. France and Germany, who had little success in the inter-war period, never laid claim to an autonomous style. On the contrary, in France the 1930s was simply a long period of withdrawal from England, whose football had inspired the French game in the 1920s, and a period in which there was a rise in the number of players recruited from Central Europe. At the 1936 Berlin Olympics, the Swedish football writer Carl Linde observed a clear distinction between the nations of north-west Europe who used the English system and the remainder of the football-playing world who played a more flowing and improvised game.[28] This was underlined by the Amsterdam fixture in June 1937. The Western Europe team was made up of players from Belgium, France, Holland and Germany while the Central European side, which easily dominated the game, featured Italians, Hungarians, Austrians and Czechs: that is, players from countries which had developed their own style of a game originally brought in from elsewhere.

26. Christian Bromberger, with Alain Hayot and Jean-Marc Mariottini '"Allez l'OM, Forza Juve": The Passion for Football in Marseille and Turin', in S. Redhead, *The Passion and the Fashion: Football Fandom in the New Europe*, Aldershot: Avebury, 1993, pp. 103–51.

27. For a discussion of the growth of the European sporting media, see Bill Murray, *Football: A History of the World Game*, Aldershot: Scholar Press, 1994, pp. 87–90.

28. Bill Sund, 'The British and Continental Influence on Swedish Football', *International Journal of the History of Sport*, 14, 2, August 1997, p. 169.

The Anatomy of National Styles

In many, though not all, of the major European and South American territories, the notion of a national style was well developed by the 1940s. As we have noted, the Danubian school emerged in the 1920s, reaching its apex in the success of the Austrian *Wunderteam* of the early 1930s; the Italian model followed it in the 1930s. Across the Atlantic, the success of the Argentinian and Uruguayan teams in the 1928 Olympic Games and the first World Cup two years later contributed to the creation of the concept of a 'River Plate' football. In Brazil, references to a national way of playing became common after the 1938 World Cup.[29] Yet these national styles did not emerge organically: they developed in relation to one another, becoming influenced by, or defined against, an international 'other'. This tension between the emergence of national interpretations within the context of burgeoning international competition raises a fundamental question. To what extent has it been possible to talk about the import and export of styles of play alongside the import and export of players?

The English (sometimes erroneously referred to as a corporate British) style of play was for many nations the most significant 'other'. Often defined as a brand of football based on speed, courage, stamina and above all physical strength, the English game in the early decades of the twentieth century was copied, adapted and more often than not eventually rejected, by continental Europeans and South Americans who developed an alternative game based on individual skill, ball control and thoughtful passing. However, as Tony Mason has recently reminded us, English football was never purely a 'kick and rush' game.[30] Not only was it more varied than has often been portrayed, but it did alter significantly over time to fit changing circumstances. The first major development in the late 1860s and 1870s, from a dribbling to a passing game, was partially a result of the influence of Scottish teams and players. Whereas previously it had been based on the individualistic talent of forwards who dribbled until they lost the ball, association football was transformed into a game of teamwork in which forwards combined closely to outflank and outmanoeuvre opposing defenders. Although opinion differs on the exact origin of this change, it is clear that the short passing game favoured by

29. Sergio Leite Lopes, 'Les Origines du jeu à la brésilienne', in H. Hélal and P. Mignon (eds), *Football: jeu et société*, Paris: INSEP, 1999, pp. 65–84 and 'The Brazilian Style of Football and its Dilemmas', in Armstrong and Giulianotti (eds), *Football Cultures and Identities*, p. 87.

30. Tony Mason, 'Grandeur et déclin du "kick and rush" anglais ou la révolte d'un style', in Hélal and Mignon (eds), *Football: jeu et société*, pp. 47–64. The text has not yet been published in English but a version entitled 'Kick and Rush or Revolt into Style?: Football playing among English professionals from Great Power to image of decline' was delivered at the INSEP conference in April 1998.

Scottish clubs such as Queen's Park and Vale of Leven – who frequently met English sides in friendly fixtures and cup competitions – was to have a significant impact on the style of club sides south of the border.[31] As we saw in Chapter 2, during the final decades of the nineteenth and beginning of the twentieth centuries, some of the most successful English teams imported Scottish professionals along with the latters' short passing game. The Newcastle United team of the early 1900s, for one, was described as 'a side of strong physique . . . [which] began to dominate English football with skilful play, short passing, pattern weaving and an admixture of power'.[32] While still based on speed and bodily strength, this was hardly what most commentators mean when they refer to the 'traditional' English game. It was an amalgam of English and Scottish styles which were, however, perceived right from the outset of the English and Scottish game to be different. As Alan Bairner has noted, the 'idea that Scots have imparted to the game of football their own innate qualities' and that 'there exists a particular Scottish style of play . . . identified with aggression, passion and, in particular, skill' has been, and remains, widely accepted.[33]

The second major stylistic development in English football followed the alteration of the offside rule in 1925. Previously a player was offside if there were fewer than three defenders between him and the goal when the ball was released but, in an effort to increase goalscoring and prevent the systematic use of the offside trap, this was altered to two. The change in law had a dramatic impact on the number of goals scored and the way in which the game was played. Defensive play, it was thought, needed to change to combat the increased emphasis on attack. So a new approach was devised which involved the recasting of the centre-half, a pivot between defence and attack before 1925, as a third back whose role it was to mark the centre-forward and stop offensive advances. Whatever the precise origins of this tactical innovation, known as the 'third back game' or the WM system, it became associated with Herbert Chapman's Arsenal side of the late 1920s and

31. Dave Russell, *Football and the English*, Preston: Carnegie, 1997, pp. 20–21.

32. Arthur Appleton, *Hotbed of Soccer: The Story of Football in the North-East,* London: Rupert Hart-Davis, 1960, p. 133.

33. Alan Bairner, 'Football and the Idea of Scotland', in G. Jarvie and G. Walker (eds), *Scottish Sport in the Making of the Nation: Ninety-Minute Patriots?*, Leicester: Leicester University Press, 1994, p. 12. In the same collection, Richard Holt, 'The King over the Border: Denis Law and Scottish Football' notes the emphasis placed on 'the individualistic, impudent style' of Scottish players such as Jim Baxter and the domestic debate over a national style which oscillated between 'effort and inspiration', pp. 65–6. For Bob Crampsey, *The Scottish Footballer*, Edinburgh: William Blackwood, 1978, the Scottish style is more clear-cut and defined in reference to the 'auld enemy': 'The style of the two national sides [England and Scotland] has . . . reflected the supposed national characteristics of their peoples. English sides have tended to be phlegmatic, disciplined, instructed, while the Scots have relied heavily on mood and feats of brilliance', p. 55.

early 1930s and was often replicated by teams with less talented players, in Britain and abroad.[34] A style of play conceived during English football's period of 'splendid isolation', the WM system was by the 1950s widely recognized as an 'essentialist' English way of playing.[35] But it had long had its critics at home and abroad, and they got to have their say in the aftermath of English football's *annus horribilus* of 1953/54, especially the famous 6–3 Wembley defeat by Hungary and the even more shocking 7–1 reversal in Budapest.[36] In his book *Soccer Revolution*, Willy Meisl, younger brother of the better known Hugo, launched a blistering attack on what he termed the 'safety first' policy of English teams 'built mainly on destructive, defensive, spoiling tactics, in short, on negative football'.[37] Meisl argued that it was only in the previous quarter of a century that a 'traditional' English game based on guile, anticipation and the combination of teamwork and individual skill had been replaced by an approach which focused on speed, power and, above all, caution.

Meisl's polemic could be interpreted as a rather crude and stereotypical analysis of English playing styles. Whereas he bemoaned the inflexibility of the English playing 'system', the journalists Archie Ledbroke and Edgar Turner felt that 'in this country, we have too many styles'.[38] There was certainly evidence of a range of different methods and tactics emerging among English club sides from the early 1950s. Matt Busby's first Manchester United side with the 'man over' tactic, Tottenham's 'push and run' style under Arthur Rowe and Wolverhampton Wanderers' long passing game all indicated the variety of playing styles in English football and the capacity for innovation. Indeed, Manchester City developed a style of play directly based on that of the Hungarians, with Don Revie taking the role of Hidegkúti, as a deep-lying centre-forward. Looking further ahead, it could be argued that Liverpool's success in European competition in the 1970s and early 1980s, with a team which was genuinely British and not just English, was partly the result of an ability to marry the 'traditional' tackling and pressuring game

---

34. Mason, 'Kick and Rush'; Tony Say, 'Herbert Chapman: Football Revolutionary?', *The Sports Historian*, 16, May 1996, pp. 81–98.

35. Eduardo Archetti has proposed two approaches – an 'essentialist' and a 'relativist' – to national football styles. The 'essentialist' vision suggests that there is an 'ideal' national style, while the 'relativist' develops as a result of confrontation with 'others'. Eduardo Archetti, 'Argentina and the World Cup: In Search of National Identity', in J. Sugden and A. Tomlinson (eds), *Hosts and Champions*, Aldershot: Arena, 1994, pp. 37–63.

36. Mason, 'Kick and Rush', pp. 7–8; Jeff Hill, 'England v Hungary: November 1953', Paper presented at the 19th Annual Conference of the British Society of Sports History, University of Liverpool, 29–30 April 2000.

37. Meisl, *Soccer Revolution*, p. 31.

38. Archie Ledbroke and Edgar Turner, *Soccer from the Pressbox*, London: Sportman's Book Club, 1955, p. 82.

with the movement and accurate distribution of 'continental football'.[39] Crucially, however, these variations on the 'orthodox' English style were developed in a league with no foreign coaches and almost no foreign players. Although the English game was probably more hetergeneous than it was often portrayed, Tom Finney was still forced in his autobiography to wonder whether foreign stars such as Garrincha, Schiaffino, Puskas and Héctor Rial would, despite their incredible talent, have been tolerated in a league which placed so much emphasis on the 'English' qualities of incessant pace and workrate.[40]

In each national discourse there is a dialogue between proponents of individual virtuosity and skill on one hand, and advocates of a more collective style based on organization and bodily strength on the other. In Sweden, major debates over the most suitable approach to the game took place first between the wars and then again from the 1970s. As in England, the change in the offside law led to comprehensive debate over different playing systems, much of which took place in the sports paper *Idrottsbladet*. Under coach Bill Petterson, Helsingborgs IF pioneered a defensive system in opposition to the English third-back game whereby the wingers of the opposing team were closely marked by wing-halves with full-backs protecting the rear. Attacks were launched through rapid passes to quick forwards, an early version of counter-attacking football. If it showed tactical similarities to the emerging Italian game and the Swiss *verrou* system, it was nonetheless interpreted as a distinctly 'Swedish model' of football and was taken on by a number of Swedish club sides as well as by the national team for a decade from the mid-1920s. Yet it never achieved hegemony domestically and amid opposition from those who saw the imported English approach as more suited to the less technically gifted indigenous players, the Helsingborgs/Swedish model was jettisoned by club and country in the mid-1930s.[41]

From the mid-1970s, a tactical battle emerged in Sweden between a new 'systematic football' pioneered by the English coaches Bob Houghton and Roy Hodgson and an alternative form of 'joyful football' which allowed players greater scope to express themselves individually. It was the 'systematic' model which won through, partly because Houghton and Hodgson achieved success with their clubs Malmö FF and Halmstad BK, but also due to the apparent compatibility between the imported ideas of organization and planning and the traditional Swedish values

39. Geoffrey Green, *Soccer: The World Game*, London: Sportsman's Book Club, 1954, pp. 140–9; Eamon Dunphy, *A Strange Kind of Glory: Sir Matt Busby and Manchester United*, London: Heinemann, 1991, pp. 185–92; Rogan Taylor and Andrew Ward, *Kicking and Screaming: An Oral History of Football in England*, London: Robson Books, 1995, pp. 114–24; Chas Critcher, 'Putting on the Style: Aspects of Recent English Football', in J. Williams and S. Wagg (eds), *British Football and Social Change*, Leicester: Leicester University Press, p. 69.

40. Tom Finney, *Finney on Football*, London: Sportsman's Book Club, 1960, pp. 97–8.

41. Sund, 'British and Continental Influence on Swedish Football', pp. 163–73.

of teamwork, rationality and loyalty.[42] This approach was formally recognized as the national style through the publication in 1980 of a document entitled 'The Swedish Model' by the governing body. The philosophy of the two English coaches had in only five years become the 'only officially correct and approved way of playing the game in Sweden'.[43] Yet, the division between these two styles of football was probably more imagined than real. It is more accurate to talk about the creation of a hybrid style, for which Tomas Peterson coined the term 'Swinglish'. Similarly Norwegian football, in spite of its close geographical and historical links with the British game, has not simply copied British playing styles. While no doubt influenced by 'British' traditions and the importation of British coaches, Norwegian club and national sides have also been inspired by a more indigenous theoretical approach to the game, which has led to the evolution of a direct and pragmatic style of play, characterized in the late twentieth century by the success of the national side under Egil Olsen.[44] Norway has in fact had relatively few of its best players earning their living as professionals abroad. The most-capped player and one of the best-known international names of the 1950s, Thorbjørn Svenssen, spent his entire career in domestic football with Sandefjord BK.[45]. Yet in recent years, the geographical proximity and linguistic affinity, along with a similar approach to the game and the culture which surrounds it, has made the Norwegian league a kind of reserve territory for English recruiters. Between 1992 and 1999, more than eighty Norwegians signed for English clubs and came to represent, after the French, the second largest non-British group. More than this, the central role of English football within Norway – the broadcast of weekly Premiership matches and the proliferation of supporters clubs, even for the smaller English clubs – has led to the strengthening of formal links between the two countries. Wimbledon FC is now Norwegian-owned, have installed Olsen as manager and have intensified the recruitment of players from Norway. In media interviews, some Norwegians seem to speak as if they are less 'foreign' than other non-British recruits.[46]

Commentators have been doubtful that such a thing as a national style of football can exist in today's global culture in which, it seems, one can play anywhere in the world for teams who increasingly seem to play in the same way. As long ago as 1960 the British journalist Bob Ferrier had observed a gradual standardization

42. Torbjörn Andersson and Aage Radmann, 'Everything in Moderation: The Swedish Model', in Armstrong and Giulianotti (eds), *Football Cultures and Identities*, pp. 67–76; Alan Bairner, 'Sweden and the World Cup: Soccer and Swedishness', in Sugden and Tomlinson (eds), *Hosts and Champions*, pp. 195–217.

43. Andersson and Radmann, 'Everything in Moderation', p. 73.

44. Goksøyr and Hognestad, 'No Longer Worlds Apart?'.

45. Guy Oliver, *The Guinness History of World Soccer*, London: Guinness Publishing, 1992, p. 400.

46. See interview with Jan Age Fjortoft in *When Saturday Comes*, February 2000.

of footballing styles: 'All the nations are narrowing down their differences, levelling up their standards. No longer can we categorize. The international game nowadays is closely intermingled'.[47] Recent World Cups have led some to argue that we are witnessing an homogenization of playing styles in which the distinct qualities of national 'schools' or 'systems' have been subsumed within a universal quest for results. The 1990 World Cup in Italy convinced some critics that as far as styles of play were concerned 'We are all Europeans now'. Four years on, it seemed that even the simple dichotomy between the South American and the European way of playing was by then more imagined than real. A well-organized and cautious Brazilian side won the Final on penalty kicks against an unfortunate Italian team inspired by the individual talent of Roberto Baggio.

Amateurs at Home, Stars Abroad

The flip side of the treatment of football migrants in the receiving country is to consider the effect of migration on the country of origin. Looking at national teams allows us to consider the different attitudes towards foreign-based players, the kind of links they retained with their land of birth and how they were regarded by their national federations. In countries such as Holland, Sweden and Norway – rich societies with high standards of living but no professional football leagues – emigration until recently meant automatic exclusion from national duties. In the post-war decades, *professional* footballers were regarded as deserters in these Protestant-dominated countries, where openly making a living from kicking a ball was a source of humiliation. These professional exiles embodied the complex relationship between loyalty (to country of origin and employer) and achievement. In certain respects, their status at home is more revealing than their experience in the host society.

Dutch football at the end of the Second World War was not known particularly for its success or for a distinctive style of play. Nonetheless, after some good individual performances, the best players began to leave the country. The amateur rules at home had made it impossible for these players to earn their living playing football. Professionals employed abroad were considered in the Netherlands to be 'legionnaires' or 'mercenaries', unfit to defend the colours and the spirit of the nation. The majority of the exiles moved to France: in 1950/51, there were seventeen Dutchmen amongst a total of ninety-one foreigners in the French league.[48] The best-known Dutch player of this period was Faas Wilkes, who had moved to Inter in 1949 and later played for Valencia in Spain. The Dutch weekly *Sportief*, reporting in 1951 on his progress in Italy, emphasized Wilkes's conspicuous wealth but was particularly impressed by the fact that the player could

47. Bob Ferrier, *Soccer Partnership*, London: Sportsman's Book Club, 1960, pp. 178–9.

command a full-page feature in a daily newspaper and that, like other professional footballers, he was regarded as a wonderful artist. The paper saw his success abroad as a source of national pride but observed that this was not the case for the federation, which had failed to call him up to play for Holland since his exile. *Sportief* began a campaign for the rehabilitation of migrants such as Wilkes, arguing that

> When a young Dutch boy has such musical talent that the Paris Opera offers him a contract as a professional violinist, we consider it as an honour. It is very different for football players . . . Dutch professionals in France are considered here as inferior humans because they earn their bread playing football. We seem unable to recognise that they are showing real talent in the exercise of their profession.[49]

The Dutch national team, composed entirely of home-based amateurs, won only two out of twenty-seven matches (both friendlies against Belgium) played between June 1949 and April 1955. The superiority of the 'legionnaires' became evident during a charity match organized in 1953 between the French national side and a selection of Dutch professionals with foreign clubs. The Dutch team, drawn entirely from French clubs with the exception of the goalkeeper De Munck of FC Cologne, won 2–1. A two-year battle ensued between the conservative federation (KNVB) and an independent professional-league-in-waiting (NBVB), which eventually led to the acceptance of professionalism, with professionals thereafter permitted to wear the national shirt. By following the events in the press over the period, one can detect a distinction between the rigid application of an amateur agenda by the leaders of the KNVB, who considered professionals as unsuitable inferiors, and the press, which saw the success of the players abroad as an expression of the quality of domestic products. The serialized biography of Wilkes, and the weekly articles concerned with the professionals in France, focused on the experience these migrants gained in meeting the world's best players, in understanding new tactics and training methods and in learning how to conduct themselves as professionals.[50] *Sportief* highlighted the ineptitude of the KNVB in ignoring these benefits of living abroad. In an interview in 1954, Wilkes acknowledged his commitment to the national side which he had not played for in five years but recognized that his loyalties lay with his Spanish employers: 'I have missed playing for the Dutch team so much but, you know, I am paid in pesetas and I have to be

---

48. *Sportief*, 3 August 1951.

49. *Sportief*, 8 January 1953. Further to this, see Gabri de Wagt, *Eerst de Man, dan de Bal*, Amsterdam: Sijthoff, 1984, pp. 63–5.

50. Martin W. Duyzings, *Faas Wilkes: Een Voetbalcarrière*, Baarn: De Boekerij, 1951, was serialized in *Sportief* throughout 1951.

fair to my club'.[51] Within six months, however, Wilkes was back in the Dutch team, scoring twice in a 4–1 victory against Switzerland in Rotterdam.

Following the introduction of professionalism, almost every migrant returned to finish his career at home and by the 1960s the two major Dutch clubs, Ajax and Feyenoord, were beginning to make an impact on European club football. These clubs established a system which involved the training and formation of young local talent in preference to the bringing in of foreign labour. In particular, the Ajax model of moulding players from nursery to international football was a striking feature of the European Cup winning sides of the early 1970s. With professionalism, all Dutch clubs had engaged foreigners but did so in conjunction with their youth policies. Budgets were not expended on a few star imports; rather, foreigners were recruited for specific purposes. When the sweeper Velibor Vasovic was signed from Partizan Belgrade he was the first foreign international to have played for the Ajax side for some years and was instrumental in improving the defensive performance of the team. The German Horst Blankenburg, a modest buy from 1860 Munich, replaced Vasovic in a role which required a particular skill. They were bought not because they were foreigners but because they were sweepers with more experience and better prospects in that position than home-grown products.

The concept of 'Total Football' which developed in this period under coaches Rinus Michels and Stefan Kovacs at Ajax (and under Michels in the national side) had a significance beyond its tactical ramifications. 'Total Football' was definitively 'modern'. Not only were the players part of a new flexible approach, which allowed them a freer role to slot into any position on the field, but they also *looked* modern. With long hair and shirts worn outside the shorts, the Dutch players resembled student activists rather than professional footballers. Yet 'Total Football' was never considered a uniquely Dutch style. Because it became associated with the aesthetics of the play and the players themselves, it was not exclusive on the basis of nationality and so could easily be exported. Indeed the impact of Ajax and the Dutch side which reached the final of the 1974 World Cup led to the dispersal of players across Europe. Johan Cruyff had already left for Barcelona in 1973 and others soon followed to Spain, France, Germany, and later Britain. Cruyff's arrival in Barcelona signalled the liberation of the club from Spanish traditionalism and acknowledged its willingness to become recognized as a modern city. Cruyff and Johan Neeskens did not cut their hair or change their appearance – in some respects, the club adapted to its Ajax imports as much as they adapted to Catalonia. For this first generation, 'style' had various meanings: style of play, style of dress and style of life. And the impact of the Ajax model was manifest. It represented

---

51. *Sportief*, 16 December 1954.

something akin to a cultural revolution in football, which the protagonists were keen to disseminate and the rest of Europe was disposed to adopt.[52]

The Ajax style could be embodied by players of different nationalities. In the 1970s, the club recruited two Danish teenagers, Frank Arnesen and Søren Lerby.[53] These 'foreign' players were integrated into the Ajax system, graduated to the first team and were successful members of the squad for a number of years. Lerby married a Dutch television personality, and while both were transferred to major European clubs, they returned to Holland at the end of their careers. Jan Mølby was another Danish Ajax product, who continued a successful career in England, and more recently the Finn Jari Litmanen has followed a similar route through the Ajax academy before recently joining the Ajax colony at Barcelona. Since the 1970s the club has innovated by proposing a specific career path for its players. More similar to the Yugoslav than to the Western model, Ajax has been prepared to offer its best first-team players a good transfer abroad at a reasonably young age. From Van Basten to Bergkamp, the club has exported high-quality players to the elite of the international market and continues to have its products engaged by major European clubs such as Barcelona, Milan and Arsenal. In the case of Ajax, the trademark 'style' has maintained its value for the last thirty years.

As in Holland, the strict amateur regulations of the Swedish federation meant that footballers employed by clubs abroad could not play for the national team. The years of the Second World War marked the ascent of Swedish football. The country remained neutral and competition continued unaffected. As a consequence, the national side enjoyed unprecedented success when international competition resumed, winning the gold medal at the 1948 London Olympics and coming third at the 1950 Brazilian World Cup. The immediate consequence of this was the loss of the best players to the wealthy leagues of Southern Europe. All but two of the Swedish gold medallists in 1948 had moved abroad by the time of the World Cup, including the celebrated forward trio 'Grenoli', composed of Gunnar Gren, Gunnar Nordahl and Niels Liedholm, who all joined Milan. Eight of the 1950 team were also signed up by Italian clubs, including Lennart 'Nacka' Skoglund who moved to Inter and Hans Jeppson, who played for Atalanta and Napoli after his short spell with Charlton Athletic.

Many of these players had long careers abroad. Dan Ekner enjoyed the most extraordinary professional journey across Europe and beyond. After five games as an amateur at Portsmouth, he travelled to Marseilles, then played a few seasons at Fiorentina and Spal in Italy before moving across the Atlantic to the Chicago Vikings for a season, returning to Atlético Madrid in Spain, Rot-Weiss Essen in

---

52. Stefan Kovacs, *Football Total*, Paris: Calmann-Lévy, 1975, pp. 33–83.
53. Evert Vermeer, *90 yaren Ajax, 1900–1990*, Utrecht: Luitingh, 1990, p. 179.

Table 7.1a Swedish Professional Footballers Abroad, 1948–65

Destination	Number
Italy	31
France	11
Spain	4
England	2
West Germany	2
Holland	1
USA	1
Switzerland	1

Source: Data elaborated from *Fotball Boken '94*

Table 7.1b Swedish Professional Footballers Abroad, 1966–93

Destination	Number
Germany	30
Switzerland	21
Belgium	18
Holland	15
USA	13
Italy	12
Portugal	11
France	8
England	8
Canada	5
Greece	4
Spain	4
Scotland	3
Austria, Hong Kong, Turkey	2
Australia, Cyprus, Czechoslovakia, Denmark, Japan, Poland, Saudi Arabia, Yugoslavia	1

Source: Data elaborated from *Fotball Boken '94*

Germany and PSV Eindhoven in Holland.[54] The term 'mercenary' may have applied in his case but most exports remained loyal to their first destination. Liedholm played fourteen seasons at Milan, married a Piedmontese aristocrat and coached for some thirty years in Italian football but kept a strong Swedish accent. After

54. Lars-Gunnar Björklund, *Fotboll Boken '94*, Stockholm: Futura Media, 1994, p. 76.

seven years at Milan, Nordahl (nicknamed 'The Fireman' after his first profession in Sweden) returned to Norrkoping but died while on his annual holiday in Sardinia. Kurt Hamrin and Jeppson still live in Italy, while Gunnar Andersson died in Marseilles where he had played for a decade, and Skoglund's sons played professionally in Italy after his death.[55] By the time the Swedes were ready to host the World Cup in 1958, they were aware of the necessity of calling their 'foreign' players to the national cause. The ban on foreign-based players was overturned in time for the competition. The forward line of the team which reached the final consisted of Liedholm, Skoglund and Hamrin who were based in Italy, Gren who had recently returned and Agne Simonsson, who was to join Real Madrid a couple of years later. During the 1960s and 1970s, the main destinations of the top Swedish players changed: Germany and Holland replaced Italy and France (Tables 7.1a and b). Of the team that reached the quarter-finals of the 1974 World Cup, eight played in Germany or Holland, following similar patterns of lengthy exile as the previous generation. The two stars of the team, the goalkeeper Hellström and the centre-forward Edström, played for Kaiserslauten and PSV Eindhoven respectively. In Germany, Swedes competed with Yugoslavs throughout the 1970s as the most desirable foreign players. Indeed, Bayern Munich's 1974 and 1975 European Cup winning sides included two Swedes – Andersson and Torstensson – as its foreign entitlement. For over fifty years, then, there has been a constant request from Europe for Swedish centre-forwards and central-defenders and playing for the Swedish national team has effectively acted as a passport for a good foreign transfer.

Exclusion and xenophobia affect not only immigrant but also emigrant footballers. The situation of players leaving their home country has evolved from complete or partial marginalization into a more open access to national honours. The composition of national teams has changed. Until the 1950s, playing for the national squad in many countries required permanent residency and a willingness to comply with the designated standards of membership: to be an amateur, for example, if the federation did not accept professionalism. The Dutch, Swedes and Norwegians we have discussed were obliged to stay in their country of origin if they wanted to play international football. Only later did the view alter to accept, and even encourage, the inclusion of players living and working abroad. In recent years expatriate footballers employed in different national leagues, and influenced by a variety of approaches to the game, have been regarded as essential to the improvement of standards at home.

55. A. Pécheral and L. Grimand, *La grande histoire de l'OM*, Paris: Robert Laffont, 1984, pp. 121–7.

Bosman: A Real Revolution?

Jean-Marc Bosman was not an itinerant footballer. He was born in Liège in 1964, and had played his football exclusively for clubs in his native city. A promising young midfielder, he had captained the Belgian Youth team and moved through the junior ranks at Standard before making his debut as a teenager in the first team. His only transfer had been to local rivals Royal Football Club (RFC) Liège. In short, he had enjoyed a fairly modest career, attaining caps at under-21 national level but failing to progress into the senior side. In 1990, he came to the end of his contract with RFC Liège. The club offered him a further one-year contract on minimum terms, equivalent to one-quarter of his previous salary, which he rejected. But he seemed to have found new employment at US Dunkerque-Littoral, a French second-division club situated a few miles from the Belgian border and less than 200 miles from his home. Under the terms of his contract with Dunkerque, Bosman was responsible for organizing his release from Liège before the beginning of the season. Yet having received no request from RFC Liège, who had come to doubt Dunkerque's ability to pay the agreed transfer fee, the Belgian federation refused to release his clearance certificate on time, and thus Bosman's contract with his new club was automatically cancelled. Finding himself expelled from the Liège squad and without work, Bosman took his Belgian employer to the local court of appeal on the grounds that they had impeded his engagement. In the meantime, he was only able to secure a short-term contract at a lowly French second-division club, St Quentin. Two years later, Bosman's case reached the European Court of Justice and the final ruling was given a further two years later, on 15 December 1995.[1]

Two aspects of the decision were relevant to the migration of footballers. First, restrictions on the use of citizens of other European Union (EU) member states were ruled to be a clear discrimination on the grounds of nationality which contradicted Article 48 of the Treaty of Rome relating to the free movement of workers. For UEFA, the European governing body, and the Belgian federation, the arguments against the applicability of EU law to football had been threefold:

---

1. Case C-415/93, *Union Royale Belge des Sociétés de Football Association ASBL v. Jean-Marc Bosman* and others, judgement of 15 December 1995. Also see Roger Blanpain and R. Inston, *The Bosman Case: The End of the Transfer System?*, Brussels: Bruylants, 1996.

first of all, footballers were considered to be workers *sui generis* – not comparable with other workers; second, it was argued that domestic football needed to be preserved as the basic resource for national teams; third, it was suggested that UEFA regulations applied to an area beyond the jurisdiction of the fifteen EU members and therefore the application of EU law would create an unfair advantage for non-EU UEFA countries. Each of these points was rejected, although the Court of Justice accepted that Community law could not be applicable to national teams. The second connection of *Bosman* to the migration of players was the Court's objection to transfer fees being applicable to out-of-contract players, and its decision that the transfer system constituted a restriction on the free movement of workers. Without doubt, the most revolutionary implication of the *Bosman* ruling was that community law applied to sport. The notion that 'sports law' existed autonomously, and could contradict general law, was henceforth redundant. As a result, professional sportspeople could not, theoretically at least, be impeded from litigation with employers and federations. As such, according to the ruling of Advocate General Lenz, football was a normal economic activity comparable to others with all the implications of employment law.

Before Bosman

Lombrette

In 1949 a case had arisen concerning a Belgian footballer playing in France which contained many elements comparable to *Bosman*. Its resolution, however, was somewhat different. On 24 February Henri Delaunay, General Secretary of the French Football Federation, received a curious letter from his Belgian counterpart asking for clarification of the status of a young national playing in the French first division. René Lombrette was a full-back who had just made the first team at CO Roubaix-Tourcoing. Born in Belgium in 1928, he had apparently played for the junior teams of Roubaix since 1943. Yet Mr Demy of the Belgian federation had noticed that the player had never received a transfer permit to leave his first club, Mouscron.[2] In response, Delaunay asked the secretary of the Ligue du Nord to provide him with further details about Lombrette's status. From his reply, we learn that Lombrette had played as an amateur for Roubaix since 1944 and a police certificate confirmed that he was resident in Wattrelos, a town bordering Roubaix.[3] On 10 March, following its normal procedures, the French league suspended

---

2. FIFA Archives, Affaires de joueurs liquidées (A–Z, up to 31 December 1950), Lombrette, Letter from Demy to Delaunay, 24 February 1949.

3. FIFA Archives, Lombrette, Carin to Delaunay, 1 March 1949.

Lombrette provisionally. The secretary of Roubaix expressed his dismay that a player who had joined the club at sixteen and renewed his licence annually should now be reclaimed by a club which had 'only recognised the value of the player when it was realised they could make a pecuniary benefit from him'.[4] Convinced by the Roubaix protest, Delaunay wrote to his Belgian counterpart asking him to withdraw the protest and give Lombrette the necessary clearance allowing him to continue to play in France. The Belgian federation refused, arguing that Lombrette had persistently declined to return to Mouscron.[5] With deadlock reached, the French approached FIFA to appoint a mediator. They chose the Englishman Arthur Drewry, vice-president of FIFA.

Like *Bosman*, the Lombrette case involved consideration of the freedom of movement of footballers across national borders, the limits of the responsibilities of national federations, as well as the ethics of financial recompense for a migrating employee. Significantly, Lombrette's case was dealt with entirely internally, with no recourse to legal arbitration. Moreover, it anticipated the Treaty of Rome by some eight years but shows that these issues were common long before *Bosman*.

The peculiarity of the Lombrette case regarded the distance of his movement. Mouscron and Roubaix are just ten miles apart but, crucially, are intersected by a border. The language spoken on both sides of the border is the same while the large textile factories recruit workers from both the French and the Belgian side. As with *Bosman*, in Lombrette's case the moral and ethical aspects were at least as important as the strictly regulatory and legal considerations. Neither footballer seems to have been a mercenary: they were simply workers seeking employment in the region in which they lived. Indeed, there is evidence that Lombrette moved to Roubaix primarily to find work in one of the town's knitting factories, even if it turns out that the factory was owned by the president of the football club. One of the arguments put by the French club was that international transfer regulations took no account of the structure of the general labour market, or of the peculiar conditions of wartime when migration and exile were both more common and more frequent. Such cases illustrate the limitations of national regulations which disregard the existence of a border economy.

The personal effect of the cases on the players involved was massive. From March to September 1949, Lombrette's promising career was interrupted. In the words of the secretary of Roubaix 'Lombrette was under intense pressure from Mouscron' and did not see any hope of his case being resolved. Similarly, Bosman faced mounting personal and financial difficulties, and as Stephen Weatherill has noted, 'one may wonder whether the real impact of the judgement may be to warn

4. FIFA Archives, Lombrette, Desrousseau to Delaunay, 4 April 1949.

5. FIFA Archives, Lombrette, Delaunay to Demy, 21 April 1949; Demy to Delaunay, 16 June 1949.

potential litigants of the costs of challenging the game's structure'.[6] Perhaps because he had no legal team to support him, Lombrette was forced to sacrifice his professional career, initially returning to Mouscron but then hanging up his boots during late summer. By the end of October, Drewry had made his recommendations, adjudging that without a transfer permit 'the registration of René Lombrette for the Club Olympique Roubaix-Tourcoing must be declared void'.[7] FIFA, in turn, endorsed Drewry's report and Lombrette's career was effectively over.

Lombrette's case is symptomatic of the existence of a long-standing struggle waged over the issues of human rights, employment law, international sporting regulations and the realities of a footballer's career. In both cases, the Belgian clubs took advantage of the particularly restrictive regulations of their federation, which denied players any of the fundamental rights of workers to decide when and where to be employed. For Lombrette, the Belgian federation made no distinction between junior and senior players or amateurs and 'independents' (players who received broken-time payments) as far as international transfers were concerned. In *Bosman*, the end of a contract did not signify that a player was free to move: his employer was still entitled to receive compensation and to block the transfer. In both cases, the player saw his career ruined. The Lombrette case is an early indication of the ethical and moral questions connected to the operation of the international transfer system. In many respects, it is hardly surprising that Lombrette failed where Bosman succeeded. Football authorities at the time considered themselves autonomous. They maintained jurisdiction over their own business irrespective of general law. Most importantly, footballers were not regarded as workers and so were not subject to employment law. Lombrette had contravened international football regulations even if his action of migrating to find work was hardly uncommon outside football.

The International Transfer System

From the late nineteenth century the movement of footballers from club to club within and between national federations has been regulated by the transfer system. As we have seen, the establishment of agreements between national federations which recognized the registration and contractual rights of clubs paved the way for its development. The foundation of FIFA led to the formalization of the transfer system on an international level. Accordingly, a player was not permitted to move freely between clubs once his employment contract had ended. To be able to field a player, a new employer had to secure his registration from his previous employer,

6. Stephen Weatherill, 'European Football Law', in *Collected Courses of the Academy of European Law, Volume 1: 1996*, The Hague: Martinus Nijhoff, 1999, p. 350.

7. FIFA Archives, Lombrette, Drewry to FIFA, 27 October 1949.

a process which often involved the payment of a transfer fee. Moreover, international exchanges required the release of an international transfer certificate from the donor national association to the recipient.

In spite of this, the migration of players has not always been accompanied by the exchange of transfer documents or the payment of a fee. The hundreds of South American and European players who moved to Colombia in the late 1940s and early 1950s were erroneously called 'outlaws' because they infringed the jurisdiction of FIFA. Yet they were not outlaws. Having signed regular contracts, these players were legally entitled to move and, providing they did not break contracts at home, could not be taken to court. In fact, all the clubs under FIFA jurisdiction who 'lost' their players resolved the matter in sporting courts. Other leagues independent of FIFA – therefore avoiding the international transfer system – have existed from time to time. At the end of the 1950s, a large number of Austrian, Dutch and Czech players migrated to Australia to play professional football with the rebel New South Wales Federation of Soccer Clubs. Likewise, in the United States, as we have seen, where anti-trust regulations have determined the operation of all organizations including sport, various leagues have operated independently, or at a distance from FIFA, since the 1920s.

All these examples emphasize the peculiar situation of football, where there has always been a struggle between the universal and the particular. It is not, and has never been, an obligation for football clubs, leagues or federations to join FIFA or even to play to the same rules. In the same way, there is no reason why a footballer moving from one club to another or one country to another should need to be transferred. In July 1969, an agreement between the French Players' Union and the French league abolished the 'life contract' which had bound players to a club until the age of thirty-five. For the next season, regulations stipulated that at the end of a contract 'whose duration was agreed by both parties', the player was free to sign with whichever employer he chose. His former club was entitled neither to oppose the transaction nor to ask for compensation.[8] For twenty years, France was the only country without a formal transfer system.[9] Indeed, when Michel Platini was transferred from Saint-Etienne to Juventus in 1982, the selling club received a nominal fee under UEFA regulations even though the player was out-of-contract. No fee would have been necessary under French regulations. If regulations in other

8. *Annuaire de la FFF*, Statut professionnel, 1969–70, Paris: FFF, pp. 133–5.

9. There were, however, two regulations which limited the free movement of players. First of all, a player who had stayed three years as an apprentice at a club was bound to sign his contract with them. Secondly, for a player's first move an 'indemnity of formation' was required to recompense his first employers for the money and time spent in training the player. Charte du football professionnel. Différents status et dispositions transitoires pour la saison 1973–74, *Annuaire de la FFF 1973–74*, p. 127; Jean-Michel Faure and Charles Suaud, *Le football professionnel à la française*, Paris: Puf, 1999, pp. 193–236.

European countries moved towards a less rigid conception of the economic control of player movement, the legitimacy of the transfer system was never directly challenged.

International Freedom of Movement

The freedom of movement of footballers across national borders has been restricted at the points of both departure and arrival. On one hand, there have been limitations on the number of non-nationals entitled either to be contracted or to actually play. On the other hand, regulations have been established which have impeded or limited players from moving away. Moreover, the concept of the 'non-national' or 'foreign' player has evolved differently and been interpreted in a variety of ways by different national federations. For a long time, international sporting institutions did not interfere with national regulations, thus allowing teams to field a range of players. A new concept emerged after the decision taken by FIFA in 1964 that a footballer could only play for a single nation in international competition, irrespective of whether he might have dual or multi-nationality.[10] A restrictive form of sporting nationality was thus created which could discriminate against players who not only move from one country to another but change citizenship (see Chapter 3).

Even after the signing of the Treaty of Rome, international freedom of movement has been restricted by national federations. To understand this situation, we need to remember that from the 1960s to the 1990s sporting federations remained convinced that EU law did not apply to sport. This was despite the fact that two sporting cases which had reached the European Court of Justice in the 1970s – *Walrave and Koch v. UCL* in 1974 and *Donà v. Mantero* in 1976[11] – confirmed that it was illegal to restrict movement on the basis of nationality.

There was no Europe-wide agreement over what constitued a 'national' player or a 'foreigner', or about how many of each category should be allowed. As Table 8.1 shows, at the beginning of the 1980s there were significant differences in the regulations regarding foreign imports across the major European leagues, from Italy's restrictive 'one foreigner quota' to Belgium's traditionally more liberal and inclusive interpretations. In addition, the rules of national federations fluctuated over time. Whereas Italian clubs were prohibited from signing 'new' foreigners between 1966 and 1980, one player from a foreign federation (including Italian citizens) was allowed between 1980 and 1982, although only, as we have noted, in *Serie A*. Between 1982 and 1988, this was increased to two and in 1989 to three (with Italians registered abroad no longer included as foreigners). For some twenty-

---

10. FIFA Archives, Minutes of the Players' Status Committee, 20 October 1963.
11. Case 36/74, *Walrave and Koch v. Union Cycliste Internationale*; Case 13/76, *Donà v. Mantero*.

Table 8.1 Regulations concerning foreign players in the major European leagues 1980/81

Belgium	3 foreign players plus an unlimited number of those with foreign passports who have played for five years in Belgium – the so-called 'Football Belgians'.
England	2 foreign players (UK and Republic of Ireland players not considered as foreigners). Foreigners require a work permit to enter the country. All EU individuals are automatically entitled to a work permit but non-EC players had to have reached a designated international standard.
France	2 foreign players in divisions 1 and 2.
Germany	2 foreign players in divisions 1 and 2. Foreign players who have played in German youth teams are not considered to be foreigners.
Greece	2 foreigners in division 1. No foreigners in division 2.
Holland	3 foreign players in division 1, subject to work permit.
Italy	1 foreign player in division 1. No foreign players allowed in the other professional divisions.
Portugal	2 foreigners in divisions 1 and 2.
Scotland	Same regulations as in England.
Spain	2 foreigners and one *oriundo* in division 1 and division 2. The *oriundi* must not have been capped by their country of birth.

five years, the sixty professional clubs in *Series C1* and *C2*, meanwhile, were banned from engaging a single foreign professional.

Some federations have also placed restrictions on the movement of players abroad. The Soviet Union gave its first clearance certificate in 1980 to Anatoly Sinchenko, which allowed him to leave Zenith Leningrad for Rapid Vienna, although the terms of the agreement assured his return after two years. *Glasnost* clearly had its effect on Soviet football. From the late 1980s, clearance certificates began to be delivered for the best Soviet players. Other Eastern European countries, particularly Czechoslovakia and Romania, have had cyclical phases in which the doors were either open or firmly shut. However, the most orthodox Communist countries in Europe, the German Democratic Republic (GDR) and Albania (before 1990), did not issue a single clearance certificate. At other times, the federations of nations with liberal economies have likewise decided to prohibit the migration of specific players, often in preparation for major international tournaments, as the West Germans did prior to the 1978 World Cup. The main restriction in many countries was, as we have seen in the Yugoslav case, the age clause. Since the early 1970s, Polish players could only move abroad once they had reached the age of thirty, although the political authorities were keen to make an exception with Zbigniew Boniek's move to Juventus in 1982. Other Eastern European countries operated a similar age clause with the addition that the player should have distinguished himself as a member of the national team. The real turning-point here came with the transfer of Alexander Zavarov at the age of twenty-seven from Dynamo Kiev to Juventus in the summer of 1988, after which East-West migration accelerated substantially.[12]

Within the European Union itself, EU citizens have not always been treated in the same way. In Britain, since the opening of doors to foreigners in 1978, a distinction was made between EU players, who were free to join any club, and non-EU players, who had to apply for a work permit.[13] From 1982, French clubs were allowed to sign two foreign players plus an optional EU player, but only two could step on the field at any time. This particular distinction between the various categories of 'foreign' player came into being following the signing of three foreign internationals by Paris Saint-Germain in 1982 – Ardiles, the Argentinian from Tottenham, the Yugoslav Safet Susic and the Dutch striker Kees Kist. Only Ardiles and Kist began the season because, as we saw in Chapter 4, Susic's move was temporarily banned by the Yugoslav federation. Nevertheless, because the signing of three foreign players contravened football regulations, the club threatened to take the matter to the courts, forcing the French league to adopt this new rule. From the mid-1980s, the majority of EU federations passed regulations which differentiated EU imports from other foreigners. And even if restrictions were relaxed in favour of the former, federations continued to apply discrimination on grounds of citizenship between nationals and other EU citizens.

The first significant intervention from the European Commission came in 1985, when the new commissioner, Peter Sutherland, directed all football authorities coming under Common Market legislation to 'stop all restrictions on non-national EEC players'.[14] In April 1989, the European Parliament voted through a resolution regarding the freedom of movement of footballers within the European Community. In this resolution, the Parliament noted football's clear breach of European law and asked for an adaptation of the football industry to European law.[15] In April 1990 the European Commission mandated vice-president Martin Bangemann to find an agreement with UEFA for a standard regulation relating to the free movement of players inside the European Union. An agreement (the so-called 3+2) was found in April 1991 which prescribed that

12. Vic Duke, 'The Flood from the East?: Perestroika and the Migration of Sports Talents from Eastern Europe', in J. Bale and J. Maguire (eds), *The Global Sports Arena*, London: Frank Cass, 1994, p. 158.

13. PFA Archives, Work Permit File, 1978–80, Cliff Lloyd to J.A. Shakesby, 19 July 1978; A.J. Gulliver to Cliff Lloyd, 2 August 1978.

14. PFA Archives, Minutes of PFA, 2 December 1985 (AGM).

15. OJ, no. C, 120, 16 May 1989, p. 33.

1. There should be no restrictions on the signing of EU players.
2. Three non-national professionals plus two non-nationals who have taken part in the youth team for at least three years could play in every competitive match.
3. This is applicable to all national associations affiliated to UEFA (not only EU countries).[16]

The European Parliament examined a second proposal in 1991 which insisted that professional football was a 'normal' activity, and firmly condemned the 3+2 agreement signed between the Commission and UEFA, 'reaffirming its strong opposition to any kind of restriction which would diminish or impede the freedom of movement of professional footballers in the Community'. They also 'considered . . . that a limitation of the number of EU players allowed to play was in flagrant violation of the fundamental principles of the Treaty of Rome'.[17] This proposal, however, was not adopted.

Players' associations throughout Europe were divided on the issue. If the Dutch union headed by FIFPRO[18] chairman the Euro MP Janzen van Raay saw in this proposal the opportunity for a broadening market for players (at the time of successful Dutch exiles such as Gullit, Rijkaard and Van Basten at Milan and Koeman at Barcelona), the unions in countries which were traditional importers of football labour, such as Italy and Spain, were concerned to protect the jobs of their members. In most cases, a compromise position was found. Thus in Italy, the union proposed that no restrictions should be imposed on EU players but that a maximum of three non-EU players should be allowed in *Serie A* teams, and none in *Serie B*.[19]

At the time of this debate over freedom of movement within the EU, the geopolitics of Europe were changing dramatically. Eastern Europe in particular was in the process of liberalizing its football. Skilled and experienced players were no longer bound by age restrictions and their clubs were in desperate need of cash. In addition, social unrest in Albania and the beginning of the war in Yugoslavia saw the arrival to the West of a wave of talented and relatively inexpensive footballers. On top of this, the nations of South America, especially Brazil and Argentina, experienced massive currency devaluation, so weakening the negotiating power of clubs and increasing the opportunity for players to find contracts in Europe (see Chapter 3). The debate within the EU could not ignore this broader context, particularly the increasing prominence of a competent labour

16. 'Joueurs de football professionnels: le dossier progresse', *Agence Europe*, Press Release IP(91)316, 18 April 1991.
17. Resolution B3-1784/91, European Parliament 157.274, 21 November 1991.
18. The international federation of players' associations.
19. *La Repubblica*, 14 April 1992.

force arriving in increasing numbers from outside. This situation excluded de facto the scenario of a resolution which guaranteed freedom of movement inside the EU at the same time as increasing restrictions on non-EU foreigners. The deregulation of the football economy outside Europe has had repercussions within the continent which are often neglected.

After Bosman

As far as it relates to the migration of footballers, the *Bosman* judgement has been less revolutionary than is often assumed. To regard the case as a major watershed in the nature and scale of football labour migration is to misunderstand the scope of the ruling and ignore the broader international context. Indeed, our main argument is that changes in the international football economy, particularly the deregulation of the player market, had an essential impact which must be recognized alongside the ramifications of the case itself. As Rick Parry, Chief Executive of the FA Premier League, commented shortly after the ruling: 'The Premier League's interpretation in changing our rules on the number of foreign players was simply to substitute EU for UK; we still have restrictions on non-EU citizens'.[20] *Bosman* did not revolutionize the migratory practices of professional footballers but merely gave added impetus to a trend already set in motion. This is equally true of the role of player's agents. This semi-legal profession existed long before 1995. An international status of the profession, recognized by FIFA, was adopted in May 1994. Agents are crucial in offering to the European football market cheap South American and African players *who are unaffected by the Bosman ruling* as well as in opening the foreign markets to players with little knowledge of other European legal systems and languages. As Fiona Miller rightly observes, many agents are legal consultants who have made real a *potential* international market.[21]

In many European countries, the *Bosman* ruling can be seen as an *excuse* for deregulation, rather than its cause. The evolution of foreign recruitment in Italy from 1995 to 2000 shows that alongside a general increase in foreign recruits, there was a significant rise in the number of non-EU imports. As Table 8.2 shows, while the number of foreign players since 1995 has multiplied almost fourfold, the percentage of EU citizens has proportionately diminished. It is South Americans and Africans, rather than players from within the EU, who are more conspicuous than they were before *Bosman*. One of the indirect consequences of *Bosman* has been the Italian league's decision to allow clubs in the lower professional divisions to employ foreign players. These clubs, in turn, have looked outside the EU – to

20. Raymond Farrell (ed.), *F.A. Premier League Seminar on the Bosman Case*, London, 6 January 1996, London: FA Premier League, 1996, p. 12.
21. Fiona E.C. Miller, 'Not Every Agent is a Bad Guy', *Sport and the Law Journal*, 4, 1, 1996.

Table 8.2 Country of origin of foreign players in the Italian League before and after *Bosman*

Place of origin	Season 1994/95	Season 1999/2000*
European Union	25 (40.0 %)	65 (28.5 %)
Rest of Europe	16 (25.0 %)	56 (24.6 %)
South America	17 (27.0 %)	75 (32.9 %)
Africa	3 (4.8 %)	26 (11.4 %)
Other	2 (3.2 %)	6 (2.7 %)
Total	63 (100 %)	228 (100.1 %)

* Figures relate to players who actually took the field during the 1999–2000 season.

Source: Data from Fabrizio Melegari (ed.), *Almanacco illustrato del calcio 1996*, Modena: Panini, 1995; *Calcio 2000*, June 2000

South America, Africa and Croatia – in order to acquire the contracts of young and inexpensive players.

Moreover, the impact of the *Bosman* ruling on the investment in foreign players seems to have varied from country to country within the EU. In France, the proportionate increase of EU players among the non-national contingent occurred some time before the 1990s. If EU imports represented 9.5 per cent of all migrants in 1977, this figure had doubled by 1983, immediately after the three-foreigners rule (including one EU player) was introduced. In 1988 EU players represented 33 per cent of all non-nationals, a percentage almost unchanged in the figures for the year 2000 (36 per cent). As shown in Table 8.3, Britain has concentrated its foreign investments within the European Union and in European Economic Area (EEA) countries such as Norway. In the season 1994/95, the year before *Bosman*, there were only four French players in the Premier and Football League; by 1998/99, sixty French players were under contract with English clubs.[22] Instructive, too, is the number of players from Eastern Europe who have migrated to Germany. In 1999/2000, German clubs employed the highest percentage of non-nationals in the EU (40.6 per cent), followed by Belgium (39.6 per cent) and England (38.8 per cent). The main groups of foreigners in the *Bundesliga* were Croatians (17), Poles (16) and Hungarians (10).

As shown in Table 8.4, the movement of professionals within the EU after *Bosman* has been less significant than the arrival of players from non-European countries with a good football tradition and a poor economy. Indeed what is striking about the data relating to the late 1990s is the continuity in migratory trails from earlier periods. *Bosman* alone can surely not explain why seventy-four Brazilians were playing in the Portuguese first division in 1999/2000, many of whom had the possibility of acquiring dual citizenship.

22. Jack Rollin (ed.), *Rothmans Football Yearbook 1995–96*, London: Headline, 1995; Glenda and Jack Rollin (eds), *Rothmans Football Yearbook, 1999–2000*, London: Headline, 1999.

Table 8.3 The distribution of foreigners by geographical area in the European Union leagues, 1999/2000

Geographical area	As percentage of total no. of foreigners in the league
European Union	England (76%)
	Scotland (73%)
	Holland (40%)
	Italy (28%)
Eastern Europe	Belgium (44%)
	Germany (40%)
Africa	France (48%)
South America	Portugal (54%)
	Spain (44%)
	Italy (34%)

Source: Data from Paolo Piani, 'Studio sull'incidenza degli stranieri nelle rose dei club europei', *News letter del settore tecnico FIGC*, 1, 2000, 2.

Table 8.4 Migrants by nationality in the major European Union leagues, 1999/2000

	BEL	FRA	ENG	GER	HOL	ITA	POR	SCO	SPA	Total
BRA	10	7	1	11	7	18	74	0	19	147
ARG	2	7	4	1	3	17	8	1	42	85
FRA	6	n/a	21	4	1	20	2	10	12	76
YUG	20	5	0	8	8	8	4	0	13	66
HOL	10	0	15	12	n/a	2	0	6	14	59
CRO	10	0	6	17	1	12	2	0	3	51

Source: Data from Paolo Piani, 'Studio sull'incidenza degli stranieri nelle rose dei club europei', *News letter del settore tecnico FIGC*, 1, 2000, 2

Significantly, the two countries which export the most players within the Union, France and Holland, are also countries whose taxes for footballers are among the highest, reaching between 55 and 70 per cent of their gross salaries. Significant as well is the success of these two nations at international level. The national teams composed almost exclusively of emigrants do not seem to have suffered from the displacement of their best players. During the last two international competitions, the 1998 World Cup and the European Nations Cup in 2000, these were the most successful EU nations. France won both competitions while Holland reached the semi-final on both occasions. The importance of the emigrant experience in football seems to be part of a much wider recognition of the value of living and working abroad. The French international relations specialist Pascal Boniface acknowledged as much in a recent article in *Le monde*. In his view, footballers should be seen as the first symbols of a single European market, but as well of a European space that replaces, in many ways, the national frame . . . But footballers are not unique. French students who spent a year abroad in the 1980s were 'marginals', but now this is becoming common and in some branches it is almost necessary.[23]

It is also important to note the resistance against the flow of foreign players which has emerged in some European countries. Piacenza in Italy, Athletic Bilbao in Spain and, until recently, Wimbledon in England, have continued to propose an autarkic, sometimes anti-economic, policy which has rejected the presence of 'foreign' imports. In the Spanish case particularly, the internationalization of the football market has had to compete with a further shift towards regionalization, symbolized by the re-foundation of a Basque selection. After poor national team results, Spanish critics chose not to blame the preponderance of foreigners but to focus on the regional identities of many of the squad who 'have doubts about winning for Spain rather than for Catalonia or *Euzkadi* a title which would reinforce the Spanish nation'.[24]

Migration and the Structure of European Club Football

In order to understand the patterns of football migration in Europe at the beginning of the twenty-first century, we need to be aware of the evolving structure of football

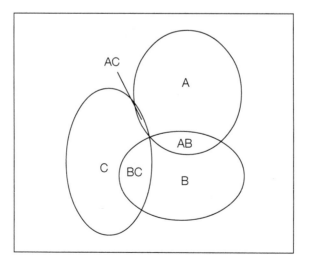

Figure 8.1 Categories of Professional Footballers in Europe

23. Pascal Boniface, 'Le football, miroir de l'Europe', *Le monde*, 20 June 2000.
24. Vicente Verdú, 'Una selección de españoles', *El Pais*, 13 September 1998.

in the continent. Figure 8.1 outlines the main categories of professional footballer and the interconnections between these groups. We are not suggesting that these categories are rigid: on the contrary, they are by their very nature fluid, allowing a player to move within or between these different 'sets' or 'groups' over the course of his career. Set A represents the top five hundred or so players from the top twenty to twenty-five clubs. Like their employers, this group moves in a space which takes little account of national borders. Regular members of their respective national teams, they take part in the Champions League and major international tournaments, and play around fifty competitive matches each year, a significant proportion outside their national boundaries. Like Hollywood film stars, these players live in exclusive areas and the only possibility to meet them is in Five-Star hotels and airports. Within this category, two groups of players are easily identifiable: the elite nationals and the elite migrants. The first group is composed mainly of the major English, Italian and Spanish players. Once they have reached the top of their national hierarchy, playing for one of the major clubs, their career expectation is to conserve their position within that club, or more commonly in the Italian case to move within the elite circle of national clubs. An extreme example of this career path was the movement of the Italian striker Christian Vieri, who acquired A status on his transfer to Juventus, and then moved on to Atlético Madrid, Lazio and Inter in consecutive seasons. For players of other nationalities, once an A contract has been acquired with an A-status club, the aim is to be mobile within this elite transnational group. Thus Ronaldo, who reached his A status at PSV Eindhoven, then moved to Barcelona and a year later to Inter. Coming from Marseilles, which was transformed to A status after winning the Champions Cup in 1993, Didier Deschamps moved to Juventus, became more prominent with the French national team, and is now playing for Chelsea.

As we noted in the introduction of Anelka, players who have reached A status have a limited choice of possible employers. What is new in this situation is that the choice is not restricted to the national elite but to the European elite. If a decade ago there existed a number of national A groups with a comparable number of players and clubs, today there is an integrated transnational A set which is becoming increasingly autonomous. If we observe the transactions in the mid-1990s between Borussia Dortmund and Juventus, both finalists of the Champions League in 1997, it becomes evident that the two became regular business partners and potential employers for one another's players. This involved not only the German players of Juventus (Möller, Kohler, Reuter) but even the Brazilian Julio Cesar and the Portuguese Paulo Sousa. This type of movement is made more natural by the regularity of the contests between the clubs, the meetings of the boards of directors, joint television interests, common sponsors and common agents. In many respects, such players and clubs now have more in common with one another than with players and clubs in their own domestic leagues who fight each year to avoid relegation or even those who endeavour to qualify (often unsuccessfully) for European competition. It is this elite A group, above all, which in its activity suggests the model of a global labour market. The crucial point, however, is that this group is far from representative of the profession as a whole.

The B Group is composed of those players and clubs who compete in the major divisions of their national leagues but do not enjoy regular international or European experience. The aim of the players of this group is to graduate to the A set and compete in the international arena. B players often reach national representative level, being selected for youth or under-21 national teams, but fail to receive full international recognition. Their market is still predominantly national and the logic of the clubs of this category is also to acquire and then preserve national status. On the transfer market, players and clubs of this category rarely compete with opponents of the A group. In most of the major European leagues this group includes around 500 players and twenty-five clubs representing average division-one and leading division-two organizations – a total of some 3,000 to 4,000 professional players across Europe. Bosman himself was part of this B category. The internationalization of the market has had an important impact on this group. If the mobility of players remains mainly national, the move towards an international market has affected emerging young players (such as the Italians Gattuso who moved from Salernitana to Rangers and Materazzi who left Perugia for Everton) as well as players from other nations who, as a part of their career strategy, choose to spend one or two seasons at aspiring elite clubs to display their talent and secure a first-team place. Like the A-category players, B players have tended, since *Bosman,* to sign long contracts and move when they are still under contract.

The intersection between group A and B (AB) is becoming a crucial space for emerging players and clubs. Young internationals and squad members of clubs such as Parma and Fiorentina in Italy, Leeds United and Newcastle United in England, Deportivo La Coruña or Real Zaragoza in Spain compose this group of emerging players. Highly competitive at national level, these players and clubs struggle to find affirmation in the global market. One could argue that a club such as Lazio, which was in the AB intersection three or four years ago, is now very much part of the A group, while Olympique Marseille, an A club some years ago, has dropped back into this intersection. AB clubs deal on the transfer market with counterparts of both groups A and B. If the vast majority of the Marseilles squad of the early 1990s moved to A clubs in Italy and England, and the club recruited internationally, now their trading partners are less representative of the European elite. The same can be said for Newcastle United, who after years of major deals with emerging clubs of the A group, such as the transfers of Ginola and Domi (Paris SG), Asprilla (Parma), Hamann (Bayern Munich), Pistone (Inter) on the international market and Shearer and Batty (from Blackburn Rovers) and the sale of Andy Cole to Manchester United on the domestic scene, are beginning to restrict their 'market area' to the B group. Transfers now tend to come from peripheral nations such as Greece (with Dabizas and Ketsbaia), B-category clubs such as Auxerre (Guivarc'h) and Metz (Terrier) in France or from elderly players who have retired from the international elite, like the two former Liverpool stars Ian Rush and John Barnes. A transfer to Newcastle for an emerging international talent is no longer a major investment for the future. Rather, clubs such as Newcastle are becoming ideal starting points for players from peripheral nations and clubs. Thus the Georgian Timour Ketsbaia and the Peruvian Nolberto Solano may have found in the club an ideal trampoline for a possible jump towards the A class. Coming from countries who failed to qualify for major international competitions, their international reputation and visibility was minimal and no elite club would have taken the risk of offering them a major contract. Success at Newcastle could secure access to the elite.

The C category represents those players and clubs from lower professional divisions in the major European leagues and players from the marginal European (principally Eastern European and Scandinavian) countries. These players could be defined as 'precarious professionals'. Their exact number is difficult to know precisely, but clearly amounts to some 20,000 in Europe at the present time. Before 1995, most enjoyed a relatively short professional experience, between two and four years on average, and little access to the main market. Their employment market is mainly regional, possibly national. More than any other group, we would agree that the average player from this category seems to have suffered from the implications of *Bosman*. More relevant, however, to the fortunes of these players has been the changing football economy. Thus while players' wages represented 26 per cent of the turnover of Manchester United in 1997, this was superior to the total incomes of some division-three clubs such as Brighton or Cambridge.[25]. Television revenues, merchandising and marketing have only marginally touched the minor clubs which employ these players. Indeed, a recent study has outlined the lack of structure and the paucity of revenue derived from non-playing activities at the majority of lower-division clubs in England.[26] As a result, these 'precarious professionals' have been excluded from the non-footballing incomes enjoyed by their more illustrious counterparts and have been unable to promote their image so as to secure a lucrative contract abroad.

There is little doubt that long before *Bosman* elite players tended to move within a closed environment. During the 1994/95 season, for instance, transfers between the Premier League and division-two and -three clubs in England were only worth

25. Gerry Boone (ed.), *Deloitte & Touche Annual Review of Football Finance*, Manchester: Deloitte & Touche, 1998, p. 52.

26. David Hudson and Brahim Herbane, *Marketing in English Professional Football Clubs*, Leicester: De Monfort University, 2000.

£2 million, while the transactions between Premier League clubs amounted to £65 million.[27] Anybody searching for the impact of the *Bosman* ruling should steer clear of Europe's lower-division clubs, where the recruitment of foreign players has been relatively slow, and in some cases negligible. At this level, contacts between clubs, agents and players and the confidence required to deal with one another on a regular basis have been insufficient to allow the development of an integrated international market. Indeed, it is perhaps ironic that those footballers who are the least secure in their employment are also the least mobile. Today it tends to be the stars rather than the journeymen who travel.

Although the foregoing discussion is only intended as a sketch of the evolving structure of European football, it provides some important clues for assessing the effect of the *Bosman* ruling on patterns of football labour migration. Emphasis on the 'global' dimension of migration is almost exclusively directed to those in the elite of the profession. To the majority of these players, mobility has become a necessary part of the profession. To reach the top, it is essential to move to the leading clubs in the most prestigious leagues. With few exceptions, the world's best footballers today are migrants.

Yet this elite group was on the move long before the *Bosman* case was settled. The volume of migration may have increased after 1995 but this is the result not of revolution but of a gradual evolution. And it is a process which extends far beyond the relatively narrow focus of the freedom of movement of footballers within the fifteen countries of the European Union. In fact, the opening of football borders within the EU as a result of *Bosman* needs to be considered alongside broader political and economic developments in different parts of the world, particularly Eastern Europe, Africa and South America, all of which have contributed to the apparent migration frenzy which we now seem to witness each summer.

27. Gerry Boone (ed.), *Deloitte & Touche Annual Review of Football Finance*, Manchester: Deloitte & Touche, 1996, p. 25.

Conclusion

In the middle of January 1958, Leo Baumgartner and his family boarded *The Flaminia* at Genoa to begin their long passage to Australia. A professional footballer with Austria Vienna, Baumgartner had, along with team-mate Karl Jaros, signed contracts with the Prague club in Sydney. The players had toured Australasia the year before and been captivated by the sun, the beaches and the hospitality of the people, if not the standard of the football. They had not decided to move at the time but financial disputes with their club when they returned home encouraged them to consider emigration. According to Baumgartner, the passengers on the voyage were 'a mixed lot of migrants, Italians, Germans, Austrians and many other nationalities, young and old, male and female; a motley [collection] of persons, all seeking a future in the new land, Australia'.[1] The families evidently learned English on the boat while the players attempted to keep fit. Despite bringing three footballs from Austria, with which they practised on the children's play deck, their sessions were often disturbed by fellow passengers, including one young boy who kicked one of the balls overboard. On their arrival in Sydney, the two families were greeted by club and federation officials and driven to a six-bedroom house which they shared for six months, rent free. They were amazed by the size of the house and the fact that the refrigerator had been filled with 'sausages, salami, meat and . . . many other foods'. Baumgartner seemed to settle well, playing and coaching over the subsequent six years for various New South Wales clubs, and acting as a contact for the importation of other European footballers. However, he also suffered some hostility and had to endure abuse from rival officials and supporters, including one opposing coach who shouted 'Why don't you go back to Austria?' during a match. Alongside his football, Baumgartner managed a canteen at the Unanderra Migrant Hostel and, while originally only intending to stay a few years, made Australia his permanent home when he retired from the game in the mid-1960s.[2]

Baumgartner's story highlights a number of the experiences common to football migrants in the twentieth century. His move was affected by both push and pull factors, it was organized by intermediaries and made possible by developments in

1. Leo Baumgartner, *The Little Professor of Soccer*, New South Wales: Marketing Productions, 1968, p. 50.

2. This section is based mainly on Baumgartner, *Little Professor*, pp. 50–101.

transport and communications. In addition, he faced the problems of adapting to a different approach to football as well as a new language and lifestyle. Frustrated by the more relaxed attitude to training and match preparation, Baumgartner admitted that in the early days he and Jaros 'missed the drill, the exactness, the attention to detail that we were used to . . . We realized though that the Australian way of living and consequently the attitude towards the game was entirely different to ours'.[3] But Baumgartner's story cannot possibly be understood without reference to its specific historical and political context. He was just one of thousands of Eastern and Southern Europeans who were attracted by the large-scale immigration programme of the Australian government in the decades following the Second World War. According to the chairman of the Australian federation, these were 'bona fide migrants' who happened to be footballers by profession.[4] As an Austrian, Baumgartner was one of the 'acceptable European races' at a time when the White Australia Policy was still in force.[5] His passage was arranged by the Immigration Officer in Vienna and, as we have seen, he travelled on a migrant ship, although his treatment on arrival was hardly typical of the majority of 'less skilled' migrants with whom he travelled. Baumgartner's decision to go to Australia, and that of the other Europeans who followed him in the late 1950s and early 1960s, can also be explained by developments in international football politics. His new club, one of the most powerful 'ethnic' teams formed around the post-war immigration of 'displaced persons' from Europe, was a member of the New South Wales Federation of Soccer Clubs, which in 1957 had split from the Australian Soccer Football Association, and therefore had no affiliation with FIFA. As such, clearance from his former club was not obtained and no transfer fees were paid. The continuation of this practice by Prague, and an outstanding transfer bill totalling £46,000, led to the suspension of the Australian federation in 1960. The migration of European professional footballers was to be much more difficult after 1963, when the bill was paid and Australia was re-admitted to FIFA.[6]

The international movement of footballers over the course of the twentieth century should therefore not be regarded as a linear phenomenon. Like all migration, it has ebbed and flowed in response to economic and political processes and the restrictions of states and governments as well as the regulations of national

3. Baumgartner, *Little Professor*, p. 58.

4. FIFA Archives, 55.9, Suspensions de joueurs jouant en Australie, Letter from the chairman of the Australian Football Soccer Association Ltd to the Secretary of the OFB, 12 May 1960.

5. Stephen Castles and Mark J. Miller, *The Age of Migration: International Population Movements in the Modern World*, London: Macmillan, 1993, pp. 74, 101.

6. Philip Moseley and Bill Murray, 'Soccer', in W. Vamplew and B. Stoddart (eds), *Sport in Australia: A Social History*, Melbourne: Cambridge University Press, 1994; Roy Hay, 'Marmaras' Oyster or Seamonds' Baby: The Formation of the Victorian Soccer Federation, 1956–64', *Sporting Traditions*, 10, 2, May 1994, pp. 3–24.

and international football federations. Above all, the vital control which states have maintained in deciding whether to let migrants in, and under what circumstances, has had a crucial impact on the movement of footballers and the composition of football labour forces.[7] In spite of the opening of national borders which now allows EU citizens to live and work anywhere in the Union, labour markets remain mainly national. As one sociologist has recently admitted, we are some way short of a global labour market: 'No other area of economic life remains so much under the thrall of states and so resistant to globalizing effects'.[8] Footballers are rarely exempt from the systems of work permits, green cards and other immigration controls which exist throughout the world in the twenty-first century.

The movement of professional footballers has tended to be from the periphery to the centre. However, the periphery and centre in football are clearly different from the conventional economic centre based around the industrialized countries of North-western Europe and North America and the peripheral countries of the Third World, or the unindustrialized South. A discussion about centre-periphery models in football cannot afford to rest solely on economic factors at the expense of cultural differences and the variables of language, religion or colonial (and post-colonial) relations. The case of African football migrants showed that language and culture were at least as important as economic considerations. Although African players were recognized as the most cost-effective acquisitions for European club sides in the 1960s, they were exclusive to three countries – Belgium, France and Portugal – all of which had a colonial past and, unlike Britain, a tradition of assimilation.

Over the last twenty years, the combination of economic factors and cultural traditions has formed the matrix of the transfer stream. Even though their clubs are of a similar economic status, the foreign players in Turkey, for example, are drawn from very different origins from their counterparts in Austria. Similarly, the most common foreign nationals in British football over the last decade, the Dutch and the Norwegians, share with their hosts a number of key cultural values, as well as a close political and diplomatic history. As English is effectively the second national language in both countries, these imports have had few problems in communicating with team-mates, managers, the board or the press. More importantly, perhaps, they were familiar with what might be termed 'the British way of life' before arriving in Britain. Not only are there few cultural or religious barriers to overcome, but the general style and standard of life is similar. Food,

7. For a powerful analysis of the role of the nation state in determining migration see Carl Strikwerda, 'Tides of Migration, Currents of History: The State, Economy and the Transatlantic Movement of Labor in the Nineteenth and Twentieth Centuries', *International Review of Social History*, 44, 1999, pp. 367–94.

8. Malcolm Waters, *Globalization*, London: Routledge, 1995, p. 89.

entertainment and social life, for instance, are not fundamentally different in Oslo, Amsterdam and Manchester. Likewise, it is much easier for an Algerian to play his football in Marseilles than any of the cities of Northern Europe. The importance of cultural norms connected with leisure time, food and youth culture often seem to be ignored, or else trivialized, in the arguments of those who take homogenization as their point of reference. The failure of Jimmy Greaves and Paul Gascoigne in Italy, for example, can be explained to some extent by their inability to shed their attachment to the British drink and pub culture. Conversely, players such as Di Canio, Tarantini and Emerson all experienced difficulties in adapting to the cultural models of British footballers. The apocryphal story that Ivano Bonetti's demise at Grimsby Town was pre-empted by a dispute over his insistence on eating spaghetti in the dressing room is testament to this. Moreover, the style and interpretation of the game is naturally an important factor when a footballer chooses a place to work abroad or a coach chooses where to buy. 'Interpretation' in this sense refers broadly to refereeing, links with supporters, training methods and matchday customs, as well as the actual style of play itself. Hence, the Italian tradition of *ritiri* was detested by generations of Northern European imports who disliked being 'imprisoned' in retreats and being forced to spend time away from their families. This type of cultural distance has not been significantly reduced in today's supposedly homogenized world.

Throughout the book we have insisted that the migration of professionals footballers needs to be understood in terms of broader patterns of labour migration. This is still true today. In the year 2000, South Americans represented 54 per cent of the foreign footballers in Portugal, 44 per cent in Spain and 34 per cent in Italy, whereas Eastern European citizens accounted for 40 per cent of foreign players in the Bundesliga.[9] Cultural as well as geographical proximity goes some way to explaining these figures. That the large numbers of Africans in France and Belgium, East Europeans in Germany and EU citizens in Britain is reflected on football team sheets shows that the game is not divorced from broader migratory trends.

We have also stressed the striking continuity in the destinations of footballers in the last hundred years as well as football's continued Eurocentrism, which still pulls much of the best talent in the world to the richest European leagues. However, it would be foolish to deny the profound changes of the last decade or so of the twentieth century. Certainly, the football migrant of the early twentieth century was a very different character from his early twenty-first century descendant. First of all, the career patterns of the most talented footballers changed dramatically in the 1990s. Whereas for a long time emigration was frowned upon at home and often meant exclusion, it had by then become almost a requirement, a vital profes-

---

9. Paolo Piani, 'Studio sull' incidenza degli stranieri nelle rose dei club europei', *News letter del settore tecnico FIGC*, 1, 2000, 2.

sional experience to put on one's curriculum vitae. Secondly, most professional players acquired a status which distanced them from mass migration. The notion of footballers as skilled workers seeking their fortune abroad was no longer appropriate. The top players in the early twenty-first century fly business class and, in the frequency with which they travel to different places of work, have more in common with the international businessman than with the footballer of previous generations. Nonetheless, it would be wrong to generalize. The break-up of the Eastern European bloc and the growth of the African market combined to create a kind of professional-football *lumpenproletariat* with career patterns and privileges as distinct from those of the international superstar as the movie extra is from the Hollywood star. This is a group which is rarely visible in the media and has few of the benefits of publicity, sponsorship and national honours enjoyed by the star migrant. Many of the world's football migrants, employed on the margins of the professional game – in semi-professional or even amateur leagues – and with precarious working contracts, fit into categories which can be more easily located within general patterns of mass labour migration.

Some observers of the late twentieth- and early twenty-first-century football scene have been impressed by the apparent integration of European and world football resulting from the migration of players. The success of foreign imports such as Vialli at Chelsea, Gullit and Van Basten in Milan and the non-national composition of teams such as Barcelona with its Dutch contingent (popularly known as *Barçolanda*), has convinced many that a new era has been entered in which nationality and national feelings become less and less relevant in a football world which is increasingly European, even global. Yet, as we have tried to demonstrate, the dichotomy between the increasing movement of players and the enduring importance of national teams means that we must be careful in making sweeping generalizations about the direction in which we are heading. As historians, we are neither qualified nor willing to predict the future, especially as recent developments seem to suggest both an increase *and* a decrease in migration. Certainly, it is evident that national federations are no longer so free as they once were to control their own labour market. The case of Britain, where there have been profound changes in the attitude towards foreign players, is the best example of this. The increasing number of non-British players in the Premiership in the early twenty-first century is well known but is less instructive than the changes occurring at lower levels of the profession. While the impact of foreign players has been limited, the beginnings of an international presence can be noted in the second and third divisions of the Football League which was non-existent ten years earlier. Developments of this kind can be observed in the football of almost every European nation. On the other hand, however, some national federations are reintroducing measures which restrict access to the profession. While it is no longer possible to prohibit EU players, the number of foreigners on the field has been regulated so as to circumscribe the effects of the Bosman ruling. This should come as no surprise. In football as elsewhere, there was a tendency throughout the twentieth century to resist, control and channel migration. The movement of professional footballers across national borders has never been completely free and there is little to suggest that it will become so in the twenty-first century.

As we have argued, the *Bosman* ruling can only provide a partial explanation of the international transfer boom of the 1990s. The role of agents, the rise of leagues at the expense of federations and the development of new cheap markets have all contributed to this boom. It is the financial and cultural impact of television more than anything else, however, which has helped to create today's segmented football industry, in which the national market is still predominant for the large majority of players and clubs but in which a supranational elite has emerged, involving the major players who appear to operate under a different logic, seemingly in a different market. The move towards an international labour market is certainly more obvious for this elite than for small, provincial clubs such as Northampton Town, Gueugnon, Carrarese, Sabadell or Aschaffenburg, where evidence of change is less easy to find. Yet these clubs have also been touched by developments in the pattern and intensity of migration, in terms of the appearance not so much of *football* migrants as of mainstream immigrant groups more generally. The impact of arrivals from the Caribbean in England, children of North African migrants in France, emigrants from the poorer south in Spain and Italy and Turks, Italians, Greeks and refugees from the former Yugoslavia in Germany, have all radically changed the complexion of these towns and their football teams in the late twentieth century. But this would be the subject of a quite different book.

Bibliography

Abrams, N.D. (1995), 'Inhibited but not "crowded out": The Strange Fate of Soccer in the United States', *International Journal of the History of Sport*, 12, 3, pp. 1–17.

Adam, P. (1907), *La morale des sports*, Paris: Librairie mondiale.

Adamson, R. (1996), *Bogotá Bandit: The Outlaw Life of Charlie Mitten*, Edinburgh: Mainstream.

Alabarces, P., Di Giano, R. and Frydenberg, J. (eds) (1998), *Deporte y sociedad*, Buenos Aires: Eudeba.

Alabarces, P. and Rodríguez, M.G. (1996), *Cuestión de pelotas: Fútbol, deporte, sociedad, cultura*, Buenos Aires: Atuel.

Allison, G. (1948), *Allison Calling*, London: Staples.

Allison, L. (1978), 'Association football and the Urban Ethos', *Stanford Journal of International Studies*, 13, pp. 203–28.

Almanah ya Fudbal 88–89 (1989), Belgrade: Tempo.

Alonso, F. (ed.) (1993), *Cien años con el fútbol*, Buenos Aires: Manrique Zago.

Anderson, B. (1983), *Imagined Communities: Reflections on the Origin and Spread of Nationalism,* London: Verso.

Andersson, T. and Radmann, A. (1999), 'Everything in Moderation: The Swedish Model', in G. Armstrong and R. Giulianotti (eds), *Football Cultures and Identities*, London: Macmillan, pp. 67–76.

Antonucci, G. (1998), *Bari 90, 1908–1998*, Bari: Corcelli.

Appleton, A. (1960), *Hotbed of Soccer: The Story of Football in the North-East*, London: Rupert Hart-Davis.

Arbena, J.L. (1994), 'Dimensions of International Talent Migration in Latin American Sports', in J. Bale and J. Maguire (eds), *Global Sports Arena*, London: Frank Cass, pp. 99–111.

Archdeacon, T.J. (1983), *Becoming American: An Ethnic History*, New York: Free Press.

Archer, R. and Bouillon, A. (1982), *The South African Game: Sport and Racism*, London: Zed Press.

Archetti, E. (1994), 'Argentina and the World Cup: In Search of National Identity', in J. Sugden and A. Tomlinson (eds), *Hosts and Champions*, Aldershot: Arena, pp. 37–63.

Bibliography

Archetti, E. (1995), 'Estilos y virtudes masculinas en El Gráfico: la creación del imaginario del fútbol argentino', *Desarollo económico*, 35, pp. 412–42.

Archetti, E. (1997), 'Argentinien', in C. Eisenberg (ed.), *Fußball, Soccer, Calcio*, Munich: DTV.

Archetti, E. (1998), 'Tango et football dans l'imagerie nationale argentine', *Sociétés et représentations*, 7, December, pp. 117–27.

Archetti, E. (1999), *Masculinities: Football, Polo and the Tango in Argentina*, Oxford: Berg.

Archetti, E. (1999), 'Fútbol, imágines y estereotipos', in F. Devoto and M. Madero (eds), *Historia de la vida privada en Argentina*, vol. 3, Buenos Aires: Taurus.

Armstrong, G. and Giulianotti, R. (eds) (1999), *Football Cultures and Identities*, London: Macmillan.

Aspinwall, B. (1985), 'The Scots in the United States', in R.A. Cage (ed.), *The Scots Abroad*, London: Croom Helm, pp. 80–110.

Baggioli, V. (1943), *Storia del calcio italiano*, Rome: De Carlo.

Bains, J. and Johal, S. (1998), *Corner Flags and Corner Shops: The Asian Football Experience*, London: Victor Gollancz.

Bairner, A. (1994) 'Football and the Idea of Scotland', in G. Jarvie and G. Walker (eds), *Scottish Sport and the Making of the Nation: Ninety-Minute Patriots?*, Leicester: Leicester University Press, pp. 9–26.

Bairner, A. (1994), 'Sweden and the World Cup: Soccer and Swedishness', in J. Sugden and A. Tomlinson (eds), *Hosts and Champions*, Aldershot: Arena, pp. 195–217.

Bale, J. (1980), 'The Adoption of Football in Europe: an Historical-Geographic Perspective', *Canadian Journal of Sport History*, 2, 11, pp. 56–66.

Bale, J. (1983), 'From Ashington to Abingdon?: Some Regional Changes in Post-War British Professional Soccer', in A. Tomlinson (ed.), *Explorations in Football Culture*, Eastbourne: LSA Publications, pp. 73–93.

Bale, J. (1991), *The Brawn Drain: Foreign Student-Athletes in American Universities*, Urbana: University of Illinois Press.

Bale, J. and Maguire, J. (eds) (1994), *The Global Sports Arena: Athletic Talent Migration in an Interdependent World*, London: Frank Cass.

Barberis, M. (1986), *La leggenda di Silvio Piola*, Milan: Sugarco.

Bardi, G. de (1580), *Discorso sopra il giuoco del calcio fiorentino*, Florence.

Barkan, E.R. (1996), *And Still they Come: Immigrants and American Society, 1920s to the 1990s*, Wheeling: Harlan Davidson.

Barnes, D. (1982), *The Game of the Century*, London: Sidgwick & Jackson.

Barreaud, M. (1998), *Dictionnaire des footballeurs étrangers du championnat professionnel français (1932–1997)*, Paris: L'Harmattan.

Bartram, S. (1956), *His Autobiography*, London: Burke.

Baudoin, G. (1985), *Histoire du FC Sochaux*, Roanne: Horvath.

Baumgartner, L. (1968), *The Little Professor of Soccer*, New South Wales: Marketing Productions.

Bayce, R. (1970), *100 años de fútbol*, Montevideo.

Bayce, R. (1983), 'Deporte y sociedad', in *El Uruguay de nuestro tiempo 1958–1983*, Montevideo: CLAEH.

Bayer, O. (1990), *Fútbol argentino: Pasión y gloria de nuestro deporte más popular*, Buenos Aires: Editorial Sudamericana.

Beardsley, P. (1985), *My Life Story*, London: Collins Willow.

Beccantini, R. (ed.) (1990), *Dizionario del calcio*, Milan: Rizzoli.

Beck, P.J. (1999), *Scoring for Britain: International Football and International Politics, 1900–39*, London: Frank Cass.

Beck, P.J. (1999), 'Projecting an Image of a Great Nation on the World Screen through Football: British Cultural Propaganda between the Wars', in B. Taithe and T. Thornton (eds), *Propaganda, Political Rhetoric and Identity, 1300–2000*, Stroud: Sutton.

Betts, R.F. (1991), *France and Decolonisation, 1900–1960*, London: Macmillan.

Bianchini, S. (1992), 'La transizione post-communista in Jugoslavia, Albania e Romania', in R. Spanò (ed.), *Jugoslavia e Balcani: una bomba in Europa*, Milan: FrancoAngeli.

Björklund, L.-G. (1994*), Fotball Boken '94*, Stockholm: Futura Media.

Blain, N., Boyle, R. and O'Donnell, H. (1993), *Sport and National Identity and the European Media*, London: Leicester University Press.

Blanpain, R. and Inston, R. (1996), *The Bosman Case: The End of the Transfer System?*, Brussels: Bruylants.

Boin, V. (1945), *Het Jubilaeumboek van het KBVB*, Brussels: Leclercq & De Haas.

Boli, B. (1994), *Black Boli*, Paris: Grasset.

Bonizzoni, L. (1989), *Calciatori stranieri in Italia: ieri e oggi*, Rome: Società stampa sportiva.

Bradford Burns, E. (1993), *A History of Brazil*, New York: Columbia University Press, 3rd edn.

Brailsford, D. (1991), *Sport, Time and Society: The British at Play*, London: Routledge.

Bredekamp, H. (1995), *Calcio Fiorentino. Il Rinascimento dei giochi*, Genoa: Il Melangolo.

Breitner, P. (1980), *Ich will kein Vorbild sein*, Munich: Copress.

Brera, G. (1994), *Il mestiere del calciatore*, Milan: Baldini and Castoldi.

Brera, G. (1997), *Il calcio veneto*, Vicenza: Neri Pozza.

Brera, G. and Tomati, F. (1991), *Genoa, amore mio*, Florence: Ponte alle grazie.

Bromberger, C. (1994), 'Foreign Footballers, Cultural Dreams and Community Identity in some North-western Mediterranean Cities', in J. Bale and J. Maguire (eds), *Global Sports Arena*, London: Frank Cass, pp. 171–82.

Bromberger, C. (1995), *Le match de football: ethnologie d'une passion partisane*, Paris: MSH.

Bromberger, C. with Hayot, A. and Mariottini, J.-M. (1993), '"Allez l'OM, Forza Juve": The Passion for Football in Marseille and Turin', in S. Redhead (ed.), *The Passion and the Fashion: Football Fandom in the New Europe*, Aldershot: Avebury, pp. 103–51.

Brubaker, R. (1992), *Citizenship and Nationhood in France and Germany*, London: Harvard University Press.

Brunori, P.L. (1981), *AS Roma: dal Testaccio alla dimensione vertice*, Florence: M'Litograph.

Brunori, P.L. (1981), *Torino: Superga nella sua storia*, Florence: M'Litograph.

Buchanan, R.A. (1985), 'Institutional Proliferation in the British Engineering Profession, 1847–1914', *Economic History Review*, 38, pp. 42–60.

Bunzl, J. (1987), *Hoppauf Hakoah. Jüdischer Sport in Österreich. Von den Anfängen bis in die Gegenwart*, Vienna: Junius.

Burns, J. (1996), *The Hand of God: The Life of Diego Maradona*, London: Bloomsbury.

Cage, R.A. (ed.) (1985), *The Scots Abroad: Labour, Capital, Enterprise, 1750–1914*, London: Croom Helm.

Cain, P.J. and Hopkins, A.G. (1993), *British Imperialism: Innovation and Expansion, 1688–1914*, London: Longman.

Caldas, W. (1990), *O pontapé inicial: memória do futebol Brasileiro (1894–1933)*, São Paulo: Ibrisca.

Caminiti, V. (1967), *Juventus 70*, Turin: Juventus FC.

Campbell, T. and Woods, P. (1987), *The Glory and the Dream: The History of Celtic FC, 1887–1987*, London: Grafton.

Cannadine, D. (1995), 'British History as a new subject: Politics, Perspectives and Prospects', in A. Grant and K. Stringer, *Uniting the Kingdom*, London: Routledge.

Cante, D. (1996), 'Propaganda e sport negli anni trenta. Gli incontri di calcio tra Italia e Austria', *Italia contemporanea*, 204, pp. 521–44.

Capelli, S. (1990), 'Il calcio fiorentino', in Azzurri, 1990, *Storia della nazionale italiana di calcio e del calcio a Firenze*, Rome: Meridiana.

Carder, T. and Harris, R. (1993), *Seagulls!: The Story of Brighton and Hove Albion FC*, Hove: Goldstone.

Cardoza, A.L. (1997), *Aristocrats in Bourgeois Italy: The Piedmontese Nobility, 1861–1930*, Cambridge: Cambridge University Press.

Carlson, A.W. (1985), 'One Century of Foreign Immigration to the United States: 1880–1979', *International Migration*, 23, 3, September, pp. 309–33.

Carter, F.W. and Capel-Kirby, W. (1933), *The Mighty Kick: The History, Romance and Humour of Football*, London: Jarrolds.

Casaus, N. (1984), *Gamper*, Barcelona: Labor.

Castles, S. and Davidson, A. (2000), *Citizenship and Migration: Globalization and the Politics of Belonging*, Basingstoke: Macmillan.

Castles, S. and Miller, M.J. (1993), *The Age of Migration: International Population Movements in the Modern World*, London: Macmillan.

Catton, J.A.H. (1900), *The Real Football: A Sketch of the Development of the Association Game*, London: Sands.

Chambat, P. (1986), 'Les fêtes de la discipline: gymnastique et politique en France (1879–1914)', in P. Arnaud and J. Camy (eds), *La naissance du Mouvement Sportif Associatif en France*, Lyon: Presses Universitaires de Lyon, pp. 85–96.

Chandos, J. (1984), *Boys Together: English Public Schools, 1800–1864*, Oxford: Oxford University Press.

Charles, J. (1957), *King of Soccer*, London: Stanley Paul.

Charles, J. (1964), *Gentle Giant*, London: Soccer Book Club.

Chartier, R. and Vigarello, G. (1982), 'Les trajectoires du sport', *Le Débat*, 19, February, pp. 35–58.

Cholvy, G. (ed.) (1986), *Mouvements de jeunesse*, Paris: Le cerf.

Cholvy, G. (ed.) (1988), *Le patronage: Ghetto ou vivier?*, Paris: Nouvelle Cité.

Ciuni, R. (1985), *Il pallone di Napoli*, Milan: Shakespeare and Company.

Closa, A. and Blanco, J. (1999), *Diccionari del Barça*, Barcelona: Enciclopèdia catalana.

Colley, L. (1992), *Britons: Forging the Nation 1707–1837*, London: Cambridge University Press.

Colley, L. (1992), 'Britishness and Otherness: An Argument', *Journal of British Studies*, 31, January, pp. 309–29.

Collinson, S. (1993), *Europe and International Migration*, London: Royal Institute of International Affairs.

Colome, G. (1992), 'Il Barcelona e la società catalana', in P. Lanfranchi (ed.), *Il calcio e il suo pubblico*, Naples: Edizioni scientifiche italiane, pp. 60–5.

Colovic, I. (1999), *Campo di calcio, campo di battaglia: il calcio dal racconto alla guerra. L'esperienza iugoslava*, Reggio Calabria: Mesogea.

Cordoba, P. (1990), 'Exercices et jeux physiques: repères pour une analyse', in A. Redondo (ed.), *Le corps dans la société espagnole des XVIe et XVIIe siècles*, Paris: Editions de la Sorbonne, pp. 267–76.

Corti, G.L. and Bet, A. (1991), *Tuttogenoa, partita per partita*, Genoa: Lo Sprint.

Council of Europe (1992), *People on the Move: New Migration Flows in Europe*, Strasbourg: Council of Europe.

Crampsey, B. (1978), *The Scottish Footballer*, Edinburgh: William Blackwood.

Crampsey, B. (1988), *The Scottish Football League: The First 100 Years*, Glasgow: Scottish Football League.

Bibliography

Critcher, C. (1991), 'Putting on the Style: Aspects of Recent English Football', in J. Williams and S. Wagg (eds), *British Football and Social Change*, Leicester: Leicester University Press, pp. 67–84.

Crolley, L., Hand, D. and Jeutter, R. (1998), 'National Obsessions and Identities in Football Match Reports', in A. Brown (ed.), *Fanatics!: Power, Identity and Fandom in Football*, London: Routledge, pp. 173–85.

Cronin, M. (1999), *Sport and Nationalism in Ireland: Gaelic Games, Soccer and Irish Identity Since 1884*, Dublin: Four Courts Press.

Dal Lago, A. and Moscati, R. (1992), *Regalateci un sogno*, Milan: Bompiani.

Da Matta, R. (1982), *Universo do futebol: Esporte e sociedade brasileira*, Rio de Janeiro: Pinakotheke.

Davids, R. (1990), *Coming to America: A History of Immigration and Ethnicity in American Life*, Princeton: Harper Perennial.

Davidson, B. (1994), *Modern Africa: A Social and Political History*, London: Longman, 3rd edn.

Delic, M. (1974), *Enciclopedija jugoslavenskog nogometa*, Zagreb: Spektar.

Delumeau, J. (1989), *Rassurer et protéger: Le sentiment de sécurité dans l'occident d'autrefois*, Paris: Fayard.

Demolins, E. (1897), *A quoi tient la supériorité des Anglo-Saxons?*, Paris: Firmin-Didot.

Deville-Danthu, B. (1997), *Le sport en noir et blanc*, Paris: L'Harmatthan.

Devine, T.M. (ed.) (1992), *Scottish Emigration and Scottish Society*, Edinburgh: John Donald.

Devoto, F. and Rosoli, G. (eds) (1988), *L'Italia nella società Argentina*, Rome.

De Wagt, G. (1984), *Eerst de Man, dan de Bal*, Amsterdam: Sijthoff.

Dietschy, P. (1997), 'Football et société à Turin 1920–1960', Unpublished PhD Thesis, University of Lyon.

Dini, V. and Nicolaus, O. (eds) (1991), *Te Diegum: Genio, sregolatezze e bacchettoni*, Milan: Leonardo.

Dini, V. (1994), 'Maradona, héros napolitain', *Actes de la recherche en sciences sociales*, 103, pp. 75–8.

Djordjevic, D. (1992), 'The Yugoslav Phenomenon', in J. Held (ed.), *The Columbia History of Eastern Europe*, New York, Columbia University Press.

Düblin, J. (1968), *75 Jahre Fußball Club Basel, 1893–1968*, Basle: Ganzmann.

Ducret, J. (1994), *Le livre d'or du football suisse*, Lausanne: L'âge d'homme.

Dudzik, P. (1987), *Innovation und Investition: Technische Entwicklung und Unternehmerentscheide in der schweizerischen Baumwollspinnerei 1800 bis 1916*, Zurich: Chronos.

Dujovne Ortiz, A. (1992), *Maradona, c'est moi*, Paris: La découverte.

Bibliography

Duke, V. (1994), 'The Flood from the East?: Perestroika and the Migration of Sports Talents from Eastern Europe', in J. Bale and J. Maguire (eds), *The Global Sports Arena*, London: Frank Cass, pp. 153–67.

Duke, V. and Crolley, L. (1996), *Football, Nationality and the State*, London: Longman.

Dummett, A. and Nichol, A. (1990), *Subjects, Citizens, Aliens and Others: Nationality and Immigration Law*, London: Weidenfeld & Nicolson.

Dunphy, E. (1991), *A Strange Kind of Glory: Sir Matt Busby and Manchester United*, London: Heinemann.

Dupont, Y. (1973), *La Mecque du football ou les mémoires d'un dauphin,* Nîmes; Bène.

Duverger, C. (1978), *L'esprit du jeu chez les aztèques*, Paris: Mouton.

Duyzings, M.W. (1951), *Faas Wilkes: Een Voetbalcarrière*, Baarn: De Boekerij.

Ehrenberg, A. (1991), *Le culte de la performance*, Paris: Calmann-Lévy.

Eichberg, H. (1983), 'Einheit oder Vielfalt am Ball? Zur Kulturgeschichte des Spiels am Beispiel der Nuit und der Altisländer', in O. Gruppe, H. Gabler and U. Göhner (eds), *Spiel–Spiele–Spielen*, Schorndorf: K. Hoffmann, pp. 131–53.

Eisenberg, C. (ed.) (1997), *Fußball, Soccer, Calcio. Ein englischer Sport auf seinem Weg um die Welt*, Munich: DTV.

Eisenberg, C. (1997), 'Sportgeschichte: Eine Dimension der modernen Kultur-geschichte', *Geschichte und Gesellschaft*, 23, pp. 295–310.

Eisenberg, C. (1999), *'English Sports' und deutsche Bürger: Eine Gesellschafts-geschichte, 1800–1939*, Paderborn: Schöningh.

Elias, N. and Dunning, E. (1986), *Quest for Excitement: Sport and Leisure in the Civilizing Process*, Oxford: Blackwell.

Elton, C. (1989), *Hull City: A Complete Record, 1904–1989*, Derby: Breedon Books.

Encyclopédie des Sports (1924), Paris: Librairie de France, vol. II.

Escarra, E. (1908), *Le développement industriel de la Catalogne*, Paris.

Escobar Bavio, E. (1923), *El football en el Rio de la Plata (desde 1893)*, Buenos Aires: Editorial Sport.

Fabrizio, F. (1973), 'Funzione e strumentalizzazione dell'attivà ginnico-sportiva dilletantistica e professionale in Italia nei contesti del regime fascista: dalle olimpiadi del 1924 a quelle del 1936', Unpublished Doctoral Thesis, Università Cattolicà Milan.

Fabrizio, F. (1976), *Sport e fascismo: la politica sportiva del regime, 1924–1936*, Rimini/Florence: Guaraldi.

Fachinetti, P. (1982), 'Sport e pubblicità', *I Problemi di Ulisse*, special issue, 'Lo Sport', May.

Fahmy, M. (1991), 'Organizzazione amministrazione', in *Proceedings of the Conference 'Africa 2000'*, Florence: FIGC.

Farrell, R. (ed.) (1996), *F.A. Premier League Seminar on the Bosman Case*, London, 6 January 1996, London: FA Premier League.

Faure, J-M. and Suaud, C. (1999), *Le football professionnel à la française*, Paris: PUF.

Favrod, C.-H. (1990), 'La Suisse des négociations secrètes', in J.P. Rioux (ed.), *La guerre d'Algérie et les français*, Paris: Fayard.

Fernández Santander, C. (1990), *El fútbol durante la guerra civil y el franquismo*, Madrid: San Martín.

Ferns, H.S. (1973), *National Economic Histories: The Argentine Republic 1516–1971*, Newton Abbot: David & Charles.

Ferrier, B. (1960), *Soccer Partnership*, London: Sportsman's Book Club.

Finn, R. (1969), *A History of Chelsea FC*, London: Pelham.

Finney, T. (1955), *Football Round the World*, London: Sportsman's Book Club.

Finney, T. (1960), *Finney on Football*, London: Sportsman's Book Club.

Firmani, E. (1960), *Football with the Millionaires*, London: Sportsman's Book Club.

Fishwick, N. (1989), *English Football and Society 1915–1950*, Manchester: Manchester University Press.

Fitzpatrick, D. (1998), *The Two Irelands, 1912–1939*, Oxford: Oxford University Press.

Fontan, A. (1963), *Divin football brésilien*, Paris: La table ronde.

Foster, J. (1992), 'A Proletarian Nation? Occupation and Class since 1914', in T. Dixon and J.H. Treble (eds), *People and Society in Scotland: Volume 3, 1914–1990*, Edinburgh: John Donald, pp. 201–40.

Franklin, N. (1956), *Soccer at Home and Abroad*, London: Stanley Paul.

Frydenberg, J.D. (1998), 'Redefinición del fútbol aficionado y del fútbol oficial; Buenos Aires 1912', in P. Alabarces, R. Di Giano and J. Frydenberg (eds), *Deporte y sociedad*, Buenos Aires: Eudeba.

Fußball und Rassismus (1993), Göttingen: Werkstatt.

Garcia Candau, J. (1996), *Madrid–Barça: Historia de un desamor*, Madrid: El País Aguilar.

Garcia Castell, J. (1968), *Història del futbol català*, Barcelona: Aymà.

Gardner, P. (1974), *Nice Guys Finish Last: Sport and American Life*, London: Allan Lane.

Gargani, F. (1935), *Italiani e stranieri alla mostra della rivoluzione fascista*, Rome: Saie.

Gatti, H. (1977), *Yo, el único*, Buenos Aires: Abril.

Gaussent, J. (1987), 'L'Eglise protestante de Sète 1851–1905', *Bulletin de la société de l'histoire du protestantisme français*, 135, pp. 25–40.

Gausti, C. (1919), 'Il giuoco del calcio a Prato', *Archivio storico pratese*, pp. 59–70.

Geertz, C. (1973), *The Interpretation of Cultures*, New York: Basic Books.

Gehrmann, S. (ed.) (1997), *Football and Regional Identity in Europe*, Münster: Lit.

Gerald, E. (1988), 'Battling Siki: The Boxer as Natural Man', *Massachusetts Review*, 29, 3, pp. 451–72.

Ghirelli, A. (1990), *Storia del calcio in Italia*, Turin: Einaudi, 3rd edn.

Gibson, J. (1984), *Kevin Keegan: Portrait of a Superstar*, London: W.H. Allen.

Gillmeister, H. (1997), 'The First European Soccer Match: Walter Bensemann', *The Sports Historian*, 17, pp. 1–13.

Glanville, B. (1961), *Soccer Round the Globe*, London: The Sportman's Book Club.

Glanville, B. (1969), *Soccer: A Panorama*, London: Eyre and Spottiswood.

Glanville, B. (1978), *The Puffin Book of Footballers*, Harmondsworth: Penguin.

Glanville, B. (1999), *Football Memories*, London: Virgin.

Glenny, M. (1992), *The Fall of Yugoslavia*, London: Penguin.

Goksøyr, M. and Hognestad, H. (1999), 'No Longer Worlds Apart: British Influences on Norwegian Football' in G. Armstrong and R. Giulianotti, *Football Cultures and Identities*, London: Macmillan, pp. 201–10.

Goldgrub, F. (1990), *Futebol: Arte ou Guerra?: Elogio ao drible*, Rio de Janeiro: Imago.

Golesworthy, M. (1957), *The Encyclopaedia of Association Football*, London: Sportsman's Book Club.

Gouberville, Sire de (1892), *Journal*, Caen: Beaurepaire.

Grant, A. and Stringer, K. (eds) (1995), *Uniting the Kingdom? The Making of British History*, London: Routledge.

Greaves, J. and Gutteridge, R. (1971), *Let's Be Honest*, London: Pelham.

Green, G. (1954), *Soccer: The World Game*, London: Sportsman's Book Club.

Grendi, E. (1983), 'Lo sport, un'innovazione vittoriana?', *Quaderni storici*, 17, 2, pp. 679–94.

Grief, J. (1999), 'Major League Soccer versus North American Soccer League: The Improvement of the American Player', Tufts University Student Essay, http://www.sws.bu.edu/palegi/jason.html

Grimaud, L. and Pécheral, A. (1984), *La grande histore de l'OM*, Paris: Robert Laffont.

Grimault, D. and Champel, E. (1988), *Montpellier La Paillade SC: Histoire d'une passion*, Montpellier: Montpellier PSC.

Gutman, H.G. (1977), *Work, Culture and Society in Industrializing America: Essays in American Working-Class and Social History*, Oxford: Blackwell.

Guttmann, A. (1978), *From Ritual to Record: The Nature of Modern Sports*, New York: Columbia University Press.

Guttmann, A. (1994), *Games and Empires: Modern Sports and Cultural Imperialism*, New York: Columbia University Press.

Guzmán, J.A. (1952), *Historia del fútbol de Guatemala*, Guatemala: FNF.

Halperín Donghi, T. (1993), *The Contemporary History of Latin America*, London: Macmillan.

Handlin, O. (1953), *The Uprooted: From the Old World to the New*, Boston: Watts and Co.

Hapgood, E. (1944), *Football Ambassador*, London: Sporting Handbooks.

Hardaker, A. (1977), *Hardaker of the League*, London: Pelham.

Harding, J. (1985), *Football Wizard: the Story of Billy Meredith*, Derby: Breedon.

Harding, J. (1991), *For the Good of the Game: The Official History of the Professional Footballers' Association*, London: Robson Books.

Harris, J.E. and Zeghidour, S. (1993), 'Africa and its diaspora since 1935', in A.A. Mazrui and C. Wondji (eds), *General History of Africa Volume 8: Africa since 1935*, Oxford: Heinemann/UNESCO, pp. 705–23.

Harvie, C. (1994), *Scotland and Nationalism: Scottish Society and Politics, 1707–1994*, London: Routledge, 2nd edn.

Hay, R. (1994) 'Marmaras' Oyster or Seamonds' Baby: The Formation of the Victorian Soccer Federation, 1956–64', *Sporting Traditions*, 10, 2, May, pp. 3–24.

Hélal, H. and Mignon, P. (eds) (1999), *Football: jeu et société*, Paris: INSEP.

Held, D., McGrew, A., Goldblatt, D. and Perraton, J. (1999), *Global Transformations: Politics, Economics and Culture*, Cambridge: Polity Press.

Hermet, G. (1996), *Histoire des nations et du nationalisme en Europe*, Paris: Seuil.

Higham, J. (1975), *Strangers in the Land: Patterns of American Nativism*, New York: Antheum.

Higham, J. (1984), *Send These to Me: Immigrants in Urban America*, Baltimore: Johns Hopkins University Press.

Hill, J. (1994), 'Cricket and the Imperial Connection: Overseas Players in Lancashire in the Inter-war Years', in Bale and Maguire, *Global Sports Arena*, pp. 49–62.

Hill, J. (2000), 'England v Hungary: November 1953', Unpublished paper presented at the 19th conference of the British Society of Sports History, Liverpool.

Hirst, P. and Thompson, G. (1999), *Globalization in Question*, Cambridge: Polity, 2nd edn.

Hobsbawm, E. (1990), *Nations and Nationalism Since 1780: Programme, Myth, Reality*, Cambridge: Cambridge University Press.

Hockings, R. and Radnedge, K. (1993), *Nations of Europe: A Statistical History of European International Football 1872–1993*, Vol. 2, Emsworth: Articulate.

Holmes, C. (1988), *John Bull's Island: Immigration and British Society, 1871–1971*, London: Macmillan.

Holroyd, S. (1999), 'The First Professional Soccer League in the United States: The American League of Professional Football (1894)', US Soccer Archives, http://www.sover.net/-spectrum/alpf.html

Holt, R. (1989), *Sport and the British: A Modern History*, Oxford: Clarendon.

Holt, R. (1994), 'The King over the Border: Denis Law and Scottish Football', in G. Jarvie and G. Walker (eds), *Scottish Sport in the Making of the Nation: Ninety-Minute Patriots?*, Leicester: Leicester University Press, pp. 58–74.

Holt, R. (1997), 'Football and Regional Identity in the North of England: The Legend of Jackie Milburn', in S. Gehrmann (ed.), *Football and Regional Identity in Europe*, Münster: Lit, pp. 49–66.

Holt, R., Mangan, J.A. and Lanfranchi, P. (eds) (1996), *European Heroes*, London: Frank Cass.

Horak, R. and Maderthaner, W. (1996), 'A Culture of Urban Cosmopolitanism: Urudil and Sindelar as Viennese Coffee-House Heroes', in R. Holt, J.A. Mangan and P. Lanfranchi (eds), *European Heroes*, London: Frank Cass, pp. 139–55.

Horak, R. and Maderthaner, W. (1997), *Mehr als ein Spiel: Fussball und populare Kulturen in Wien der Moderne*, Vienna: Locker.

Horne, J. and Jary, D. (1994), 'Japan and the World Cup: Asia's first World Cup Final hosts?', in J. Sugden and A. Tomlinson (eds), *Hosts and Champions*, Aldershot: Arema, pp. 161–82.

Hubscher, R., Durry, J., and Jeu, B. (1992), *L'histoire en mouvements: le sport et la société en France (XIXe–XXe siècle)*, Paris: Armand Colin.

Hudson, D. and Herbane, B. (2000), *Marketing in English Professional Football Clubs*, Leicester: De Montfort University.

Huizinga, J. (1955), *Homo Ludens: A study of the play-element in culture*, Boston: Beacon Press.

Hurseau, P. (1977), *L'histoire du football Nordiste*, Lille: Ligue du Nord de Football.

Jaun, R. (1986), *Management und Arbeiterschaft. Verwissenschaftlichung, Amerikanisierung und Rationalisierung der Arbeitsverhältnisse in der Schweiz, 1883–1959*, Zürich: Chronos.

Jenkins, R. (1990), 'Salvation for the Fittest?: A West African Sportman in Britain in the Age of the New Imperialism', *International Journal of the History of Sport*, 7, 1.

Jessurun d'Oliveira, H.U. (1992), 'Calcio e nazionalità: le Olimpiadi, la Coppa del Mondo', in P. Lanfranchi (ed.), *Il calcio e il suo pubblico*, Naples: ESI, pp. 353–67.

Joannou, P. (1990), *Wembley Wizards: The Story of a Legend*, Edinburgh: Mainstream.

John, M. (1997), 'Österreich' in C. Eisenberg (ed.), *Fußball, Soccer, Calcio*, Munich: DTV, pp. 65–93.

Johnes, M. (1998), 'That Other Game: A Social History of Soccer in South Wales c. 1906–1939', Unpublished Ph.D. Thesis, University of Wales.

Jolinon, J. (1932), *Le joueur de balle*, Paris: Ferenczi.

Jones, M.A. (1960), *American Immigration*, Chicago: University of Chicago Press.

Jordan, G. (1947), *Football européen*, Paris: Triolet.

Jose, C. (1989), *NASL: A Complete Record of the North American Soccer League*, Derby: Breedon Books.

Jose, C. (1998), *American Soccer League, 1921–1931: The Golden Years of American Soccer*, Lanham: Scarecrow Press.

Jose, C. (1998), *Keeping Score: The Encyclopedia of Canadian Soccer*, Vaughan: Soccer Hall of Fame.

Joutard, P. (1986), *L'invention du Mont Blanc*, Paris: Gallimard.

Jusserand, J.-J. (1901), *Les sports et jeux d'exercice dans l'ancienne France*, Paris: Plon. [facsimile edition, Geneva: Slatkine, 1986].

Kearney, H. (1989), *The British Isles: A History of Four Nations*, Cambridge: Cambridge University Press.

Kivisto, P. (1990), 'The Transplanted then and now: the reorientation of immigration studies from the Chicago School to the new social history', *Ethnic and Racial Studies*, 13, 4, pp. 455–80.

Klein, A.M. (1994), 'Trans-nationalism, Labour Migration and Latin American Baseball', in J. Bale and J. Maguire (eds), *Global Sports Arena*, London: Frank Cass, pp. 183–205.

Klippstein, F. (ed.) (1925), *Festschrift zum 30 Jährigen Bestand des Schweiz. Fussball- und Athletik-Verband*, St Gall: Tschudy.

Korr, C.P. (1986), *West Ham United: The Making of a Football Club*, London: Duckworth.

Koser, K. and Lutz, H. (eds) (1998), *The New Migration in Europe: Social Constructions and Social Realities*, London: Macmillan.

Kovacs, S. (1975), *Football Total*, Paris: Calmann-Lévy.

Kramer, F. (ed.) (1992), *Hrvatski nogometni savez 80. obljetnica*, Zagreb: HTZ.

Kraut, A.M. (1982), *The Huddled Masses: The Immigrant in American Society, 1880–1921*, Arlington Heights: Harlan Davidson.

Krulic, J. (1993), *Histoire de la Yougoslavie: de 1945 à nos jours*, Brussels: Editions Complexe.

Kuper, S. (1995), *Football Against the Enemy*, London: Phoenix.

Lafond, P. and Bodis, J.-P. (1989), *Encyclopédie du rugby français*, Paris: Dehédin.

Lamming, D. (1987), *A Scottish Soccer Internationals' Who's Who*, Beverley: Hutton.

Lane, A.T. (1980), 'The British and American Labour Movements and the Problem of Immigration, 1890–1914', in K. Lunn (ed.), *Hosts, Immigrants and Minorities: Historical Responses to Newcomers in British Society*, Folkestone: Dawson, pp. 343–67.

Lanfranchi, P. (1989), 'Les footballeurs-étudiants yougoslaves en Languedoc', *Sport Histoire*, 2, 3, pp. 43–59.

Lanfranchi, P. (1990), 'Die Entwicklung eines europäischen Netzwerks, 1920–38', in R. Horak and W. Reiter (eds), *Die Kanten des runden Leders*, Vienna: Promedia.

Lanfranchi, P. (1991), 'Bologna, the team that shook the world!', *International Journal of the History of Sport*, 8, 3, pp. 336–47.

Lanfranchi, P. (ed.) (1992), *Il calcio e il suo pubblico*, Naples: Edizioni scientifiche italiane.

Lanfranchi, P. (1998), 'Football et modernité: La Suisse et la pénétration du football sur le continent', *Traverse, revue d'histoire*, 5, 3, pp. 76–88.

Lang, F. (1952), *Das ist Rapid. Der Weg der Grünweissen Meistermannschaft*, Vienna: Josef Faber.

Langenus, J. (1943), *En sifflant par le monde. Souvenirs et impressions de voyage d'un arbitre de football*, Gent: Snoeck-Ducajou.

Lattes, A.E. (1987), 'An overview of International Migration in Argentina', in A. Lattes and E. Oteiza (eds), *The Dynamics of Argentine Migration (1955–1984): Democracy and the Return of Expatriates*, Geneva: United Nations Research Institute for Social Development.

Laurens, G. (1990), 'Qu'est-ce qu'un champion? La compétition sportive en Languedoc au début du siècle', *Annales: Economie, Sociétés, Civilisations*, 45, September, pp. 1047–69.

Law, D. with Bale, B. (1999), *The Lawman: An Autobiography*, London: Andre Deutsch.

Lecic, B. (1996) 'Participation of Yugoslav Athletes in International Competitions, 1992–95', *Yugoslav Survey*, 37, 2.

Ledbroke, A. and Turner, E. (1955), *Soccer from the Pressbox*, London: Sportsman's Book Club.

Leguineche, M., Unzueta, P. and Segurola, S. (1998), *Athletic 100: Conversaciones en La Catedral*, Madrid: El País Aguilar.

Leite Lopes, S. (1998), 'La disparition de "la joie du peuple": Notes sur la mort d'un joueur de football', *Actes de la recherche en sciences sociales*, 79, pp. 21–36.

Leite Lopes, S. (1999), 'Les Origines du jeu à la brésilienne', in H. Hélal and P. Mignon (eds), *Football: jeu et société*, Paris: INSEP, pp. 65–84.

Leite Lopes, S. (1999), 'The Brazilian Style of Football and its Dilemmas', in G. Armstrong and R. Giulianotti (eds), *Football Cultures and Identities*, London: Macmillan, pp. 86–95.

Leite Lopes, S. and Faguer, J.-P. (1994), 'L'invention du style brésilien: Sport, journalisme et politique au Brésil', *Actes de la recherche en sciences sociales*, 103, pp. 27–35.

Lémenon, E. (1911), *Naples: Notes historiques et sociales*, Paris: Plon.

Lemmi Gigli, R. and Turrini, G. (1959), 'La lunga linea Rossoblu' in *Il Mezzosecolo del Bologna*, Bologna: Poligrafia del Resto del Carlino.

Lever, J. (1983), *Soccer Madness*, Chicago: Chicago University Press.

Levinsky, S. (1995), *El negocio del fútbol*, Buenos Aires: Corregidor.

Bibliography

Lewis, R.W. (1993), 'The Development of Professional Football in Lancashire, 1870–1914' Unpublished PhD Thesis, Lancaster University.

Lidtke, V. (1984), *The Alternative Culture: Socialist Labor in Imperial Germany*, Oxford: Oxford University Press.

Lopez, R. (1987), 'Les Suisses à Marseille: une immigration de longue durée', *Revue européenne des migrations internationales*, 3, 1–2, pp. 149–72.

Lord, B. (1963), *My Fight for Football*, London: Stanley Paul.

Lydall, H. (1984), *Yugoslav Socialism: Theory and Practice*, Oxford: Oxford University Press.

MacBride, E., O'Connor, M. and Sheridan, G. (1994), *An Alphabet of the Celts: A Complete Who's Who of Celtic FC*, Leicester: ACL and Polar Publishing.

Macnaghton, R.E. (1898), 'The Eton Wall-Game', *Badminton Magazine of Sports and Pastimes*, Vol. 6, London: Longmans.

Magas, B. (1993), *The Destruction of Yugoslavia: Tracking the break-up, 1980–92*, London: Verso.

Magee, J. (1999), 'Historical Concepts of Football and Labour Migration in England', unpublished paper presented at the 18th conference of the British Society of Sports History, Eastbourne.

Maguire, J. (1999), *Global Sport: Identities, Societies, Civilizations*, London: Polity.

Maguire, J. and Stead, D. (1998), 'Border Crossings: Soccer Labour Migration and the European Union', *International Review for the Sociology of Sport*, 33, 1, pp. 59–73.

Mahmood, R.A. (1996), 'Labour Crunch, Foreign Workers and Policy Responses: The Experience of Japan', *International Migration*, 34, 1, pp. 97–114.

Majoub, F. (1988), *Trente ans de Coupe d'Afrique des nations*, Paris: Jeune Afrique.

Malatos, A. (1989), *Il calcio professionista in Europa. Profili di diritto comparato*, Padua: CEDAM.

Manson, M. (1982), 'La choule (soule) en Normandie au XVIe siècle d'après le Sire de Gouberville', in L. Burgener (ed.), *Sport und Kultur; Sport et civilisations*, Bern: Lang, pp. 97–106.

Marcacci, M. (1998), 'La ginnastica contro gli sport', *Traverse*, 5, 3, pp. 63–73.

Marchesini, G. (1988), *La storia del Bologna*, Florence: Casa dello sport.

Marco, J.L. and Hernaez, A. (1974), *CF Barcelona Campeones*, Madrid: Mirasierrea.

Marinkovic, M. (1988), *Almanah Fudbalskog Saveza Jugoslavije 1978–1986*, Vol. 2, Belgrade: FSJ.

Markovic, T. (1977), *1976–77 Godisnjak Fudbalskog Saveza Jugoslavije*, Belgrade: FSJ.

Markovits, A.S. (1990), 'The other "American Exceptionalism": Why is there no Soccer in the United States?', *International Journal of the History of Sport*, 7, 2, pp. 230–64.

Markovits, A.S. and Hellerman, S.L. (1997), 'USA' in C. Eisenberg (ed.), *Fußball, Soccer, Calcio*, Munich: DTV, pp. 185–212.

Marri, F. (1983), 'Metodo, sistema e derivati nel linguaggio calcistico', *Lingua nostra*, 44, 2–3, pp. 70–83.

Marschik, M. (1998), *Vom Nutzen der Unterhaltung. Der Wiener Fußball in der NS-Zeit: Zwischen Vereinnahmung und Resistenz*, Vienna: Turia und Kant.

Mason, T. (1980), *Association Football and English Society, 1863–1915*, Brighton: Harvester Press.

Mason, T. (1986), 'Some Englishmen and Scotsmen Abroad: The Spread of World Football', in A. Tomlinson and G. Whannel (eds), *Off the ball: The Football World Cup*, London: Pluto, pp. 67–82.

Mason, T. (1990) 'Football on the Maidan: Cultural Imperialism in Calcutta', *International Journal of the History of Sport*, 7, 1, pp. 85–96.

Mason, T. (1994), 'The Bogotá Affair', in J. Bale and J. Maguire (eds), *Global Sports Arena*, London: Frank Cass, pp. 39–48.

Mason, T. (1995), *Passion of the People? Football in South America*, London: Verso.

Mason, T. (1999), 'Grandeur et déclin du "kick and rush" anglais ou la révolte d'un style' in H. Hélal and P. Mignon (eds), *Football: jeu et société*, Paris: INSEP, pp. 47–64.

Matthews, S. (1952), *Feet First Again*, London: Nicholas Kaye.

McKibbin, R. (1998), *Classes and Cultures: Britain 1918–1951*, Oxford: Oxford University Press.

Meisl, W. (1957), *Soccer Revolution*, London: Panther.

Melcon, R. and Smith, R. (eds) (1961), *The Real Madrid Book of Football*, London: Consul.

Meroi, R. (1989), *Storia dell'Udinese calcio*, Udine: Campanatti.

Metcalfe, A. (1989), *Canada Learns to Play: The Emergence of Organized Sport, 1807–1914*, Toronto: McClelland & Stewart.

Miles, R. (1989), 'Nationality, Citizenship and Migration to Britain, 1945–1951', *Journal of Law and Society*, 16, 4, Winter, pp. 426–42.

Miller, F. (1996), 'Not Every Agent is a Bad Guy', *Sport and the Law Journal*, 4, 1.

Molenaar, H. (1969), *Top Voetbal '67–'68*, Baarn: de Boekerij.

Moorhouse, H.F. (1994), 'Blue Bonnets over the Border: Scotland and the Migration of Footballers', in J. Bale and J. Maguire (eds), *The Global Sports Arena*, London: Frank Cass, pp. 78–96.

Moorhouse, H.F. (1996), 'One State, Several Countries: Soccer and Identities in a "United" Kingdom', in J.A. Mangan (ed.), *Tribal Identities: Nationalism, Europe, Sport*, London: Frank Cass, pp. 55–74.

Bibliography

Morgagni, T. and Brusca, V. (1907), *Annuario Sportivo 1907–1908*, Milan: Corriere della sera editore.

Mormino, G.R. (1982), 'The Playing Fields of St. Louis: Italian Immigrants and Sport, 1925–1941', *Journal of Sport History*, 9, 2, Summer, pp. 5–19.

Moseley, P. (1994), 'Balkan Politics in Australian Soccer', in J. O'Hara (ed.), *Ethnicity and Soccer in Australia*, Sydney: ASSH, pp. 32–43.

Moseley, P. and Murray, B. (1994), 'Soccer', in W. Vamplew and B. Stoddart (eds), *Sport in Australia: A Social History*, Melbourne: Cambridge University Press.

Murray, B. (1984), *The Old Firm: Sectarianism, Sport and Society in Scotland*, Edinburgh: John Donald.

Murray, B. (1994), *Football: A History of the World Game*, Aldershot: Scholar Press.

Murray, B. (1995), 'Cultural Revolution: Football in the Societies of Asia and the Pacific', in S. Wagg (ed.), *Giving the Game Away*, London: Leicester University Press, pp. 138–62.

Murray, B. (1998), *The World's Game: A History of Football*, Urbana: University of Illinois Press.

Musso, D. (1999), 'Conséquences de l'arrêt Bosman: Réflexions sur la situation juridique du sportif', in H. Hélal and P. Mignon (eds) *Football: jeu et société*, Paris: INSEP, pp. 245–55.

Naudin, P. (1961), *La foire aux muscles*, Paris: Editeurs Français Réunis.

Néré, J. (1975), *The Foreign Policy of France from 1914 to 1945*, London: Routledge.

Nicolini, G. (1967), *La storia del Napoli*, Rome: Editrice Italiana.

Nogowa, H. and Maeda, H. (1999), 'The Japanese Dream: Soccer Culture towards the new Millennium', in G. Armstrong and R. Giulianotti (eds), *Football Cultures and Identities*, London: Macmillan, pp. 223–33.

Oliver, G. (1992), *The Guinness History of World Soccer*, London: Guinness Publishing.

Ollier, F. (1992), *Arsenal: A Complete Record, 1886–1992*, Derby: Breedon Books.

Onofri, S. and Ottani, V. (1990), *Dal Littoriale allo Stadio: Storia per immagini dell'impianto sportivo bolognese*, Bologna: CCC.

Panayi, P. (1999), *Outsiders: A History of Minorities in Europe*, London: Hambledon.

Papa, A. and Panico, G. (1993), *Storia sociale del calcio in Italia*, Bologna: il mulino.

Pastore, F. (1999), 'Droit de la nationalité et migrations internationales: le cas italien', in P. Weil and R. Hansen (eds), *Nationalité et citoyenneté en Europe*, Paris: La découverte, pp. 95–116.

Patton, J. (1994), *Il Basket d'Italia*, New York: Simon and Schuster.

Pefferkorn, M. (1944), *Football, Joie du monde*, Paris: Susse.

Pele, with Fish, R. (1979), *My Life and the Beautiful Game*, Oxford: Oxford University Press.

Pellegrino, A. (1987), 'Argentines in Venezuela' in Lattes and Oteiza, *The Dynamics of Argentine Migration*, pp. 95–104.

Pérez de Rozas, E. (1992), 'Bar-ça, Bar-ça, Bar-ça! ou l'amour foot', in A. Sanchez (ed.), *Barcelone 1888–1929: Modernistes, anarchistes, noucentistes ou la création fiévreuse d'une nation catalane*, Paris: Autrement.

Perman, M. (ed.) (1990), *Perspectives on the American Past*, Lexington: DC Heath.

Peucelle, C. (1975), *Fútbol todo tiempo e historia de 'la Maquina'*, Buenos Aires: Axioma.

Piérard, P. and Dubois, M. (1992), *Standard, une épopée*, Alleur-Liège: Le Perron.

Pieth, F. (1979), *Sport in der Schweiz*, Olten: Walter.

Pinto, F.T. (1956), *História do futebol português no campo internacional*, Lisbonne: Garfitécnica.

Pirjevec, J. (1995), *Serbi, Croati, Sloveni: Storia di tre nazioni*, Bologna: il mulino.

Pivato, S. (1990), 'Foot-ball e neotomismo', *Belfagor*, 16, 5, pp. 579–86.

Pivato, S. (1991), 'Il football un fenomeno di frontiera. Il caso del Friuli-Venezia-Giulia', *Italia contemporanea*, 183, pp. 257–72.

Polley, M. (1998), *Moving the Goalposts: A History of Sport and Society since 1945*, London: Routledge.

Pooley, J.C. (1976), 'Ethnic Soccer Clubs in Milwaukee', in M.M. Hart (ed.), *Sport in the Socio-cultural Process*, Dubuque: William C. Brown.

Potts, L. (1990), *The World Labour Market:: A History of Migration*, London: Zed.

Powell, J. (1993), *Bobby Moore: The Life and Times of a Sporting Hero*, London: Robson Books.

Pozzo, V. (1960), *Campioni del Mondo. Quarant'anni di storia del calcio italiano*, Rome: CEN.

Price, C. (1969), 'The Study of Assimilation', in J.A. Jackson (ed.), *Migration*, Cambridge: Cambridge University Press, pp. 181–237.

Puskas, F. (1961), 'A Few Precious Years', in R. Melcon and S. Smith (eds), *The Real Madrid Book of Football*, London: Consul, pp. 52–61.

Rabier, R. (1985), *Allez SOM: cinquante ans de football montpellierain (1919–1970)*, Montpellier: Private Edition.

Ramírez, P.A. (1988), 'Politica y fútbol', *Todo es historia*, 21, 248, pp. 34–43.

Ramírez, P.A. (1990), 'Alzas y bajas en el fervor por el fútbol', *Todo es historia*, 23, 272, pp. 88–96.

Ramos Ruiz, A. (1973), *Nuestro fútbol: grandeza y decadencia*, Buenos Aires: LV Producciones.

Rauch, A. (1989), 'Des jeux aux sports. Pour une histoire des différences', *Cahiers d'histoire*, 34, 1, pp. 156–63.

Rauch, A. (1995), 'Les vacances et la nature revisitée', in A. Corbin (ed.), *L'avénement des loisirs (1850–1960)*, Paris: Aubier, pp. 81–117.

Ricci, F.M. (1999), *African Football Yearbook 1999*, Fornacette: Mariposa.

Robbins, K. (1988), *Nineteenth-Century Britain: Integration and Diversity*, Oxford: Clarendon.

Robbins, K. (1995), 'An Imperial and Multinational Policy: "The scene from the centre", 1832–1922', in A. Grant and K. Stringer, *Uniting the Kingdom*, London: Routledge.

Roden, D. (1980), 'Baseball and the Quest for National Dignity in Meiji Japan', *American Historical Review*, 85, 3, pp. 511–34.

Romanato, L.C. and Marmiroli, R., *Il gioco del calcio dalle origini al 2000*, Modena: Dini, 1949.

Romero, A. (1985), *Deporte, violencia y politica (crónica negra 1958–1983)*, Buenos Aires: CEAL.

Roques, J.D. (1974), 'Nouveaux aperçus sur l'Eglise protestante de Nîmes dans la seconde moitié du XIXe siècle', *Bulletin de la société de l'histoire du protestantisme français*, 120, pp. 48–96.

Rotschildt, J. (1977), *East Central Europe between the Wars*, Seattle: University of Washington Press.

Rouquié, A. (1977), *Pouvoir militaire et société politique en République Argentine*, Paris: Presses de la fondation des sciences politiques.

Rovelli, A. (1997), 'Il romanzo degli stranieri' in L. Giannelli (ed.), *100 anni di campionato di calcio*, Florence: Scramasax.

Rowlands, A. (1991), *Trautmann: The Biography*, Derby: Breedon Books.

Roy, J.-A. (1958), *Histoire du Jockey-Club de Paris*, Paris: Rivière.

Rumiz, P. (1993), 'Armi, droga, mafia: la guerra come affare', *Limes*, 1–2, pp. 117–23.

Russell, D. (1997), *Football and the English: A Social History of Association Football in England, 1863–1995*, Preston: Carnegie.

Ryswick, J. de (1962), *100 000 heures de football*, Paris: La table ronde.

Saïd, A. (1977), 'Les trois âges de l'émigration algérienne en France', *Actes de la recherche en sciences sociales*, 15, January, pp. 59–79.

Saint-Martin, M. de (1989), 'La noblesse et les sports "nobles"', *Actes de la recherche en sciences sociales*, 80, pp. 22–32.

Sallmann, J.-M. (1982), 'Il santo patrono cittadino nel 1600 nel regno di Napoli e in Sicilia', in *Per una storia sociale e religiosa del mezzogiorno d'Italia*, vol. 2, Naples: Guida, pp. 191–210.

Samuel, R. (1995), 'British Dimensions: "Four Nations History"', *History Workshop Journal*, 40, pp. ii–xxii.

Say, T. (1996), 'Herbert Chapman: Football Revolutionary?', *The Sports Historian*, 16, May, pp. 81–98.

Scher, A. and Palomino, H. (1988), *Fútbol: pasión de multitudes y de elites*, Buenos Aires: CISEA.

Schidrowitz, L. (1951), *Geschichte des Fußballsports in Österreich*, Vienna: ÖFB.

Schweickard, W. (1987), *Die Cronaca calcistica. Zur Sprache des Fußballberichterstattung in italienischen Sportzeitungen*, Tübingen: Niemeyer.

Sebrelli, J.J. (1998), *La era del fútbol*, Buenos Aires: Editorial sudamericana.

Seed, J. (1957), *The Jimmy Seed Story*, London: Phoenix.

Seidler, E. and Parienté, R. (1964), *Dictionnaire des sports*, Paris: Seghers.

Serra, L. (1964), *Storia del calcio 1863–1963*, Bologna: Palmaverde.

Shenton, J.P. (1990), 'Ethnicity and Immigration', in E. Foner (ed.), *The New American History*, Philadelphia: Temple University Press, pp. 251–70.

Shumway, N. (1991), *The Invention of Argentina*, Berkeley: University of California Press.

Singleton, F. (1976), *Twentieth Century Yugoslavia*, London: Macmillan.

Skoblar, J. (1977), *Chasseur de buts*, Paris: Olivier Orban.

Smith, D. and Williams, G. (1980), *Fields of Praise: The Official History of the Welsh Rugby Union*, Cardiff: University of Wales Press.

Solinas, P. G. (1997), 'Le sort, le hasard, la lutte: le Palio de Sienne', *Ethnologie française*, 2–3, pp. 170–77.

Soremekun, F. (1986), 'Portugal, Mozambique and Angola: Trends Towards Future Relationships', in A. Sesay (ed.), *Africa and Europe: From Partition to Independence?*, London: Croom Helm, pp. 86–103.

Soulier, M. (1969), *Le football gardois*, Nîmes: Bène.

Spivak, M. (1987), 'Un concept mythologique de la Troisième République: Le renforcement du capital humain de la France', *International Journal of the History of Sport*, 4, 2, pp. 155–75.

Stallart, H.B. (1930), 'The Olympic Games', in Amateur Athletic Association, *Fifty Years of Progress 1880–1930*, London: Amateur Athletic Association.

Stock, A. (1982), *A Little Thing Called Pride*, London: Pelham.

Stora, B. (1991), 'Algérie, années coloniales: quand le sport devient un facteur de mobilisation politique', in *Jeu et sports en Méditerrannée. Actes du colloque de Carthage, 7–9 novembre 1989*, Tunis: ACIF, pp. 143–53.

Strikwerda, C. (1999), 'Tides of Migration, Currents of History: The State, Economy and the Transatlantic Movement of Labor in the Nineteenth and Twentieth Centuries', *International Review of Social History*, 44, pp. 367–94.

Sugden, J. and Bairner, A. (1993), *Sport, Sectarianism and Society in a Divided Ireland*, Leicester: Leicester University Press.

Sugden, J. and Tomlinson, A. (eds) (1994), *Hosts and Champions: Soccer Cultures, National Identities and the USA World Cup*, Aldershot: Arena.

Sund, B. (1997), 'The British and Continental Influence on Swedish Football', *International Journal of the History of Sport*, 14, 2, August, pp. 163–73.

Sutcliffe, C. E. and Hargreaves, F. (1928), *History of the Lancashire Football Association, 1878–1928*, Blackburn: George Toulmin.

Bibliography

Sutcliffe, C.E., Howarth, F. and Brierley, J.A. (1938), *The Story of the Football League, 1888–1938*, Preston: The Football League.

Tavella, R. and Ossola, F. (1997), *Il romanzo della grande Juventus*, Milan: Newton and Compton.

Taylor, M. (1997), '"Proud Preston": A History of the Football League, 1900–1939', Unpublished PhD Thesis, De Montfort University.

Taylor, P. and Smith, D. (1995), *The Foxes Alphabet: A Complete Who's Who of Leicester City Football Club*, Leicester: Polar Print.

Taylor, R. and Ward, A. (1995), *Kicking and Screaming: An Oral History of Football in England*, London: Robson Books.

Termes, J. (1999), 'Barça y Història', in R. Besa (ed.), *Amb blau sofert i amb grana intens: cent anys del Barça*, Barcelona: Proa.

Thébaud, F. (1975), *Pele: une vie, le football, le monde*, Paris: Hatier.

Tornabuoni, G. (1932), *L'ascesa del calcio in Italia*, Milan: Gazzetta dello sport editore.

Torre, J. (1972), 'Mario Esteves Coluna: Schwungard der Benfica Elf' in K.H. Huba (ed.), *Die Großen am Ball*, Munich: Copress.

Tramontana, E. and Virnicchi, G. (1970), *Il Napoli dalle origini ad oggi*, Naples: Arte tipografica.

Trento, A. (1992), 'Le associazioni italiane a São Paulo', in F.J. Devoto and E.J. Minguez (eds), *Asociacionismo, trabajo e identidad étnica. Los italianos en America Latina en una perspectiva comparada*, Buenos Aires: Cemla, pp. 31–57.

Trindade, M.B.R. (1979), 'Portugal', in R.E. Krane (ed.), *International Labor Migration in Europe*, New York: Praeger.

Turner, A. (1998), '25 miliones des Argentinos: Fútbol y discurso en el Mundial 78', in P. Alabarces, R. Di Giano and J. Frydenberg, (eds) *Deporte y sociedad*, Buenos Aires: Eudeba, 143–50.

Turner, D. and White, A. (1993), *Football Managers*, Derby: Breedon Books.

Unzueta, P. (1999), 'Fútbol y nacionalismo vasco', in S. Segurola (ed.), *Fútbol y pasiones politicas*, Madrid: Debate, pp. 147–67.

Valdano, J. (1994), *Sueños de fútbol*, Madrid: El País Aguilar.

Vamplew, W. (1988), *Pay up and Play the Game: Professional Sport in Britain 1875–1914*, Cambridge: Cambridge University Press.

Vamplew, W., Moore, K., O'Hara, J., Cashman, R. and Jobling, I.F. (eds) (1992), *The Oxford Companion to Australian Sport*, Oxford: Oxford University Press.

Vamplew, W. (1994), '"Wogball": Ethnicity and violence in Australian soccer', in J. Williams and R. Giulianotti (eds), *Games Without Frontiers: Football, Identity, Modernity*, Aldershot: Arena.

Varela Gómez, J.G. (1998), *Historia de la selección de fútbol de Euskadi*, Bilbao: Beitia.

Varley, N. (1997), *Golden Boy: A Biography of Wilf Mannion*, London: Aurum Press.

Varrasi, F. (1999), *Economia, Politica e Sport in Italia, 1925–35*, Florence: Fondazione Franchi.

Vasili, P. (1998), *The First Black Footballer: Arthur Wharton, 1865–1930*, London: Frank Cass.

Vasili, P. (2000), *Colouring over the White Line: The History of Black Footballers in Britain*, Edinburgh: Mainstream.

Veisz, A. and Molinari, A. (1930), *Il giuoco del calcio*, Milan: Corticelli.

Verdú, V. (1980), *El fútbol: mitos, ritos y símbolos*, Madrid: Allianza editorial.

Vermeer, E. (1990), *90 yaren Ajax, 1900–1990*, Utrecht: Luitingh.

Vial, F. and Ruffin, F. (1988), *FC Sochaux Montbéliard*, Lyon: La manufacture.

Vukadinovic, L. (1950), *Yugoslav Football*, Belgrade: Jugoslovenska Knjiga.

Waddington, I. and Roderick, M. (1996), 'American Exceptionalism: Soccer and American Football', *The Sports Historian*, 16, pp. 42–63.

Wagg, S. (ed.) (1995), *Giving the Game Away: Football, Politics and Culture on Five Continents*, London: Leicester University Press.

Wahl, A. (1986), 'Le footballeur français: de l'amateurisme au salariat (1890–1926)', *Le mouvement social*, 135, pp. 7–30.

Wahl, A. (1989), *Les archives du football*, Paris: Gallimard.

Wahl, A. and Lanfranchi, P. (1995), *Les footballeurs professionnels des années trente à nos jours*, Paris: Hachette.

Waldstein, D. and Wagg, S. (1995), 'Unamerican Activity: Football in US and Canadian Society', in S. Wagg (ed.), *Giving the Game Away: Football, Politics and Culture on Five Continents*, London: Leicester University Press, pp. 72–87.

Walton, J. (1999), 'Football and Basque Identity: Real Sociedad of San Sebastián, 1909–1932', *Memoria y Civilización*, 2, pp. 261–89.

Walvin, J. (1975), *The People's Game: A History of British Football*, London: Allen Lane.

Walvin, J. (1994), *The People's Game: A History of Football Revisited*, Edinburgh: Mainstream.

Waters, M. (1995), *Globalization*, London: Routledge.

Weatherill, S. (1999), 'European Football Law', in *Collected Courses of the Academy of European Law, Volume 1: 1996*, The Hague: Mijhoff.

Weber, E. (1971), 'Gymnastics and Sport in Fin de siècle France', *American Historical Review*, 76, 1, pp. 70–98.

Weil, P. (1991), *La France et ses étrangers: l'aventure d'une politique de l'immigration 1938–1991*, Paris: Calmann-Lévy.

Weil, P. and Hansen, R. (eds) (1999), *Nationalité et citoyenneté en Europe*, Paris: La découverte.

Wendt, J. (1975), 'Grundzüge der Geschichte des Deutschen Fußball-Bundes und des bürgerlichen deutschen Fußballsports im Zeitraum von 1918 bis 1933', Unpublished PhD Thesis, University Halle/Witteberg.

Whitacker, S.B. (1994), 'Leandro Arpinati, anarcoindividualista, fascista, fascista-pentito', *Italia contemporanea*, 196, pp. 471–489.

Whitcher, A.E. (1947), *The Voice of Soccer*, Brighton: Southern Publishing.

Whittaker, T. (1958), *Tom Whittaker's Arsenal Story*, London: Sportsman's Book Club.

Williams, G. (1984), *The Code War: English Football Under the Historical Spotlight*, Harefield: Yore.

Williams, J. (1999), *Is It All Over?: Can English Football Survive the Premier League*, London: South Side Press.

Williams, J. and Wagg, S. (eds) (1992), *British Football and Social Change: Getting into Europe*, Leicester: Leicester University Press.

Wilson, D. (1980), *Tito's Yugoslavia*, Cambridge: Cambridge University Press.

Wyman, M. (1993), *Round Trip to America: The Immigrants Return to Europe, 1880–1930*, London: Cornell University Press.

Young, P.M. (1964), *Football in Sheffield*, London: Sportsman's Book Club.

Young, P.M. (1964), *Football on Merseyside*, London: Stanley Paul.

Subject Index

Subject Index

Subject Index

Singapore 12
Social mobility 180
South Africa 6, 9, 177–8
Soviet Union 219–20
Spain
  Argentinean players in 97–9
  Athletic Bilbao 4
  Basque emigration 4, 87
  Basque protectionism 225
  Civil War 4, 87
  Clubs in Barcelona 28, 195–6
  Development of Football 20–1
  Dutch players in 105, 208, 235
  FC Barcelona 4, 24, 26–30, 104, 195–6, 235
  Moroccan in 173
  National Federation 34
  Oriundi in 97–9
  Real Madrid 4, 91–3, 104
  South American players 86, 93, 103–05
  Yugoslav players in 137–8
Sporting Press 29, 200
Standardization 15
Stadiums 105, 123, 193, 197
Sweden 117, 209–11
  English managers in 204
  National style 204
Swedish players
  in Britain 50–1
  in the United States 145
Switzerland 19–20, 23–6
  Argentinean players in 107
  Border Residents 11
  Education 19–20, 24–5, 28–9
  English Tourists in 47
  Matches with Germany 35
  Yugoslav players in 132
Swiss players
  in France 23–5
  in Italy 28–9
  in Spain 23–4

Tango 69–70, 77
Television 8, 96–7
Tennis 28
Titoism 116
Total Football 208
Transfer Fees 1–2, 53–4, 60, 63, 75, 82, 91, 93, 107, 118–9, 123

Transfer Market 131–2, 225–9
Transfer Regulations 214–8
Turkey
  Bosnian players in 136
  Yugoslav players in 132

UEFA 213
UEFA Champions League 8
United States of America 3, 6, 141–66
  Austrian players in 145, 148–9
  British players in 51, 142–49
  Clubs in 145–6
  Croatian Ethnic clubs in 124
  Dutch players in 158
  Hungarian players in 145
  Indoor Soccer 164
  Initial football migrants
  Latin American players in 165
  Local players in 155–6
  Major Soccer League (MSL) 165–6
  Migration flow to 3, 142–4
  National team 149, 151, 156
  Swedish players in 145
  Yugoslav players in 118, 120, 164
Uruguay 69–70, 72, 85–7, 92–3, 95–6
  Intracontinental migration 95–6
  Foreign players in 95

Venezuala 89

Welsh players 2
World Cup 25, 38, 78, 79, 86, 93, 96, 100–01, 103, 114, 119, 134, 149, 152, 168, 173, 184–5, 191, 198, 201, 224
World War I 3, 24, 35, 44
World War 2 49–50, 84, 87, 115–16, 133

Xenophobia 9, 21, 84

Yugoslavia 1, 6, 111–39, 221
  Chinese players in 132
  Economic Reforms of 118
  FK Sarajevo 136
  French Influence in 112–15
  Hajduk Split 120–4
  International transfer regulations 118–9
  Introduction of professionalism 117
  Migration to Germany 137

Subject Index

Author Index

Author Index

Author Index

Author Index

Author Index